DESIGN AND PLANNING OF RESEARCH AND CLINICAL LABORATORY FACILITIES

DESIGN AND PLANNING OF RESEARCH AND CLINICAL LABORATORY FACILITIES

LEONARD MAYER, AIA

JOHN WILEY AND SONS, INC.
New York / Chichester / Brisbane / Toronto / Singapore

Copyright © 1995 by John Wiley & Sons, Inc.

Library of Congress Cataloging in Publication Data:
Mayer, Leonard, 1929–
    Design and planning of research and clinical laboratory facilities
    / Leonard Mayer.
        p.   cm.
    Includes bibliographical references.
    ISBN 0-471-30623-1
    1. Laboratories—Design and construction.   I. Title.
TH4652.M39   1995
727'.5—dc20   94-28955

*"Aye, it is Magic, but not as
you know it. Not the Magic of
the Gods and Wizards, but the
Magic of the Stars and Men.*

*White Magic, the Infinite Fire
that feeds the Stars themselves
for Eternity with Power that
no God can match.*

*Black Magic, infinite Black and
Cold as the Space between the
Stars and in the Hearts of Men
when they go to War.*

*Brought together by Men who
challenge the Universe with the
Magic of Science and
Technology."*

Ronald Frederick Mayer – 1985

PREFACE

The information in *Design and Planning of Research and Clinical Laboratory Facilities* is based on the author's 33 years of experience, including almost 20 years experience in his specialty consulting practice programming and planning laboratory and health care facilities. The book is intended to be a primer for administrators, researchers, facility managers, and architects and engineers.

The author extends his thanks to associates and friends who encouraged this task and "adventure." The author also extends special thanks to his wife, Alice Marcella, who edited and inputted much of the material, for her patience and time spent over many weekends and late nights assisting with the completion of the manuscript.

Additional and equal thanks are extended to Robert Thaddeus (Thad) Braddock of Arlington, Virginia. Thad is the artist for the great sketches that appear in the book. He is not only a very talented artist but is also a budding architect (Associate Member of the American Institute of Architects). Thad is currently employed as an intern architect by Cannon, the nationally renowned architectural and engineering firm (Washington, DC office). The author met Thad while collaborating with Cannon on several research laboratory projects.

The intent of the book is to assist administrators, researchers, facility managers, and design professionals (the architect and engineer) develop planning and design criteria. An extensive list of publications is included. Reasonable effort has been made to provide current and accurate information. The information is not intended to be used as a substitute for detailed design criteria and calculations related to a specific project.

The information and data contained in the standards, guidelines, and other publications listed have been compiled by various governmental agencies and recognized authorities and represents their opinions and experience. Since laws, regulations, and codes are subject to frequent changes, readers are advised to confer with appropriate local, state, and federal authorities for latest editions prior to recommending specific designs for a proposed facility.

CONTENTS

INTRODUCTION

This book is intended to be a primer for administrators, researchers, facility managers, architects, and engineers. It presents biomedical, environmental, physical, and basic sciences research laboratory programming, planning, and design criteria based on the experience of the author. The book focuses on what may be considered as wet laboratory environments, such as chemistry and biology including related subspecialties. There are those in the laboratory community who contend that the wet laboratory may eventually disappear—that computer modeling technology, imaging, data transmission, networking, fiber optics, and other yet-to-be-defined investigative techniques will replace the test tube, beaker, and flask approach. It is emphasized, however, that the basic programming and planning principles indicated are equally applicable to *all* research, clinical, teaching, and production-type laboratory facilities.

Numerous master plans, facility programs, functional programs, and programs of requirements were prepared and developed by the author to accommodate a wide variety of scientific disciplines and related spaces, including:

- Administrative office facilities
- Basic and physical sciences laboratories
- Biomedical research laboratories
- Central audiovisual and library facilities
- Central computer facilities
- Conference and education facilities
- Core, support, and building services facilities
- Engineering and testing laboratories
- Laboratory animal facilities
- Materials management and handling facilities
- Pathology and clinical laboratories

Included is an extensive list of codes, regulations, standards, guidelines, and other reference publications. Also included are architectural, structural, mechanical, electrical, and plumbing criteria. The information is intended to illustrate the myriad of factors that must be considered during the programming, planning, design, and construction process for laboratory, laboratory service and support, and related facilities.

Laboratory facilities are considered to be the most complex and costly structures to program, plan, design, construct, operate, and maintain. Financing laboratory facilities is a complex and costly activity compared to financing other building types. Environmental studies, zoning requirements, hazardous materials analysis, and waste management (collection, processing, holding, disposal, etc.) are only a fraction of the many complex factors that have a significant impact on the design of laboratory facilities. All these factors—and more—must be considered during the programming and planning phase.

PROGRAMMING CRITERIA

The space program criteria present the range of work areas expressed in net or usable square feet required for a variety of laboratory functions and activities. Estimates for functional net square feet requirements should include space needs to meet guidelines and regulations governing accommodations for disabled persons and safety for all persons in the laboratory workplace environment. The "traditional standard" of 5'-0" wide aisles (based on a 10'-0"-wide module) between laboratory work counters is questionable and should be considered obsolete. Some sources indicate that 3'-6" to 4'-0" aisle clearances are adequate. These clearances are inadequate and can restrict egress during an emergency. Space standards that are being developed to meet the requirements of the Americans with Disabilities Act will make traditional and most current standards obsolete.

Architectural barriers requirements and guidelines should be considered as one of the many factors that must be considered and applied when developing space criteria. Many of these requirements and guidelines cannot be accommodated within traditional and current space planning standards and factors. The general intent of the Americans with Disabilities Act is to remedy inequities encountered by individuals with disabilities in employment and facilities under current laws.

The impact on space allocation requirements will be significant—and costly.

Most casework and work counter units (including the utility service chase) are 2'-6" deep. Aisle widths are usually measured from face to face of the casework and/or equipment face. Many items of equipment (chemical fume hoods, biological safety cabinets, refrigerators, ovens, incubators, autoclaves, centrifuges, autoanalyzers, etc.) are 3'-0" to 3'-6" deep. These items protrude into the aisle, reducing the circulation space between the work counters and equipment. Analytical and test equipment, supplies, and so on, are often transported to the work counter on mobile utility carts further restricting aisle space and can cause egress problems if an emergency occurs. Many electronic equipment items, whether floor or counter mounted, require service access on all sides. Aisle widths of 5'-6" to 6'-0" (and more) will have to be considered and may become the new traditional standard.

Chemical fume hoods and biological safety cabinets appear in corner locations or adjacent to the door (entry/exit) of the laboratory in published plans of many laboratory projects. Office spaces open to the laboratory work areas are considered functionally appropriate. It has been traditional practice in medical schools to locate faculty offices adjacent to or within research and clinical laboratory work areas. These traditional practices are not only questionable from a safety standpoint but may violate certain guidelines, standards and regulations relating to exposure of staff to hazardous environments. Again, these are only a few of the many factors that determine the space requirements and functional relationships for laboratories and related spaces.

PROGRAMMING JUSTIFICATION

To provide an efficient and safe laboratory work environment, mechanical, electrical, and plumbing systems are becoming increasingly complex, sophisticated, space consuming, and costly. Building space(s) required for services and utilities to supply many laboratory work areas include:

- Service personnel access and clearance for maintenance, replacement, or modification of mechanical, electrical, plumbing, valves, equipment, and so on.
- Auxiliary heating, cooling, and ventilation units to control

or supplement laboratory processes and equipment energy output.

- Electrical cabinets and panels, telecommunication/data conduits, and cable trays.
- Filter boxes for fume hoods and biosafety cabinets. These items of equipment are becoming more frequent. Some weigh as much as 100 lb (or more). Some filters may trap and contain hazardous particles—both biological and radioactive. Adequate space and clearances *must* be provided for servicing, testing, and replacement of motors, fans, and filters.
- Other motors, pumps, fans, and similar equipment.
- Plumbing pipes, gas lines, and drains.
- Supply and exhaust air ducts.

It is important to note that utility space requirements (ductwork, fans, motors, filter boxes, pipes and redundant systems, etc.) to service certain scientific disciplines and processes *may equal the floor area and volume requirements of the individual laboratory work area(s).*

The administration of the institution is a key ingredient to the successful completion of a functional, efficient, and safe laboratory or health care facility. The rationalizations most often cited to accelerate the programming and planning process (or eliminate them because "we know what we want") are:

- "The cost of the consultant fees and the length of time it takes to program and plan is not worth the expense," and/or
- "We cannot take the time to program and plan because every day that passes, construction costs are increasing and we are losing money."

COMMENTS

1. Facility programming and planning *must* be regarded in the same context and as having the same importance as financial and budgetary planning. Facilities are an important asset and resource and are second only to personnel in cost. They must be managed as other assets and resources. Facility programming and plan-

ning cannot be accomplished successfully after the fact. It is then usually too late and too costly to remedy the results of a lack of planning.

2. There is no longer justification or reason to dispute the fact that properly programmed, planned, and designed work spaces and facilities for employees increases efficiency, productivity, safety, and profitability—regardless of the function and activity to be accomplished. It is in an institution's self-interest to devote the time and resources for programming and planning *any* proposed facility. Implementation of laws and regulations virtually mandate that detailed programming and planning be part of the facility acquisition process.

3. It is *critically important* that the architect-of-record and the engineer participate in the initial programming and planning phases of a proposed laboratory facilities project. If the architect-of-record has not been engaged, one should be selected as soon as possible. It is the author's recommendation that the programming and planning consultant be a member of the architect-of-record's team.

4. The cost of consultant fees, including participation by representatives of the institution, is *always* a small fraction (usually less than 1%) of the total cost of the facility. Assistance of experienced and knowledgeable consultants as members of the design professionals' (architect-of-record and engineer) team during the programming and planning process *always* results in savings that far exceed the time invested and fees paid. These costs should be considered an investment with significant returns rather than lost or unrecoverable overhead costs.

5. Laboratory consultants must be selected carefully. Some are untrained or do not have the education and experience in planning, design, and construction. Some approach the problem of planning and design with preconceived concepts and ideas that often have no relation to the specific nature of the scientific discipline to be accommodated. Avoid representatives of equipment or casework companies offering free planning services. Free services are never free. The laboratory consultant should be a member of the architect-of-record's team.

6. Construction costs are increasing with each passing day. However, what is often overlooked by an institution is the fact that the money invested during this time usually has a greater return than is supposedly lost through construction cost escalation. This is another indication of the importance of total project planning. The emphasis must be to integrate all facets of the total facilities acquisition process, including strategic planning, financial planning, long-range master facilities planning, programming and planning, design, construction, occupancy, and operations.

PARTICIPANTS IN THE PROCESS

Functionally efficient, safe, and cost-effective laboratory facilities *cannot* be planned and designed without input from many sources, including:

- The architect, and structural, civil, mechanical, electrical, plumbing, and sanitation engineers
- Chemical and reagent manufacturers
- The construction manager and contractor
- Consultants in laboratory programming and planning, environmental engineering, biosafety procedures, acoustics, vibration control, computer information systems and networks, telecommunications, audiovisual systems, security, interior design, animal facilities planning, hazardous materials analysis, waste management, construction cost analysis, graphics and signage, safety engineers, radiofrequency/electromagnetic/gamma radiation shielding and protection, and food services
- Financial planning, sources and methods of financing, grantsmanship
- Laboratory apparatus and equipment manufacturers
- Materials handling and management systems
- Representatives from local, state, and federal agencies (life safety, fire marshal, building inspectors, zoning, architectural review, etc.); and depending on the location of the facility, representatives from community groups
- Representatives from the institution, including the board of trustees; general administrators, research administra-

tors, and development and grants administrators; scientists and researchers/investigators; physicians and nurses (clinical research); laboratory workers; technicians and technologists; paramedical, service, and support staff; safety and disaster planning officer(s); facility managers; plant engineering and maintenance, environmental services (housekeeping), infection control, and human resources personnel; and so on.

Not all of the disciplines listed above would be involved throughout the entire project process. The design professionals (architect and engineer) and key members of the institution's staff would form the core planning and design team. Other disciplines would participate at various intervals during the process.

The institution must make the commitment to invest adequate time, personnel, and resources in the programming and planning process. Sufficient time must be allocated for periodic review sessions during the programming and planning process. The users (researchers, operations and maintenance staff, etc.) must be permitted time for second thoughts during the development of space criteria, functional relationship diagrams, space schematics and schematic design, and design development documents.

The usual impatience to secure departmental sign-offs at the completion of the programming and planning phases without adequate time intervals for review will always result in changes and complications that cause costly delays during the preparation of design and construction documents. There are no shortcuts or easy methods to program and plan laboratory facilities.

Those facilities that are functionally and operationally successful are the direct result of the institution's commitment to the programming, planning, and design process.

THE METRIC SYSTEM

The use and application of the metric system has been the law of the land since passage of the *Metric Conversion Act of 1975*, as amended by the *Omnibus Trade and Competitiveness Act of 1988*. These acts establish the modern metric system (Systemè International or SI) as the preferred system of measurement in the United States. Since September 30, 1992, the act has required that to the extent feasible and practical, the metric system is to be used in all federal procurement contracts for services, supplies, and so on; grants; and business-related activities.

Many industries have begun the process of conversion. Many large corporations such as General Motors are now completely metric. Many institutions are teaching use of the metric system. Since all facets of the economy and society are affected, the process of conversion has been and probably will continue to move slowly. However, experience since conversion began indicates that conversion is occurring without significant problems. Since January 1994, the federal government has required that virtually all documentation (drawings and specifications) for federal construction projects be produced using metrics. This requirement appears more and more frequently, as evidenced in *Commerce Business Daily* (CBD) announcements of construction projects.

The American Society of Heating, Refrigerating, and Air-Conditioning Engineers, Inc. (ASHRAE), American Society of Mechanical Engineers (ASME), American Society for Testing and Materials (ASTM), Construction Specifications Institute (CSI), National Fire Protection Association (NFPA), and others publish metric editions of many of their standards. Several of the code groups, including the Building Officials and Code Administrators International, Inc. (BOCA), publish their codes in dual units (both metric and inch-pound measurements). Many handicapped accessibility and product standards are published with dual units. The metric measurements in these publications are all virtually exact or "soft" conversions. These conversions will eventually become "hard" metric units as more industries complete the conversion to metric.

Soft metrics may be described as direct mathematical conversions of Imperial (English—feet/inches, etc.) measurements: for example, 1 inch (in.) = 2.54 millimeters (mm). Hard metric would convert this to 2.50 mm or 2.60 mm. What hard unit should be used? The standard reference is National Technical Information Service NBS Technical Note 990, *The Selection of Preferred Metric Values for Design and Construction.*

The following publications are considered the standards on the metric system:

- ASTM E380, *Standard Practice for the Use of the International System of Units (SI)*

- ASTM E621, *Standard Practice for the Use of Metric (SI) Units in Design and Construction*
- ANSI/IEEE 268, *American National Standard Metric Practice*

An excellent publication entitled *Metric Guide for Federal Construction* is available from the Construction Metrification Council of the National Institute of Building Sciences (NIBS), 1201 L Street, NW, Washington, DC 20005. The publication summarizes metrics, discusses metrics in construction, metric usage, and length/area/volume; civil/structural/mechanical/electrical engineering; education, management and training, definitions, rules (conversion and rounding), and metric documentation. Included is an extensive bibliography of metric references. Call (202) 289-7800 to order. Also inquire about their *Metric in Construction Newsletter.*

Additional useful and informative metric publications are:

- ASTM E713, *Guide for Selection of Scales for Metric Building Drawings*
- ASTM E557, *Guide for Dimensional Coordination of Rectilinear Building Parts and Systems*
- *Metric Units of Measurement and Style Guide*, U.S. Metric Association, 10245 Andasol Avenue, Northridge, CA 91325, (818) 363-5606
- *Metric-X Conversion Software*, Orion Development Corp., P.O. Box 2323, Merrifield, VA 22116, 1-800-992-8170
- NIST, Special Publication 330, *The International System of Units (SI)*, Superintendent of Documents, U.S. Government Printing Office, Washington, DC 20402, (202) 783-3238
- *The Architect's Studio Companion: Technical Guidelines for Preliminary Design* (includes dual units), Edward Allen and Joseph Iano, John Wiley & Sons, Inc., Professional Reference and Trade Group, 605 Third Avenue, New York, NY 10158, 1-800-225-5945

Addresses not indicated for sources above are listed in Appendix C.

All dimensioning in this book is in Imperial measurements.

OBJECTIVES

This is not a "how-to" book. Laboratory facilities are far too complex to be designed from a book. Numerous opinions and experiences exist about how laboratory facilities should be planned and designed. The information contained herein presents the author's experience, new and updated criteria based on recent laws, and rules and regulations for consideration in the facilities programming and design process. Data that is often overlooked or not considered during the facilities programming and planning process is presented and highlighted. The author welcomes comments that readers may have regarding the material presented and suggestions for additional topics to be included in updates to this book and to future planning monographs.

■ CHAPTER ■

1 PROGRAMMING AND PLANNING CRITERIA

The criteria presented in this book are applicable to the several building service and utility systems concepts used to plan and design laboratory facilities, including:

- Interstitial space, 6' to 8' high clear (±)
- Multiple service cores or shafts, x'-x'' on-center (o.c.) vertical, horizontal, interior (in-board/out-board), and/or exterior of the building
- Services corridor, 10' to 12' to 14' wide clear (±)
- Mechanical space at the ceiling (unfinished—exposed services) or above the finished ceiling, 4' to 6' clear (±)
- Combinations of the systems described above

The building services or utilities concept developed should provide sufficient *space and clearances for changes and maintenance* of all conduits, pipes, valves, ducts, filters, motors, pumps, telecommunications, data, electronic wire, fiber optic cable and cable trays, and other service and support systems for laboratory work areas (Figures 1.1a–d). The services should be installed in an orderly and rational pattern to ensure access for maintenance, operations, and replacement of components, use of test equipment (static pressure in ducts, airflow, etc.), and maximum flexibility for future additions and deletions to each laboratory module. Ease of access must be provided to duct inspection and cleanout panels, observation ports, electrical distribution panels, and so on. Access to shutoff, control valves, and electrical master switches in times of emergency can be a critical factor. Locating services within wall systems is not considered an efficient means to distribute required ser-

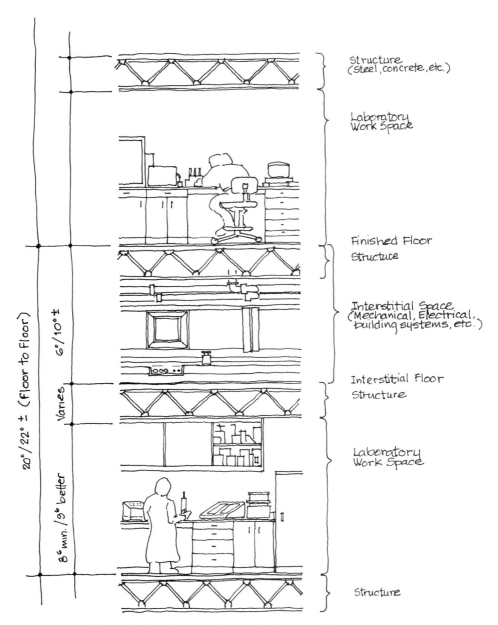

Figure 1.1a Example interstitial space utility concept.

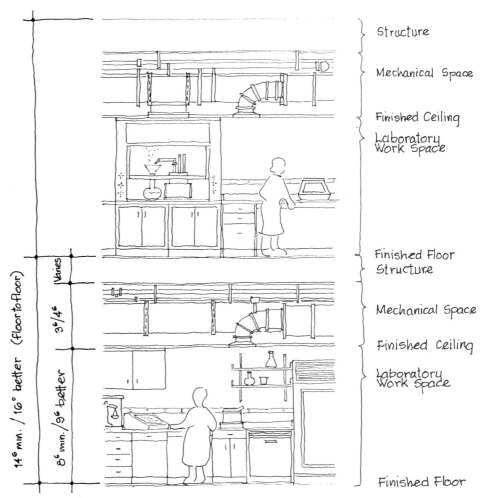

Figure 1.1b Example ceiling space utility concept.

vices for laboratory facilities. All service elements, including ducts, pipes, valves, panel boxes, switches, conduits, and so on, *must be identified clearly and legibly.* The American National Standards Institute, Inc., publishes a guideline (ANSI A131-81) for identifying piping systems.

Whether or not the services (pipes, ductwork, conduits, etc.) should be exposed at the ceiling in laboratory work areas must be considered carefully. Exposed services at the ceiling may provide ease of access for changes, maintenance, and so on. However, the top surfaces of these elements will accumulate dust and dirt particles. Over time, these particles, including the minute flaking of the coatings (paint, insulation, etc.),

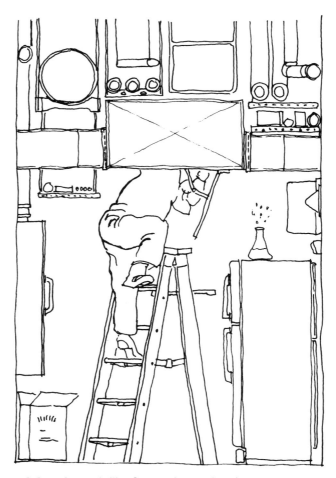

Figure 1.1c Accessibility for service and maintenance must not be compromised.

will begin to raindown on the tables, equipment, and experiments in progress.

Exposed service systems may not be appropriate in certain biomedical or chemical research laboratory work areas where size of dust particles may be of concern. Size of particles is of particular concern in various production and manufacturing facilities (e.g., pharmaceuticals and electronic components). Exposed services and utilities, however, may be satisfactory and economical in various engineering, environmental, and some physical science (physics, etc.) laboratories. Again, it is during programming meetings with researchers and investigators that design criteria for special environments can be identified.

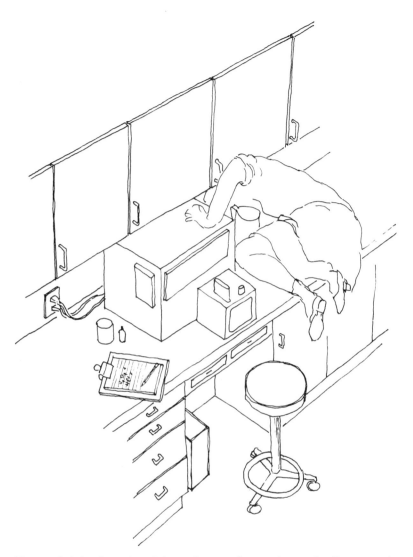

Figure 1.1d Access to lab equipment for service and adjustment is equally vital as access to lab services and utilities.

Floor penetration in laboratory work areas is a subject of considerable discussion. Many laboratory workers and safety officers contend that they should be avoided. Floor penetrations provide an opening for spills to flow to spaces below and tunnels for insects and vermin. It is difficult to prevent punctures to the waterproofing membrane during installation and construction. Floor drain traps may dry out, creating odor and hazardous gas problems.

In one laboratory facility it took several months of almost daily investigation to locate the source of a very malodorous condition. The source turned out to be a dried-out floor drain that had been covered and hidden from view by a piece of equipment. Fortunately, the odorous gas emissions were not hazardous. This condition, in many instances, can be solved through careful placement on the design and construction documents, and follow through during construction. Finally, a well-managed building maintenance and operations program to fill the drain trap periodically will eliminate dry drain traps. Certain research functions and processes, however, may require an island work counter arrangement with a sink and resultant drain line through the floor.

In another laboratory facility, floor drains were provided convenient to the emergency safety deluge showers, presumably to drain the water if the shower was used in an emergency. During a weekend when the building was virtually unoccupied, one of the shower valves failed. The resulting flood [flow pressure of 5 to 50 pounds per square inch (psi) and flow rate of 20 to 135 gallons per minute (gpm)] inundated and destroyed a computer facility that was located on the floor below. The equipment loss alone was several thousands of dollars. The floor drain could not cope with the volume of water released. We are all familiar with the operating principles of Murphy's laws. These types of systems and equipment failures almost never happen during normal business hours.

Since all laboratory work areas and service and support spaces may be subject to a wide variety of functions, activities, and range of environmental and security controls, each should be serviced independent of the other. Each laboratory work area module should have access to all services, regardless of the service concept developed. This permits shutdown of services to make changes to specific laboratory work areas or to respond should an emergency occur. Separation of control systems permits shutdown of selected laboratory work areas without forcing cessation of operations in other laboratory work areas. However, this standard should be considered carefully in the context of its impact on program criteria, flexibility to permit future change, maintenance and operating costs, and most important, initial facility construction costs. It may be that the least expensive initial cost solution is to provide shutdown controls for two to three modules instead of each module. Most laboratory planning and design professionals, including facility managers and engineers, would recommend that each module be provided shutdown controls.

All control systems, however, must also be designed carefully to avoid inadvertent shutdown in adjacent laboratory work areas. An ongoing experiment can be ruined completely if interrupted for any reason. Certain research grant restrictions and conditions may also prescribe that if an experiment is interrupted, the researcher may face loss of the balance of the grant. The researcher (institution) may also have to make restitution of the grant monies already expended. Thus the people responsible for administration of the grant(s) should be included during the initial programming interview phase of the project. This is extremely important during remodeling and renovations to an existing laboratory building. Construction phasing becomes paramount to ensure that accidental service interruptions and shutdowns do not occur or can be controlled.

COMMENTS

1. Interstitial mechanical and equipment space is perhaps the most controversial and costly of the building services systems concepts. Interstitial space consists of a floor devoted to mechanical, electrical, and plumbing service systems and equipment above each occupied floor. For example, a 10-story building would contain five floors of usable functional space (laboratories, service and support, offices, etc.) and five floors of building systems and equipment space. The floor-to-floor height of the interstitial space is usually less than the occupied space. The most significant advantage of this concept is the virtual unlimited access and flexibility to accommodate functional changes in the occupied laboratory work space below (see Figure 1.1a).

2. Disadvantages of an interstitial space concept may include:

   a. The addition to the building of considerable volume (cubic feet) per gross square foot compared to other services systems. An interstitial services concept can add 15 to 20% (or more) to the construction cost compared to a building with comparable gross square feet and a different services concept.

   b. Difficulty to conform with fire codes (type of materials selected to separate the interstitial space from the occupied space below, etc.).

c. Floor loading of the interstitial space must be sufficient to accommodate maintenance personnel, movement of replacement equipment (motors, fans, filter boxes, etc.). Certain filter boxes may weigh more than 100 lb, requiring a small hand electric lift truck to remove or move the filter boxes.

d. If the building structure is a steel frame, certain diagonal braces and struts may interfere with duct runs, location of filter box access panels, fans, motors and so on.

3. A service corridor concept has the advantage of providing space for certain items of equipment that may not be accessed often, such as refrigerators, freezers, and centrifuges, immediately adjoining the laboratory work area. The service corridor can also become the horizontal transport corridor for movement of supplies, equipment, and animals. Waste products can also be transported through the service corridor. Such use eliminates the conflict of movement of these items from the public and staff circulation corridor. Valuable space in the laboratory work area is available for direct experimental activities. Gas cylinders (CO_2, N_2, NO_2, O_2, He, mixed gases, etc.) can also be located in the service corridor.

4. The apparent advantages of the service corridor concept is not without disadvantages, hazards, and safety and security problems. The doors from the laboratory work areas to the service corridor can permit unauthorized and untrained persons access to the mechanical and electrical equipment. This can create a dangerous situation causing severe injury to an innocent person. A person with intent to cause problems and damage has the opportunity to do so, creating hazards for others. Placing laboratory equipment in the service corridor can also create problems with access to the mechanical and electrical equipment during remodeling and renovations or in an emergency situation.

5. Each services concept has advantages and disadvantages. Each must be evaluated within the context of

the program criteria, design, construction costs, and operational and maintenance costs and efficiencies. Consideration must also be given to the strategic and long-range master plans for the institution. There is no ideal services concept that will be optimum for all research activities. There is, however, an optimum concept for a given series of program criteria. The key to developing this optimum concept is the initial commitment to detailed interactive programming and planning involving all the key players. These programming sessions provide the opportunity to determine specific program criteria and then to design the optimum services system.

6. Every researcher, investigator, administrator, facility manager, and maintenance engineer will probably cite flexibility or adaptability as the most important criterion for a laboratory facility. The researcher and investigator will cite the constantly changing nature of scientific activity. The administrator will cite the need for flexible laboratory space to attract first-class researchers and investigators. And last but certainly not least, the facility manager and maintenance engineer will cite the ease to make changes and adapt the laboratory work space to satisfy all of the above.

7. Flexibility is not without its price. Building systems and spaces designed to accommodate many different types of scientific functions and activities are generally not economically feasible or practical. Attempts to accommodate such widely divergent activities may result in remodeling and renovation costs that exceed the costs of new space. The resulting space may contain many facility and environmental compromises that ultimately have a negative effect on the activity to be accommodated. It is therefore extremely important to determine the variety of activities to be accommodated and the building systems required— *and, of course, let's not forget the little item called the construction budget.*

8. The equipment elements of the mechanical, electrical, and plumbing systems—ductwork, fans, motors, pumps, filter boxes, conduits, panel boxes, pipes, drains, shutoff valves, cable trays, and services capped for future extension—must be carefully planned, or-

ganized, and identified. The location of these items must be coordinated on the respective architectural and engineering construction documents. Frequently, these building elements conflict with each other and the building structural members. For example, fume hood exhaust duct filter boxes are often located where access is restricted by building structural members, making filter replacement difficult and dangerous. Existing ductwork, fans, and filter boxes had to be removed—and reinstalled—in order to replace the fume hood filters. Proper care and thoughtfulness during design—and construction administration—can provide an opportunity to remedy a costly and dangerous condition.

9. It cannot be overemphasized that the architectural and engineering design and construction administration team members must have significant knowledge and experience with laboratory facilities design and construction *before they are selected as team members*. The design team should be selected based on the following criteria:

   a. Relevant design experience with similar facilities not only in scale and scope, but functions and activities as well. Experience with a high-energy physics laboratory is not sufficient qualification for the planning and design of a pharmaceutical research laboratory and production facility.

   b. Experience in master planning of large academic university or corporate facilities indicates that the design firm has an understanding of and sensitivity to the strategic and long-range goals and objectives of the potential client. Since many research laboratory facility projects are part of a university environment, the facility often has to provide space for undergraduate and graduate education and teaching programs. A strategic goal might be, for example, to develop and establish a "center of excellence" in a particular area of science.

   c. The design firm should have an understanding of the preferences of the administration and the scientific community at the institution, including a keen awareness of the politics that is an extremely important element at any university.

d. The design firm must have superior and high-quality references from similar and representative clients. The references should reflect a cross section of the participants in a research laboratory project, including the highest administrative level (board members, dean, chief executive officer, provost, etc.), department chairpersons, chief investigators, chief technologists and technicians, facility managers and building plant engineers, and so on.

e. The design firm should exhibit a stable staff of key or core professionals experienced with research laboratory planning, design, and construction. Many times, projects listed in a firm's brochure may indicate substantial project experience. Often, however, no one remains at the firm who may have been involved with certain projects.

f. Awards may be a significant factor for selection. However, awards from peer groups are usually not as significant or meaningful as awards conferred by recognized special industry groups, scientific organizations, etc. A design award is not nearly as important as an award for an innovative building services system or an energy conservation system that provides significant savings for the institution over the life of the building. This is not to imply that aesthetics are not an important factor in the design team selection process.

10. Space and clearances must be provided for maintenance personnel to sit, stand, crouch, bend, kneel, reach, twist, turn, or lift and to manipulate wrenches, screwdrivers, saws, hammers, welding equipment, and other tools. Space must also be provided to deploy ladders and mechanical lifts to remove and service equipment, change light bulbs and tubes, clean and dust, use test equipment, etc. It is not only frustrating for personnel to work in cramped mechanical spaces but can be dangerous as well. OSHA regulations mandate that safe and adequate work spaces of all types be designed and provided for all building occupants. A few minutes' discussion with many building engineering and maintenance staff will reveal how little thought is given during the planning and design process to the time when building systems maintenance, operations, and replacements are required. Several of these key persons should be included during the programming interview phase. An architectural or engineering design system or element that cannot be operated, serviced, maintained and replaced in a safe and efficient manner is a *failure*. The design professional may face severe liability responsibilities for injuries that may occur because of such poor (thoughtless and dangerous) nonfunctional planning and design features.

11. It is considered good practice to include in a specifications of a construction contract documents the requirement that each building construction discipline (mechanical, electrical, and plumbing contractors or subcontractors) develop and prepare installation and coordination drawings to minimize conflicts in the placement of building systems components (ductwork, pipes, conduits, etc.). However, responsibility for determining adequate space allowances for scientific research functions and activities, including adequate space for the building systems to support these functions and activities, *rests initially with the design professionals. The programming and planning activities of a laboratory project are the most important phases of the entire facility acquisition process.*

The latest buzzword with reference to laboratory facilities is state-of-the-art. A few years ago the phrase was on the cutting edge. Presumably, this means that the facility incorporates the latest in building systems design, equipment, and casework technology, flexibility to accommodate a variety of research functions and activities, and so on. The following items might be considered as attributes of a state of the art research laboratory facility:

1. Sufficient building systems and laboratory services that are representative of the program criteria (not in order of priority).

   a. Adequate clean and uninterruptible power source (UPS), including emergency power and building watts per square foot vs. laboratory work area watts per square foot.

b. Built-in temperature-controlled spaces/rooms vs. prefabricated units and "reach-in" units.

c. Creation of a generic or basic modular plan to permit accommodation of a wide variety of scientific research functions and activities; should adhere to previously established planning principles.

d. Data and telecommunications systems (CCTV, computer networks, fiber optics, microwave/satellite transmission, cable trays, etc.).

e. Energy-efficient facilities (variable-volume systems, computerized building environmental control systems, etc.) and heat recovery systems.

f. Flexibility to permit ease of responding to changing functions and activities, equipment, and response to regulations (ADA, EPA, OSHA, etc.).

g. Individual laboratory work area/space module temperature, humidity, and lighting controls.

h. Life safety and emergency systems (fire and smoke suppression, flame and smoke detectors, spill containment materials, etc.), emergency eye wash and showers, fire blankets, and disaster planning.

i. Materials management systems (ordering; purchasing; receiving; holding; storage; inventory; distribution; and maintenance, repair, and calibration of equipment; etc.).

j. Natural, special, and mixed gases (gaseous and liquid states, cryogenics, dewars, storage/distribution systems, low-temperature systems, etc.), used helium storage and reclamation facilities, and gas cylinders.

k. Proper air quality (near-zero emissions standards, chemical exposure limits), changes per hour, pressure differentials, filters, scrubbers, and air movement and distribution within a space (laminar flow, etc.).

l. Proper functional relationships among the principal activities, adjacent offices and core facilities (shared work areas, equipment, staff), and service and support spaces.

m. Special environmental requirements [radiation, magnetic and electromotive force (EMF) shielding, microwave, vibration control, etc.].

n. Waste management systems (containers, collection,

holding, processing, transportation, disposal, recycling, hazardous and nonhazardous).

o. Water quality, chemical purity, volume, pressure, and temperature.

2. Spatial volume (three dimensions) reflecting functional relationship requirements (modular planning) and building service and utility systems concepts.

3. Attention to regulatory building code, safety and security requirements outlined in BOCA, EPA, NFPA, OSHA, and so on, regulations, including laboratory practice guidelines, and standards contained in AAALAC, AALAS, CLIA, JCAHO, NCCLS, NIH, NIOSH, and other publications.

4. Attention and accommodations to ADA requirements to provide accessibility to all persons, including staff and visitors.

5. Aesthetically pleasing and functional work environment, including color, texture, lighting, vistas (views from the building), spatial relationships, acoustics, and so on, to foster interdisciplinary interaction and exchange of ideas, including integrated research, teaching, and public relations activities, if part of the program.

6. Energy-efficient designs to reduce operating costs, and selection of materials to minimize the impact on the immediate site and surrounding environment, and improvement in the interior building environment (control of the sick building syndrome).

7. Convenient vehicular access for service, deliveries (loading dock), and trash dumpsters (control of insects and vermin); fire and staff emergencies; adequate parking facilities; accommodations for public transportation; and so on.

8. The two most outstanding qualities of a state-of-the-art research laboratory facility appear to be:

    a. Capacity, flexibility or adaptability to accommodate a wide variety of initial program functions and activities.

    b. Capacity, flexibility or adaptability to accommodate future changes in research functions and activities with a minimum of remodeling and renovation expense.

Users (researchers and investigators) are generally concerned that the facility should provide adequate utilities and services, including proper lighting levels, minimum building vibrations, optimum functional relationships and adjacencies, space efficiencies [net square feet (nsf) to gross square feet (gsf) ratios—*maximum nsf* and *minimum gsf*]; and maximum built-ins. Care must be exercised in response to requests for built-in casework, equipment, controlled environment spaces, refrigerators, and so on. Built-in elements can reduce flexibility, making changes time consuming, difficult, and expensive. Built-in elements are often included in the initial construction budget estimates and can result in significant cost increases. Built-in elements are usually not included and paid for by research grants. Most users feel that their laboratory should be custom designed and often do not support generic laboratory planning concepts. The other precaution relative to satisfying individual preferences relates to the fact that the individual investigator requesting such customization often has left his or her position at the institution before the laboratory facility is completed.

Administrators at universities or corporations are most concerned with the cost and quality of the proposed facility. They are also concerned with the building efficiency relative to the nsf/gsf ratio. They focus on flexibility and ease of remodeling and renovations that inevitably occur on an increasingly frequent basis. Other factors include generic design and compliance with the explosion of regulations applicable not only to life and fire safety items but also to the working environment of the laboratory, management of hazardous materials and reagents, operations and maintenance costs, and so on. The proposed laboratory facility must also conform to and complement the strategic and long-range goals, objectives, and mission of the institution.

It is not the intent of this book to present any one services system concept as being more advantageous than another. The building services concept should evolve as a function of the program of requirements or the design program. An interstitial services concept may be practical for an environmental research facility that may use a large number of fume hoods with redundant exhaust fans and filter boxes. A corridor (or ceiling) services system concept may be more efficient and less costly for biomedical or physical sciences disciplines. Each system has advantages and disadvantages. Each must be analyzed within the context of the program criteria. An institution should avoid approaching the planning and design of a laboratory facility with a preconceived idea or plan that presumes the ability to accommodate *all* types of research functions and activities.

The facilities must be designed to have a measure of flexibility to accommodate future program and technological changes and remain economical to construct and operate. Building systems excess design capacity for research facilities may be as little as 10 to 15% and as much as 40% or more. Changing a laboratory work area (module) to accommodate a different scientific discipline may not involve additional space requirements to perform the new functions and activities. However, the services requirements may be several times as great as the former activity. The building systems' built-in flexibility (excess design capacity) must also be cost-effective and meet proposed capital and operational budget limitations or restrictions.

A research facility designed primarily to accommodate biomedical or environmental disciplines may not be economically adaptable to high-tech electronic, pharmaceutical clean room production activities, or a physics research project requiring high-bay space to accommodate lifts and cranes. It may be significantly less expensive and more functionally efficient to design and build a new facility than to rehab an existing building. Again, this highlights the importance of the programming and planning phase process and the development of the basic building systems design criteria prior to making such determinations.

How much flexibility should or can be designed into a facility? What is the impact on first and life-cycle costs? Should the foundations be stressed for vertical expansion? Should an exterior wall be designed to accommodate horizontal additions or bridge connections? Are the costs of the additional structural elements to provide this flexibility justified? Each of these items must be viewed and analyzed in the context of the specific research program criteria requirements. There is no single solution, whether it involves a utilities services concept, a particular laboratory module dimension, or other arrangement, that suits all proposed laboratory facilities.

It is not always possible, practical, or even desirable to build a facility with "shell space" (unassigned/unfinished space). Often, initial costs preclude such an investment. In certain instances the anticipated scientific research discipline to be accommodated may require building services criteria that are not available in the existing shell space. It may be too costly, and therefore not practical, to rehab the shell space economically. Remodeling often results in many compromises that can handicap the intended research activity. Experience indicates that shell space is almost always allocated and filled even before the building is completed.

The traditional criteria related to wet vs. dry laboratory work areas are becoming less distinct and may no longer provide a feasible classification or standard. Microanalysis techniques used in biomedical and clinical laboratories reduce the need for large volumes of reagents and specimen fluids. Regulations governing the use of various reagents may accelerate the application of microanalysis techniques. Many autoanalyzers can perform multiple tests on a minute quantity of a specimen. Specimens can be collected, inserted in specially designed containers, tested, stored, processed, and disposed of without the specimen being removed from the test container. Use of smaller amounts of reagents and specimens for laboratory processes has the added benefit of reducing waste volumes and further minimizing hazardous conditions for staff. However, electrical power requirements to service the new electronic equipment are increasing at a rapid rate.

Many of the new electronic test equipment may also require a clean electrical power source, further complicating design of the basic electrical power system. Fortunately, there are many devices on the market that can provide clean power to the equipment, computer, and so on. These devices plug into any outlet. Specially designed electronic circuits monitor and control power surges and electrical "noise." The equipment serviced is provided with clean and stable power. Emergency power requirements can also create expensive backup building systems and space requirements (generators, controls, fuel storage, service areas, etc.). Many of these new machines also require a more controlled and stable space environment. These machines are often more sensitive to changes in temperature, humidity, and vibration. Such environmental and operational criteria will increase demands for more sophisticated and costly building systems.

The problem of hazardous reagents and materials purchase, transport, storage, use, processing, and disposal has become very complex and costly. Government regulations are becoming more restrictive and costly to follow. The safest, most effective, most efficient, and least costly methodology in the management of such hazardous products is to limit and minimize the initial use. Many institutions have established research review committees to examine the proposed research program and develop basic hazardous materials protocols and criteria. These criteria or standards provide the framework that governs the use of such materials. Key members of this committee *must* participate in the initial programming and planning process.

Perhaps the most overlooked item in the equation to program and plan functional, efficient and economical laboratory facilities is the human factor. As research becomes more sophisticated and complicated, the need for service and support functions, activities and staff multiplies. New electronic test equipment requires complex levels of service, maintenance, and calibration. Service technicians now require expensive and extended training periods. Bioengineering facilities at some institutions are large and expensive departments. All these elements require staff and space to function that were not even conceived of several years ago.

Let's not forget the impact of government regulations. Spaces are now required so that staff can review safety materials and manuals [e.g., material safety data sheets (MSDSs)]. What have these factors to do with programming, planning, and design of laboratory facilities? Full-time staff is required to develop, monitor, and record protocols to conform to safety regulations. Space needs include offices, conference rooms, and classrooms to conduct staff safety orientation sessions, secretarial and support staff areas, and storage areas for supplies. All of these factors have generated entire occupations and specialties that never existed before. The answer to the question above is obvious—additional and increased space factors have to be applied to develop adequate space programs to accommodate these new functions and activities.

ROBOTIC SYSTEMS

Robots or smart machines have been used by manufacturing industries for many years. The auto manufacturers have developed many sophisticated machines that accomplish a wide variety of tasks formerly done by human workers. The advent and development of the computer has produced a variety of even more sophisticated machines that can perform many complicated tasks. Robots are generally stationary or have limited mobility. Newer robots have been equipped with TV cameras permitting the machine to see its environment. The computer program provides the ability for the machine to make choices to accomplish its assigned tasks.

Karel Capek, a Czechoslovakian playwright, invented the word *robot* in a play he wrote in 1920. Although it may have been total imaginative fantasy at the time, the word *robot* has become a permanent word in the world's technical and literary language bank. The noted scientist and author Isaac Asimov has written many stories incorporating robots. Asimov formulated his now famous *Three Laws of Robotics* in a story he wrote called "I, Robot":

1st Law   A Robot may not injure a Human Being, or, through inaction, allow a Human Being to come to harm.

2nd Law   A Robot must obey orders given it by Human Beings except where such orders would conflict with the First Law.

3rd Law   A Robot must protect its own existence as long as such protection does not conflict with the First or Second Law.

—(from the *Handbook of Robotics*, 56th Edition, 2058 A.D.)

Intelligent automated machines are rapidly becoming an important part of the functioning research and clinical laboratory, particularly those involved with hazardous processes and production (pharmaceutical) activities. Various human-like arm or finger extenders and manipulators called *Elmers* are used in nuclear physics (radioisotope "hot labs," etc.) and chemical laboratories to provide a safe and protected means for personnel to handle dangerous chemical and radioactive reagents. Other robots perform repetitive tasks with mathematical precision. Most of these machines are operated and controlled by a computer program system. It is interesting to note that the concept of manipulators to handle hazardous materials was developed by a science fiction author in a story he wrote many years before the need was perceived; this author named the manipulators "Elmers." When such manipulators were developed in high-hazard laboratories to handle radioactive materials, scientists and technicians named these machines Elmers in his honor.

The University of Nebraska Medical Center at Omaha has pioneered the development of laboratory automated systems. These systems are currently designed primarily for application within clinical laboratory testing functions and activities. The systems could, however, be adapted to certain research and production laboratory functions and activities. Also, the facility manager and designer should use caution when considering existing automated systems. Many are proprietary, copyrighted, or patented systems. Use may be restricted or forbidden.

Continued miniaturization of microelectronic components portends even more startling advances in the area of robotic machines. One of the more fascinating developments is in the area of computer-voice-activated software. Such software permits voice inputting of data and computer recognition of voice commands. In essence, the computer becomes a specialized tape recorder and transcriptionist: executing commands, processing voice input to text, and so on. This particular software development will permit an entire new generation of laboratory automated equipment. The fantastic "droids" of the *Star Wars* movie trilogy may not be as fantastic as portrayed. Companies producing automated equipment include the General Electric Company, Westinghouse Corporation, United States

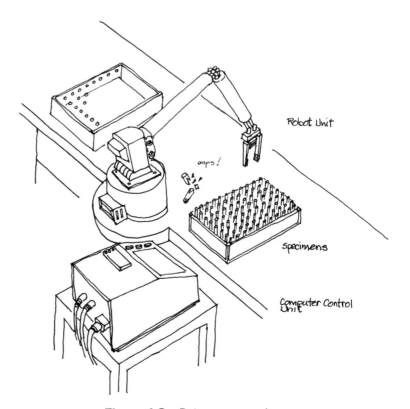

Figure 1.2 Robot arm reach.

Robots, Storage Technology Corporation, GCA Corporation, and Texas Instruments. These companies are a few of the growing industries in the area of robotics.

Space requirements for robots may consist of a series of partially overlapping circular, semicircular, or linear workstations. The reach or radius may be 3' to 4' and as much as 8' to 12' or more, depending on the scope of the activity (Figure 1.2). The robotic system may also include a mechanical rail or transport system connecting a series of robotic workstations with human workstations. Space must be provided for the computer hardware components and peripherals, maintenance and repair of the machines (workshops or bioengineering facilities), sufficient access and clearances for adjustments and repair during operations, and space for equipment and spare parts. The computer control room may not have to be adjacent to the operating or production area.

EFFICIENCY AND COST FACTORS

Several factors that affect and help determine the efficiency and cost of service and utility systems include:

1. Scale and scope of the program [e.g., single-story vs. multistory facilities, campus plan vs. megastructure (single building)].
2. Scientific disciplines, functions, and activities to be accommodated will vary at each institution and may include*:
   a. Basic sciences
      - Anatomy, biochemistry, comparative anatomy or medicine (animal facilities), microbiology and immunology, pathology, pharmacology, and physiology

---

*This list is not all-inclusive. The traditional boundaries between and among many of the basic sciences (e. g., biology, chemistry, and physics) are rapidly disappearing. Subspecialties now include biochemistry, biophysics, neurophysiology, and many others. The expanding and overlapping gray area between and among the sciences has been lending the need to incorporate more interactive spaces convenient to laboratory work areas. Such spaces encourage discussions, exchange of ideas, and requests for assistance to solve problems between or among researchers and investigators. Spaces may include conference/classrooms, research/reference libraries, lounge areas, cafeteria/snack/vending areas, and lobby/courtyard/atrium areas.

    b. Clinical sciences
- Anesthesia
- Community medicine
- Dentistry
- Diagnostic imaging (radiology, ultrasonics, CT/CAT/PET scan, MRI)
- Family medicine and family practice
- Medicine, including allergy, cardiology, dermatology, endocrinology, general medicine, gastroenterology, hematology, immunology and rheumatology, infectious diseases, nephrology, oncology, and pulmonary medicine
- Neurology including neuropsychology and pediatric neurology
- Obstetrics and gynecology
- Pediatrics, medical genetics
- Psychiatry
- Surgery, including cardiothoracic, emergency medical services, general surgery, neurosurgery, ophthalmology, orthopedics, otolaryngology, and plastic and reconstructive surgery
- Urology

    c. High tech
- Electronics research, manufacturing, production, storage, and distribution

    d. Pharmaceuticals
- Research, manufacturing, production, storage, and distribution

    e. Physical sciences
- Astronomy, botany, chemistry, computers, electronics, engineering, geology, mathematics, physics, seismology, etc.

    f. Combinations of the foregoing disciplines and subdisciplines, sections, functions, and activities (e. g., chemical engineering, biotechnology, physical chemistry, biophysics, etc.)

3. Initial financial and budgetary constraints and limitations.

4. Planned or future facilities growth and expansion, both horizontal and vertical.

5. New (freestanding) vs. remodeling and renovation of existing facilities vs. combination of new (addition) and remodeling and renovation of existing facilities.

6. Future use of the facility—changes in occupancy and classification (offices to laboratories, etc.). Changes in occupancy may not be practical in certain instances. It may be too costly to decontaminate a laboratory facility for office use.

7. Site, location, contours, orientation, environmental impact, neighbors, transportation (public/private), and zoning restrictions.

In view of the many regulations to be followed, guideline criteria to be incorporated, and questions to be answered, we present several laboratory work area module units representing a range of square feet. The range of areas will provide the laboratory worker, facility manager, and architect with basic guidelines to use when developing and quantifying the space requirements, testing the program criteria, and developing the suitable laboratory work area module unit(s). These basic planning criteria are extremely important in establishing the building structural bay size and building envelope. See Appendix C for a comprehensive list of codes, regulations, standards, guidelines, and reference publications.

A wide variety of scientific research functions and activities can be accommodated within a system of laboratory work area modular units (Figures 1.3a–e). Concepts of modular building organization have many advantages. However, determination of the exact size of the laboratory work area module unit and its arrangement can become a complex and often an arbitrary (political) process. The most common modules (laboratory work areas only) are usually between 10′ × 20′ (200 nsf) to 12′ × 24′ (288 nsf) exclusive of partitions. Other modules may be based on multiples of 10′ × 35′ (350 nsf) to 12′ × 40′ (480 nsf). The latter modules may include adjacent (but separate) office, administrative, service, and support work areas. The 10′-0″-wide module for new laboratory facilities is no longer considered a feasible option. It is recommended that all areas in a laboratory building, including nonlaboratory spaces (e.g., office areas, conference rooms, classrooms, etc.), be designed to permit conversion to laboratory activities. This recommendation should be analyzed carefully for each facility design. Although the concept permits utilization of all building space for laboratories, the initial construction costs may be difficult to

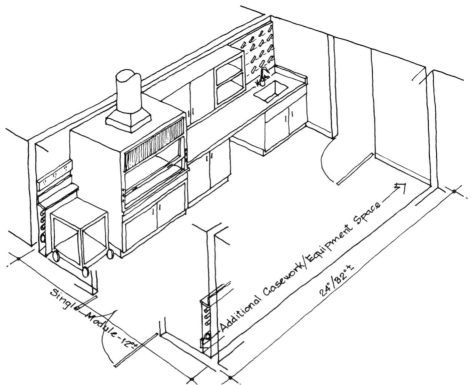

Figure 1.3a Example single module. See also Figures 7.1–7.10 for additional details.

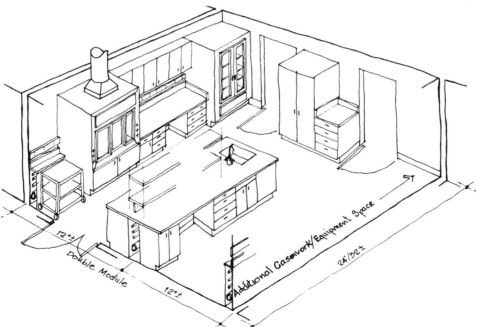

Figure 1.3b Example double module. See also Figures 7.1–7.10 for additional details.

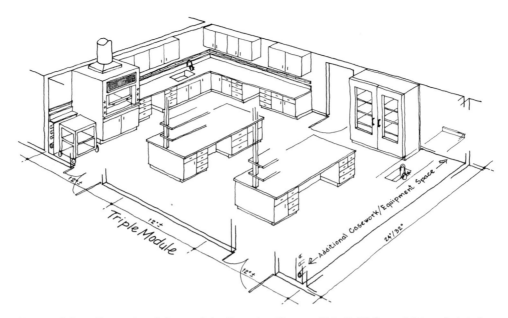

Figure 1.3c   Example triple module. See also Figures 7.1–7.10 for additional details.

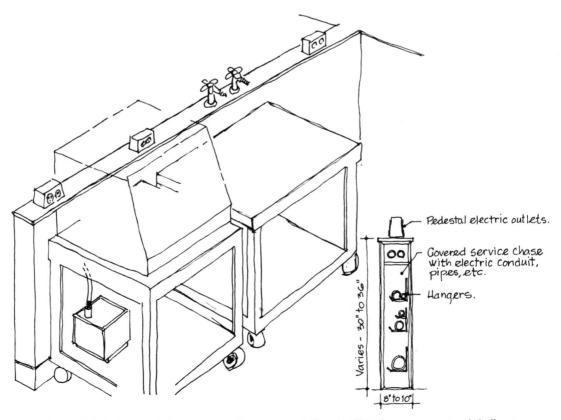

Figure 1.3d   Example lab work station concept. Fixed utility chases set at module lines with mobile casework areas. Sinks located along fixed wall areas.

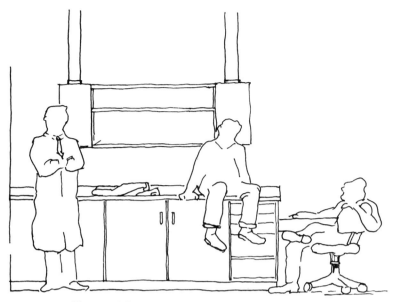

Figure 1.3e   *Realities of the lab environment.*

justify. Scale or size of the project will also determine whether the entire facility should be designed for laboratory functions and activities, zoned vertically or horizontally, or separate facilities—with bridge connections—provided.

COMMENTS

1. It is extremely important to understand that the concept of modular planning applies to the three dimensions (volume) of a building and its structure and not just to the floor plan or plate.

2. A 12'-0" × 32'-0" laboratory module may have a vertical dimension of 16'-0" finished floor-to-floor height to include a ceiling services distribution system and the building structure.

3. A laboratory facility employing an interstitial services distribution system may have a finished floor-to-floor height as great as 20'-0" (±) to include the services distribution system.

4. A services corridor distribution system may have a lower finished floor-to-floor height than each of the former systems, but not necessarily. The finished

floor-to-floor dimension for *any* services system that is selected should be based on (but not limited to) several factors, including:

a. Program requirements and criteria of the functions and activities to be accommodated

b. The services concept developed (interstitial, services corridor, etc.)

c. Structural system to be developed (concrete, steel, combination, etc., clearances under beams and from other structural members)

d. Whether the facility is an addition to an existing building, matching floor-to-floor heights

e. A new building connected to an existing building by bridges, also matching the existing building floor-to-floor heights

f. Budget limitations and constraints

The decision to match existing building floor-to-floor heights in a new laboratory facility—for whatever reason—must be made with detailed analysis and extreme care. The consequences can be immediate and/or long term. The existing building floor-to-floor height may be obsolete in terms of contemporary laboratory planning standards (state-of-the-art). This dimension may limit the flexibility in the new building to accommodate a more extensive variety of research functions and activities.

Other modules may be as large as 24′ to 32′ wide and 28′ to 36′ long (deep). The need for a wide basic module may make a module multiple of 10′ wide practical if the module is limited to 20′ wide minimum. These modules may be appropriate for physics research activities that require larger, more open free space to set up experimental apparatus. Such activities may include engineering/automobile/engine test facilities, high-energy physics, and condensed-matter and low-temperature experiments. Such laboratories may require a moving crane on rails to lift heavy equipment. Machine fabrication shops may be needed to design and manufacture the equipment to be used during the experiment. Other experimental activities may have to be accommodated in high-bay spaces. Clearances required may exceed 20′ to 30′ or more. High energy (linear accelerators) or experiments using radioactive elements (cobalt irradiation/therapy) may require concrete shielding several feet thick. Certain laboratory areas may have to be buried below grade to utilize the shielding properties of the surrounding earth fill.

COMMENTS

1. All dimensions indicated in this book are nominal or statistical, for planning purposes. Construction document dimensions (after the structural system has been designed) may be 10'-6" × 20'-6" centerline to centerline to allow for partition thickness. Actual construction as-built dimensions will also vary.

2. Architects and engineers should heed the following important note—that the time to convert to and use the metric system of measurement is now. Most federal government agencies require that the construction documents be prepared in metric units.

3. The development or evolution of the laboratory work area module should consider many factors, including:

   a. Type of research (discipline) to be accommodated

   b. Size (area) of the facility

   c. Design structural bay size (the laboratory work area module should be a multiple of the structural bay size, or vice versa)

The 10' module width has been based on the standard casework depth of 2'-6", including the rear service or utility chase. When the casework is placed at the partition face or on the module line, it results in a 5'-wide aisle (less partition thickness). This aisle width has been accepted for many years as adequate to permit personnel to work at either counter and allow another person to walk between them. However, the impact of the requirements of the Americans with Disabilities Act (ADA) and the use of equipment deeper than 2'-6" renders the 10' module width—as a *basic* module width—virtually obsolete for all practical purposes.

An aisle width of 5' (between work counters) is subject to some concern in view of the necessity to accommodate people with disabilities within the laboratory work area. The requirements indicated in many accessibility standards publications would prohibit such aisle widths because of the space restrictions created for those in wheelchairs, the sight impaired, or those who have difficulty in walking (leg braces, crutches, neurological disorders, etc.). What may be perceived as an ideal laboratory work area module unit to accommodate staff (both able-bodied and disabled), casework, and equipment may translate into a costly and complicated structural framing, service, and utility system.

ACCESSIBILITY SPACE FACTORS

The Americans with Disabilities Act of 1990 (ADA) is often referred to as the most significant civil rights legislation enacted since the Civil Rights Act of 1964. Although the ADA will have a significant impact on facilities design, it should be understood that it is not a national building code. Alterations made to existing facilities since January 26, 1992, and new buildings occupied since January 26, 1993, must be made accessible according to standards for design, construction, or alteration issued by the U.S. Department of Justice (DOJ). The various definitions, requirements, and guidelines have been prepared by the U.S. Architectural and Transportation Barriers Compliance Board (ATBCB) to serve as minimum requirements for regulations issued by the DOJ. Those institutions receiving federal grants, funds, loans, and assistance are presently required to comply with similar accessibility requirements under Section 504 of the Rehabilitation Act of 1973. The ATBCB has issued various guidelines to conform with the interpretations of the requirements of ADA.

Compliance with the *Uniform Federal Accessibility Standards* (UFAS-FS-795-1988) will probably most likely continue to be accepted (as revised) (Figures 1.4a–e). The UFAS is a minimum standard. Architects are to be cautioned, however, as some state regulations are more restrictive than the UFAS. The facility manager and architect must be prepared to determine what will be required for any proposed laboratory facility that is planned. The DOJ and ATBCB should be contacted before the programming of a laboratory facility is begun, to determine the latest requirements.

Hospitals and health care facilities are considered as public accommodations under the ADA and must therefore comply

Figure 1.4a Accommodations must be made for staff not confined to a wheelchair.

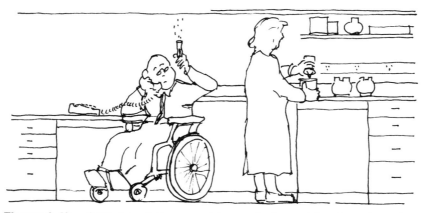

Figure 1.4b Accommodations must be made for multilevel work stations.

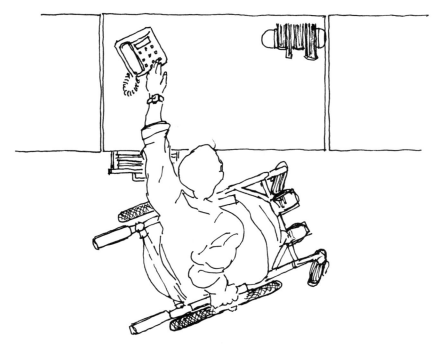

Figure 1.4c   Reach is important for a person in a wheelchair.

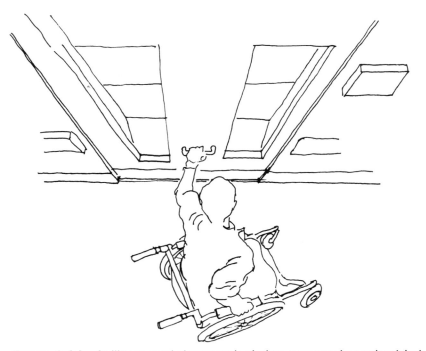

Figure 1.4d   Ability to apply leverage is vital to a person in a wheelchair.

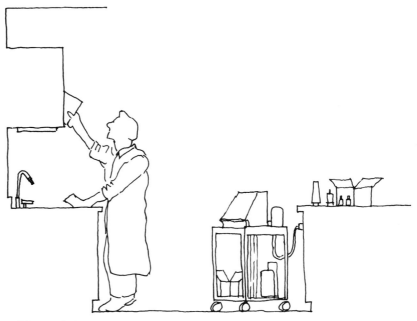

Figure 1.4e As aisle space becomes cluttered with equipment carts, accessibility becomes hazardous.

with the regulations. Research facilities perhaps may not be public accommodations. Potentially hazardous functions and activities conducted in a research facility may make confor-mance difficult, dangerous, and costly. These are definitions and conditions that may require discussion and review with the appropriate agency and building official(s).

However, since many institutions receive funding and grants from federal government sources, presumably, they will be required to comply with the ADA regulations. Architects should also be cautioned, depending on the circumstances, that de-sign errors and omissions insurance may not apply in cases that may allege noncompliance with ADA requirements.

Persons with disabilities alleging discrimination under the ADA may file complaints with the Equal Employment Oppor-tunity Commission (EEOC). They may also file a private lawsuit after exhausting administrative remedies. Remedies are the same as those available under Title VII of the Civil Rights Act of 1964. The court may order the employer (institution, etc.) to hire or promote qualified disabled individuals, to reasonably accommodate their disabilities, and to pay back wages and attorneys' fees, as applicable.

One of the most significant aspects of the ADA is perhaps its impact on life-safety egress requirements outlined in building codes and the NFPA 101 Life Safety Code. The ADA states that life-safety egress features *must be equal for all building occupants, including the disabled.* According to the NFPA, the language in the ADA may result in significant modifications to recent life-safety code guidelines relative to "defend-in-place" and "areas-of-refuge" concepts. The implication that segregating or treating the disabled differently *for any purpose* may now be considered a discriminatory practice under the ADA.

Standards being considered for possible revision by the NFPA due to the language contained in the ADA include:

- Consideration of sprinkler requirements for areas not currently included in codes
- Designation of elevators for egress of occupants when no life-safety-referenced standards exist for ensuring a level of protection in elevators equal to areas of refuge in stairwells
- Egress stair and ramp increased from 44"-wide minimum to 51"-wide minimum
- Equivalency of areas of refuge and access to stairwell and corridor egress for able-bodied and disabled occupants
- Disabled persons refuge areas within stairwells in new and existing buildings
- On-demand access by disabled occupants to designated areas of buildings, affecting existing designs for egressing unimpaired occupants to the detriment of established egress times in stairs, aisles, and corridors

It is suggested that prior to starting the programming and planning process, facility managers and architects contact the various agencies, including the NFPA, involved with the preparation, issuance, and interpretation of ADA regulations. Many new regulations, standards, and guidelines have been published since the preparation and publication of this book.

CHANGES IN SPACE ALLOCATIONS

Space program allocations can no longer be based on normal or able-bodied ambulation criteria. The facility manager and architect must be prepared to modify an entire spectrum of planning standards that affects the three-dimensional space within the building envelope. Virtually all buildings must be designed (or remodeled and renovated) to provide access to and accommodate all persons, including those with hearing, sight, and walking disabilities (physical or orthopedic and neurological disabilities, etc.).

Planning criteria mandated or implied by accessibility regulations and standards affecting space allocations may include:

- Access to emergency eye and face washers, deluge showers, fire blanket cabinets, and fire extinguisher locations.
- Clearances between work counters, work counters and equipment, and aisle widths between modular and rolling storage shelving units.
- Corridor widths, ramps, stairs, elevators, horizontal and vertical egress, railing heights, dead-end limitations, and areas of refuge and safe areas.
- Door swings, revolving doors, sliding doors, clearances, corridor rest alcoves, approach and access to doors, door openers and closers, door assist mechanisms, and type of door hardware.
- Emergency controls and equipment, electrical cabinets, fire hose cabinets, fire alarm stations, emergency alarm lights, textured "Braille" control buttons, hardware, room signs, emergency signs, elevator controls, and so on.
- Floor, wall finishes, colors, textures, depth of carpet pile, and height of thresholds.
- Heights of work counters, equipment (hoods, biosafety cabinets, autoanalyzers, etc.) wall shelves, desks, file cabinets, and other furniture. Not all disabled persons are confined to wheelchairs. Certain disabilities preclude the person from assuming a "seated" position because of leg braces, degree of disability, and other factors.
- Public telephone locations, mounting height, and so on.
- Protruding objects, overhead hazards, overhanging objects, headroom, low lintels and structural members, drinking fountains, corridor and lobby display cabinets, and fire extinguishers (surface mounted).
- Reach extension for persons in a wheelchair or with other disabilities.
- Sight lines; tactile, sensory, and auditory controls; alarm devices and mechanisms (lights, bells, raised characters, vibrator-type beepers, Braille, etc.); illumination levels;

reflectance; light frequencies; divisions between surfaces; materials; and so on.

- Telecommunication devices for the deaf (TDDs) permit hearing- and speech-impaired persons to communicate effectively with visually displayed typed messages transmitted over standard telephone lines. Decontamination shower facilities may have to be provided for disabled persons.

- Toilet and shower facilities, grab bars, thermostat water controls, paper and soap dispensers, lavatories, and waste receptacles.

- Wheelchair maneuvering clearances, accessible routes, corridor resting spaces or alcoves, elevators, and chair lifts.

DESIGNER ATTITUDES

Often during the planning and design of facilities to accommodate the physically disabled or patients confined in a hospital, the individual designer or architect responsible for development of the plans may have had little or no contact with these patients. Many designers have never experienced the research laboratory work environment other than during a visit. Few have experienced the hospital environment as a patient. Some designers may lack the perception and sensitivity to understand the obstacles and problems faced by disabled persons and patients, particularly the very young, the elderly, and others who are both a patient and disabled. What may be considered as a simple task for an able-bodied person [e. g., turning a round (spherical) door knob to open a door] may be a formidable obstacle for a patient or disabled person to accomplish. In an emergency situation, such mechanical devices become insurmountable barriers and may create life-threatening conditions.

The designer should never lose sight of the fact that the particular building in question is not his or hers. The building design solution should never be the product the designer "likes," the latest architectural design fad, or "what everybody is doing." The designer should avoid the attitude that he or she "knows what the owner wants" or, worse, "knows what is best for the owner and user because they don't know what they want." It is the designer's (architect's) responsibility to assist the owner and user with the development of the design criteria. It is the designer's (architect's) responsibility to plan and design a safe, functional, efficient, economical, and aesthetically pleasing facility.

COMMENTS

1. Several physically disabled researchers (wheelchair confined, leg braces and crutches, walking with the aid of a cane, etc.) were interviewed by the author about hazards encountered because of architectural design conditions that pose virtually no hazard to an able-bodied person. One scenario was as follows:

   a. The flooring specified for many biomedical research laboratories is sheet vinyl with welded seams. Sheet vinyl is a suitable choice because of its resistance to a wide variety of reagents, impervious surface, ease of cleaning, choice of generally pleasing colors and patterns, easy installation, and so on. One disadvantage with sheet vinyl, however, is its relatively higher cost compared to other floor materials.

   b. Staff members carrying coffee cups, glasses of water, and the like, in the corridors invariably will spill a few drops on the floor. If a person on crutches traversing the corridor happens to place the tip of a crutch (usually hard rubber, presumably for safety and its nonslip qualities) on the drops of liquid, the result almost invariably will be a fall. Because of the small surface area of the pressure exerted is several hundreds of pounds per square inch. The liquid acts as a lubricant, causing a crutch to fly out from under a disabled person, resulting in a fall.

   c. Situations such as that described above have happened not only in corridors, but in laboratory work areas as well. Again, the amount of the liquid need be no larger than droplets.

   d. This is a situation that probably would not create a hazard for a nondisabled person.

   e. What is the answer? What substitute floor material

should be specified? Should the floor material have a texture like sandpaper to prevent such incidents? How would such floor materials be cleaned? Would such materials create other, more hazardous problems? The answers to these questions are not readily obvious. Different materials with different properties would most certainly create other problems, and some may be even more hazardous.

f. Because of the variety of reagents and materials used and the processes involved in both chemical and physical reactions, the research laboratory work area is a hazardous environment. It is dangerous to all its occupants. The architect must consider an entire range of conditions and incidents that may occur that may not have existed previously.

2. Although the following circumstance occurred in a hospital/health care setting, the principles and applications to research laboratory facilities are apparent:

   a. In a survey of hospital inpatients, the questions focused on patients' perceptions and concerns regarding the hospital physical environment (e. g., shape and size of the bedroom, orientation of the bed relative to the door and window, etc.). The responses were surprising and enlightening. The perceptions and concerns were quite different from the design approach typically used to plan hospital spaces.

   b. Traditional design practice dictated that a patient bed be oriented so that the patient could see out the window, observe whether it was sunny or raining, and enjoy the view, if one existed. Patients surveyed responded that they were more concerned with the activity in the corridor. They wanted to be able to see the nurse and have the nurse able to see them. Being able to look out the window had very low priority.

   c. Nurses were also included in the survey. Their comments were even more critical regarding the design standards and the architects' perceptions used in planning nursing units and other areas of the hospital. However, some words must be said in defense of members of the architectural profession. There are many who have the sensitivity, aesthetic sense, and talent and experience to design facilities that accommodate the physical and psychological needs of hospital patients.

3. It is interesting to note that the design standards of hospitals were developed for the most part by well-persons using their perceptions of what was best for the patient. Virtually no input was solicited from the patient and very little from nurses or patients' relatives. In some instances the nursing staff is not included in the planning process. Unfortunately, many new health care facilities continue to reflect this approach. However, a bright side of the facilities picture is emerging. Due to market forces, competition, and increasing consumer awareness and sophistication, many hospitals are responding to these changes. Administrators, physicians, and others are radically changing their view of hospital facilities. Architects are being encouraged to develop innovative and aesthetically pleasing hospital facility designs.

4. The traditional hospital-green glazed-tile corridors are rapidly disappearing. New medical techniques and technology permit many more procedures to be accomplished on an outpatient basis that were inpatient procedures three or four years ago. Obstetric facilities are no longer cold and sterile-looking stainless steel facilities. Many are now called "birthing units" and have the attractiveness of a home setting. Much research has been and is being done regarding the planning and design of hospital and health care facilities by the health care industry and the design professions.

5. Inconsistencies with the application of various design criteria continue, however. Patient room toilet and shower facilities (and other spaces) are often planned using able-bodied-person standards. Many do not contain a lavatory within the toilet and shower space to permit the patient to wash after performing bodily functions. The necessity to wash is particularly important for patients who have undergone urological or abdominal surgery. The lavatory is usually placed in the patient bed space, which is, for all

practical purposes, a public space. Double-bed patient rooms further complicate the ability to provide
for personal privacy. Single-patient bedrooms, fortunately, are becoming the principal choice in many
new, replacement, and retrofit hospital projects.

6. Shower stalls are almost always too small and narrow.
   The standard used appears to be 3' × 3' or less. The
   architect should discuss medical protocols with the
   nursing staff prior to design of nursing units. Incidents involving an ill and obese patient fainting and
   becoming wedged in the shower can be life threatening for the patient and dangerous for the hospital staff
   trying to extricate a patient in this situation. A transfer or roll-in type of shower may be sufficient to meet
   these situations and accessibility requirements.
   Knurled surface grab bars for shower and tub areas, a
   sink in a countertop, shelves, robe hook on a door or
   wall, and so on, although seemingly inconsequential
   and unimportant, are just a few of the very necessary
   items for the safety, comfort, and convenience of
   patients.

7. Another planning standard that should be abolished
   is the practice of not including a lavatory in the same
   space as the toilet in patient rooms, hotel rooms, and
   so on. Many health and safety protocols clearly state
   that a person should wash his or her hands immediately after using the toilet, handling hazardous
   materials, and so on. OSHA requires lavatories in all
   clinical laboratory work areas. Staff members are
   required by law to wash hands before leaving such
   work areas. Awareness of this requirement has been
   heightened since HIV, AIDS, and other contagious
   diseases have become so prevalent. The same standard is applied to research laboratories, particularly
   biomedical processes, including tissue culture, processes, using bodily specimens (blood, urine, tissue,
   feces, etc.), and the like. Presumably, the hand washing requirement reduces the incidence of disease
   transmission.

8. The old standard for toilet stalls of 3' × 5' and the
   practice of doors swinging into the stall space should
   be made illegal in the author's opinion. It is ridicu-
   lous that the architectural design profession con-

tinues to use standards in public facilities that are not only obsolete, but create a situation that does not permit the exercise of a natural function in at least a reasonable measure of convenience and dignity. It is no wonder that the design profession is held in such low regard by many members of the public.

9. Again, although the comments above refer to experiences at health care facilities, the same principles apply to research laboratory facilities. They are very graphic representations, again and again, of the importance of the programming and planning process in its totality. The programmer, researcher, investigator and staff, facilities manager, architect, designer, engineer, safety officer, building engineer, and others must be involved in the programming, planning, and design process. The ADA, CDC, NIH, OSHA, and other government agency regulations are having profound effects on facility environments. Design professionals must become aware of the regulations and their far-reaching implications.

10. The author, through his consulting practice experience as a laboratory programming and planning specialist, has had an opportunity to work with many nationally recognized architectural and engineering firms. Perhaps the most outstanding is Cannon, Architects, Engineers and Planners. The firm has offices in Boston, Massachusetts; Grand Island, New York; Los Angeles, California; New York City, New York; St. Louis, Missouri; and Washington, DC. The firm's commitment to excellence and focus on laboratory and health care facility planning and design reflects the basic philosophy of their experienced and dedicated professional staff.

ALTERNATIVE PLANNING FACTORS

Providing natural light (directly or indirectly) to laboratory work areas is the subject of endless discussion. Many solutions developed often create a functional compromise between laboratory work areas and adjoining administrative office areas. Natural light can affect ongoing experiments, create a heat load within the laboratory and on sensitive instruments, cause annoying reflections in cathode ray tubes (CRTs), and make it difficult to read instrument dials and create problems for controlling lighting conditions and the quality and type (frequency and color) of artificial light. In many instances, equipment is placed in front of windows or they are covered over with posters. Glass installed in interior partitions to borrow light from exterior sources is also often covered over (e.g., with posters) by the laboratory staff to provide privacy. It has been documented that the 60-hertz (Hz) frequency and oscillation of fluorescent lights and their ballast can cause stress in persons within the space. The EMF radiation of fluorescent lights and its ballast can also affect sensitive electronic equipment.

The controversy regarding natural light in laboratory work areas will probably be an ongoing topic of discussion. It is another important programming and planning design criterion that must be resolved during the initial phases of the development of the laboratory facility. Laboratory facility design should not be based on preconceived ideas. Solutions should develop and evolve based on design criteria. This methodology is the *only* way to achieve a successful laboratory facility that meets the design criteria, providing the proper and safe environment for the researcher and investigator.

COMMENTS

1. The author contends that because of the potential hazardous nature of research activities and the high cost of laboratory work spaces, there should be no compromise in the safe, functional, and efficient use of all laboratory work areas. The research laboratory facility perhaps exemplifies the statement that "form follows function." This does not imply that aesthetics, proper functional planning and design, and selection of laboratory casework and furnishings, materials, colors, textures, finishes, lighting, and sound control be ignored in laboratory work areas. On the contrary, these areas should command the same design commitment given to the boardroom or other spaces in the institution. The exterior of the building should reflect the high-technology processes and activities that are conducted within.

2. The challenges and opportunities that exist for imagina-

tive planning and design solutions for research and health care facilities have yet to be fully exploited. There are no valid reasons functionally or otherwise not to devote a similar kind of creative design intensity and energy to these facilities as is expended for other building types. On the contrary, particularly for the hospital and health care environment, more creative design should be devoted because of the very nature of the physical and psychological stress and trauma that is experienced by the individual patient and his or her relatives. Let's not forget the staff physicians, and others that work and occupy the facility, as well.

Relief from the intensity of research activities should be accomplished *outside* the laboratory work areas. This is partly because of the difficulty in controlling the air quality in the laboratory work areas due to the many hazardous reagents and processes. Personnel should be encouraged to leave the laboratory work areas periodically. This encouragement can come from the attraction of well-planned and designed administrative office work areas, conference and brainstorming spaces, lounges, cafeterias, coffee and snack areas, research and reference libraries, balconies, and computer workstations located convenient to the laboratory work areas. These alternative work and relaxation spaces can provide the opportunity for personnel from different scientific disciplines to communicate, interact, exchange and share ideas, and discuss and develop solutions to problems. Such spaces do not necessarily have to be outdoors. However, if the climate, location, and site views permit, several of these spaces should be located outdoors.

In view of the increasing data and information regarding the long-term effects of exposure to various chemicals and reagents, the continuing practice of providing desk work space for technical staff, graduate students, and so on, within the laboratory work areas should be avoided as a matter of basic programming and planning principles. These functions and activities should be accommodated in spaces outside the laboratory work areas. More consistent control can be maintained of the office working environment that is separate from the laboratory environment. However, there are certain scientific functions and activities that do not use hazardous reagents except perhaps in very infrequent circumstances and almost always in a controlled fume hood or biosafety cabinet. Many of the subdisciplines in physics and engineering involve machine activities. Another precaution to keep in mind is that electric motors, electric arc equipment, in fact, any electrical equipment that creates an electrical spark—generates ozone. This compound can be hazardous in confined and inadequately ventilated spaces.

DIVERSE FUNCTIONS AND ACTIVITIES

A research and hospital facility must accommodate a wide variety of functions and activities that are not readily compatible from physical environmental criteria and operational factors. Except for special research laboratory facilities, the hospital remains the most complicated building type. A community hospital facility encompasses the entire spectrum of human activity from birth through death. Also, persons representing virtually every human activity must be accommodated within a hospital. Teaching hospitals are even more complex.

The research laboratory building envelope must provide a safe and efficient environment to accommodate many functions and activities, such as:

- Administrative offices, conference rooms and classrooms, lecture halls, audiovisual facilities, computer facilities, public areas, gift shops, cafeterias, and snack, vending, mail, and printing facilities
- Animal holding, breeding; materials, supplies, animal receiving, holding, processing; cage washing, sterilizing, repair; surgery, recovery, isolation, necropsy, pathological waste; feed storage, mixing, distribution; animal bedding, waste holding and processing; specialized research laboratory facilities
- Clean rooms, electromagnetic shielded rooms, high-energy particle shielding (gamma radiation, cobalt, linear accelerators), anechoic chambers, biohazard rooms (BSL-1, 2, 3, and 4; P1, P2, P3, and P4; class 100, 1000, 10,000, etc.), controlled-temperature spaces, specialized testing and production facilities
- Collection, receiving, staging, holding, processing, storage, disposal and removal of waste (hazardous and nonhazardous), recycling materials.

- Facilities for carpentry, electronics, mechanical, electrical, plumbing, and machine shop activities; maintenance, repair, calibration and testing facilities, model building, experiment equipment fabrication
- Laboratories for many diverse scientific disciplines, including biomedical and physical sciences, engineering and environmental sciences, production and testing activities
- Materials management systems for ordering, purchasing, receiving, staging, holding, storage, inventory, distribution of materials, supplies, equipment
- Physical plant and energy facilities (boilers, chillers, transformers, emergency power, fuel storage—above and below ground, cogeneration facilities, energy recovery systems)
- Service and support spaces, including files and records storage, staff facilities, toilets, showers, environmental services (housekeeping), infection and isolation control, decontamination, instrument and equipment storage, safety and security
- Special equipment rooms for magnetic resonance imaging (MRI), radiology, electron microscopy, spectroscopy, special tests, photo and film processing
- Special holding, processing, and storage areas for hazardous and nonhazardous waste; recycling facilities

SECURITY CONSIDERATIONS

Security of and access to the laboratory work areas must be carefully planned and controlled. Certain functions and activities may consist of extremely sensitive, delicate, hazardous, and confidential processes. The circulation patterns of personnel and flow of specimens to be analyzed, including the location of equipment and casework, are very important for safe, efficient, and secure operations.

Security access can be controlled using electronic computer-based systems, including special card access devices, biometrics, voice, fingerprints, thumbprint, palm print, proximity access, and a variety of mechanical systems. All security access and control systems must comply with the NFPA Life Safety Code requirements. Security systems and controls must permit safe egress for occupants and access by security and fire personnel during emergency conditions.

The increase in assaults occurring to patients, visitors, and staff in the hospital environment has generated the need for security systems and policies. If security guards are employed, do they come to the hospital in uniform, or do they come to the hospital in street clothes and then change in the hospital? What is the requirement for security facilities, lockers, and change areas? Are they armed? If armed, are the weapons stored at the hospital or do the guards take the weapons home? These are a few of the policy matters that generate space requirements.

People espousing animal rights have broken into research laboratory facilities, destroying valuable equipment and records. This has resulted in the loss of months, sometimes years of research work. In some instances, researchers themselves were attacked and injured and animals removed or destroyed.

Security is not just a matter of placing guards in a building after the fact. If the facilities are not planned to accommodate or permit implementation of the security program, the building occupants may be placed at risk. The architect's design (or lack thereof) may also be cited by the victim as a major contributing factor to an assault.

TYPICAL LABORATORY MODULE AND STANDARD LABORATORY MODULE WORK AREAS

Typical laboratory modules (TLMs) are 10' to 12' wide × 20' to 24' and 35' to 40' long (deep). These dimensions provide a range of areas between 200 and 480 nsf for a TLM. The standard laboratory module (SLM) may consist of two to four adjacent TLMs. The SLM provides a range of 600 to 1440 nsf. Hoods may be permitted in single enclosed TLMs. Supply air requirements and capacities, cooling, heating, and room air changes per hour may be based on placing 2–6'-wide chemical fume hoods for each three or four TLMs. Due to the increasingly restrictive safety requirements for handling certain reagents, a biological safety cabinet (class II, type B2, 100% exhaust) may also have to be accommodated within the TLM and at least one per SLM. *This requirement is in addition to the chemical fume hood.* Some laboratory planners and safety offices suggest providing two 6'-wide hoods (chemical and/or biosafety) for each 350 nsf of laboratory work area. This is consistent with the suggestions discussed above.

COMMENTS

1. The typical laboratory module is based on a laboratory work area allocation to accommodate one or two persons. Experience indicates that this basic laboratory work area unit (or multiples) can satisfy most biomedical, physical, and environmental sciences research grant objectives and facility requirements. The smaller TLM (10′ to 12′ wide × 20′ to 24′ long at 200 to 288 nsf) does not include laboratory service and support spaces (instrument and equipment rooms, storage, temperature-controlled rooms, glassware wash, etc.) or administrative office support space(s).

2. Consider that the laboratory work area module may be a derivative of an architectural, structural, or design modular grid. For example, the integrated architectural and structural design grid for the building may have evolved from a 2′ × 2′ (±), 4′ × 4′ (±), or 5′ × 5′ (±) grid. Modules of 15″, 16″, or 18″ may also be efficient. The TLM for the 5′ × 5′ grid would be 12′-6″ wide × 25′ long or 30′ to 35′ long (or more). If a 4′ × 4′ module is established, it would produce a TLM 12′ wide × 24′ long or 28′ to 32′ long (or more), and so on.

3. It bears repeating that the concept of modular planning applies to the three dimensions (volume) of a building, not just to the floor plan or plate.

4. The translation of the laboratory work area module into a building is based on a number of factors. Site size or area available and location has perhaps the most significant impact (next to the project budget, of course) on the building shape (volume, massing, number of floors, etc.). The space program establishes the total net and gross square footage required to accommodate the program requirements of the building. Certain functional relationships may determine the building height and number of floors. Other program criteria may determine whether more than one building is required. As a rule of thumb, a floor plate of approximately 12,000 to 16,000 gsf and 24,000 to 28,000 gsf can generally provide a reasonably efficient ratio between nsf and gsf, laboratory

work areas to service and support spaces, and to office spaces, for most biomedical research laboratory facilities. The ground rules may change considerably if the facility is an addition to an existing building, how it may be connected, and so on. Buildings proposed for urban sites will have to conform to various zoning requirements, fine arts commissions, architectural review boards, and so on, as well.

5. Determination of the structural grid (bay size) can have a significant impact on construction costs: whether a concrete or steel frame is employed and whether adequate clearances under beams for ductwork and piping are possible without increasing floor-to-floor heights unduly. Other factors include the availability of steel or concrete materials in the region and the contractor and construction worker skills and experience levels in the area. The program requirements may indicate that a certain low vibration level or frequency be maintained in the building. Concrete is generally the first choice to achieve such criteria in a structure. If concrete is not readily available in the area and the concrete construction worker experience is lacking, the costs of the building may become prohibitive to meet certain functional and environmental criteria.

6. The TLM assumes a 9'-6" minimum clear ceiling height with or without a finished ceiling. The laboratory work area ceiling height may range between 8'-6" and 10'-6". Certain activities (MRI, spectroscopy, high-energy physics, engineering testing, etc.) will require higher ceilings (high-bay space) to provide clearance for large and tall equipment, hoists or cranes to lift heavy equipment components, and so on. Consideration may be required for access holes in the floor (or ceiling) to lower (raise) certain pieces of equipment and to provide access for maintenance, recharging liquid gas dewars, and the like. The latter requirements must be carefully coordinated with activities conducted in spaces above and below, particularly when remodeling and renovating existing facilities.

7. Before a decision is made to upgrade the infrastructure of an older existing laboratory building to correct insufficient HVAC, electrical, and plumbing

services, careful analysis must be accomplished to ensure that the finished space will actually provide efficient and contemporary laboratory work areas. The idea of rehabbing an existing building is usually most attractive to the institution's administration. The first thought is that money can be saved because the building structure is still in good condition. Initial cost estimates may indicate that savings can be achieved by remodeling and renovating. Upgrading the HVAC systems, however, may result in limited ceiling heights of 8' or less because of larger air-handling duct sizes. Existing floor-to-floor heights may be much less than recommended for new laboratory buildings. A ceiling height of 8' should be considered the *absolute minimum* for research laboratories of any type.

8. Considerable floor space may have to be allocated to mechanical equipment rooms, further reducing an efficient nsf/gsf ratio. The number and type of hoods may have to be limited, restricting the variety of scientific functions and activities that can be accommodated. The existing structural bay size may not permit development of an adequate laboratory module to meet functional criteria for efficient laboratory work areas and to accommodate regulatory (ADA, OSHA, etc.) requirements. The shape of the existing building (long, narrow floor plate) may also be of such dimensions that functional relationships among laboratory work areas, service and support spaces, and office areas may be seriously compromised. The rehab and upgrade may result in similar inefficient laboratory work space. The major difference may turn out to be that the remodeled and renovated space now has new finishes.

9. Many institutions allocate between 800 and 1400 nsf (1200 to 1800 nsf and more in other institutions) of laboratory work area as a basic assignable space unit to each principal researcher or investigator. This area assignment or allocation usually includes administrative office work space(s) for the principal investigator only and his laboratory technical staff. Assigned laboratory support personnel may vary between one or two and four to six (or more) technicians per principal investigator, depending on the

nature and scope of the research grant and project. Trends appear to indicate that working groups of as large as 12 to 18 persons are not uncommon. These trends, if they continue, will have a significant impact on service and support spaces, particularly proximity and functional relationship to the laboratory work areas.

10. Consideration should be given to the fit-out (casework installation, etc.) of selected service and support spaces (core areas): electron microscopy, dark rooms (photo processing), special procedures (balance/weight measurement, irradiation, image analysis, flow cytometry, molecular biology, etc.), tissue culture, equipment rooms (centrifuge, freezers, etc.) and so on. Fit-out of certain laboratory spaces assigned to new investigators or those who had not participated in the initial programming interviews would not be completed. Fit-out would be accomplished when the investigator arrived at the institution. This will avoid changing the casework layout to suit the new occupant. Those generic laboratories that may be fitted-out with casework may follow the author's "$\frac{1}{3}$ Rule," consisting of $\frac{1}{3}$ sit-down and $\frac{1}{3}$ stand-up casework work counter, and $\frac{1}{3}$ free wall space to accommodate equipment, mobile carts, and so on.

11. Factors for other service and support spaces (e.g., core areas, including instrument and equipment spaces, other technical service and support spaces, secretarial and clerical support, files and records storage, conference spaces, etc.) may have to be added. A Laboratory core services and support facilities concept may reduce the total area allocated or required for a specific principal investigator's research facility (space) program needs. However, the total building gross square feet requirement may not be significantly reduced if all other investigator requirements are included in the space equation. Care must be exercised to avoid permitting investigators' tendency to customize their laboratory space. This occurs most frequently in remodeling and renovation projects. It is important to establish certain standards for services, type of casework, equipment,

finishes, and so on, that are used to analyze requests for planning individual laboratories.

12. Recent experience indicates that the ratio between spaces for service and support functions and activities and laboratory work spaces is increasing. Ratios between laboratory work space and service and support space has been approximately 3 to 4 (laboratory) to 1 to 2 (service and support), although some laboratory facilities experience the reverse ratio. Service and support spaces exceed the laboratory work areas by as much as 60% service and support spaces to 30 to 40% laboratory work areas. This should not arbitrarily change programming and planning principles or factors. Determination of the needs for laboratory work areas and service and support spaces should be based on the research protocols, processes, and design criteria. It is also interesting to note that the ratio of office spaces to laboratory, service, and support spaces has remained stable.

13. Such space assignment standards or allocations may be totally inadequate for certain functions and activities. A specific research program may often require the basic space allocation to accommodate the activity or process. A high-energy physics research project may require several thousands of program net square feet to accommodate the necessary equipment. The research laboratory space required may best be provided in large, open, clear-span (space-frame), high ceiling spaces (20′ to 30′ more or less) similar to a high-tech production, fabrication, and maintenance machine shop. Such functions and activities may best be segregated in a separate free-standing building or an addition attached to the basic laboratory building. The specific program activity; type, number, and size of the equipment; and number, and qualifications of the research staff will dictate the size and type of space (s) required, again demonstrating how important it is that the programming and planning process precede the design process.

14. Careful consideration should be accorded the level of the building systems and utility services technology and sophistication required to support a particular research function and activity. As indicated

above, certain physics research laboratory space needs may be satisfied with high-tech machine shop space available in a preengineered or prefabricated type of structure. Long-span, column-free, high ceilings, aircraft hanger doors, and so on, can provide the ultimate in flexible space for certain research projects. Special rooms, full-scale mockups, and so on, can be constructed within the open space of such prefab buildings to conform to specific and varied individual space and facility needs. These custom spaces can be heated/cooled/humidity/electrical power controlled on an individual basis using portable units. The possibility of responding to such research activities is virtually endless. The cost of such prefab structures is many times less than that of traditional and permanent types of buildings.

15. Many hospital clinical laboratories are designed and constructed with materials and services similar to those specified for biomedical research laboratories. In reality, clinical laboratories for most general community hospitals are "high-tech-kitchen" spaces. Some of the author's pathologist friends will cringe at this designation, but *all* of his architect associates will scoff. Benchtop materials usually specified are of the composition resin type because of its rather high resistance to many chemicals and reagents. Very few, if any, of these highly corrosive or caustic reagents are ever used in a clinical laboratory. The best top material to use for such applications is laboratory-grade plastic laminate. It is durable, easily replaced, and inexpensive compared to composition-type material. A workstation designed for reagent preparation, including composition top material, a chemical resistant-type utility sink, and a resistant drain pipe should be provided. This reagent preparation, workstation need not be more than 8 to 10 linear feet (lf) in length. Also, acid-resistant drains are not required at each sink in a clinical laboratory—another major cost savings.

16. Limiting the number of hoods per fixed number of modules is always a controversial subject for researchers and investigators. The architect and engineer should be aware that safety rules and regulations indicate it may become a requirement that

virtually all research work involving biological or chemical reactions and processes be performed within a chemical fume hood or a biological safety cabinet, and in addition, that laboratory personnel wear special protective clothing and connected or self-contained breathing apparatus.

DEVELOPING THE TYPICAL LABORATORY MODULE

Figure 1.5 presents typical laboratory module (TLM) space allocation range examples. Although a service corridor concept is indicated, the net square footages for the TLMs, corridors, and office work areas are equally applicable to other service concepts. The arrangement and relationship of the TLMs, corridors, and office work areas may vary relative to the service concept developed.

TLM-A indicates the most commonly used basic laboratory work area unit, 10′ wide × 20′ long (200 nsf). TLM-B indicates the basic laboratory work area unit, 12′ × 24′ (288 nsf), that will meet contemporary laboratory research program criteria. This module will satisfy many more of the new safety and accessibility regulatory requirements than will the former module. The range of net square feet for space programming estimating purposes is indicated at 200 to 288 nsf exclusive of the laboratory staff corridor, office work area, and public corridor; and 420 to 624 nsf, including the laboratory staff corridor, office work area, and public corridor for the basic laboratory work area units.

COMMENTS

1. The net square footage equals the area contained within the face of the surrounding partitions. This figure is generally referred to as the free floor area or net usable floor area. It also includes the floor space occupied by group I (fixed) and group II (movable) equipment. Countertop equipment items are not included.

2. Department gross square feet (dgsf) includes nsf plus floor area occupied by partitions within the department space and intradepartment circulation space.

All dimensions indicated are nominal.

Diagram assumes a services corridor concept (12' to 14' wide; 12'-wide clear minimum). Door swing into service corridor at 4'-6" opening (3'-wide active leaf with 1'-6"-wide inactive leaf) to permit easy equipment access. The service corridor concept permits two exits from a single module.

If an interstitial or ceiling services concept is used, services must be extended through the floor (not as desirable) or from the ceiling to the casework. This services concept permits only one exit from a single module.

Placement of a chemical fume hood or biological safety cabinet (32" to 34" deep) results in space between the face of the hood/cabinet and the opposite work counter/equipment of less than 4'-6" (30" counter depth at each wall and 4" to 6" for partitions). This is unsatisfactory from a safety viewpoint and disability clearances—5'-wide minimum clearance is required for wheelchair turnaround. Test equipment on carts, etc., will reduce the clearance between the fixed work counters to approximately 2'-6" (assuming a utility cart size of 24" to 30" wide × 36" long).

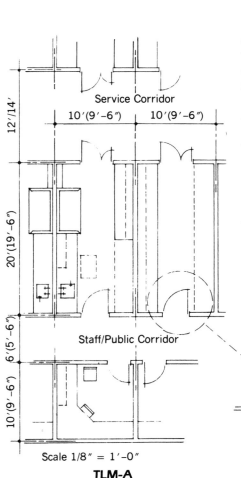

Door swing into laboratory work area: should swing into corridor for safety reasons. If staff/public corridor designated as an egress corridor, proper clearance must be provided to avoid door swing. The door may be placed in an alcove to reduce corridor width. This creates dead-end spaces within the laboratory work area.

Basic office module—across the corridor from the laboratory module or in adjacent areas on each floor. Multiple modules may be combined for conference, meeting spaces, and brainstorming meeting spaces as alcoves off the corridor.

Service Corridor

10'(9'-6") | 10'(9'-6")

12'/14'

20'(19'-6")

6'(5'-6")

10'(9'-6")

Staff/Public Corridor

Scale 1/8" = 1'-0"

TLM-A

This traditional laboratory work area module contains 200 nsf (nominal). If partitions enclose a single module, actual total nsf (face to face of partitions—assuming partition width between 4" and 6") will be approximately 185 nsf (usable). Basic office module at 100 nsf (nominal)—actual total nsf (face to face of partitions) will be approximately 90 nsf (usable). *Module dimensions may or may not include partition thickness; this example includes the partition thickness within the module dimensions.*

Figure 1.5 Typical laboratory work area space allocation ranges.

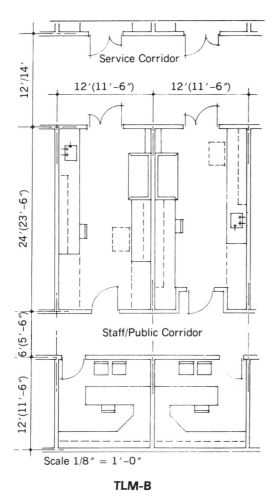

Service Corridor

12'(11'-6")   12'(11'-6")

12'/14'

24'(23'-6")

Staff/Public Corridor

6'(5'-6")

12'(11'-6")

Scale 1/8" = 1'-0"

TLM-B

All dimensions indicated are nominal.

Diagram assumes a services corridor concept (12' to 14' wide; 12'-wide clear minimum). Door swing into service corridor at 4'-6" opening (3'-wide active leaf with 1'-6"-wide inactive leaf) to permit easy equipment access. The service corridor concept permits two exits from a single module.

If an interstitial or ceiling services concept is used, services must be extended through the floor (not as desirable) or from the ceiling to the casework. This services concept permits only one exit from a single module.

Placement of a chemical fume hood or biological safety cabinet (32" to 34" deep) results in space between the face of the hood/cabinet and the opposite work counter/equipment of approximately 6'-6" (30" counter depth at each wall and 4" to 6" for partitions). This is satisfactory from a safety viewpoint and clearances for a disabled person—5'-wide minimum clearance is required for wheelchair turnaround. Test equipment on carts, etc., will reduce the clearance between the fixed work counters to approximately 4' (assuming a utility cart size of 24" to 30" wide × 36" long).

Door into laboratory work area: should swing into corridor for safety reasons. If staff/public corridor is designated as an egress corridor, proper clearance must be provided to avoid door swing. The door may be placed in an alcove to reduce corridor width. This creates dead-end spaces within the laboratory work area.

Basic office module—across the corridor from the laboratory module or in adjacent areas on each floor. Multiple modules may be combined for conference, meeting spaces, and brainstorming meeting spaces as alcoves off the corridor.

This recommended laboratory work area module contains 288 nsf (nominal). If partitions enclose a single module, actual total nsf (face to face of partitions—assuming partition width between 4" and 6") will be approximately 270 nsf (usable). Basic office module at 144 nsf (nominal)—actual total nsf (face to face of partitions) will be approximately 132 (usable) nsf. *Module dimensions may or may not include partition thickness; this example includes the partition thickness within the module dimensions.*

Figure 1.5 Typical laboratory work area space allocation ranges.

3. Building gross square feet (gsf) includes:

   a. Nsf plus dgsf and floor area occupied by building elements, interdepartment circulation (public corridors, stairs, elevators, etc.)

   b. Structural members (columns)

   c. Mechanical, electrical, and plumbing elements

   d. Electrical and telecommunications equipment

   e. Partitions surrounding these building elements

   The gsf is the total building area, which also includes the exterior walls of the building envelope, balconies, canopies, and other overhanging covered projections.

4. The American Institute of Architects (1735 New York Avenue, Washington, DC 20006) publishes guidelines for estimating building areas. Copies of AIA Document D101, Architectural Area and Volume of Buildings, may be obtained directly from the AIA.

Laboratory Utilities, Casework, and Equipment

The following summarizes the utilities and services that should be considered and made available for a typical laboratory module:

GENERAL

[It is recommended that services (e.g., gas, air, vacuum outlets/petcocks, etc.), be installed above and off the benchtop work surface.]

1. Central natural gas (butane may be used if natural gas not available); special gases (O_2, N_2, He, CO_2, mixtures, etc.) supplied from gas cylinders located in the service corridor or central gas cylinder distribution facility. Location of gas cylinders within the laboratory work area should be avoided. Liquid gas storage/supply facilities may also be considered. Helium recovery facilities may also be required. (If the volume of helium used is relatively large, recovery facilities will save considerable cost.)

2. Central vacuum at 18″ to 22″ mercury (oil and water free). Although an administrative matter, consideration

must be given to the fact that some laboratory staff will use the vacuum system to suck-up spills, etc.

3. Electric power:

   a. Bus duct system

   b. 120/208-volt (V) panelboards with 25 to 35% additional capacity for future expansion

   c. Two 120-V three-wire polarized grounding duplex outlets each 2 to 3 lf average at work counters, metal multiple-channel raceway (plug-mold type) or individual receptacles, 15-ampere (A) capacity minimum, 20 A suggested

   d. Two 208-V single- and two 208-V three-phase outlets

   e. One 120-V 1200- to 1500-watt (W) emergency power outlet available at each module line

   f. Special service(s) available for individual equipment from the service corridor, interstitial services space, etc. Space and clearances in the utilities services spaces to permit extension of certain services that may not have been installed during construction.

4. Ground busbar in each laboratory module connected to the building ground grid system. Consideration should also be given to experimental requirements or equipment that may need an independent ground.

5. Individual room or module thermostat control. Humidity control may also be required.

6. Individual lighting control, with special requirements for dimmers, timers, and so on, to meet program requirements, particularly for animal facilities.

7. Negative pressure for laboratory work areas relative to public/staff corridors and nonlaboratory spaces (offices, etc.); positive pressure for designated laboratories (tissue culture, etc.).

8. Water (potable—hot at 120°F and cold), and high-purity distilled water at each sink. Other special water provided by stills, cartridge systems, and so on, located in support spaces (glass wash, etc.) or individual laboratories (wall mounted or under counter). High-purity dual-bed deionized water system as feedwater for distilled water system(s). Consider plastic pipe water distribution system. Material selected for water distribution

systems (plastic, copper, glass, etc.) can be a significant item of concern for certain research activities.

9. Steam (primary for autoclaves, steam baths, etc., secondary for media preparation, special glassware wash).

10. Building structure designed to minimize vibrations. Certain heavy or vibration-sensitive equipment might best be located at grade (within the building) on isolation concrete pads or slabs.

SINGLE MODULE (Casework and Generic Equipment)

1. Chemical fume hood 5' to 6' wide. Type and materials selected to meet program requirements.

2. Biological safety cabinet (class II, type B2, 100% exhaust) 5' to 6' wide.

3. Flexible exhaust duct ("elephant trunk" or "snorkel") to remove point sources of heat generated by certain equipment (e.g., atomic absorption units, etc.), and heavier than air gases.

4. Vented acid and corrosive reagents storage cabinets located under the chemical fume hood. This location, however, may not be the safest place to store hazardous reagents. An explosion in the hood could be multiplied by the reagents in the cabinet.

5. $\frac{1}{3}$ lf of 36" to 37"-high work counters (stand-up with minimum one 36"-wide knee space). Consideration may have to be given to provide an adjustable (vertical) workstation/work counter to accommodate disabled personnel.

6. $\frac{1}{3}$ lf of 27" to 30"-high work counters (sit-down with minimum one to two 36"-wide knee spaces). Consideration may have to be given to provide an adjustable (vertical) workstation/work counter to accommodate disabled personnel.

7. $\frac{1}{3}$ lf of open wall space to accommodate equipment (refrigerators, centrifuges, incubators, ovens, carts, etc.), in addition to shared or core service and support areas.

8. Sink with hot and cold water, plastic utility sink faucet, and high-purity distilled water faucet. Other special water derived from cartridge systems, for example. Hand wash lavatory with hot and cold water faucet, soap and paper towel dispenser, trash container.

9. Deluge emergency shower and eye-wash stations. Eye wash may be located at service sink or designated eye-wash station. Accessible to disabled staff.

10. Smoke and flame detector and alarm. Sprinkler system may be required.

11. Emergency equipment (fire extinguisher, fire-blanket, first-aid kit). Accessible to disabled staff.

12. Hazardous waste storage cart (stainless steel, 2' deep × 3' wide × 4' high, with three or four tub-type shelves).

APPLICATION OF STANDARDS

Space standards and guidelines should be used with care and applied with seasoned judgment. Unfortunately, the tendency is to use standards without understanding how the standards may have been developed and the implications on the total program of requirements. Each institution has its own unique experience with space allocations just as each research project has different objectives and requirements. When standards and guidelines are applied in the proper context, they can provide valuable assistance in establishing initial program and planning criteria. Standards can also assist with the development of accurate concept costs for budget purposes.

Space standards and guidelines may be used to develop a program quickly for a hypothetical biomedical research laboratory facility. For example, assuming a staff of 15 to 20 principal investigators, 30 to 35 technicians and laboratory assistants (graduate students, etc.), and 10 to 15 administrative support staff, a conceptual preliminary space program might be set up as outlined in Table 1.1.

COMMENTS

1. The total area for this example facility would probably range between 85,000 and 125,000 gsf when detailed programming has been completed. Construction costs would range between $15,725,000 and $28,125,000 (1994 costs at $185 to $225 per square foot, depending on area of the country, construction, methodology, program criteria, etc.). Total completion time from start of programming, through design and con-

struction, to occupancy is estimated to be 26 to 32 months.

2. Total project costs would include financing and interest, bonds and assessments, professional fees (attorneys, architects, engineers, specialist consultants, interior design, graphics, etc.), equipment and furnishings, taxes, surveys, permits, insurance, environmental impact study, land acquisition, rights-of-ways, and appraisals. These costs usually range between 25 and 35% of construction costs. Thus, for the example in Table 1.1 the total project budget cost estimate (see Table 1.2) would be approximately $19,656,250 to $37,968,750.

3. It is quite simple to begin the arithmetical process of dividing the number of staff into the areas assigned for offices, laboratories, service/support spaces, and so on, to arrive at x number of square feet per principal investigator, technician, and so on. These figures or factors can be useful, but they can also be misleading and if applied out-of-context can produce seriously flawed net square feet figures. Again, space program development must be based on the specific requirements and criteria for each institutional research facility.

4. The author cautions against the application and use of these example data and emphasizes that the steps above do not eliminate the need for detailed programming or reduce the time required to complete the programming process. The experience factors used to prepare the example facility program can assist with the preparation of a conceptual program outlining the general scope and scale for a proposed project. Experience factors can be useful to prepare a response for a grant application and other estimates prior to commitments for the formal project acquisition process.

Table 1.2 indicates the various items that constitute the total project cost.

The TLMs generally can be accommodated within efficient and economical structural framing systems (bay sizes) to minimize space planning conflicts with column locations, depth of beams, and so on. TLMs may be combined in any numbers to provide service and support functions (instrumentation, equipment, computer, controlled-environment rooms, photography processing, biosafety laboratories, animal facilities, etc.) to satisfy a wide range of specific program function and activity requirements.

TABLE 1.1 **Example of Facility Space Program**

Functions and Activities	Space Allocation
Principal investigator offices: 15–20 at 180 nsf each	2700–3600 nsf
Research laboratories at 1200–1600 nsf each	18,000–32,000 nsf
Laboratory core service/support spaces (electron microscopy, photo darkroom, tissue culture, controlled temperature/humidity/ light rooms, refrigerator/freezer rooms, supplies storage, autoclave/washing, instrument/machine room, medium preparation, computer room, BL2,3,4 biocontainment rooms, machine shop, etc.)	5000–8000 nsf
Technician workstations: 30–35 at 80 nsf each	2400–2800 nsf
Administrative/secretarial staff: 10–15 at 120 nsf each	1200–1800 nsf
Administrative service/support spaces (reception, waiting, public toilets, coat closet, telephones, records, files, copy/mail/FAX work area, coffee, computer/printing, supplies storage, etc.)	3000–5000 nsf
Estimate for Research grant requirements	3000–5000 nsf
Conference/seminar, classroom, library/reference, reading/ periodicals, interactive (brainstorming) spaces, staff safety publications display space (MSDS, etc.), audiovisual storage, etc.	3000–5000 nsf
Staff facilities (lockers, lounge, snacks, toilets, showers, etc.)	2000–3000 nsf
Animal facilities [administration, staff facilities (lockers, showers, toilets, etc.), holding, laboratories, surgery, radiographic, refrigerator/freezer, feed/bedding storage, cage wash, cage/cart staging, receiving/quarantine, animal waste process/hold, etc.]	5000–8000 nsf
General service/support [waste management, collection, transport, process, decontamination, storage, recycle/sort, disposal, reagent storage, gas cylinder storage, loading dock, receiving/shipping, spill containment materials storage cart, environmental services (housekeeping), etc.]	3000–5000 nsf
Subtotal	48,300–79,200 nsf
Building services/net to gross space factor 1.45 to 1.55 average (1.58 to 1.65 considered more accurate)	35,235–43,560 nsf
Total building gross square feet	83,535–122,760 gsf

TABLE 1.2 Total Project Budget Cost Estimate Checklist

Items	Costs	
Project name:		
Project number:		
Date:		
Building Costs		
Construction _____ gsf × $____ /gsf =	$	
Demolition	$	
Fixed equipment	$	
Site development	$	
Utilities	$	
Subtotal		$
Project Costs		
Land acquisition/rights-of-way	$	
Surveys, soil borings, materials tests	$	
Programming/planning fee	$	
A/E planning/design/construction documents fees	$	
Interior design/graphics fees	$	
Landscaping/site design fees	$	
Project management fees	$	
Construction management fees	$	
Specialty consultant fees:		
Acoustics/vibration	$	
ADA assessment	$	
Asbestos survey	$	
A/V planning	$	
Construction cost analysis	$	
Environmental assessment	$	
Environmental/hazardous	$	
Equipment planning	$	
Food facilities planning services	$	
Materials management	$	
Waste management/recycling	$	
Other(s)	$	
Asbestos containment/removal	$	
Movable equipment + furnishings	$	
Reproduction costs	$	
Legal, administrative + advertising	$	
Interest during construction	$	
Insurance during construction	$	
Additional construction services	$	
Miscellaneous costs	$	
Contingency: ____ % of building cost	$	
Escalation: ____ years at ____ %/year	$	
Subtotal		$
Total project budget cost estimates		$

COMMENTS

1. Several industries, particularly in petroleum and chemical engineering, construct working models at sufficient scale to analyze, test, and confirm the design of facilities for specific processes. This practice saves hundred of thousands, if not millions, of dollars in construction, operational, and maintenance costs. The two-dimensional medium of a drawing cannot illustrate design features in the same space detail as that of a three-dimensional model.

2. The same consideration should be given to this technique or methodology in the testing, confirmation, and verification of the programming, design, and construction solutions developed for laboratory work spaces (module size $12' \times 24'$, etc.), services systems concepts (service corridor, interstitial space, ceiling systems, etc.), arrangement of services and utility runs behind the laboratory casework, and so on. If warehouse space is not readily available on campus, the space to construct a full-size mockup can be rented for this purpose. Mockups should be considered for spaces in the hospital as well as those in the laboratory environment.

3. Full-size mockups of the laboratory work area module can highlight not only design problem areas and provide the opportunity to develop solutions but also construction problems that may only become evident during construction. Laboratory casework systems can be studied to develop flexible systems to simplify future changes.

4. A three-dimensional clear plastic model with the floor plans inked on outlines of the floor plates should also be constructed. The model should be at an appropriate scale horizontal and vertical). The model will be indispensable to assist in visualizing such factors as inter- and intrafunctional relationships and vertical and horizontal circulation of staff, visitors, patients, materials and supplies, etc. (stairs, elevators, escalators, corridors, dumbwaiters, pneumatic tube, and other carrier systems).

5. Many of the new CAD/CADD/CAM computer draw-

ing programs with three-dimensional capabilities can duplicate or simulate much of what can be achieved with a three-dimensional scale model. However, a two-dimensional or three-dimensional simulated model on a computer monitor can never replace the visual impact and versatility of a scale model. As the planning and design progresses, full-scale working models or mockups should be constructed to test certain laboratory work area criteria or services concepts.

SPACE PROGRAM DIFFERENCES

As the design documents (space schematics, schematic design, and design development drawings) evolve, the distinction between nsf, dgsf, and gsf becomes less clear and more complicated. Many of the building elements become integral parts within department areas. Determining the true or actual area figures becomes a matter of judgment as to how the final-plan scaled nsf, dgsf, and gsf figures relate to the original statistical space program figures. These matters must be reviewed carefully and discussed with the facility manager, administration of the institution, and users (researchers and investigators) to avoid any confusion that may occur as the plans develop and especially, during occupancy. This is a particularly important topic to review during the initial programming kickoff meeting with the interviewees present.

Department chairpersons, managers, and principal investigators usually compare the original statistical space program figures with the plan area figures as the planning progresses into the drawing phases. These people do not always understand how differences develop between the several program and plan (design or construction) drawing figures. Unfortunately, many programmers and architects are not aware or sensitive to the important significance of how total department area allocations relate to the prestige and standing of the chairperson's position, particularly at university academic institutions. These factors are in addition to specific departmental space requirements.

COMMENTS

1. As the statistical space program is developed and the figures are used to prepare the design documents defining the three-dimensional characteristics of the building (shape, size of the floor plate or building "footprint," floor-to-floor heights, and services and utilities systems), the volume of the building generated has a major impact on building costs, including construction and operations. Construction and operational costs are a direct function of building area and volume and, of course, the complexity of the functions and activities to be conducted within the building.

2. Valid construction costs can be developed early in the programming and planning process by using conceptional functional cost factors. These cost factors relate to specific disciplines or functions (e.g., laboratory spaces are more expensive than office spaces) and include building systems cost factors. The cost estimate should evolve with the building design. Cost estimates should not be based solely on building total gross square feet.

3. The architect should not proceed with the space planning process until all major fixed building elements have been defined and located. This is especially important when planning existing building spaces in remodeling and renovations projects. Nothing undermines the planning process and confidence in the architect than to return to the user or researcher after securing approval of the plan and state that changes must be made because of conflicts with existing building elements (pipes, ducts, conduits, etc.) that may not have been known at the time of initial planning.

LABORATORY AND EQUIPMENT USAGE FACTORS

Factors for estimating laboratory and equipment usage (LEUFs) to determine mechanical, electrical, and plumbing design criteria and loads are indicated in Table 1.3. These factors are also referred to as the *demand/diversity factors* or *group diversity factors* by some sources.

TABLE 1.3 Laboratory and Equipment Usage Factors

TLM Module(s)	Usage Factor (%)
1	100
2/12	100/85
12/45	85/55
45/120	55/35
120+	35/25

COMMENTS

1. The factors are based on general and average laboratory operations and equipment use. They should be reviewed and confirmed with the principal investigators and the facility manager. Experience indicates that a LEUF of 75%/65% may be used to estimate initial conceptual construction costs for building systems demands and requirements prior to the development of specific systems design criteria.

2. The architect should note that LEUFs may vary during the same period of time for different scientific disciplines, processes, and types of laboratories (e.g., research vs. clinical vs. teaching vs. production facilities).

BUILDING CLASSIFICATIONS

Building or occupancy classification and types of construction for scientific research laboratories vary according to the jurisdiction (location), applicable codes, and regulations. How these regulations may be interpreted and applied are additional factors affecting planning and design criteria. Careful review and analysis of the proposed laboratory functions and activities, type and classification of reagents to be used, and procedures to be performed will generally establish the extent of the hazards to be contained and controlled. The building classification and type required by the code(s) can be determined from these factors. It is also important to determine the zoning classification of the proposed building site. Although the zoning may be determined to permit construction of the laboratory, the adjoining property owners may challenge the project, resulting in costly delays and even cancellation of the project.

Various codes, regulations, and guidelines are not always in agreement on the classification or degree of hazard to be contained within a particular building type. Some sources classify laboratories under a business or educational category. There are also subclassifications determined by the extent of the hazards involved. The building classification and type of construction have significant design and cost implications. The facility manager and architect must determine the classification based on the nature of the functions and activities to be conducted in the proposed facility within the requirements of the applicable code(s). The assistance of local building officials may have to be secured for interpretations of the codes and regulations. Whether the proposed building is an addition or freestanding structure has an impact on the classification. Distance from existing buildings and connections (bridges, etc.) are other factors.

COMMENTS

1. Significant construction cost savings can be achieved by designing separate building types and classifications to house discrete groups of functions and activities. For example, one structure might house the laboratory work areas and animal facilities. Another structure may be designed to accommodate the administrative office, conference, classroom functions, and activities.

2. Savings can be achieved in the design of the structural, mechanical, electrical, and plumbing building systems, including the selection of materials and finishes. Circulation between or among the buildings can be accomplished through tunnel and bridge connections.

3. This concept may be possible if the various program elements are of sufficient size and scale. Functional relationships, available site and configuration, zoning restrictions, future expansion, and personnel environmental and safety considerations are other factors that affect the decision to implement a separate structures concept.

4. At one medical center, the administrative functions,

faculty offices and support spaces, conference rooms, and so on, were of sufficient scale to justify a facility separate from the laboratory and clinical facilities. The faculty initially resisted the separation of their offices from laboratory and clinical activities. However, as the planning developed, each clinical department was located functionally at the same level as the respective clinical and laboratory activities. Convenient connections were made at all levels. After completion and occupancy, the faculty were well pleased with the functional relationships. The offices being separated from the clinical and laboratory activities provided the needed escape for the faculty to manage and attend to administrative and teaching activities that were previously interrupted or overshadowed by the immediate adjacency of the laboratory and clinical activities.

5. It was estimated that almost 35,000 gsf more office space was purchased for the same dollars spent by separating the office functions into an office-type structure than to combine offices in the laboratory or clinical (hospital) structure.

6. It may be possible to develop exterior circulation spines or elements to solve circulation problems at existing facilities. As an institution (medical center with medical school, teaching hospital, research facilities, etc.) expands, existing corridors become major circulation elements, even though they may not have been designed for such a function. Exterior (enclosed) circulation elements can be constructed to provide a pedestrian bypass to reach other buildings without using buildings as connecting corridors. These exterior corridors may not necessarily be at the same elevation and perhaps even hung from the exterior of existing buildings. If at all possible, they should be wide enough to accommodate electric vehicles similar to those used at many airports. These vehicles are ideal to transport individuals, patients, materials, equipment, and so on, from parking structures to the main entry, to laboratory and teaching facilities, or to patient care facilities.

7. The author program-planned such elements in a master strategy plan developed for a major medical center more than 20 years ago. Circulation spines were incorporated in the first phase of the expansion program.

The spines were designed wide enough for pedestrians and airport-type electric vehicles. The electric vehicles were introduced several years ago and are highly praised by staff, visitors, and patients. They save time and aggravation traveling among the several buildings on campus.

Laboratory and health care facilities must be designed for continuous 24-hour operations. When initiated, many laboratory tests and processes must be maintained in continuous operation until completed. Animal facilities must also be maintained in continuous operation and be provided with redundant systems. Many functions in health care facilities must be available to respond immediately to patient needs.

LABORATORY FINISHES

Certain laboratory walls and floors may have to be washed or steam cleaned frequently. Epoxy finishes (troweled, rolled, brushed) or seamless vinyl (welded seams) materials may be appropriate. Although the traditional standard gypsum board and stud wall system can be very serviceable and cost-effective for laboratory use, the concrete masonry partition has superior resistance to high-humidity and high-moisture conditions, particularly in animal cage rooms and in cage wash, surgery, and necropsy facilities.

Seamless floor and wall materials provide good protection against contamination from spills and satisfactory resistance to many chemicals, and are easier to walk and stand on for long periods of time (many are manufactured with a resilient core or backing). However, such materials have a higher initial cost than that of other floor materials, are more subject to physical damage (cuts and abrasions) because they are usually softer, and are difficult to patch and repair when damaged. If the seams are not welded properly, separation can occur at the joints. Separation can also occur between the sheet vinyl and subfloor, creating bubbles.

As mentioned earlier in this section, certain materials and finishes can also cause problems for disabled persons and must be selected carefully. Bright colors may create problems for persons with certain eye conditions. Color-blind persons may have difficulty distinguishing colors that may be used to designate hazardous conditions or for other purposes.

Composition tile materials ($9'' \times 9''$, $12'' \times 12''$, etc.) are relatively inexpensive, easily repaired or replaced when damaged, and resistant to a wide range of chemicals. The primary disadvantage is that of the many joints between tiles. If a particular reagent or contaminant is spilled, it is very difficult, if not impossible, to clean or decontaminate the tiles because of the many joints. The entire floor may have to be removed. However, in laboratories not using such reagents, composition tiles are a satisfactory floor material. Resilient tiles are available to provide a similar soft flooring surface.

Waterproofing floor slabs can be a difficult and costly design, installation, and construction problem. Also, floor drains may not be permitted in certain areas because of possible contamination from the open drain. Drains may have to be located in adjoining spaces. Consider locating spaces that require such cleaning protocols at grade level.

COMMENTS

1. There are many opinions about the type of floor material that should be specified and installed in laboratory work areas. Many sources recommend a seamless plastic (vinyl) material with an integral coved base. This material may be the most expensive floor finish from a unit cost, installation, and maintenance standpoint. It is not easy to repair damage to seamless floor materials caused by reagent spills, equipment cuts and indentation caused by table and equipment legs, tears, and scars.

2. Many institutions have had considerable success with plastic (vinyl) tile floor materials adhered to the structural slab. The tile is less expensive per unit cost than seamless material and relatively simple to replace. Maintaining an inventory of tiles to replace and match different areas is also reasonably simple.

3. However, the facility manager, architect, and materials specifier should be aware that certain laboratory work areas may require a seamless floor and wall material (e.g., to contain radioisotope spills and maintain the integrity of clean rooms).

4. It should be noted that the selection of finishes and materials can have severe consequences on the ability and safety of disabled people to maneuver within the building spaces. The selection of the flooring material(s) is critical not only from the functional standpoint of resistance to contaminants and chemical reagents, ease of cleaning, decontamination, and maintenance but to a nonslip and safe walking surface.

STRUCTURAL CONSIDERATIONS

Determination of the structural system (bay sizes, materials, etc.) depends on several factors, including:

- Proposed size, volume, shape, and height of the building.
- Structural materials (concrete, steel, wood, or combinations).
- Regional location (availability of materials, experience, and skills of local contractors and workers).
- Nature of the research activities (requirements for vibration-free work areas, height required for the laboratory activities, sensitivity and influence of steel structural members on instruments and experiments, etc.).
- Type of building services concept (service corridor, interstitial space, ceiling, through floor, combination, etc.).
- If the building is planned for expansion, is the structure stressed to accommodate the vertical or horizontal addition(s), bridge connection(s), and so on?

Structural bay sizes may vary from 28' to 32' square to 32' to 36' square. These dimensions may also be totally inappropriate in certain circumstances. The structural engineer should determine what the optimum frame/bay size may be based on the program requirements. A rectangular structural bay may also be economical. Beam and joist depths can be critical to ventilation and exhaust duct system layouts and other building services elements. Clear-span laboratory work areas may be accomplished with space frames or bridge girders. Minimum suggested live loads are listed in Table 1.4.

TABLE 1.4   Suggested Values for Structural Live Loads

Design Element	Minimum Load
Offices (incl. partitions)[a]	100 psf
Assembly spaces	100 psf
Computer and data storage	150 psf
Laboratories, service, support, storage[b]	150 psf
Mechanical equipment rooms	200 psf
Rolling files/x-ray films	400 psf
Roofs (25 psf live load + 20 psf for future roof work)[c]	45 psf
Staff corridors	100 psf
Service corridor	150 psf
Concrete mixes[d]	
Footings and walls	3000 psi
Caissons	3000 psi
Columns	5000 psi
Other concrete	4000 psi

[a]Floor slabs of offices part of typical laboratory modules (TLMs) should be designed as laboratory work areas to facilitate future expansion. Consideration should be given to design exterior wall structure to accommodate future horizontal additions. Footings may be stressed for future vertical expansion. Note, however, that only approximately one-third of buildings stressed for additional floors are ever completed.
[b]Certain equipment items can impose a live load that may exceed this value. Early identification during programming will minimize disruptive changes to structural designs. Floor loadings of 400 to 600 psf may be required to minimize vibrations.
[c]Add allowances for loading of any roof-mounted mechanical equipment, fans, motors, pumps, pipes, ducts, cable trays, chillers, and tanks suspended on the underside of the roof structural slab.
[d]Strength of concrete mixes may vary with the structural design system.

Wind loads may be based on a velocity of 100 mph/33 psf times a shape factor of 1.3. Local conditions relating to prevailing winds, topography, historical meteorological conditions, and shape, size, and height of adjacent buildings will modify these parameters. Areas of the country subject to tornadoes and hurricanes may have developed specific structural requirements.

SEISMIC CONSIDERATIONS

The 1994 earthquakes in California again focus attention on the importance of seismic design for laboratory and health care facilities. The author was living in the Los Angeles area (less than 2 miles from the epicenter) when the earthquake of February 1971 occurred and participated in several site visits to hospitals damaged during the earthquake. The experience resulted in the author revising various programming space factors and criteria. The earthquakes of January 1994 in southern California have yielded additional structural experience of criteria applied since the 1971 earthquake.

The facility manager, architect, and structural engineer should be aware of potential problems or hazards that may occur as a result of seismic activity, regardless of the frequency of such activity:

- Access to and security of sensitive research laboratory areas, including hazardous reagents and materials storage, particularly areas using biohazardous, virulent, infectious, and radioactive materials, and animal facilities

- Doors and partitions (partial and full height)

- Emergency electrical power, communications control center and systems, transformers and switchgear, building systems control centers, major aboveground and underground utility service tunnel interfaces and distribution systems (conduits, pipes, cables, etc.), aboveground and underground fuel storage tanks

- Entrance canopies, balconies, overhangs, parapet walls, exterior non-load-bearing walls, steeples, building veneer finishes (brick and stone)

- Equipment suspended from underside of structural slab and on partitions (television sets, shelves, cabinets, cranes and hoists, etc.).

- Exiting and egress (horizontal and vertical), including corridors, stairs, elevators, escalators, and lifts. Closed doors may become impossible to open because of deformed walls, floors, structural frame, and so on.

- Landscaping features, including ponds, sculptures, trees, and plants

- Location and methods of attachment of items, including TV monitors, patient monitoring equipment, signs, water fountains, fire extinguishers, and other equipment

- Placement, size, and type of furnishings and equipment

- Suspended ceiling systems, light fixtures, speakers, and diffusers

- Suspension methods for building services, including pipes, pumps, motors, chillers, tanks, fan coil units, filter boxes, fire and smoke detection systems, fire suppression systems, smoke removal systems, primary electrical cables, conduits, and ducts
- Wall- and floor-mounted shelving units (fixed or rolling)
- Windows and curtain walls

Many codes include recently revised seismic structural design requirements. Geologists and seismologists are concerned that regions of the country that have not experienced damaging earthquakes may be subject to this phenomenon. Although the occurrence of earthquakes on the west coast is highly publicized, every area of the country is subject to earthquakes. The most severe earthquakes have occurred in the eastern regions of the country. Fortunately, they occurred many years ago, prior to the development of large urban centers and caused little damage or injury. Seismologists believe that we may be within the geological time frame or window for a damaging earthquake to occur in the eastern regions of our country.

The knowledge or technology to predict with any accuracy when an earthquake will occur does not exist at this time. The facility manager, architect, and structural engineer must be aware of seismic code requirements applicable to the region of the proposed facility. Other recommendations are published by the *Building Seismic Safety Council*, indicating basic architectural design features that can be included in the building to minimize structural damage and injury to occupants.

Structural engineers must review the latest seismic design codes and current published data to determine what structural methodologies should be considered and presented to the facility manager for inclusion in the building design. This may mean exceeding current specific code requirements for seismic structural design.

A relatively simple and successful method for securing laboratory equipment and office furnishings and equipment (PCs, files, etc.) is available using Velcro fasteners. Several hospitals reported virtually no damage occurred during the recent San Francisco earthquake to equipment that had been secured with Velcro fasteners. Unsecured equipment was a total loss. The laboratories with secured equipment were able to begin operations almost immediately after the earthquake, when debris had been cleared away. Institutions with unsecured equipment sustained hundreds of thousands of dollars in equipment losses. They were unable to resume operations until damaged equipment was replaced. Information about one type of Velcro fasteners may be obtained by writing to "Q" Sales, 2341 East Foothill Boulevard, Pasadena, CA 91107.

ACOUSTICAL CONSIDERATIONS

Noise in the workplace environment is considered by safety and medical authorities and physiologists as an equally dangerous pollutant as airborne contaminants. Unnecessary noise (not only loud noise) can cause progressive, irreversible, and irreparable hearing loss, impair concentration, and create undue fatigue, stress, and irritability. Occupational hearing loss is a function of the noise level(s) and the time of exposure to the noise. Damage due to exposure to high noise levels is cumulative. It is similar to exposure to gamma radiation. Small doses over time can produce the same trauma as that caused by an equally large single dose.

The Occupational Health and Safety Administration (OSHA) has specific regulations governing noise levels produced in the workplace. Certain protective measures and devices are also mandated in the regulations. The best method to prevent hearing damage is to eliminate the source(s) creating the excessive noise levels. The second method is to reduce, contain, or control the source of the noise. The third method is the use of protective devices and limiting the exposure time. Most noise abatement programs focus on the second and third methods. Perhaps the greatest obstacle to occupational hearing loss prevention programs is to persuade employers and employees to recognize that there is a problem and to regard it seriously.

Laboratory work areas and health care facilities are not usually considered noisy work environments. However, during the past several years noise levels have been steadily increasing, due to the introduction of various types of equipment (electronic and mechanical) and processes. Research laboratories, particularly those involved with the physical sciences, can produce noise levels 85 decibels (dB) and higher. Electric motors, vacuum pumps, high-pressure gas moving through pipes, vessels, and so on, can create harmful noise levels.

Unfortunately, many acoustical materials that are used successfully to reduce and control noise levels in office work areas are not compatible or practical in laboratory work areas. The soft and porous acoustical materials absorb liquids and moisture and can become a medium to propagate dangerous biological organisms. Acoustical materials also lose sound control properties when wet. These acoustical materials also flake and the particles fall to equipment and work surfaces below.

The perception of noise is perhaps as much psychological as it is physiological. Its manifestation in a hospital environment is magnified because of the medical traumatic condition of the patient. Sounds that may be considered annoying or not even heard (noticed) at all by the staff and visitors (well persons) can become almost painful to some patients.

All too often, many materials, equipment, furnishings, casework, and building systems are designed, purchased, selected, installed, and used with little or no thought to its impact and contribution to the noise environment within the facility. Something apparently as simple as the type of drawer slide specified for a cabinet drawer can make the difference between a noisemaker and a quiet element. Purchasing departments can assist in this process by requiring equipment to meet certain sound-level standards.

Building systems and equipment sound levels are functions of the fabrication quality of the unit and how it is installed or mounted (spring mounted, vibration pads, flexible couplings, etc.). Other sound sources may be the result of staff and visitor actions. These sound sources are difficult to control and are more administrative and work habit related.

Every building system and its design, items of equipment (fixed and movable), furnishings, and materials should be reviewed and analyzed during the programming, planning, design, and preparation of the construction documents and specifications phases. Careful thought must be given to the acoustic properties of all these elements to minimize the impact that each has on the total noise environment of the facility. The same principles apply for the programming, planning, and design of laboratory facilities.

The following list summarizes a range of the many sound sources within a laboratory facility:

- Mechanical equipment: boilers (noise output depends on design and fuel type), roof ventilators, blowers, fans (intake, exhaust), louvers, chillers, compressors, radiators, elevators, dumbwaiters, automatic valve systems, air movement through ductwork and grills

- Electrical Equipment: transformers, motors, switchgear, solenoids, timers, light fixture ballast, radios, TV sets, voice paging systems, telephones, handbells, intercoms, warning devices and alarms, monitoring equipment, emergency power generators, computer printers (impact type), copy machines

- Plumbing equipment: toilets, lavatories, showers, washers, pipes for air, gases, liquids, steam, pumps (circulating, condensate return, steam and water hammer, etc.)

- Service equipment: carts (noise generated depends on items carried on carts, type of wheel, surface rolled on, etc.), metal pans, gas tanks and regulators, suction equipment, refrigerators, icemakers, drinking fountains, dishwasher, glass washers, sterilizers, autoclaves

- Furnishings: cabinet doors and drawers, metal sinks and cabinets

- Housekeeping Equipment: vacuum cleaners, floor scrubbers and polishers, metal mop and scrub buckets, trashcans, pails

- Exterior Sounds: vehicles, aircraft, trains, loading dock activity, birds, weather, insects, animals, people, athletic playing fields, industrial facilities

COMMENTS

1. Acoustical consultants are not often engaged to assist in the planning and design of a laboratory or health care facility. Architects, in general, are not experienced in acoustical analysis and design. The extent of acoustical design on most projects is usually limited to the application of suspended acoustical ceiling tile systems. An acoustical consultant can be a valuable team member assisting in the design of safe working environments.

2. Covering the entire ceiling with acoustical tiles in a room or corridor can compound the problem instead of reducing reverberation time. A more effective method is to place a 2' to 4' foot strip of acoustical material on the walls and ceiling at the intersection of these surfaces. Reducing reverberation time can reduce sound transmission.

3. This treatment uses essentially the same amount of acoustical material and results in greater reduction in reverberation time. Carpeting can be used effectively and safely in many laboratory work, service, and support areas. Acoustical "clouds" or baffles can also control sound in laboratory work areas. Massive and dense materials (concrete masonry, poured concrete, etc.) may be required to isolate certain noise sources. Isolation pads, staggered stud walls with insulating batting and unequal thickness of wallboard material, and sealing wall and floor joints are several methods to minimize and control sound reverberation and transmission.

4. Voice and sound transmissions can have far-reaching and severe liability consequences in certain instances. Conversations between a patient and a psychiatrist are protected and confidential. In one facility, the voices in the psychiatrists' offices were transmitted through the ventilation system and could be heard clearly in other areas of the building. The lack of acoustical privacy resulted in compromise of the patients' conversations with the psychiatrists. The patients and physicians were successful in the legal suits brought against the building designers, constructors, and owners. The same situation could occur if private discussions about proprietary experiments and processes could be overheard by unauthorized persons who may be in adjacent or other spaces in the building.

The facility manager and architect must be aware that occupational hearing loss in the laboratory environment is a serious problem. Possible noise generators due to the laboratory experiment, equipment, or process, including building systems equipment, must be identified during the programming process. Manufacturers should be required to provide data about the acoustical output in addition to the power requirements, Btu output, and size and weight of the equipment. The acoustical data should be analyzed to determine what treatment may have to be included in the design of the facility to alleviate the problem. Occupational hearing loss due to hazardous noise levels in the work environment should be considered as part of the sick-building syndrome problem.

WASTE CONSIDERATIONS

Recycling selected waste products can be cost-effective. Hospital employees may generate between 0.75 and 1.5 lb of waste paper per day. Recycling waste paper and corrugated cardboard can reduce overall waste handling costs. Definition of the waste management policy and allocation of adequate space and facilities for the various classifications of waste must be accomplished during the initial programming and planning process. Revenues received can offset costs for handling, processing, and storage space, including compacting and baling equipment. Other waste materials, including aluminum, plastics, and glass, can also become part of the waste recycling stream.

It is important that proper facilities be provided for the items to be recycled. Storage areas and bins should be protected from the weather. Waste paper storage areas should be sprinkled. Regulations from federal agencies (OSHA, EPA, NIOSH, etc.) must be reviewed when waste-handling facilities are planned. Regulations require that certain hazardous waste materials be stored in separate containers and, in some instances, separate spaces and buildings. Mixing certain types of hazardous waste materials can result in toxic fumes and gases, fires, and explosions.

Improper mixing can also result in significant fines and penalties for failure to follow regulations. Classifications of hazardous materials; processing, holding, and recycling facilities; incinerator facilities, and so on, will also have to conform to site zoning regulations. Some institutions are combining resources with local or regional governments to develop large incinerator facilities and waste-to-energy generation systems.

Liquid waste handling facilities (including some solid waste holding) may require multiple tanks for holding, processing (cooking, etc.), and treatment (pH balance, etc.) prior to release into the sanitary sewer system or holding after processing for removal by an outside contractor for proper disposal. Certain treatment processes may require heat or generate heat. The materials may also have to be held until the proper temperature is reached before disposal. The tanks require adequate pumps, mixers, and access and view ports to monitor the treatment process. Shielded waste holding facilities may be required for radioactive material until it decays to a safe level for handling, transport, and disposal.

Because of the increased awareness and proliferation of regulations, it may be necessary to engage an environmental consultant experienced in hazardous waste management to assess the research programs and assist with the planning and design of proper waste management protocols and facilities. The best method of hazardous waste control is in the laboratory. Minimum amounts of hazardous materials should be used to accomplish the test results.

SAFETY CONSIDERATIONS

The requirements for planning and designing safe working environments for personnel who may be exposed to hazardous substances, gases, and so on, has become extremely complex. Regulations from several federal government agencies are quite specific regarding how personnel are to be protected. The regulations are also specific about penalties that may be assessed for violations.

The Occupational Safety and Health Administration (OSHA) regulations are voluminous and complex and have significant impact on facilities requirements. As an example, OSHA Employee "Right-to-Know" Standards or OSHA 29 CFR 1910.1200, 1450, 1915, 1917, 1918, 1926 and 1928, Hazards Communications Standards, Standards for Employee Safety Educational Programs, and Hazards Associated with Toxic and Dangerous Chemicals, state the requirements for conference and classroom facilities. These facilities are required to conduct general staff meetings, in-service education programs, and so on, to explain employees rights and the dangers to be encountered handling or being exposed to toxic and dangerous chemicals. A reference library should be provided with space to display MSDS (material safety data sheets) and equipped with a TV/VCR to view safety, educational tapes, and so on.

The National Committee on Clinical Laboratory Standards (NCCLS) publishes many documents related to health and safety issues related to clinical laboratories. Many of these documents also apply to the biomedical research laboratory environment. NCCLS Document I17-P, Vol. 11, No. 15, *Protection of Laboratory Workers from Instrument Biohazards* (Proposed Guideline, September 1991), lists standards that apply to the use of many laboratory instruments. Most standards relate to management and operational protocols. Standards that relate to facilities include the following:

> "Laboratory space should be sufficient to minimize crowding, which may contribute to laboratory accidents."

"Facilities for hand washing should be provided in each laboratory area. These should be separate from those used for washing equipment or for waste disposal."

"There are sufficient space, equipment, supplies within the laboratory work areas to perform the required volume of work with optimal accuracy, precision, efficiency timeliness, and safety."

Several applicable OSHA standards are:

- OSHA 29 CF 1910.101-152 defines flammables cabinet specifications based on reagent classifications, carcinogenic chemicals, volumes to be stored, chemical compatibility, etc.
- OSHA CFR 2236 lists standards for materials handling and storage.
- OSHA 29 CFR 1910.120, which lists standards for hazardous waste operation, indicates requirements for adequate storage of materials.
- OSHA 29 CFR 1910.1030 lists standards for regulated medical waste. The storage room must also meet 29 CFR 1910.155-165 standards for fire suppression systems.
- OSHA 29 CFR 1910.1200, 1450 refers to standards for exposure to hazardous chemicals in laboratories.
- The proposed performance standards for laboratories using toxic substances are outlined in 51 FR 26660.
- Standards for working with carcinogens (hoods, etc.) are also listed in Subpart Z.

The list above cites only a few of the OSHA standards and regulations. OSHA also encourages employers to follow centers for Disease Control (CDC) guidelines for engineering Controls for ventilation, local exhaust, and so on. The architect must research all the applicable regulations that may apply to the specific research facility being designed.

OSHA has revised the permissible exposure limit (PEL) for formaldehyde from 1.0 per million parts of air (ppm) to 0.75 ppm on an 8-hour time-weighted average (TWA) basis. Respiratory protection must now be offered to employees exposed above the new PEL (since September 24, 1992). Engineering and work practice controls must be in place since June 26, 1993. If tests indicate concentrations over the limits, the facilities must be modified to reduce the levels. Air quality tests should be performed by a professional engineer. OSHA 29 CFR 1910.1000-1500 standards limit employee exposure by inhalation to various agents. See proposed OSHA 29 CFR 1910.1450 for additional standards.

An emergency shower, eye wash station (OSHA 29 CFR 1910.133), fire extinguisher types (OSHA 29 CFR 1910.157), and fire blankets are required in all laboratory work areas. OSHA Standard 29 CFR 1910.106 defines fire extinguishers and distance from flammables stored in the laboratory.

Research laboratories involved with handling blood specimens (HIV, AIDS, etc.) must conform to OSHA Bloodborne Pathogen Standard 1910.130. This standard requires that shields (bench and face types), gloves, masks, and protective clothing be provided and worn by staff. OSHA 29 CFR 1910.134, *Standard for Respiratory Protection*, also applies. NCCLS Document M29-T2, Vol. 11, No. 14, *Protection of Laboratory Workers from Infectious Disease Transmitted by Blood, Body Fluids, and Tissue*, 2nd Ed. (Tentative Guideline, September 1991) is consistent with OSHA and CDC standards.

Designation and allocation of space(s) for safety equipment, apparatus, and storage units are often overlooked during development of the program space list. To comply with this requirement, employers must provide storage for the protective clothing and equipment, change areas, lockers, toilets, showers, and management and processing of soiled clothing. These items must be added to the total supplies, materials and equipment purchasing, receiving, storage, distribution, usage, and disposal stream. These items may have to be added to the hazardous waste management stream, including decontamination processing. Final regulations were issued by OSHA in May 1991. See Appendix A, Checklist 2, Safety Programming Considerations, for additional criteria. The employer must also keep detailed records of all related activities involving hazardous substances. This may involve a full-time staff person to meet the record-keeping requirements. Therefore, an office area may be required that includes records storage.

MISCELLANEOUS CONSIDERATIONS

All services should be available at each laboratory module line whether or not partitions are installed. Hood number should be limited to two in each standard laboratory module (SLM). This limitation may appear restrictive, but it will assist in lowering building mechanical systems costs. If additional hoods are required in a SLM, the capacity can be borrowed from adjoining modules. This will restrict or eliminate hoods in these adjoining modules. In essence, this hood limitation standard limits the number of hoods that can be accommodated per floor. The mechanical system should be designed to permit a broad range of location and combination of hoods on each floor. The frequency of the use of hoods will also be a determining factor for the number of hoods that may be accommodated (see Table 1.3).

Special Hoods and Facilities

Perchloric acid- or explosion-proof hoods should be strictly controlled and permitted only in specifically designed areas. Separate exhaust ducts fabricated from special materials with wash-down features may be required for hoods designated to contain certain hazardous substances (radioisotopes, etc.).

Exceptions to established program systems design criteria and protocols must be carefully reviewed and approved by the facility manager and safety officer. Special research activities may cause extraordinary demands on and create hazardous conditions difficult to control within the designed building systems capabilities. Designing a facility to accommodate many diverse scientific disciplines may result in a very expensive building that would be difficult and costly to control, balance systems, and operate. Special research activities may be accommodated more efficiently, safely, and cheaply in separately designed facilities.

Administrative office spaces contained within standard laboratory modules should be designed for conversion to laboratory work areas. However, personnel safety considerations and requirements of codes, regulations, and guidelines may not recommend or permit office spaces within and open to laboratory work areas. If these spaces are included, they may have to be environmentally isolated (e.g., enclosed with full-height partitions and provided with separate mechanical ventilation systems to prevent exposure of personnel to chemical and biological hazards). Office work space in laboratory work areas should, in fact, not be permitted.

Laboratory work areas that involve high-, medium-, or low-risk carcinogens, recombinant DNA molecular investigations, potentially explosive reagents, and tissue culture work may require special design features. The building service systems

should be capable of accommodating selected special requirements as they may develop in the future, such as:

- Controlled staff access, changing rooms with air locks to
  biological safety level 3 and 4 laboratories
- Negative or positive pressures relative to adjacent spaces
- Separate controlled and redundant air supply, filtration,
  booster fans, and exhaust systems with emergency power
  systems to maintain special environment(s) during power
  failures or power interruptions

Typical laboratory modules that use biological safety cabinets may require direct connection to a separate exhaust system with sufficient static pressure capability to overcome
redundant and multiple filter requirements. Class II, type B
biological safety cabinets require bag-in, bag-out filter hous-
ings with prefilter, charcoal, and HEPA filters installed in the
exhaust ducts.

Instrument and equipment rooms may serve as support
work areas to one or more TLMs or other special laboratory
work areas. The instruments and equipment may vary in each
room. These rooms may be a single or multiple TLMs. All services and utilities should be available to these rooms. Supplemental cooling units may be required to maintain reasonable
environmental ranges and manage the excessive heat loads
generated by ovens, furnaces, incubators, atomic absorption
units, and other high-heat-producing equipment.

Computer/Data Processing

Computer rooms may consist of one or more TLMs. All services
and utilities should be available to these rooms. Computer
rooms should be maintained at a design temperature of 68°F
($\pm$) and 50% humidity ($\pm5\%$). Low-humidity conditions increase the static electricity potential. Air should be supplied
from the main air-handling system. Supplemental cooling units
may be required to maintain the environmental ranges under
high-heat-producing equipment conditions.

Raised floor systems may be required to accommodate certain mainframe computer equipment selected. Exhaust fans
may be required to reduce heat buildup in underfloor system
spaces. Computer rooms with mainframe systems should have
a minimum air exhaust rate of 3 to 5 cubic feet per minute

(cfm). Personal Computer (desktop units) technological capabilities may equal mainframe system capabilities.

The building fire suppression, extinguishing systems, and alarms and controls may have to be modified to accommodate the computer systems. If a water sprinkler system is not used, space may be required for the fire suppressant tank system (e.g., carbon dioxide or foam). Halon 1211 and 1301 gases contain bromine, which is alleged to deplete the ozone layer. Alternative fire suppressants may have to be considered. It should be noted that the Environmental Protection Agency (EPA) has classified Halon 1211, 1301, and 2402 gases as "indirectly toxic". The manufacture of the gases will eventually be restricted and forbidden. Smoke and fire detectors and fire suppressant systems are also required within the raised floor areas.

Hazardous Operations

Reagent preparation and storage facilities may require special ventilation and other protective devices, including fire safety and environmental controls, alarms, flame and smoke sensors, and explosion blowout panels. Hazardous reagents, cryogens, and flammable gases may have to be stored in separate facilities located away from other structures or buildings.

Special Conditions

Certain functions and activities may require a vibration-free work area (e.g., electron microscope suites, seismographs, optical laser and balance equipment, and spectroscopic analysis). Because of the weight of spectrographic and MRI equipment, the most practical location may be at grade on concrete isolation pads. The pads will also reduce transmission of vibrations. High-energy linear accelerators may require many feet of special dense concrete for shielding. Such facilities may also be located below grade to use the earth as supplemental shielding.

Prefabricated Equipment

Walk-in controlled-temperature environmental workrooms must be carefully designed. These rooms require special systems, sophisticated controls, sensors, and alarms to ensure proper operation. The same services should be available in walk-in environmental rooms as in the typical laboratory modules. Provisions for chilled water return with secondary pumping for the refrigeration condenser water system may be required. A drain should also be provided for the condenser water.

Consider the advantages and disadvantages of built-in vs. prefabricated modular walk-in environmental rooms. A built-in unit may require a depressed structural slab and cannot be relocated without considerable expense. Walk-in units require additional space and volume for circulation that must be heated or cooled. Prefabricated units can be assembled and relocated relatively easily. Some units with insulating floor panels may require a ramp to enter. Reach-in chambers may also satisfy program requirements. They can be moved easily and are less expensive than built-ins or prefabricated units of equal volume. All such units generate considerable heat that must be removed from the laboratory working environment.

Laboratory personnel must be made aware of the hazards of walk-in chambers. To maintain the controlled environment, air supply and exchange may be virtually nonexistent. People may succumb from lack of oxygen. Safety protocols should require a person to monitor the activities within the chamber from the outside. Subzero-controlled environmental chambers require an anteroom chamber before entering the subzero chamber. Space for storage of cold weather gear (parka, gloves, boots, etc.) must be provided.

Clean rooms can be secured as prefabricated units. If the basic building systems have been designed with a measure of excess capacity, such units can be accommodated within the laboratory work module. A distinct advantage of prefabricated facilities is the ability to classify them as capital costs (construction cost items) or as movable equipment not included in the construction budget. This permits the institution a measure of financial flexibility in maintaining and meeting limited construction budgets. However, this may impose an additional burden on the equipment budgets. Also, many grants will not permit the costs of such items to be included as part of the grant application.

Working Gear

Many institutions require laboratory personnel to wear a lab coat while working. Certain activities and processes may require that laboratory personnel change from street clothes to coveralls or protective garments. OSHA and other agencies are considering this protocol to become a requirement for clinical laboratory personnel. Facilities will have to be provided for the changing and storage of clothing and laboratory protective gear. The facilities may include lockers, showers, toilets, clean protective clothing storage, soiled protective clothing containers and holding, areas, and so on, for both men and women staff members. This becomes a security matter as well. The regulations may also be extended to require laboratory personnel to remove the protective clothing and shower before leaving the laboratory work areas for any reason.

2 MECHANICAL ENGINEERING CRITERIA (HVAC)

The very nature of the functions and activities conducted in a research laboratory facility may create biological and environmental hazards not only to the occupants of the facility but to persons in surrounding buildings and neighborhoods as well. These hazards may be small to insignificant to extreme and life threatening. Some of the effects may be experienced immediately and others may not appear until many years later. Therefore, it is *imperative* from a facility design, safety, and liability view that the administration of the institution, directors of the various research programs, principal investigators, facility manager, and safety officer(s) determine the proposed reagents to be used and processes to be conducted. Identification of the reagents and processes will permit the establishment of the research and safety protocols and policy for the proposed research facility.

Many institutions have selected a research committee that reviews proposed research activities. The committee's primary function is to assess the proposed research program or activity and determine its goals and objectives relative to its ultimate value and application as basic research or applied research. Although the classification of a particular research program may be an academic question, the hazards that may be produced must be determined and detailed before the architectural and engineering systems programming, planning, and design phases can proceed.

DESIGN FACTORS

Code requirements, regulations, standards, and guidelines vs. environmentally safe facilities vs. architectural and engineering systems design costs, and other factors must be analyzed and reviewed carefully during the program development phase. The factors must be reviewed with the institution's administration, facility manager, and safety officer, principal investigators, and federal authorities, particularly those responsible for grants allocations and for the use of animals for research purposes.

Contamination control, volume, and type of hazardous waste (biological and radioactive solids, liquids, gases; electromagnetic radiation, etc.) produced begins with the researcher at the source of the experiment, not at the end of exhaust stack, drain, sewer, trash dump, and so on. At that point, the system may not be able to manage and dispose adequately of the by-products of the experiment safely. The facility manager, safety officer, and the principal investigator can assist in reducing the amount of reagents used and hazardous by-products created. Review of proposed research projects and application of microexperimentation and microtesting techniques can significantly reduce the volume of specimens and reagents required to conduct and complete an experiment or test.

These factors can be of considerable assistance to the design engineer in estimating and quantifying the fluid volumes and energy demands that the building systems must provide, manage, and control. It is *absolutely essential* that the type and scope of the proposed research activities be established during the initial programming and planning phases. The required engineering design parameters can then be developed to provide for an efficient and safe laboratory work environment.

SPACE ENVIRONMENTAL PROBLEMS

Sick-building syndrome (SBS) and building-related illness (BRI) are considered relatively new phenomena. It is estimated that perhaps as many as 30% of new and renovated buildings may have serious indoor SBS and BRI air quality problems. The classification developed from a recognition that environmental pollution occurs within the interior of a building as well as in the outdoor environment. SBS and BRI are usually the result of the concentrations of interior air contaminants, including:

- Adhesives used to attach floor and wall coverings
- Architectural materials and finishes, including paints, carpets, drapes, vinyl and rubber moldings, and wall coverings
- Cleaning solvents, solutions, floor wax, and similar products
- Emissions from office equipment (e.g., printers, etc.)
- Functions and activities conducted within the building, including food preparation, manufacturing processes, scientific research, and health care activities
- Incomplete combustion from heating equipment, furnaces, and incinerators; improperly functioning building systems; volatile fluids and lubricants from fan and other shaft bearings, escalators, elevators; ozone from electric motors; and so on
- Microfiberglass from air filtration systems and insulation; plastic foam insulation, materials containing asbestos (insulation, flooring, etc.)
- Natural physiological processes of occupants, including products of respiration, breathing (carbon dioxide, etc.), and digestion
- Pesticides used to control insects and vermin
- Polychlorinated biphenyls (PCBs) contained in nonconforming electrical transformers
- Radon gas produced from the radioactive decay of radium existing naturally in the ground, including radioactive elements in natural stone building finishes (granite, etc.)
- Tobacco smoke, with its toxic and poisonous by-products

Authorities indicate that fiberglass wool filter materials may be hazardous to humans. In 1987, the International Agency for Research on Cancer (IARC) classified fiberglass wool as a possible carcinogen. The National Institute for Occupational Safety and Health (NIOSH) has determined that small-diameter fiberglass fibers produce fibrosis in animals and respiratory irritation in humans. Alternative air filtration materials are now available produced from microsynthetic continuous polyester filament fibers that appear to eliminate these problems.

Chemicals, materials, and processes occurring within buildings can produce concentrations more than 100 times outdoor levels if the building systems are improperly designed, maintained, and operated. Insufficient dilution due to inadequate volumes of fresh ventilation supply air, clogged filters, small-capacity fans and motors, air leakage from exhaust ducts, dusty and dirty duct interiors, and improper air balancing in the HVAC systems contribute to indoor air pollution or SBS.

It may seem that the architect/designer and specifier are faced with insurmountable obstacles relating to safety and liability concerns when deciding what systems, equipment, materials, and finishes to select and specify for a research laboratory project. The traditional adage of "due professional care and judgment" must be supported with detailed investigations of product manufacturers, including research and laboratory testing, if necessary. The systems, equipment, materials, and finishes selected must be determined to be correct and conform to applicable codes and federal regulations.

IMPACT OF INDOOR AIR POLLUTION

SBS and BRI can affect building occupants in many ways. Symptoms such as headaches due to allergic sensitization may result in reduced personnel productivity and efficiency, increased illness, and time lost. It has been alleged in some extreme cases that miscarriages and death have resulted because of polluted indoor environments. Similar symptoms can also be caused by employee dissatisfaction with their work or from other illness contracted from sources outside the building. Employee lawsuits are being filed more often, and sizable monetary awards have been granted to employees, claiming health problems created by inadequate and hazardous indoor air quality.

Employees have sued their employers, architects and engineers, building owners, contractors, manufacturers, distributors, sellers of HVAC equipment, and manufacturers of office equipment, cleaning chemicals, furniture, furnishings, and finishes. Everyone involved or associated with the building design, construction, and its contents are subject to lawsuits. Building owners should test and document the quality of indoor air to provide a defense if problems occur. New buildings and newly remodeled and renovated spaces should also be tested prior to occupancy. Healthy indoor environments result from adequate ventilation provided through the proper design, maintenance, and operation of the building HVAC systems.

Improper temperature and humidity variations also contribute to indoor pollution by creating changing release rates of various contaminants. Air quality measuring instruments are available to measure concentrations of various gases and changes in temperature and humidity. The instruments can record the data for immediate review and evaluation. Remedial steps can be instituted if the building systems have been designed with the capacity to permit such operational changes. Sophisticated instrumentation is available to provide alarm signals that interface with HVAC control systems. Computer software programs are available to assist in monitoring, measuring, and controlling HVAC systems. The programs can also prepare schedules for equipment maintenance to improve operational efficiency and reduce costs. Established operational and periodic maintenance programs can be the best defense against employee SBS accusations.

REDUCING INDOOR POLLUTION

The Department of General Administration of the state of Washington has developed a series of policies to minimize polluting interior building spaces. The following list includes practices that would seem to be simple common sense and good practices:

1. Delivery trucks are prohibited from idling engines at loading docks, minimizing the volume of exhaust fumes and reducing ingestion by building fresh air intakes and also saving fuel.
2. Emphasis is placed on reducing the sources and processes within the building that produce indoor pollutants.
3. Fresh air changes per hour for interior spaces were increased significantly over current standards or code requirements as much as *four times* in certain instances.
4. Furnishings and carpets were tested for toxic emissions, including formaldehyde, airborne particulates, volatile organic compounds (VOCs), and other carcinogens that may cause gene mutations, birth defects, and so on.
5. New facilities are given a 90-day flushing-out period to remove toxic building by-products prior to occupancy.

Building HVAC systems are operated as if the building were occupied.

6. Office equipment was carefully located and the spaces provided sufficient exhaust air to contain and remove emissions.

7. Smoking is prohibited inside all buildings. Current efforts to ban smoking in all public and private buildings, including military facilities, appear to be successful. Smoking within buildings will be limited to spaces with separate exhaust directly to the outside.

8. Workstations (modular landscape-type office furniture systems) from several manufacturers were tested for hazardous chemical emissions prior to installation.

Particular attention must be given to remodeling projects for laboratory and hospital facilities. Proper design, maintenance, operations, adequate indoor air quality, and energy management control programs can reduce and prevent the SBS and BRI syndrome. Qualified and experienced design professionals and staff from the institution, including the facility manager, plant engineer, and safety and infection control officers, must interact to produce a safe and healthy indoor environment.

HAZARDOUS CONDITIONS IMPACT

Dangerous working conditions can occur through improper design and lack of knowledge of the properties that various materials exhibit with changing environmental conditions. A catastrophic accident occurred in an experimental hyperbaric (high-pressure) chamber facility. This special laboratory work space was designed to investigate the effects of a high-pressure environment on humans. A fire occurred within the chamber. What would have been a nonthreatening situation in a normal laboratory environment (sea level or local atmospheric pressure) became lethal to the technicians in the chamber. Materials selected for the floor and wall finishes flashed into flames, incinerating the technicians. Subsequent investigations determined that the materials selected were noncombustible under normal atmospheric pressures. However, because of the increased pressures (up to 15 atm) and the increased oxygen concentrations per unit volume in the chamber, the materials became highly flammable.

Most compounds normally change physical state from a solid to a liquid to a gas. However, some compounds change (sublimate) directly from a solid to a gas. Many new adhesives, paints, and other finishes developed during the past several years exhibit this property. The chemical compounds in paints become gases as the paint dries or cures. Many of these gases are highly toxic and can cause serious health problems if inhaled.

TOXIC EFFECTS OF MATERIALS

Many materials, including finishes, building components, and fabrics, produce lethal toxic fumes as they burn. Polyvinyl chloride (PVC) plastic used as an insulation for electric wire decomposes as it burns into a combination of airborne petroleum sludge and several poisonous gases. These gases have been developed and produced as ingredients for chemical warfare weapons. The same effect is true with many of the insecticides that are used to control insect pests within buildings. One of the compounds that was used in an insecticide was a compound found in chemical nerve gas weapons. This product was quickly removed from sale to consumers.

When large quantities of water are used to quench a fire, the water combines with many of these hazardous by-products and forms hydrochloric and sulfuric acids. The acid fumes can cause permanent lung damage or lethal effects when inhaled. The fumes can also cause damage to the building systems, equipment, and materials. The smoke, fumes, and gases produced by these burning materials can be more hazardous than the fire itself. The National Fire Protection Association (NFPA) Research Foundation has recently prepared reports detailing the effects of many building materials when burned.

Another tragic incident occurred in a biomedical research facility less than one year after its completion and occupancy. Experiments using boiling hydrochloric acid were conducted in accordance with established protocols and safety procedures. The fume hoods and ventilating and exhaust systems were supposedly in proper operating condition. Hood face velocities and exhaust duct air velocities were within recommended design parameters. The fume hood linings and exhaust duct materials were fabricated from stainless steel of a resistant type generally specified for use with similar corrosive reagents. Presumably, all reasonable design and operational practices had been followed. However, the following series of events highlight the importance of the initial programming and planning process:

1. During a routine inspection of the condensate trap at the bottom of one of the fume hood exhaust duct risers, the condensate fluid poured on the employee when the access panel was opened. The fluid (a mixture of hydrochloric acid and other chemicals) caused fatal burns to the employee.

2. At almost at the same time as the tragic accidental death of the employee, fluid began to leak through the ceiling tiles in several secretarial work areas. The hydrochloric acid vapors had condensed and puddled at the bottom of the horizontal exhaust ducts. The acid eventually corroded through the stainless steel duct to the ceiling tiles and then poured into the office space below. Fortunately, the acid condensate leak occurred during a lunch period and most employees were away from their workstations. No one was injured. It is also interesting to note that certain reagents are more dangerously corrosive, explosive, and flammable when in a dilute solution or mixture than in a concentrated state.

3. Subsequent investigation discovered that the stainless steel fume hood exhaust ducts suspended in the air-conditioned ceiling space above the administrative work areas had not been insulated. It was determined that the warm hydrochloric acid vapors condensed on the cold surfaces of the metal ducts. It was concluded (even though the exhaust air velocity was within recommended values) that the exhaust ducts in the cooler ceiling spaces should have been insulated on the exterior to prevent condensation of the vapors on the interior of the duct surfaces.

Should the design professional also be a physicist, chemist, or biologist knowledgeable of the properties of compounds and materials as well as an architect? Although this may be debatable, the architect and engineer should be more familiar with the unique problems related to the planning and design of research laboratory facilities. There are consultant specialists available to assist in analysis of the inherent hazards and dangers that may occur related to a particular physical process and chemical reaction. The most competent source is usually the principal investigator and the institution's safety officer. Sources at various federal agencies, including:

- The Centers for Disease Control (CDC)
- The Environmental Protection Agency (EPA)
- The National Institute for Occupational Safety and Health (NIOSH)
- The National Institute of Environmental Health and Safety (NIEHS)
- The Occupational Safety and Health Administration (OSHA)
- Several institutes at the National Institutes of Health (NIH)

can provide specific data relative to many processes that occur in most research laboratories.

At another facility, the inadequacy of the waterproofing membrane and flooring installation specifications could have resulted in significant hazardous conditions. The laboratory work area was classified as biosafety level (BSL-4). The flooring material selected was a sheet plastic vinyl type installed over the membrane. Because of the negative pressure differential between the BSL-4 laboratory and the surrounding spaces, the flooring material "floated" above the structural floor. Air pressure differential between the structural floor, membrane, and finished floor caused the finish floor material to separate and float. The laboratory cannot be used until this condition has been remedied. If the direction of the airflow between such spaces is considered critical, airflow monitoring devices should be installed to signal an alarm if the airflow drops below a certain level or reverses direction.

A recently completed research facility remains unoccupied and unusable because the solder used in the joints and connections of the copper pipe potable water system had a high lead content. The lead is leaching into the water, rendering it too dangerous for human consumption. The cost to replace the water pipe system will exceed $3 million dollars. No estimates are available regarding the costs accruing due to the lack of the use of the facility. Copper piping systems in many older buildings also used high-lead-content solder. Similar conditions may exist in older buildings, and occupants may be exposed to high-lead-level hazards.

These brief case histories highlight the critical importance of conducting detailed programming and planning sessions involving the principal investigators, the facility manager, and administrative representatives of the institution to determine the nature of the proposed research activities. Representatives of the chemical manufacturers may also have to be interviewed to determine the specific properties of the compounds they may supply to the researchers for their work. The hazards that may be generated during and as a result of the research activities can have significant implications on the ultimate responsibility and liability of the design professionals and the owners of the institution.

MONITORING THE ENVIRONMENT

Monitoring indoor air quality is critically important in hospitals, where small changes in airborne contaminants can have significant harmful impact on patients whose resistance has been compromised by illness or surgical procedures. Patients are particularly vulnerable in this impaired physiological condition. Design, maintenance, operations, monitoring, and control of HVAC systems are critical. Ventilation rates (air changes), air velocities, filtration efficiencies, air distribution, air volume controls, and heating, cooling, and humidification systems require continual monitoring. Ductwork systems, ventilation shafts, air-handling units, fans, motors, and ceiling spaces must also be inspected.

Outdoor air quality must also be carefully monitored and analyzed. Concentrations of ozone, acidic particles and fumes, hydrocarbon emissions, airborne bacteria, spores, pollen, particulates, volatile organic compounds, and other contaminants surrounding a facility can affect indoor air quality. These contaminants can be ingested by the building's fresh air intake system. The exterior air may have to be treated (cleaned or scrubbed) before being circulated within the building. Research and hospital facilities located in urban, suburban, industrial, and farming communities can be subject to a wide variety of outdoor contaminants. The contaminants produced at airports, vehicles on highways, and industrial and agricultural activities can complicate indoor air contaminant concentrations.

Outdoor contaminants can also become particularly hazardous when mixed with the fumes, vapors, and gases generated by research processes. Carbon monoxide exhausted from internal combustion engines can combine with oxygen, forming carbon dioxide. This process can reduce the volume of oxygen present in enclosed spaces. Carbon monoxide also forms other poisonous compounds in the body when inhaled.

Attached and underground parking garages are sources of carbon monoxide and nitrogen dioxide. Improperly located building fresh air intakes, windows, and other openings can create a path for these contaminants to reach indoor areas. Motor vehicle exhaust gases, particularly delivery trucks with motors idling at loading docks or at any open entry/window of a building, gases from plumbing vents, and exhaust from toilets and kitchens are other sources of pollutants that can be recycled into the ventilation system of the building. Bacteria can propagate in stagnant water in humidifiers, cooling coil condensate pans, or water that may have collected in ceiling tiles from leaking pipes, carpeting, insulation materials, and interior duct insulation.

One of the most significant problems for hospitals is the danger of cross-contamination among patients. A high level of air quality is essential to the patients' health and must be maintained. Air quality must be carefully controlled to eliminate airborne pathogens and pollutants. Air quality criteria in hospitals range from laminar airflow filtered rooms with HEPA filters, 99.97% particulate free to 0.3 micron (μm) (0.1 μm for TB isolation conditions) to a minimum standard of less than three air changes per hour. Similar conditions can occur in research laboratories involved with dangerous viruses, bacteria, and human- and other-animal-infected specimens or tissue. Certain insects can also be carriers of dangerous organisms.

Immunosuppressed patients are particularly susceptible to airborne infectious viral particles and mold spores. Protocols can be developed to minimize risk of transmission or contamination to patients with highly infectious diseases or in highly susceptible immunodeficient conditions. Inpatient care areas should be designed to include sealed isolation rooms, increased room air changes, local HEPA-filtered unidirectional supply air, and an automatic airflow monitoring device.

PREVENTATIVE PRACTICES

Authorities estimate that nosocomial infections (hospital acquired) result in approximately 30,000 deaths each year in hospitals. The dirtiest object that can be introduced into the hospital environment is the human person. It is estimated that one-third of these deaths could be eliminated by providing hand-washing facilities for personnel. Proper location, fixture type, and perhaps the most important factor of all, personnel education and adherance to medical safety protocols, are key to improving this situation.

All laboratory work areas, particularly those involved with biomedical experimentation, must be equipped with adequate numbers of properly located hand-washing sinks. Laboratory utility sinks should not be used for hand washing. New electronic no-touch or smart fixtures with automatic water turn-on-off and soap- and paper towel-dispensing features are now available. Protective gloves are also necessary; however, organisms can multiply inside the gloves, and many viruses can penetrate glove materials. Personnel hand-washing facilities are also a necessity in animal facilities. All these protocols require equipment, supplies, and space for installation and implementation.

Special attention should be given to sealing windows and wall and ceiling penetrations, including light fixtures, electrical and service receptacles, medical gas outlets, and air diffuser and register frames. Installation of high-efficiency, microsynthetic air filters at the central air-handling units and local final particulate air control (FPAC) filters at patient room ceiling air diffusers will greatly reduce the risk of infections and the transmission of diseases. Similar conditions exist in the laboratory environment. Openings between walls and floors, through wall and floor pipes, conduits, ducts, and so on, produce open pathways for fumes, gases, and fluids to traverse into adjoining spaces. Improperly designed, fabricated, and sealed fume hood ducts can leak hazardous gases and fumes into adjoining spaces.

HVAC SYSTEMS HAZARDS

The facility manager and designer must also contend with the concerns over the effects of chlorofluorocarbons (CFCs) on the environment. It is generally accepted by many authorities that these compounds contribute directly to depletion of the ozone layer, although there are many in the scientific community that disagree with this conclusion. However, the EPA has enacted regulations that will ultimately eliminate the production and use of CFCs in building mechanical equipment. The EPA has also placed an excise tax on the sale and use of CFCs. This has the net effect of substantially increasing the cost of designing, constructing, and operating new facilities. Existing facilities maintenance and operating costs will also increase. The impact on future building costs will be significant. These regulations will also spur additional research and design into more-energy-efficient systems and equipment to reduce costs or at least to reduce the rate of increase in construction costs.

Research on alternative refrigerants continues with some measure of success. Refrigerants designated HCFC-123 and HFC-134A are alternatives to CFCs and have advantages and disadvantages. These compounds are considered to have a significantly reduced negative impact on the ozone layer. These new compounds may have increased costs when used as a replacement in existing chillers because they corrode chiller components, including O-rings, seals, gaskets, flanges, and tubes. Also, because of lower thermal efficiency, they may decrease chiller capacity 10 to 15% and increase energy (kilowatts per ton) operating costs. The net effect may be larger equipment and increased energy costs to achieve the same design results.

Although HCFC-123 becomes a mild anesthetic in high concentrations, it is currently classified as a safe and nontoxic compound. HFC-134A supplies have been available from manufacturers since 1991. It is considered to be a substitute for CFC-12 or CFC-500 with minimum or no modification required to existing equipment or loss of efficiencies. However, it may not be compatible with current lubricants. The design engineer should review the findings and recommendations of the American Society of Heating, Refrigerating, and Air-Conditioning Engineers (ASHRAE) and the manufacturers of the new compounds during the design of the building systems for the proposed facility to establish if problems may exist with the new systems.

RECENT REGULATORY CHANGES

All this has been further complicated by passage of the new Clean Air Act of 1990. The new law halts production of CFCs and Halon gases by the year 2000. Recycling programs are mandated for CFCs used in air-conditioning and refrigeration equipment by 1992. Production of the less corrosive HCFCs will be stopped in 2015 and eliminates their use entirely by 2030. Certain solvents, such as carbon tetrachloride and methyl chloroform, are to be eliminated by 2000 and 2002, respectively. *Maximum achievable control technology* must be installed by emitters of 189 airborne toxins by 2003. The new Clean Air Act details and contains a list of the toxins to be controlled.

The goals of clean air are certainly laudable; however, the costs will be considerable. The hothouse or greenhouse effects of various gases produced during manufacturing processes have been touted by environmentalists to have near-term catastrophic consequences on global weather, warming temperatures, and so on. It is interesting to note that volcanic eruptions within the past several years have produced naturally many thousands of times as much volume of greenhouse gases, solid particulates, and so on, than we have produced in all of known human history. These volcanic eruptions have had no known measurable effects on the environment. It appears that our knowledge of human effects on global systems is perhaps more misunderstood because of our lack of knowledge of such systems and events.

These controversial items are perhaps clouded more by politically motivated agendas than by scientific facts and observations. This does not mean that architects and engineers should not design energy-efficient and environmentally safe systems. On the contrary, building systems for laboratory facilities, including all types of facilities, should be designed to be efficient, cost-effective, and safe—and we should not forget aesthetically pleasing as well.

The increased costs now associated with the eventual phaseout of CFCs makes it imperative that the facility manager develop detailed protocols for the maintenance and management of existing equipment. Refrigerant leaks due to normal wear and tear on equipment, deteriorating seals, and costs and difficulties of securing adequate supplies of CFCs justify conserving existing CFC supplies. Use of auxiliary equipment can also reduce CFC losses. The facility manager and design engineer are faced literally with only two choices in planning new facilities. One is to design a system to operate with HCFC-123. The other is to design a system to operate with CFC-12 or CFC-500 and gamble that HFC-134A will be an equivalent substitute for CFCs, with a minimum of conversion problems.

Ammonia (R-717 as it is known in the refrigeration industry) has been used for many years in industries such as meat and dairy processing, fruit and vegetable storage and processing, and process cooling in petrochemical and pharmaceutical research and manufacturing facilities. However, its use as a refrigerant for air-conditioning applications has been sparse. This has resulted in very few HVAC engineers with experience in designing air-conditioning systems employing ammonia. Although ammonia may be toxic and flammable, there remains considerable disagreement as to how toxic and flammable it is and what level of precautions must be taken to control and contain such properties. Its greatest attraction is that it is available now, the mechanical technology exists, and perhaps most notably, it does not have the environmentally destructive properties of CFCs.

Historically, very few serious incidents can be associated with the use of ammonia as a refrigerant. Given these brief facts, it may be a cost-effective alternative cooling system for research laboratory facilities.

NEW OSHA STANDARD FOR CONFINED SPACES

OSHA's new *Permit-Regulated Confined Space Standard* (29 CFR 1910.146) establishes criteria for the protection of personnel who may have to enter and work within areas that can pose immediate health and safety risks from asphyxiation, explosion, or toxic fumes and gases. Such confined spaces may include boilers, storage areas, fuel or water storage tanks, ductwork, incinerators, furnaces, utility pipe service tunnels and spaces, electrical manhole areas, and storm drains. Confinement may pose a risk of entrapment or exposure to hazardous conditions that they may not have been exposed to otherwise. Confinement, limited access and egress, reduced airflow or air changes, and so on, may result in a dangerous environment that would not exist in a normal, open work environment. OSHA's new Standard defines a *confined space* or *non-permit-required confined space* that provides limited or restricted means of entry and exit (access panel, small door, etc.), and it is large enough for personnel to enter and perform the required task. However, the space is not designed for continuous occupancy by personnel.

A *permit-required confined space* is similar to the definition of a confined space (above). The space, however, has the additional characteristic or *has the potential to exhibit* an immediate safety or health risk. These risks or hazards may include:

- Hazardous atmospheric conditions
- Engulfment or immersion in the contents of the space (water, chemicals, ash, waste, etc.)
- Electrocution or electrical shock from wires, cables, transformers, motors, and so on
- Entrapment within the space due to the configuration of the space (i.e., sloping floor and walls, uneven floors, tapering surfaces that converge to small-diameter openings whereby a person may become wedged within the space, etc.)
- Changes in temperature (heat/cold)
- Additional hazardous or dangerous health or safety hazards, including elevated noise levels, vibrations, and lack of proper communication (verbal or instrumentation)

It is quite conceivable that these new standards may even apply to such spaces as walk-in refrigerators, freezers, incubators, certain biohazardous isolation or containment rooms, storage and processing areas, access/service space behind built-in equipment (autoclaves, cage washers, etc.), and various test chambers. There is no question that many mechanical, electrical, and plumbing service spaces are within the definition of this standard, particularly in many existing laboratory buildings. These confined spaces will have to be reevaluated to determine if they may justify the "permit required" classification. These spaces may require additional ventilation and other safety equipment installed to render them safe under the new standard. This will certainly necessitate the institution's safety officer and mechanical and electrical engineers to survey the spaces and determine the action to remedy violations. It is critical that each institution conduct immediate surveys to develop corrective measures to render existing spaces safe under the new standard. It is vitally important during the planning and design phases as spaces develop that all designated equipment service access areas and mechanical, electrical, and plumbing rooms and spaces are designed to conform with the new standard.

AIR CHANGE RECOMMENDATIONS

Typical laboratory module air changes are suggested at 12 to 16 to 18 per hour to maintain a high-quality, safe laboratory work environment. Certain chemical processes may require as many as 24 to 26 air changes per hour. The facility manager and designer (architect and engineer) may find that various codes and regulations indicate somewhat lower air change requirements. These codes and regulations may not reflect current health and safety findings, recommendations, guidelines, and regulations of NIH, NIOSH, CDC, EPA, OSHA, NFPA, ASHRAE, and so on. The differences may appear to create a legal requirement vs. a cost choice dilemma. The lower air change rates may satisfy the design code legal requirements and would result in lower construction and operation costs. However, these rates may not provide a safe environment for laboratory personnel relative to recognized and known hazardous properties of reagents that may be used. The suggested rates for air changes per hour will certainly result in increased services and utilities systems design, construction, and operations costs.

Special laboratory work areas and service and support spaces (BSL-3 + 4, hazardous reagent preparation and storage, etc.) may require increased air changes. Animal facilities may require a minimum of 16 to 20 air changes; offices, conference rooms, classrooms, and similar spaces may require from 6 to 8 to 10 air changes (Table 2.1). The mechanical (HVAC) systems should perhaps be designed for a capacity of 20 to 24 air changes to provide a reasonable range of flexibility to accommodate a variety of research and special activities. The excess capacity will also allow for future expansion of the facility. Additional ventilation parameters are published in ASHRAE guides and standards.

TABLE 2.1   Suggested Room Air Changes

Room/Space	Air Changes/Hour
Animal facilities	16–20
Administrative offices	6–8
Conference/classroom/auditorium	8–10
Laboratory work areas (TLMs)	12–18

Note: The supply system air must meet the technical requirements of the activities and processes to be conducted in the laboratory and the requirements of the latest version of ANSI/ASHRAE 62.

COMMENTS

1. There are continuing discussions as to whether increased air changes per hour will result automatically in a cleaner and safer space. Research indicates that the design and placement of the supply and exhaust registers are just as important as the number of air changes provided. If the air supply and return registers are not located properly, the space will not achieve the safe air dilution desired (Figure 2.1).

2. Some sources indicate that the supply air should be distributed uniformly into the space from the ceiling and exhausted uniformly at the floor. This may appear to imply a laminar flow system, but not in the strict technical definition. The objective is to supply air to and exhaust it from the space with a uniform flow of air to all areas of the space and minimize turbulence, eddies, and dead areas within the space.

Many authorities recommend that a volumetric control system should be designed and installed in a laboratory facility. This system provides a greater degree of flexibility for maintaining adequate pressure relationships between laboratory

Figure 2.1 Airflow within a space with varying air supply and return register locations.

work areas and adjacent spaces. In general, all laboratory work areas should be maintained at a negative pressure relative to adjacent nonlaboratory spaces. However, certain laboratory work areas such as tissue culture and clean rooms may have to be maintained at a positive pressure relative to adjacent spaces. This prevents contamination from entering the work environment. This also means that certain spaces within the facility may have to be designed with a separate ventilation system, controls, and so on.

Much has been written about constant-volume and variable-volume systems for research laboratory facilities. A constant-volume system is exactly what the name implies. Air is supplied and exhausted to and from the laboratory spaces at a constant rate regardless of the number of hoods that may be in use at any given time. A constant-volume system does not allow much flexibility to change to accommodate varying conditions throughout the building. It is fairly obvious that under certain conditions this system can be very energy wasteful and costly to operate. However, if there are few hoods in the laboratory facility (perhaps certain physics or electronics laboratories), changes that may occur in air demand requirements may not be significant. Another advantage of the constant volume system is its lack of sophistication and number of controls. This factor reduces operations and maintenance costs. Thus the constant-volume system can be cost-effective and efficient.

A variable-volume system is espoused by many as the most efficient and least costly for *all* research laboratory facilities. This system, with its myriad of sophisticated sensors and controls, regulates the air supply to all hoods based on use, position of the hood sash controlling the opening of the hood, and can save on the volume of air supplied to the hood. This reduction in air volume presumably translates into savings of energy and initial design of HVAC equipment requirements. However, the variable-volume system requires sophisticated and expensive sensors and control systems to monitor the changes in hood use, which initiate the changes to fans, dampers, and so on, modifying the volume of air supplied to the laboratory spaces (hoods) in question. Operations and maintenance of this system are more costly than a constant-volume system.

However, the final HVAC control system, whether constant or variable, to be designed and selected for a proposed research facility should be the result of the analysis of program requirements, the nature of the scientific activities to be conducted, scope and scale of the facility, number, size and type of hoods to be used, applicable codes and regulations, practical cost considerations (budget limitations and restrictions of the owner), and efficiency of operations and maintenance (life-cycle costs). Each system has its advantages and disadvantages within the context of the research criteria.

Ventilation systems should be designed to control airflow patterns to prevent cross-contamination between exterior fresh air supply intakes and interior exhaust air ports or stacks. Codes and regulations usually specify distances between fresh air supply intake and exhaust air ports. Airflow should circulate from clean to dirty areas. Automatic airflow devices should be provided to maintain constant air volume, regardless of varying system pressure changes due to filter loading. The quantity of air supplied to and exhausted from each space should remain constant except when adjusted manually and regardless of changes in cooling and heating loads or fume hood operation.

Biological safety cabinets, chemical fume hoods, and general laboratory exhaust systems should have sufficient static pressure to exhaust the hoods located in the most remote laboratory work areas on a specific floor. Exhaust fans and ductwork for hoods must be fabricated from corrosion-resistant materials to provide protection from chemical reagents. Horizontal exhaust duct runs should have $\frac{1}{4}$ in. per foot of minimum pitch to allow for drainage and corrosion with drip-proof seams at the hood connection. Sparkproof fan motors should be specified to preclude or minimize fire and explosion hazards.

Insulation of the exterior of hood exhaust ducts should be considered to prevent or minimize the condensation of vapors generated during chemical reactions. This is particularly important for ducts that traverse air-conditioned or cooled spaces. The condensate can accelerate corrosion of the duct material and create hazardous conditions for occupants and equipment below. Increased air velocity through the exhaust duct can also minimize condensation problems.

Chemical fume hood exhaust ductwork construction should be flanged and bolted in 4' to 6' sections with all joints gasketed and sealed with a chemically resistant duct sealer. Circular exhaust ductwork also has advantages in reducing joints and seams. The objective is to provide a fume hood exhaust system that is chemically resistant and airtight. Proper air balancing dampers should be installed in the exhaust ductwork system(s). Exhaust fans for the hoods and general exhaust system should be located in the penthouse mechanical rooms. Exhaust systems with special or redundant filters may require additional pressure booster fans to maintain adequate air velocity. These booster fans should be located to minimize the transmission of fan noise to the laboratory work areas.

Chemical fume hood exhaust discharge nozzles should be located at a minimum of 16′ above the highest roof of the facility. The exhaust air should have an escape velocity of 4000 to 6000 feet per minute (fpm). Escape velocity may have to be reduced if internal condensation may occur. Exhaust fans for chemical fume hood exhaust systems must have spark-resistant wheels with motors located outside the airstreams. The location, size, height, and shape of adjacent buildings; configuration of surrounding topography; and prevailing winds can have a significant impact on the location, height, size, and exhaust air escape velocity of the discharge stack. Computer modeling or wind tunnel testing of scale models of the facility and surrounding buildings may be required to determine how and where exhaust air should be ejected to provide adequate dispersion and dilution. This will also assist in determining where the building fresh air intakes should be located. This computer modeling may also assist in determining where on the site the laboratory facility should be located in relation to its surroundings.

Exhaust filters should be installed as close to the exhaust fans as may be practical. Ductwork between the exhaust filter discharge and exhaust fan outlet should be sealed airtight. The exhaust fan and filter should be located as close as possible to the building discharge. Adequate space must be provided surrounding the fans, filters, filter boxes, and motors to permit servicing, maintenance, and replacement of filters.

The supply and exhaust systems should have self-balancing capability and controls for the laboratory work areas. This will assist in simplifying installation or removal of hoods and general remodeling and renovation of laboratory work areas that may occur in the future. A constant air supply and exhaust system concept is suggested. Installation of orifice plates or air monitoring devices should assist to simplify balancing of airflows.

A manifold-type exhaust duct system may be considered as an alternative to single (combined or grouped) exhaust ducts routed to strategically placed stacks. The manifold concept will tend to reduce the number of exhaust fans or multiple exhaust stacks. Grouping of hoods to exhaust ducts should be designed so that the exhaust system static pressure drops are similar. This should assist to simplify air balancing.

Careful analysis of the reagents to be used in the hoods must be conducted during the programming and planning phases. The analysis must consider if any dangerous or hazardous condition may be created when fumes or gasses produced in separate hoods may combine in the exhaust duct system to create a fire or form an explosive or toxic compound. The analysis may indicate, because of the nature of the research activities proposed, each hood or a designated hood(s) should have a separate exhaust duct and fan.

Outdoor fresh air supply for laboratory work areas should be filtered with high-efficiency filters of the bag-in, bag-out type (80% atmospheric dust). Laboratory work areas that may require high-quality clean air should have HEPA-type filters installed at the room terminal. Filtering efficiencies for office areas should be between 30 and 40% (50 to 60% is recommended) on atmospheric dust. Prefilters should be installed at all air intakes of primary air-handling units. This will increase the life of the filter and the time between replacement of the high-efficiency HEPA filters. These parameters are subject to modification depending on the quality of the outdoor air environment and its impact on the building systems design.

ENVIRONMENTAL DESIGN FACTORS

Mechanical systems should be designed to maintain environments within the following parameters:

Laboratory Work Areas

- 75°F (±2°F) for all seasons with 100% outside air
- 50% RH (±5% RH) in summer; and 30 to 50% RH (±5% RH) in winter

Administrative Offices, Conference, Classrooms, Corridors, Public Spaces

- 75 to 80°F (±2°F) in summer; and 65 to 72°F (±2°F) in winter
- 50% RH (±5% RH) in summer; and 30 to 40% RH (±5% RH) in winter

---

COMMENTS

1. Offices, conference, classrooms, corridors, and public spaces may be supplied with recirculated air. However, the recirculated air must never be mixed with air from laboratory work areas or the animal facilities.

2. Because of the difficulty to confine animal odors to the animal facilities, particularly if they are designed as part of the research facility, the animal facilities might best be located in a separate building. The same principles apply to the nonlaboratory functions and activities as well.

3. It is recognized that many factors have to be considered before such separate facilities are developed. However, depending on the program scale and scope, separate facilities can have many advantages to a single building concept.

The outside winter design temperature may be 0°F for 100% outside air units. When the air entering the air-handling unit coils is less than 35°F, the units must have preheat coils to prevent the coil from freezing. Preheat coils must have the capacity to preheat the air when the heat reclaiming coils are not operating. The geographic location of the facility and meteorological conditions may require modified mechanical environmental design criteria.

The concept design equipment or process load for the typical laboratory module (10' to 12' wide × 20' to 24' long; and 10' to 12' wide × 35' to 40' long, with 9' to 10' finished ceiling height) may be assumed at 8000 to 10,000 British thermal units (Btu), to 10,000 to 12,000 Btu, respectively. Figures will vary within specific criteria. This Btu load should be added to the space load to accommodate typical laboratory procedures. These parameters may be used for initial systems planning and design estimates.

A secondary cooling system should be installed to accommodate excessive cooling loads of an additional 8000 to 12,000 Btu in each of approximately half of the total number of typical laboratory modules planned for the facility. This load may be accommodated with a secondary chilled water piping system. This system can facilitate the connection of fan coil units without disrupting service to adjacent laboratory work areas.

Secondary cooling units and chilled water may be required for selected movable and semimovable equipment, including prefabricated controlled-temperature cold rooms, electron microscopes, and autoanalyzers. The design should have sufficient flexibility (shutoff valves, etc.) to permit an increase or decrease in Btu loads without interruption of services in adjacent laboratory work areas or require a major systems shutdown.

COMMENTS

1. Virtually all hospital functions and activities (patient and service and support) must operate on a 24-hour basis. The building systems must be designed to maintain operations at all times. Emergency power systems must maintain functions and activities during power interruptions and outages. This complicates remodeling and renovations. Systems must be designed to permit isolated or controlled shutdowns to accomplish changes or installation of additional or new equipment.

2. Similar principles apply to research activities. Once initiated, certain procedures cannot be interrupted or stopped. Some research grants also do not permit research activities to be stopped. The research grant may be canceled in such circumstances. Certain hazardous processes may require redundant systems to maintain safe and continuous operations until the experiment is concluded.

Energy conservation should be one of the primary systems design considerations. Several jurisdictions have energy efficiency requirements for various facilities. Use of heat reclamation devices (e.g., runaround coils, heat pipes, etc.), should be considered if design analysis indicates that application is practical and cost-effective. However, cross-contamination between supply and exhaust air must be scrupulously avoided for laboratory work areas, animal facilities, administrative office areas, and patient areas in hospital facilities.

COMMENTS

1. The results of a study by the Potomac and Electric Power Company of Washington DC, indicates that many building owners are employing energy conservation options (ECOs), including:

   a. Air economizers

    b. Automated energy management and control systems

    c. Double-entry vestibules with revolving doors

    d. High-efficiency fluorescent light fixtures and ballasts

    e. Thermal break multiple-pane windows

    f. Variable-air-volume HVAC systems

2. However, high first costs of these methods are cited as reasons not to use ECOs by other building owners. Bad management techniques were least used because of cost and lack of experience with such systems. High first costs appear to negate payback or cash flow analysis. The apparent negative first-cost aspects of ECOs should not deter an institution from considering the overall long-term advantages of using energy management systems EMSs).

CHEMICAL HOODS AND BIOLOGICAL SAFETY CABINETS

The primary function of the chemical fume hood and the biological safety cabinet is to provide a safe environment to conduct activities that are hazardous and dangerous to humans. It is perhaps the single most useful item of equipment in the laboratory and also the most abused. The chemical fume hood and biological safety cabinet can have more influence on the design and cost of the building service systems (mechanical and electrical) than any other item of equipment. The air necessary to supply the hood(s), the HVAC system controls, exhaust duct materials, filter boxes, fans and motors, and redundant systems, and so on, all compose a significant portion of the total construction and operations budget. Costs of HVAC systems for certain research laboratory facilities can comprise more than half of the construction budget.

Basic laboratory hood types include chemical fume, radioisotope, perchloric acid, and biological safety cabinets (laminar flow, glove boxes, etc.). Laminar-flow hoods may also constitute another hood type. Ductless hoods are not widely accepted in this country and their utility and safety are questionable. Canopy hoods are generally used to remove steam (water vapors), heat from equipment, and noxious odors. These hoods are useful but have limited application and efficiency. There are many manufacturers that produce variations to the general basic hood types to suit a wide range of activities and procedures.

A number of small countertop equipment (atomic absorption units, etc.) produce relatively high heat loads and require exhaust hoods to remove the heat generated. Each laboratory module should have the capability to provide a snorkel or elephant-trunk flexible duct to extend over the machine terminating in a funnel shape approximately 12″ to 18″ square. Air exhaust capacity of between 100 and 150 cfm is usually sufficient. The connection at the ceiling can be accomplished through a knockout panel if a finished ceiling is present, or an exposed duct, or to the service corridor and the appropriate exhaust duct.

The following recommendations have been summarized from the *American Conference of Governmental Industrial Hygienists* (ACGIH) publications. ACGIH publications are very useful and helpful in assisting with the preparation of hood criteria and selections. An extensive publications list is included in Appendix C.

ACGIH-VS-203 Laboratory Hoods

1. Face velocities for vertical and horizontal sash airfoil hoods may vary between 60 and 150 fpm (cfm/sf), depending on the quality of supply air distribution. Exhaust duct air velocity should vary between 1000 and 2000 fpm to suit conditions.

ACGIH-VS-204 Laboratory Hood Data (Supply Air Distribution)

1. The research investigator or technician stands or sits in front of the hood opening manipulating the apparatus within the hood. The indraft at the face of the hood opening creates eddy currents in front of the person and extending into the hood.

2. These currents can circulate contaminants being generated in the hood to the person's breathing zone. Increasing hood face velocity does not automatically result in greater protection, as might be anticipated.

3. Room air currents from supply air distribution systems (grilles, diffusers, vents, etc.) and location within the laboratory work area can have a significant impact on

hood performance. Personnel circulating near or in front of the hood opening create turbulence and eddies that affect hood efficiency and performance.

4. Hood location (e.g., near doors, high traffic areas, canopy hoods, etc.) within the laboratory work area is another significant factor affecting hood performance. ASHRAE Research Project RP-70 discusses these important factors.

5. Reduced breathing zone concentrations of contaminants can be better attained using a 50-cfm/sf face velocity with proper supply air distribution than at 150 cfm/sf with incorrect supply air distribution within the laboratory work area. When tracer gas is released at 8 liters per minute (L/min) within the hood, breathing zone concentrations of contaminants can be maintained below 0.1 ppm and usually less than 0.01 ppm with proper supply air distribution systems.

6. The terminal throw velocity of supply air jets should not exceed one-half to two-thirds of the hood face velocity. These suggested terminal throw velocities are considerably less than those recommended by other sources.

7. Considerable design thought and development must be allocated to these considerations to ensure proper and safe hood performance. Perforated ceiling panels appear to provide a more efficient supply air distribution system than grilles or ceiling diffusers.

8. Systems design criteria for perforated ceiling panels appear less complex and easier to apply, and precise adjustment of fixtures is not required (opinions may vary). Increasing hood face velocities often does not necessarily reduce the ppm of contaminants in the breathing zone within the hood operating area because the increased air volume flowing through the laboratory work area makes low-velocity supply air distribution more difficult.

Selection of Hood Face Velocity

1. Interdependence of supply air distribution systems and hood face velocities does not make establishment of standard hood face velocity factors practical for all hood installations. High hood face velocity values will result in

increased equipment, maintenance, operations, and energy costs. High values may not provide increased protection. Evidence from the ASHRAE RP-70 appears to indicate that the opposite is true.

2. ACGIH recommends hood performance test criteria developed by the ASHRAE RP-70 be used as hood specifications for the hood manufacturer to follow. The same performance criteria should be used by the engineer for design of laboratory supply air distribution systems.

HOOD PERFORMANCE SPECIFICATION CRITERIA

The ASHRAE RP-70 hood performance specification criteria are presented for convenience. An extensive list of ASHRAE publications is included in Appendix C.

xx   Tracer gas release rate in the hood using the specified diffuser apparatus. Tracer release rates defined as:

       1   1 L/min approximates pouring a volatile reagent back and forth from one beaker (container) to another.

       2   4 L/min equals an intermediate rate between 1 and 8 L/min.

       3   8 L/min approximates violently boiling water on a 500-W hot plate.

       4   Other release rates may be specified for special cases.

YYY   The control level and ppm at the breathing zone of the laboratory staff.

AU   "As used" in the laboratory work area relative to the design of the supply air distribution system and the toxicity of the reagents used in the hood.

AM   Indicates "as manufactured" and presumes that testing was conducted by the manufacturer.

GUIDELINES FOR ESTIMATING HVAC SYSTEMS COSTS

The information in Table 2.2 is summarized from ACGIH-VS-204.1, Laboratory Hood Data, and can assist in developing in-

TABLE 2.2   Guidelines for Estimating HVAC Systems Costs

Laboratory Work Area Condition	Hood Face Velocity (cfm/sf)
1. Ceiling panels properly located with average panel face velocity <40 fpm. Horizontal-sliding sash hoods. No equipment in hood closer than 12" to opening of hood. Hoods located away from doors and corridors.[a]	60
2. Same as 1 above, some traffic past hood opening. No equipment in hoods closer than 6" to hood opening. Hoods located away from doors and corridors.[a]	80
3. Ceiling panels properly located with average panel face velocity <60 fpm or ceiling diffusers properly located; no diffuser immediately in front of hood opening, quadrant facing hood blocked, terminal throw velocity <60 fpm. No equipment in hood closer than 6" to hood opening. Hoods located away from doors or corridors.[a]	80
4. Same as 3 above; some traffic past hoods. No equipment in hoods closer than 6" to hood opening.	100

Note: It is generally not considered a safe practice to leave any laboratory door open. Open doors can have a severe impact on control of supply and exhaust air, maintenance of pressure differentials between the laboratory and adjacent spaces, temperature and humidity control, containment of odors, fumes, and access by unauthorized personnel.

[a] Hoods located near or adjacent to doors are acceptable if:
  (1) There is a second exit from the laboratory work area.
  (2) Personnel circulating in front of the hood is infrequent.
  (3) The laboratory door is normally open.

itial cost estimates of HVAC systems for proposed new laboratory facilities before detailed design and equipment specifications have been prepared.

GENERIC BASIC LABORATORY HOOD DATA

It is suggested that the ventilation system be designed to accommodate no more than two hood widths in any adjacent group of two to four TLMs to meet most program requirements for general-purpose laboratory work areas. This standard will assist in establishing the basic scope of the building systems and controls that will be required for a proposed project (Table 2.3).

COMMENTS

1. Specifications, including width, height, depth, equipment, and fixtures, vary with each hood manufacturer. The list above is intended for space programming purposes. Hoods may be supplied with horizontal sliding or vertical sash openings. Hoods with horizontal sliding sash appear to be the choice among most safety officials.

2. Vertical sliding sash are the usual choice among researchers because it provides a clear opening to arrange apparatus, monitor procedures, and so on. Tests appear to indicate no significant differences between the two sash types regarding airflow or safety.

3. One of the world's largest chemical research and chemical manufacturing corporations established the horizontally sliding sash fume hood as a standard for *all* laboratories more than 25 years ago. It was reported that many of the researchers objected. However, within a very short time period, everyone adapted and this style of hood has been in continuous use since. So much for those who strongly argue the merits of the vertical sliding sash hood over the horizontal sliding sash hood, and vice versa.

TABLE 2.3 Generic Basic Laboratory Hood Widths

Hood Type	Width		
1. Chemical fume hood	60″		72″
2. Laminar flow hood	51″	63″	75″
3. Biological safety cabinet			
■ Class IIA (100% recirculating)	52″	64″	76″
■ Class IIB			
—30% recirculation/70% exhaust	54″		74″
—Class IIB2 (100% exhaust)	52″	63″	76″
4. Radioisotope hood	60″		72″
5. Canopy (warm air, odors, etc.)	Varies		

At least one each (corrosive and acid) 3'- to 5'-wide vented hazardous reagent storage cabinet should be provided in each standard laboratory module. Several laboratory casework and safety equipment manufacturers fabricate a variety of these cabinets to meet hazardous storage classifications. Several are available as base cabinets for fume hoods. The reader is reminded that under hood hazardous reagent storage cabinets can contribute to explosions or fires that may occur within the hood.

A 6'-wide chemical fume hood should contain a cup sink with hot and cold water; one each natural gas, compressed air, and vacuum outlets; four 120-V ac (duplex) and two 208-V ac (single) outlets with ground-fault protection; two-tube fluorescent sealed vaporproof light fixture; and a chemical-resistant finish. Depending on the reagents and processes conducted within the hood, the cup sink drain may have to be connected to a collection container so that the waste may be treated before discharge into the sewer system.

Allow space for a bag-in, bag-out filter box assembly on the exhaust duct. Although the filter boxes are recommended to be installed as close to the hood as possible, the filter boxes, when required, should not be located in the laboratory work space. An audible and visual alarm should be mounted on the hood face to indicate if the airflow is below the minimum value.

Allow for additional air between 350 and 850 cfm minimum to compensate for the pressure drop across filters. Additional air may be required if HEPA-type filters are used or multiple filter boxes are installed. Prefilters installed upstream from the HEPA filter(s) can extend the time between filter changes.

A 5'-wide radioisotope fume hood should contain a cup sink with hot and cold water; one each natural gas, compressed air and vacuum outlets; four 120-V ac and two 208-V ac outlets with ground-fault protection; two-tube fluorescent sealed vaporproof light fixture; and stainless steel seamless interior finish with coved corners and washdown capability. The drain in the hood may have to be connected to a container or holding tank depending on the level of radioisotopes used and the volume of wastewater produced; and a HEPA absolute-type filter (99.97%) with charcoal and prefilters to extend the life of the HEPA filter(s). A bag-in, bag-out filter box system installed in an exhaust system as close upstream from the hood as possible.

Additional air between 350 and 850 cfm minimum may have to be provided to compensate for pressure drop across filters as they become loaded with particles. Walk-in radioisotope hoods may require approximately 2000 cfm plus 350 to 850 cfm minimum to compensate for pressure drop across the filters. Additional air may also be required, depending on the type of filters and the number of filter boxes installed. Approximately 1140 cfm to 1420 cfm may be required for each typical laboratory module.

A 5'-wide chemical fume hood requires approximately 960 cfm at 100 fpm face velocity. A 6'-wide fume hood requires approximately 1250 cfm at 100 fpm face velocity. A 5'-wide radioisotope hood requires approximately 1125 cfm at 150 fpm face velocity. A specific laboratory module may require additional supply air, depending on the number and type of hood(s), type and number of filters required, and so on.

COMMENTS

1. Guidelines (NIH, CDC, etc.) indicate higher hood face velocities. Other institutions have had satisfactory experience with lower (75 to 85 fpm, even as low as 60 to 65 fpm) face velocities. Lower face velocities translate into reduced energy costs. Selection of face velocity values should be made after a determination of the reagents and procedures that are proposed to be conducted in the hood. This can be critically important relative to personnel safety practices and precautions.

2. Hoods should be located away from high traffic areas to minimize airflow turbulence. Hoods should *never* be located adjacent to the only laboratory exit or in a corner. Corner locations impair airflow. Hoods should be located 3' to 4' from a corner and as far as possible from the primary laboratory exit to permit occupants maximum time to exit in the event an emergency occurs at the hood. Some sources indicate that doors to laboratories with hoods may remain open. The author strongly suggests that laboratory doors remain *closed* at all times. See Note 1.

3. The work surface in the hood should be depressed at least 1″ to contain any spills that may occur. The cup sink should be raised from the depressed area so that spills do not initially flow into the drain. The reagent spilled may be of a classification that should not be dis-

posed of in a drain without collection and treatment prior to disposal.

4. The discussions continue regarding the number (linear feet) of hoods to be installed in a basic laboratory module. At least one 6' chemical fume hood or its equivalent should be accommodated and, further, two 6' hoods each with three modules. Some safety officials recommend that one 6' chemical fume hood and one 6' biological safety cabinet be accommodated in *every* laboratory module. Some reagents and materials must be handled in a chemical fume hood and others in a biological safety cabinet (class IIB2, 100% exhaust, 6' wide).

5. One institution installed 48 lf of hoods in each laboratory of 600 nsf. Quick approximations indicate that if the module suggested ($12' \times 24' \times 2 = 576$ nsf) is used, the hood requirement would occupy at least two walls in the laboratory. Except for the end walls (minus staff corridor and service corridor doors), not very much wall space remains for casework and equipment.

6. The author does not imply that this requirement is excessive or unnecessary. *On the contrary, the broad range of standards applied at many institutions further underscores and supports the critical importance of the initial programming and planning process to determine precisely the specific criteria and then to determine what the standard laboratory module design should be for the particular research activity.*

GENERIC BIOLOGICAL SAFETY CABINET TYPES

Refer to National Sanitation Foundation (NSF) Standard No. 49 for class II (laminar flow) biological safety cabinets, including description and design information. This standard provides guidance for design and installation of the following safety cabinets:

Type A   70% recirculated air with high-efficiency particle arrestor (HEPA-type filter(s), 30% exhaust.

Type B1   70% exhaust, 30% recirculated through (HEPA) filters. A 4'-0"-wide cabinet requires approximately 240 cfm of exhaust air. A 6'-0"-wide cabinet requires approximately 350 cfm of exhaust air. Allow space for bag-in, bag-out HEPA and charcoal filters on both cabinets. Allow for 350- to 850-cfm booster fans in exhaust ducts to overcome static pressure drop through the filters.

Type B2   100% exhaust, no recirculated air. Allow for bag-in, bag-out HEPA charcoal filters in the exhaust duct. Allow for 350- to 850-cfm booster fans in exhaust ducts to overcome pressure drop across the filters.

Containment of aerosols in the laboratory work areas has become a serious problem particularly if specimens containing tuberculosis, hepatitis B, and AIDS are present. Other hazardous microbials and contaminants are also subject to becoming aerosols. These aerosols can contaminate other experiments, creating loss of the entire procedure or incorrect data results. Special work stations and equipment must be provided to eliminate or minimize the effects of aerosols on personnel and ongoing experiments. Laminar flow biological safety cabinets are available to meet these conditions.

Custom safety cabinets can be fabricated to provide work environments for special conditions. Researchers must discuss their proposed work with the institution's radiation or biological safety officer, hygienist, or health physicist. Determination of the proper cabinet must be made based on the activity to be conducted, the reagents or agents to be used, the potential risk, and the level of protection of personnel and the environment. If the risk is determined to be high, a class III safety cabinet (glove box) may be required.

Low- to moderate-risk aerosols, without the presence of volatile toxic chemicals or radionuclides, may be contained in a type A safety cabinet (70% recirculated air and 30% exhaust through HEPA filters). The type B safety cabinet (70% exhaust, 30% recirculated air through HEPA filters) provides a reasonably safe environment to protect personnel and other experiments from a wide range of potentially hazardous aerosols.

Consider providing canopy exhaust hoods to remove heat released from laboratory processes and equipment such as refrigerators, ovens, and incubators. These hoods can also be used to control, contain, and remove or reduce the spread of nontoxic odors. This excess heat can be used in heat reclamation systems.

FUME HOOD EXHAUST DUCT MATERIALS

The material to be selected for use as fume hood exhaust ducts must be based on the nature of the chemical, biological, and physical processes to be conducted within the hood. Materials available include:

- Galvanized steel
- Stainless steel 304
- Stainless steel 314
- Borosilicate glass
- Plastic-coated steel
- Polyvinyl chloride plastic (PVC)
- Fiberglass-reinforced plastic (FRP)

Some installations have also used cementitious pipe materials, and others have used vitrified clay pipe similar to chimney flue liners. Two problems with these materials is that its weight makes it difficult to support and that airtight joint seals are difficult to secure.

Galvanized and stainless steel materials are subject to severe corrosion by many acids and other chemical compounds. Galvanized steel is not recommended for use as a chemical fume hood duct material. Plastic-coated steel, polyvinyl-chloride (PVC), and fiberglass-reinforced plastic (FRP) materials are subject to damage by many chemical solvent compounds. PVC plastics also require more supports, particularly in a horizontal position because the material is subject to flow and is susceptible to softening in high-temperature environments. Plastic materials are subject to fire damage and collapse and may emit poisonous fumes and gases in a building fire. It is often difficult to secure approval for installation of plastic exhaust ductwork from building and fire officials.

Borosilicate glass is resistant to many more chemicals than is any other duct material. Thermal expansion coefficients and fire resistance are superior to those of other duct materials. It has been in use as a laboratory drain and vent material for more than 50 years. It is virtually leakproof, although seals often deteriorate and fail. However, since it is transparent, inspection is simplified. Installation costs are also slightly less than those for stainless steel. Initial material costs may be more expensive than those for stainless steel, however.

There is no universal material that is chemically resistant to all or most chemical compounds. The type of reagents to be used in the laboratory must be identified during the programming and planning process before the duct material can be selected. Consideration must be given to initial budgets and costs. Other factors can mitigate or justify the selection of a duct material that may have low or relatively poor chemical resistance properties. The duct material connected to the fume hood and main exhaust duct line may be a more chemically resistant material. At the point that the fumes become more diluted, a less chemically resistant duct material may be used. It must be cautioned that certain chemical compounds become more chemically reactive when in a diluted state and may negate this "change of duct material strategy." Again we see the importance of determining the nature of the chemical processes to be conducted in the laboratory before selecting the duct material.

Some authorities state that each fume hood should have its own duct and fan. Others recommend a manifold system that collects fume hood ducts at each floor level into a central duct. It must be cautioned that mixing certain fumes and vapors may create explosive or incendiary conditions. However, this situation can be minimized or eliminated by providing supplemental air to further dilute the concentrations of such compounds. It is also recommended that separate hood and exhaust systems be designed and designated for hazardous and dangerous processes such as those using perchloric acid or radioactive materials. Just as it is important to select the proper duct material, it is equally important for the institution to develop strict safety procedures and protocols for the use of reagents in chemical fume hoods by the laboratory staff. It is also important to establish a regular testing and monitoring program for all hood types used in the laboratory to ensure that the equipment is functioning in an efficient and safe manner as designed.

3 ELECTRICAL ENGINEERING CRITERIA

The data in this section do not attempt to establish specific criteria but provide generic guidelines that can assist in the development of specific electrical design criteria for a wide variety of research laboratory activities. However, as the program design criteria evolve, the flexibility of research activities must be established. Building systems cannot be designed to accommodate all types of scientific research. This would not be practical or economically feasible.

Greenhouse effects, *global warming*, and *ozone depletion* are no longer buzzwords eliciting "knee-jerk" reactions from environmentalists and others concerned with the environment. Many scientists are convinced that rapidly increasing demands for energy and burning fossil fuels to meet these energy demands are creating severe global environmental problems. The discussions and arguments are seemingly endless and the rhetoric continues to flow unabated. The interpretation of data and evidence varies from no adverse environmental problems to the beginnings of a "nuclear winter." Current regulations promulgated by the EPA will cost building owners billions of dollars with no discernible benefits. All these costs will ultimately be born by the consumer. Many regulations, unfortunately, are politically motivated and cannot be supported scientifically. However, placing all the rhetoric and politics aside, it is just plain good old common sense to design and build energy-efficient and aesthetically pleasing research laboratory facilities. Satisfying these objectives will help to achieve the overall goal of improving the environment for all. Owners will also be satisfied because their needs will be met in an economical manner.

DESIGN CONSIDERATIONS

As the designers of the human-built environment, architects and engineers must use the best experience and technology to create research and health care facilities that are more energy efficient. Many factors must be considered in developing solutions for the complex facilities design puzzle. Building systems costs almost always become the driving bottom line when making choices, decisions, and designing and assembling the building envelope.

Electrical power requirements for research facilities (and certain smart office buildings) have increased dramatically during the past five to seven years. The abundance of power-hungry electrical and electronic test and processing equipment of all types requires electrical service demands that may range from 8 to 12 W/nsf (building area) to 60 to 100 W/nsf (laboratory area only) in many biomedical and biotechnical laboratory work areas. The high-tech research and production laboratory work areas may require several hundred watts per net square foot (laboratory work area only) to satisfy electrical power demands.

QUALITY POWER DEMANDS

Increasingly important is the quality of the power available not only within the laboratory work areas but from the source as well. "Dirty power" can be the result of power failures, blackouts, brownouts, interruptions, outages, harmonic distortions, frequency variations, voltage spikes or surges, and transient overvoltages and radio-frequency interference. Dirty power can cause ruined equipment, distorted test results, and lost data. In one research facility, the power lines to a series of magnetic resonance imaging equipment were "picking up" the radio-frequency signal from a local radio broadcast tower. It required seven months of "trial and error" to remedy the problem. The worst-case scenario may result in repeating an experiment that may have taken many months or several years of work. Power companies are working to resolve problems particularly to customers that require cleaner power. Electrical power systems have become a major percentage of the total cost of the building. It is not unusual for electrical power systems to be 25 to 35% of the cost of a research facility.

All these factors highlight the importance of detailed investigation, analysis, and review of the program criteria used to design electrical power systems. Research and health care facilities require adequate quantities of reliable and quality power to support laboratory and service activities. Although the objective of most research projects may be the application of its results, the electrical power required to support the building systems (HVAC, lighting, alarms, controls, security systems, fans, motors, etc.) is of equal importance.

LIGHTING FIXTURES

Ceiling lighting fixtures may be 2' × 4', four 34-W lamps or 2' × 2', two 35-W lamps with parabolic louvers in most laboratory and nonlaboratory areas (offices, conference, etc.). The fixtures may be recessed, surface or pendant, depending on the ceiling system and treatment. Dimming controls, multiple-level switching, and special lighting may be required in certain laboratories and animal facilities. Correct color presentation and representation may be additional criteria to accommodate. High-pressure sodium vapor lights are generally satisfactory to be used as outside building security lighting at night.

EMF CONSIDERATIONS

The jury is still out regarding the question of dangers and hazards of electromagnetic radiation (EMF). The Food and Drug Administration is currently conducting tests and research to determine the extent of the regulations that may be required to protect people from this form of radiation. The general consensus appears to support the view that EMF does pose a hazard. Questions remain at what energy levels, frequency, and so on, EMF is dangerous.

The proliferation of microwave transmission dishes can also create hazardous conditions. Stray radiation entering occupied space can be dangerous. Microwave radiation can also affect equipment performance and readings.

The site location of the research facility is an important factor. Electric power generating plants; electrical power transformer substations; microwave, radio, and TV transmission towers, high-tension transmission power lines; and so on, can produce electrical "noise," creating significant problems for research and experimental procedures.

Electromagnetic radiation does affect various electronic equipment. Laboratories conducting sensitive electronic research may have to be shielded with copper mesh or screening to provide the proper EMF-free environment. Design and installation of EMF-shielded rooms, including shielding entire buildings, must be very carefully monitored and supervised during the construction phase. Penetrations (ducts, pipes, cables for test equipment located outside the shielded room, etc.) into the shielded space can destroy the protection desired. Improperly installed contacts around doors can also create problems.

Such built-in facilities are also very expensive. Prefabricated EMF-shielded rooms are available for many research projects requiring relatively small shielded laboratory work spaces. The prefabricated units offer the flexibility to be moved (or removed) to suit research requirements. Many items of laboratory test and analytical equipment are designed with integral EMF shielding.

GENERIC CONSIDERATIONS

Consideration should be given to waiting before installing special electrical outlets (220 V ac three-phase, etc.) until the specific items of equipment have been identified, purchased, and *delivered.* If the services system concept has been carefully designed, extension of conduits and provision of proper outlets and plugs for the equipment, at the correct location, can be accomplished with minimum difficulty and cost.

The laboratory work area lighting system should be designed with light fixtures and equipment using energy-saving rapid-start cool-white lamps or warm-white lamps. Illumination levels should be between 60 and 70 fc at the standing work counter height of 36″ to 37″. Some sources recommend 100 fc for laboratory work areas, including the illumination levels inside chemical fume hoods and biological safety cabinets. The dilemma to be overcome is the effect that high illumination levels may have on persons with vision-sensitivity problems. Light sources with low-level ultraviolet radiation must also be selected to minimize problems for other sight-impaired persons.

Task lighting can supplement the ceiling lighting system. An assessment and evaluation should be made of the proposed laboratory work area plans to determine if the laboratory casework layouts have been coordinated with the ceiling light fixture plan. A decision can then be made whether task lighting would contribute to a balanced lighting solution for the proposed work areas. Ballasts provided should be an energy-efficient type designed to meet UL class P requirements. The ballasts should be equipped with a built-in automatic reset thermal protector and designed to have a class A sound rating.

ELECTRICAL POWER SYSTEMS

The secondary power distribution system for the laboratory work areas should be designed with free-standing 277 V/480 V switchgear. The switchgear should have draw-out air frame circuit breakers with a minimum of two stages of ground fault interrupter protection. The electrical panel boxes for each Typical Laboratory Modules (TLMs) should be designed to include a minimum of 25% additional circuit spaces for future electrical demands. The switchboards should be provided with ground-fault interrupter protection, an ampere demand meter with an instantaneous ammeter, and four-position switch for phase selection. The voltmeter should have a seven-position selection switch.

All the buses in the switchgear should be fabricated from solid copper stock. Current density for the copper bus should be designed for a maximum of 1200 A per square inch of cross-section area. The switchgear room(s) should be provided with adequate ventilation, filtered air, and heat in severe winter climates.

The 480V/277V plug-in bus duct feeders should have a rated capacity of 600V. The feeders should be installed in vertical service chases to the electrical distribution panel boxes. The distribution panel boxes should service the 480V electric motor loads and the 277V light panel boxes supplied through dry-type transformers to 120V/208V subdistribution and branch-circuit power panel boxes.

The vertical feeders should be plug-in bus duct type extended to the services corridor, interstitial space, or service chase, depending on the services systems concept adopted. The distribution and subdistribution panel boxes and dry-type transformers may be located in these services spaces. Adequate working space must be provided to permit safe access for servicing, maintenance, and equipment replacement.

Plug-in bus ducts may be used for horizontal distribution to permit reasonable flexibility to accommodate future electrical requirements. Branch-circuit light and electrical panels should be located in the services corridor, interstitial space or service chases, and so on, depending on the services systems concept adopted for the laboratory work areas.

All electrical feeders and associated electrical panel boxes should be provided with a minimum of 25% spare capacity to accommodate future growth. The design and layout of all distribution, subdistribution, branch-circuit panel boxes, and circuit breakers should be carefully coordinated. Panelboards should have rated bus extensions to each breaker position. All panel boxes should have a copper ground bus bar bolted to the panelboard enclosure. A grounding bus bar connected to a building grounding grid system should be provided in every laboratory module. Provision should be made to accommodate individual grounding capability for special conditions.

All branch circuits serving office work areas should be installed above the finished ceiling space (if provided) and concealed in walls where possible. Electrical services should be available to the laboratory work areas through the services corridor wall, interstitial space, or service chase, again depending on the services systems concept adopted. Concealment of electrical conduit within any wall systems should be carefully reviewed. Such concealment may be attractive visually but may create problems and additional costs during remodeling and renovations to accommodate changes.

Consider 277 V branch circuits for the lighting systems with local switching in the laboratory work areas, service and support areas, and office spaces, conference rooms, classrooms, and so on. The 110V (115V, 120V, etc.) duplex convenience outlets in office work areas should be planned and located to permit reasonable flexible arrangement of desks, bookcases, file cabinets, and so on. Quadruplex wall outlets should be avoided. The different-size plugs from various electrical equipment sometimes overlaps an adjoining outlet, preventing its use. This defeats the purpose of providing the additional outlets. Because of the proliferation of electrical equipment used at most office workstations, a minimum of six to eight outlets should be provided at each workstation.

Office landscape-type furniture and furnishings, low partitions, and so on, may be powered (supplied) through underfloor ducts coordinated with flexible flat wiring or wired partitions systems. The planning and design of open office landscape furniture-type work areas are being questioned by some sources as being noisy, impersonal, and an invasion of privacy. The facilities manager and the architect should carefully consider alternatives to the open plan concept. The open-laboratory concept has many more implications than simply electrical planning. The open-laboratory plan may create difficult air supply and exhaust problems which may also negatively affect safety considerations.

The electrical branch-circuit system within the services corridor, interstitial space, or service chases, again depending on the services systems concept adopted, should be reasonably flexible, to facilitate laboratory work area and office alterations. All laboratory work areas should be provided with 120V/208V single-phase and 208V three-phase electrical service. In addition, 60 A electrical service at 120V/208V should be available to each laboratory work area module when needed for designated equipment.

Electrical service convenience outlets at the laboratory work area counters may be provided in a single- or multiple-channel metal raceway system. The raceway may be surface mounted on the wall above the work counter backsplash or supported on shelf supports or brackets. The metal raceway can be installed on island or peninsula workbench units.

Many of the laboratory casework manufacturers have various systems and fixtures to meet electrical service requirements at the work counter. Outlets may be spaced at 1' to 2' on centers (single or duplex outlets). Quadruplex outlets are not recommended. Pendent outlet fixtures may block full use of the work counter.

Provide a limit of three to four outlets per circuit. Electrical service of 480V should be available for special laboratory equipment. Consider including the distribution of communications cable(s) telephone, computer networking, data, and so on, within a separate compartment of a metal raceway system. Care must be exerted when considering mixing electrical, telecommunication, and data cables within separate and adjacent compartments of a metal raceway system.

GENERAL ILLUMINATION LEVELS

General illumination [footcandle (fc)] levels are indicated in Table 3.1. The facilities manager and architect should also refer to applicable codes and regulations as required.

TABLE 3.1   General Illumination Levels

Space/Room/Area	Illumination (fc)
Laboratory spaces	60–100 (with task lighting)
Chemical fume hoods, biological safety cabinets	100 (certain hoods may require explosion/vapor/humidity/ waterproof lighting fixtures)
Laboratory corridors and stairs	15–20
Animal areas (varies)	60–80 FC (with day–night controls on timers, etc.)
Office spaces	40–50
Conference/classrooms	40–50
Office space corridors and stairs	15–20
Public areas	20–30
Mechanical rooms	30–40
Parking lots	3–5 (location in high-crime areas may require increased lighting levels to supplement security systems lighting requirements)

COMMENTS

1. Factors for recommended illumination levels should be carefully reviewed not only from the standpoint of energy conservation and savings, but of actual need.

2. Recent experience indicates that current illumination criteria may be excessive. Task lighting in many instances can be more effective and efficient than a ceiling grid lighting system.

3. Ceiling light fixtures are generally designed to provide an overall illumination level to overall work areas. However, as changes are made to the work areas (new equipment, processes, casework, height of work counters, etc.), the original ceiling lighting grid system may no longer be located and oriented correctly.

4. For many years the illumination level in hospital patient corridors was recommended to be equal to that provided in most work areas. No thought or consideration was given to the discomfort caused to a patient being transported on a stretcher and forced to

look into these bright lights. Fortunately for patients, lighting levels are changing and indirect lighting methods are being used in many corridor areas, treatment rooms, and so on.

5. Computer areas require special attention to location, placement, size, type, and quality of light provided. Glare and reflections in computer monitor screens can cause physiological and psychological stress to personnel. Studies indicate that the frequency of fluorescent lights [60 hertz (Hz)] can cause stress and fatigue. Indirect and task lighting can assist in alleviating many of these problems.

6. Many laboratory work areas do not require finished suspended ceilings. Pendent lighting systems are usually employed. This permits relative ease in relocating light fixtures to suit changing activities in the laboratory work areas.

7. Many service systems concepts have been derived from an established series of standard laboratory work areas. If the scientific activities to be accommodated in the research facility are known at the time that programming criteria are being developed, the electrical power system requirements can be developed and designed to suit these needs.

EMERGENCY POWER SYSTEMS

The emergency power system should be designed to service emergency and exit lighting; and to critical equipment, laboratory work areas, ongoing experiments, animal holding areas, and so on, during planned outages for periodic maintenance programs. Certain laboratory work areas may have to be provided with separate emergency power systems using an automatic-start diesel engine-generator unit(s). The automatic starting system should start the emergency generator(s) after a predetermined time following power failure. The generators should be capable of transferring service and assume the critical load(s) within 8 to 10 seconds, and no longer than 12 seconds. The laboratory work area generator(s) should be located within the building and near the switchgear, if possible and practical. Consideration must be given to engine and generator noise, exhaust, and vibration problems. The generators and associated equipment should be arranged with adequate clearance to facilitate servicing and maintenance. An emergency battery lighting system should be installed in this work area to provide light to work on the generator(s) and motor(s) during emergency conditions.

Testing and maintenance programs for contemporary emergency power systems must be carefully designed and executed. Testing protocols must conform to codes and regulations and be conducted under full, connected loads. Since electrical power disruption occurs during the interval of transfer from utility power to the emergency generators, testing must be accomplished so that critical experiments are not interrupted or compromised. Investigators must be made aware of the emergency generator testing schedules so that experiments or processes can be coordinated with the physical plant manager and minimize disruptions, loss of data, or ruined experiments.

The Joint Commission on the Accreditation of Healthcare Organizations (JCAHO), P.O. Box 75751, Chicago, IL 60675-5751, has published a monograph *Emergency Power: Testing and Maintenance* (PTSM-831), that provides guidance about emergency power systems programs.

The capacity of fuel storage tank(s) should allow operation at continuous load for a minimum of 3 to 5 days. Local experience with storms (tornadoes and hurricanes), length of power outages, and so on, may require fuel supplies to maintain emergency power for longer periods of time. Some authorities recommend fuel supplies for 2 weeks in such regions. Location of the tanks can present formidable safety, design, and construction problems. Silencers or mufflers should reduce engine exhaust noise to acceptable levels. Mufflers can also reduce the horsepower rating of diesel or gasoline engines. The generator(s) should be a water-cooled design with a closed system complete with heaters, antifreeze, and circulating pumps.

The emergency power system should be designed, distributed (risers, branches, panel boxes, etc.), and controlled as a separate system on each floor from the normal electrical power system. Every emergency power distribution panel box should be designed with sufficient capacity to service estimated and designed program electrical demands. A minimum of 25 to 35% additional space to accommodate future requirements should also be included. A separate emergency electrical power system must be designed to supply various building emergency systems (e. g., exit lights, alarm systems, corridor lights, ventilating systems, controls, and other building systems during a power outage or fire emergency).

The normal side of the switchboard should be connected to the emergency power system through key-interlocked circuit breakers between the network protectors, circuit breakers of the emergency power system protectors, and circuit breakers of the emergency power system source. This feature will permit servicing predetermined breakers on the normal side of the switchboard under certain emergency and program maintenance conditions where critical loads are not at a maximum and after all critical loads have been serviced.

CONNECTED EMERGENCY POWER LOADS

Emergency loads that should be connected at the time of installation are as follows:

- One duplex receptacle on each side of the laboratory work area module at approximately 1200/1500 W per receptacle.
- Fire alarm system, security systems.
- Exit lights.
- Emergency lighting at 3 fc minimum for egress and other designated areas.
- 10 fc at switchboards, security, and other communications command centers.
- Special laboratory equipment, including designated BSL-2, BSL-3, and BSL-4 rooms, animal facilities (air supply and exhaust), refrigerators, and freezers.
- Telephone relay systems.
- Controlled-temperature rooms, walk-in refrigerators, and special controlled-temperature hazardous storage units.
- HVAC and hood exhaust systems for special laboratories (BSL-2, 3, and 4, etc.).
- At least one passenger and one service elevator. Recent NFPA Life Safety Code responses to ADA requirements will affect emergency power requirements for elevators to accommodate disabled persons during an emergency situation.

- Critical sump pumps and other associated mechanical equipment, fans, motors, pumps, and controls. Selecting locations for building services equipment must be considered carefully in regions of the country subject to frequent storms, flooding, and seismic activity.
- Critical computer equipment (UPS systems may be satisfactory).
- ATC air compressors.

COMMENTS

1. The facilities manager and architect must carefully consider the requests from the principal investigators for emergency power service in the laboratory work areas. Many requests can be classified as "personal convenience" and attempts to customize laboratory work areas. Experience at many institutions indicates that during power interruptions emergency power needs were adequately met through the use of extra-long extension cords from strategically placed emergency power outlets. However, the principal investigators must be afforded the opportunity to present the emergency power needs based on the specific research activities and equipment to be used.

Consideration should be given to the installation of a static uninterruptible power system (UPS) with battery backup for central computer mainframe systems. Recent technological advances, however, have produced UPSs that are more compact, including units that install directly in the PC microcomputer expansion slots. These units can save data and equipment.

With the apparent obsolescence and phasing out of mainframe central computer facilities for many institutions and the growing application of PCs, networks, and FAX machines in laboratory work areas, sufficient power and data transmission outlets must be provided throughout the facility. In existing facilities, clean power can be provided relatively inexpensively through the use of commercially available surge suppressers, power-line conditioners, surge and dropout protectors, standby power supplies, and so on. These units plug directly into existing outlets with the equipment plugged into the unit.

Consider battery-powered wall clocks. This eliminates the need for an outlet, related wiring, conduit, junction boxes, coordination of equipment, casework and furnishings, and so on. Master clock systems are expensive, subject to synchronization and maintenance problems, and their usefulness and need are difficult to justify in many applications.

4 PLUMBING ENGINEERING CRITERIA

The specific functions and activities to be conducted in the proposed research facility will determine the specifications and materials for the plumbing, drain, and gas distribution systems. Materials previously considered safe and nontoxic are now classified as toxic and hazardous. These changes have brought about a reevaluation of the continued use of such materials as copper, and zinc. Alternative materials are being used to eliminate the hazards. Lead pipes, lead-solder connections for copper pipes, and so on, have been recognized as dangerous and are no longer used in new construction. Lead is considered very dangerous and can cause serious disabilities in children as well as adults.

Lead has been used in paints for many years. As a surface treatment, it can be removed or covered. However, lead pipe and lead-soldered pipe joints in existing buildings cannot be removed easily because most of the pipes are buried within the structure of the building. Several recently completed buildings are uninhabitable because of the high lead levels in the potable drinking water systems. A new research facility has been vacant for more than two years because of the high lead content in the water system. The pipes are being replaced with plastic pipes at a cost of several million dollars. It was determined that a plumbing mechanic used lead-based solder on the joints of the copper pipe potable water system.

Some authorities state that plastic piping is acceptable and safe for drinking water systems. Depending on the chemicals and minerals in the drinking water, it can erode the inside surface of the pipes and transport the leached materials to the person drinking the water.

The problem is further complicated in animal facilities. Some animals are very susceptible to substances in the drinking water. Chemicals in water may also distort test readings and ruin experiments. Many seemingly innocuous substances can have a serious impact on research test program results.

PROGRAMMATIC CONSIDERATION

An example case history illustrates the many factors that contribute to the success or failure of research activities. An experiment was organized to determine how the development and progress of cancer in primates may occur. Facilities were constructed to provide an isolated and sterile environment. All direct contact with other animals (and humans) was prevented. Contact was through glove boxes and similar devices. Food was carefully controlled and sterilized. Air was filtered and sterilized. However, in less than one year, a significant percentage developed a specific type of cancer.

All possible causes were examined, including hereditary factors. It was finally determined that the drinking water supplied to the primates was the primary cause of the cancer. The drinking water had not been prescreened or tested. It had been assumed initially that since it was safe for humans, it would be safe for the primates. The drinking water that was the cause of the cancer in the primates was the same drinking water that has been used by the inhabitants of the building literally since its occupancy. The only happy ending to this case history was that the cancer developed in the primates was a form of cancer unique to that species and not found in humans. There appears to be cause for some concern, however, about our public drinking water treatment and supply system.

What is the proper course and choice for the facility manager, architect, plumbing engineer, and researcher? The answer is complex and not easily discernible; however, it is another factor that reinforces the vital importance of the initial programming and planning process. It is at this time during the overall planning process that evaluations and selections can be made based on the research criteria and protocols that are to be followed and conducted in the proposed facility.

What if specific research program criteria are not available during the programming and planning process? Then the best considered judgment and experience of the administration of the institution, the investigators, and the design professionals must be applied. Building systems and materials should be selected in a generic context. As the building is being occupied and research programs are considered, evaluated, and space assignments being made, *the capabilities and limitations of the buildings systems must be used in determining what functions and activities can be accommodated safely within the facility.*

DESIGN FACTORS

Local and national plumbing codes provide the requirements for the building plumbing systems. However, many recent regulations from the Environmental Protection Agency (EPA), the Department of Energy (DOE), and so on, impose requirements that some codes have not as yet addressed. Many codes establish minimum plumbing standards and rely on the judgment and experience of the design professional, with input from the owner to decide what additional factors may be considered. It is imperative that the facility manager, architect, and plumbing engineer make themselves aware of the activities and processes that may be conducted in the proposed facility to ensure that the plumbing design provides for a safe environment for the researcher.

The recent Supreme Court decision stating that women cannot be prohibited from working at dangerous and hazardous occupations has many far-reaching liability implications for employers. The decision relates principally to the civil rights issues of women in the workplace. Does this mean that women can still sue the employer if they or their unborn children are injured by the hazards of the workplace? Can the children who may be afflicted with disabilities at birth or later in life because their mother was exposed to the hazardous conditions in the workplace sue the mother and/or the employer? Are judgments to be assessed against employers even though the employee was told of the hazardous conditions?

Again, what do these factors have to do with the programming and planning of research and health care facilities and building plumbing systems? In the opinion of the author, the implications are considerable. The building plumbing systems must meet basic minimum code requirements and must anticipate and accommodate processes that may pose a hazard to the researcher and others.

GENERIC CONSIDERATIONS

There continue to be considerable differences of opinion as to where to locate emergency deluge showers and eye washers in a laboratory facility. Should all laboratories have an emergency shower whether or not the laboratory is equipped with a chemical fume hood? Should the shower be located at the hood? Inside the laboratory work area at the door? At another location within the laboratory? In the corridor (x feet on center) outside the laboratory? Should floor drains be provided? Should the emergency shower be in the open? In an alcove? In a stall arrangement? The answers to these questions are perhaps both "yes" and "no." Much depends on the processes to be conducted and an estimate of the possible frequency emergencies that may occur, the disability or injury to the person at the site of the accident, and so on.

Every laboratory with a hood should have an emergency shower and eye washer. If it is a single module, perhaps the most logical location for both items would be at the utility sink. In a larger laboratory with multiple doors to the staff corridor, perhaps the location closest to the primary exits from the laboratory would be satisfactory. The difficulty of selecting the best location is solely dependent on the behavior of a person who may need the shower or eye washer immediately after an accident occurs. Unfortunately, in an emergency situation, the only thing that can be ascertained with any degree of certainty is that the person's response will vary—from collapsing at the site of the emergency to retaining some composure and being able to get to the shower or eye washer. The problem is further compounded if the person may be alone in the laboratory at the time of the emergency.

COMMENTS

1. It is suggested that each laboratory module be pro vided with a capped roughed-in pipe connection above the finished ceiling or in the service corridor. If a hood is installed, the emergency shower should be located at the utility sink or before the exit door from the laboratory. The eye washer should be located at the utility sink.

2. Other locations may be appropriate, depending on the processes to be conducted in the laboratory.

> Larger laboratories would follow a similar pattern. Corridor locations are not recommended because of the long travel time to get to the shower from the laboratory in the event of an emergency.

Chilled water should be available at each laboratory module (in the service corridor, interstitial space, etc.) for extension to all laboratory work areas. This chilled water system is a secondary system to be used to provide cooling for special equipment (electron microscope power supply, spectroscopy units, etc.) or to provide additional space cooling if high-heat-output equipment are installed and used in the laboratory.

The plumbing systems should also be designed to support administrative office areas, conference rooms, and other nonlaboratory functions and activities. The utility distribution systems should reflect the requirements of a unitized three-dimensional laboratory module concept to minimize disruptions caused by changes in room arrangements and location of casework and equipment.

Central utility systems should be designed to service initial demands with an excess capacity minimum of 25% to anticipate future needs. Allow space for piping not initially required but probably anticipated. Adequate personnel work space *must* be provided to permit normal maintenance and repair to be made safely. Service (shutoff) valves should be provided to permit isolation of individual laboratory modules for alteration or repair without disruption to other laboratories. All pipes, valves, cleanouts, and so on, should be clearly labeled with industry standard graphics for easy identification of contents, pressure, temperature, contents, and so on, and direction of flow.

COMPRESSED AIR SYSTEMS

The laboratory compressed air system should be designed with at least two oil-free air compressors to provide high-quality air substantially free of impurities and water. The compressors should have the capacity to provide 100% standby service. Refrigerated dryers should be used to meet dryness and temperature conditions normally expected in laboratory compressed air systems. Each compressor and refrigerated dryer should discharge to a separate header. A changeover valve should be provided between headers and at the connection to the compressed air main. Compressed air that may be supplied to special laboratories (BSL-2, BSL-3, BSL-4, etc.) may have to be filtered and sterilized.

The laboratory distribution system should be designed to provide a regulated pressure of approximately 40 psig and 1 scfm at every work counter outlet installed. Some laboratories may require 100 psig or more. The main system should provide 100 psig air pressure with pressure controlled by pressure regulators at the central air compressors.

COMMENTS

1. Laboratory and equipment usage factors (LEUFs) or standard laboratory building diversity factors are useful to determine compressed air equipment requirements. See Table 1.3. The program criteria should define the proposed functions and activities to be conducted, providing further data on compressed air requirements.

Compressed air requirements for pneumatic controls including heating, ventilating, and air conditioning systems, must use a separate controlled air system with separate air compressors and 100% standby capacity with emergency power. Compressed air for control systems should be oil-free and dried with adequate refrigeration equipment.

VACUUM SYSTEMS

The laboratory central vacuum system should provide vacuum at 18″ to 22″ of mercury and 1 cfm at each work counter outlet installed. Standard laboratory diversity factors may be used to determine requirements. See the Comment above and Table 1.3. Two (or more) vacuum pumps should be designed and installed to provide for 100% standby capacity. Air discharged from the vacuum pump must be exhausted outdoors at a safe location and height. Filters should be provided on the vacuum system air intake to prevent contaminants from entering the system. Special precautions must be considered for vacuum systems used in high-hazard spaces.

COMMENTS

1. Central vacuum provided to special laboratories (BSL-2, BSL-3, BSL-4, etc.) must be carefully filtered in the laboratory to prevent any of the hazardous materials from being ingested into the vacuum pipe system and carried to the outside of the special laboratory.

2. Depending on the specific processes to be conducted, the scope and scale of the special laboratories, and other factors, it may be more economical, efficient, and safer to provide a separate vacuum pump system for these special laboratories.

GAS SYSTEMS

Natural gas should be available to all laboratory modules. The distribution system should be designed to provide a minimum of 7 cfh per outlet at 0.6" W.C. Standard laboratory diversity factors may be used to determine requirements. See the Comment above and Table 1.3. Propane gas may be provided and used if a source of natural gas is not available. Propane gas may be secured in the liquid or gaseous state, stored in tanks. Gas in the liquid state is usually stored outside the facility.

If the decision is made to provide a central carbon dioxide and nitrogen gas distribution system, the most efficient and economical system (if volume use is sufficient) is to supply the gases from a liquid gaseous storage facility. Although there are no flammable hazards associated with carbon dioxide and nitrogen, there is some hazard from the handling of low-temperature cryogenic liquid gases. If the liquid gases come in contact with skin, serious low-temperature burns can occur.

Quenching occurs when cryogenic liquids reach the boiling point, rapidly expanding to its gaseous state instantly and explosively. This has happened in some MRI installations that use liquid helium. Mechanical venting must be provided to exhaust the gas in the event of a quench. Helium, nitrogen, and carbon dioxide are nontoxic. However, when a quench occurs, the expanding gas can displace the normal room air (oxygen), creating a suffocation hazard for the laboratory or hospital staff.

Explosions are possible due to defective pressure control regulators, valves, and so on. The *Compressed Gas Association*

(CGA) and the *National Fire Protection Association* (NFPA) publish several guidelines and standards for the storage and handling of liquid and compressed gases, including flammable and nonflammable gases. (see Appendix C).

Carbon dioxide, nitrogen, helium, argon, nitrous oxide, and other special and mixed gases supplied from cylinders should be handled and stored according to the several hazard classifications. The cylinders may be grouped in a central gas cylinder storage and holding facility with manifolds and piping of adequate capacity to supply the various laboratory work areas. Piping systems must be the same as those used for hospital medical gas systems. Gas cylinders may also be located in the service corridor. Location of gas cylinders in the laboratory work areas is to be discouraged because of hazards such as explosion, high-pressure gas release, and so on. The gas cylinder can become a dangerous missile if the valve is broken, causing a high-pressure gas release.

WATER SYSTEMS

The potable water systems must be designed so that the potable domestic water system cannot be contaminated by the laboratory industrial water system or other water systems. This protection may be provided through the installation of backflow preventers. Backflow preventers should be installed in parallel and be of the reduced-pressure zone type. Laboratory faucets must also be equipped with backflow preventers.

Separate potable water systems should be provided for laboratory work areas and toilet and office areas. Drinking fountains in laboratory areas must be on the domestic water system. Foot-operated drinking fountains in hazardous areas may be required with consideration for disabled persons. Other items in the laboratory work areas that should be on the domestic water system include emergency showers, eye washers, toilet, shower and locker rooms, janitor closets (housekeeping), and so on.

Water-saving faucets are suggested for use in toilet areas. Since many faucets are fabricated from brass, which may have a high lead content, it is suggested that plastic faucets be considered for most, if not all, sink locations throughout the facility. Automatic valves and faucets may be ideal in certain hazardous locations.

Safety showers and eye wash facilities should be provided in all laboratory areas as well as other spaces where chemicals may be used. Eye washers should be of the dish washing sprayer type, although other types are available. Eye washer requirements in areas other than laboratories may be satisfied with the use of standard eye washer units.

Emergency showers and eye washers for laboratory work areas may be serviced by water lines from the service corridor, interstitial space, ceiling, underfloor, and so on, to each laboratory. Where no shower is needed at the time of laboratory casework and equipment installation (fit-out), the end of the pipe should be valved and capped above the finished ceiling or ceiling line if services are exposed. Shutoff valves to all water lines servicing the emergency showers or eye washers should be carefully labeled to prevent an accidental shutoff of water to the shower and eye-wash fixtures. This is particularly important when an adjacent laboratory may be undergoing renovation and the services to the renovated area have to be shut off.

Emergency shower heads should be of deluge type, with valves capable of continuous operation on activation. The flow rate generally should be between 30 and 60 gpm at the shower head. Flow rates between 20 and 135 gallons may be required, depending on the processes conducted in the laboratory. See Checklist 2 in Appendix A for additional data. Water temperature should be supplied at a minimum of 72 to 74° F (±5°F). Water pressure should be between 5 and 50 psi.

Floor drains are a subject for considerable discussion and the decision should be based on the nature of the laboratory processes planned to be conducted in the facility. Dry traps are the source for contamination, gases, and so on.

Flow rates for eye washers should be 2.5 to 12 gpm. The water temperature range should be a minimum of 60°F and a maximum of 95°F (±3 to 5°F), which approximates body temperature. Water pressure should be 20 psi minimum to 125 psi maximum. Alarm systems should be installed to indicate when an emergency shower or eyewash is activated. See Checklist 2 in Appendix A for additional data.

EMERGENCY SYSTEMS

Because of the nature of the processes conducted and hazards contained in research and clinical laboratory facilities, all areas should be sprinkled. Whether a wet or dry system should be installed may depend on codes and the type of laboratory. Some laboratories may require a fire suppression system other than water (carbon dioxide, etc.). The *National Fire Protection Association* (NFPA) publishes extensive standards and guidelines on this subject (see Appendix C).

All valves, controls, switches, electrical panel boxes, circuits, and so on, must be clearly labeled (with industry standard labels and graphics) to identify function, flow direction, pressure, fluid type, and operation. Utilities, pipes, and services in concealed locations (walls, floors, ceilings, service chases, etc.) must be identified. Identification may be placed in finished spaces or adjacent to any access and inspection panels. Standpipes, fire hose cabinets, sprinkler systems, and portable fire extinguishers (ABC types) must be provided in accordance with codes and regulations of the jurisdiction where the facility is to be located.

Laboratory acid waste drain lines may be glass, plastic, or other acid-resistant material above ground and duriron below ground. Several disadvantages of glass include the tendency to crack due to thermal and physical stresses. The gasket joint materials for the glass pipe tend to rot and decay creating fluid and gas leakage. Plastic has the tendency to become soft or ductile (flows) under thermal and physical stresses. These drain pipes should be located where they may be easily inspected and serviced, if possible.

Chemical and biological waste holding, processing, treatment, and storage tanks may have to be provided. Various fluid waste materials may have to be treated to correct pH levels before being released into the sanitary sewer system. Other materials may have to be diluted or rendered biologically and chemically harmless. Some waste materials may have to be treated and processed before disposal by means other than release into the sanitary sewer system.

These tanks should be located to provide easy access, inspection, processing, treatment, and removal of the contents. All holding tanks should have inspection and sample ports. Sizes may vary from several hundred gallons to many thousands of gallons. Tank size depends on volume, type of waste, treatment, and holding and disposal requirements. It is recommended that a separate chemical retention tank or basin be provided for each photography darkroom facility. Several darkrooms may be drained into a single tank of sufficient size. Chemicals used in the process of films should not be permitted to drain directly into the sanitary sewer system. Many of the chemicals contain heavy metals. A silver recovery system should also be provided.

STEAM AND HOT WATER SYSTEMS

High-temperature hot water (HTHW) requirements may be provided from a central power plant (if one exists). Distribution may be through an underground utilities tunnel system on the site. HTHW may be used in heat exchangers to generate steam and low-temperature hot water. Uses for HTHW may include:

- Environmental heating equipment.
- Steam required for autoclaves, washers, humidification units, and related equipment.
- Areas requiring purified steam for humidification (animal rooms, media preparation, etc.) must use distilled water in a converter. Where possible, the condensate should be reclaimed and may be used as makeup water for the system.

Domestic hot water (120 to 140°F) and low-temperature hot water (180°F) supplies for dishwashers, glass washers, and so on, may be obtained from HTHW to water heat exchangers. Pumps should be installed to provide continual circulation of the low temperature and domestic hot water to assure constant temperatures within the specified limits at laboratory fixtures (emergency showers, eye washers, etc.), toilet room fixtures, and other laboratory equipment requiring a constant-temperature water supply.

SERVICE REQUIREMENTS FOR WATER PURIFICATION SYSTEMS

Pure water is required for many chemical, biological, and pharmaceutical processes, preparing solutions and mixtures, and washing glassware. One type of water may be required to be used as the feedwater to produce a higher-purity water. Reagent-grade water is generally categorized in five general types by the *National Committee for Clinical Laboratory Standards* (NCCLS):

Type I   Test methods requiring minimal interference and maximum precision and accuracy: atomic absorption, flame

	emission spectrometry, legend assays, trace metals, enzymatic procedures sensitive to trace metals, electrophoretic procedures, buffer solutions, standard solutions.
Type IIA	Test methods in which the presence of bacteria is likely to affect the test results: general reagents without preservatives and microbiology systems (not to be sterilized).
Type IIB	Test methods for which requirements leading to the choice of Types I, IIA, or Special Purpose waters do not apply: stains and dyes for histology, general reagents with preservatives, microbiology systems (to be sterilized).
Type III	General washing and feedwater for producing higher-grade water, as well as bacteriological media preparation.
Special purpose	Procedures requiring removal of specific contaminants: removal of pyrogens for tissue/cell cultures, removal of trace organics for HPLC.

The different water types may be obtained through several treatment methods. Each method (or combination) eliminates or reduces the amount of several contaminants including dissolved ionized solids and gases, dissolved nonionized solids and gases, microorganics, particulate matter, and pyrogens:

- Activated Carbon Filtration
- Deionization
- Distillation
- Electrodialysis
- Microporous filtration
- Reverse osmosis
- Ultrafiltration
- Ultraviolet oxidation

Analysis of proposed functions and activities should be accomplished during the programming and planning phase to determine the quality and quantity of the water required. The source and quality of the feedwater (raw water) supply to the facility must be determined to design the water treatment properly, conditioning ("polishing"), or purification systems. Contaminants in most water supply systems may include dissolved inorganics (solids and gases), dissolved organics, microorganisms, particulates, and pyrogens.

Central distilled water systems can be very expensive. Distribution systems, including plastic, glass, aluminum, or tinlined steel pipes, are additional costs. If the distribution system becomes contaminated, it may result in compromise to the purity of the water and ultimately in the loss of the entire system. It is virtually impossible to clean or decontaminate a central distilled water system.

Several water processing units located in the laboratory core service and support facilities or laboratory work areas should be considered. Water can be purified using various cartridge-type systems. Cartridge systems can be wall or casework mounted. The processed water can be dispensed in 1- or 5-gallon containers. The *American Society for Testing and Materials* (ASTM), the *National Committee for Clinical Laboratory Standards* (NCCLS), and the *College of American Pathologists* (CAP) have established standards for water purity and its use.

RULE-OF-THUMB FACTORS

The following list and Tables 4.1 and 4.2 provide rule-of-thumb factors to estimate size and service requirements for water purification systems. The information was summarized and developed from several sources, including water still equipment manufacturers. Capacities and specifications of various types of stills and other water purifiers may vary with each manufacturer.

TABLE 4.1 Service Requirements for Electric Stills

Still Capacity (gph)	kW	Amperes (120 V/240 V)	Cooling Water (gph)
1	3	22/12	10
2	6	50/25	15
5	12	110/55	40
10	25	220/110	80

TABLE 4.2   Service Requirements for Steam Stills

Boiler HP (gph)	Steam (lb/hr)	Cooling Water (gph)
5	2	40
10	3.5	80

Estimates for Water Purification Systems

■ 100 L/day or less volume used requires a system producing 4 to 8 L (1 to 2 gal) of treated water per hour.

■ Over 100 L/day of volume used requires a system producing 19 to 38 L (5 to 10 gal) of treated water per hour.

Several manufacturers of water purification equipment provide and have published valuable data about purification systems. They can also assist researchers and investigators design systems to meet special needs. Labconco Corporation, 811 Prospect, Kansas City, MO 64232, (816) 363-0130, is one source for such assistance.

5 ANIMAL FACILITY CRITERIA

The use of animals in biomedical research has resulted in treatments and cures for many human and animal diseases. Hundreds of thousands, perhaps millions of people are alive today because of the dedication of the researchers and the health care community in bringing the results of this research to the clinical level. The author's brother is alive today because of research work accomplished on pigs' hearts. The findings and techniques developed have been applied to humans suffering from certain diseases of the heart.

However, during the past several years there is a growing community of animal rights' advocacy groups determined to stop the use of animals for such research and experimental purposes. Most of the objections focus on alleged mistreatment of animals. Others state ethical and moral reasons to stop the use of animals for research and experimentation. Militant animal rights groups have forcibly entered laboratories, destroyed property, threatened and injured researchers and staff, destroyed and ruined experiments that have in many instances taken years of work, and removed the animals from the laboratory. In a recent case, the animals removed were infected with dangerous diseases and could infect not only their abductors, but other innocent persons and other animals they might come in contact with outside the laboratory.

The problem is complex, with many voices and opinions for and against the question of the use of animals in biomedical research activities. Many scientists and others contend that there are alternative methods to conduct biomedical research without the use of animals. However, like any alternative investigative method, it cannot become a complete substitute and achieve the same results. How do these matters affect the laboratory administrator, the facilities manager, the architect, and the engineer? Again, a complex series of responses.

Aside from the very technical building systems design problems related to animal facilities, there has been heightened attention to provide:

- Adequate and humane facilities for the animals
- State-of-the-art research facilities for the researcher, investigator, and veterinarian
- Service and support spaces for both the researcher and for the animals
- Sophisticated security systems to protect the staff and the animals

These factors have become major considerations and objectives in the planning and design of animal facilities and have a significant impact and influence on systems design, construction, and operations costs.

COMMENTS

1. The author does support the use of animals for biomedical research. However, as an architect, scientist, and consumer, that support is conditioned by the belief that the facilities provided for the laboratory animals and the research protocols developed be as humane and sensitive to the life form used as is possible.

2. The information in this section reflects the experience of many individuals and agencies concerned with this matter to ensure that the most humane facilities are designed and provided for animals involved in research experimentation.

3. Sources of information include publications from the American College of Laboratory Animal Medicine (ACLAM), American Association for Accreditation of Laboratory Animal Care (AAALAC), National Institutes of Health (NIH), U.S. Department of Agriculture (USDA), Federal Rules and Regulations, Scientists Center for Animal Welfare (SCAW), Canadian Federa-

tion of Humane Societies, and others (see also Appendix C).

4. The information contained in several of the tables in this section have been extracted and summarized from the *Guide for the Care and Use of Laboratory Animals*, NIH Publication 86-23, Revised 1985. This publication has become one of the primary resources and references for planning animal facilities. It is available from NIH.

5. Another area of legitimate scientific activity is the research conducted solely for the benefit of animal health and husbandry, including farm animals and animals classified as pets.

6. Research in veterinary medicine has also made significant strides in reducing animal suffering and improving their life and health. If left unchecked, many animal diseases could cause serious problems for animals and humans.

ANIMAL CARE AND USE COMMITTEES

Every institution using animals for research purposes must establish an Animal Care and Use Committee (ACUC). This requirement has been established by law in amendments to the Animal and Welfare Act, December 1985. The following statement by William C. Stewart, senior staff veterinarian of the Animal and Plant Health Inspection Service, U.S. Department of Agriculture, summarizes the basic responsibilities of an ACUC: "The essential functions of an ACUC are to review and assess protocols and investigative personnel, to conduct unannounced, semi-annual inspections of all sites of the research facility, and to support and advise the administration and the attending veterinarian on all issues of an animal care nature."

The members of the ACUC must be included as participants of the animal facilities planning team to interact with the facilities manager, the architect, and the engineer. The ACUC is key to assist with the interpretation of the research goals, objectives, and protocols, and in developing and establishing the proper facilities planning criteria during the programming phase. Their participation will ensure the success of the planning endeavor and the facility as well.

GOVERNING LAWS and REGULATIONS

Animal facilities *must* be planned, designed, operated, and maintained in accordance with the *Guide for the Care and Use of Laboratory Animals*, NIH Publication 86-23; the Animal Welfare Act (PL 89-544, as amended by 91-579; and PL 94-279); and other applicable federal, state, and local laws regulations and policies. The statement "and other applicable federal, state, and local laws regulations and policies" is extremely broad. However, this only emphasizes the complexity and detail that must be addressed in planning animal facilities.

The statement "and other applicable federal, state, and local laws regulations and policies" is almost a cop-out. The author has not researched all laws and regulations pertaining to animal facilities. The list of publications, agencies, and associations in Appendix C are excellent sources. Local animal humane societies can be very helpful. The following selective list highlights several sources that can provide information and data directly or provide additional sources (addresses are listed in Appendix C).

- American Association for Accreditation of Laboratory Animal Care (AAALAC)
- American Association for Laboratory Animal Science (AALAS)
- American College of Laboratory Animal Medicine (ACLAM)
- American Veterinary Medical Association (AVMA)
- Institute of Laboratory Animal Resources (ILAR)
- Animal Welfare Information Center (AWIC) of the National Agricultural Library (NAL)
- National Association for Biomedical Research (Foundation for Biomedical Research)
- Scientists' Center for Animal Welfare (SCAW)

GENERIC PLANNING CRITERIA

Many animal facilities (for small animals such as mice, rats, hamsters, rabbits, etc.) are planned and integrated as part of the total research facility. The usual location selected for the animal facility is in the basement or top floor of the laboratory building. Unfortunately, in many facilities, the smells and odors associated with the animals, permeates the entire building. This is perhaps due to the building system's inability to perform as designed and provide the HVAC separation of functions and activities as designed and anticipated.

This does not imply that all animal facilities should be located in separate facilities, whether attached or detached, from the research laboratory facility. It does underscore, however, the unique and difficult design problems that are associated with animal facility functions and activities. Many of the spaces required in animal facilities are not very similar or compatible with spaces usually part of the research laboratories. However, close examination indicates that the module for a typical laboratory work area is very similar to the animal room for small animals. Consideration should be given during the programming phase to applying the same laboratory module to the module for the animal facilities. This is particularly important if the animal facility is within the same building as the laboratory facilities.

The typical laboratory module of 12′ × 24′ (288 nsf) may be somewhat larger than the animal rooms suggested by some authorities. However, when the proposed new rules and regulations are considered, the trend is to provide more space for each animal species. The use of ventilated cage rack systems is increasing. These particular animal cage racks are larger than the nonventilated type. The 12′ × 24′ module is adaptable for use as an animal holding room.

Research laboratory work space is also required as part of the animal facility. There are many reasons not to transport animals to other areas of the research facility (e.g., cross contamination, trauma for the animals, difficulty in containing odors, etc.). The basic laboratory module can then be applied as the basic building block for the animal facilities as well. This standardization and application of the same space modules permits efficient and economical integration of animal facilities within the framework of the total research facility. Structural elements (columns) should not appear in the middle of rooms and spaces.

COMMENTS

1. It should be noted that this book focuses on the planning and design of facilities for small animals. Facilities for large animals, such as dogs, sheep, pigs, cattle,

horses, and so on, require special (different) spaces and are not discussed. Nonhuman primates are another special category and would require a separate volume devoted exclusively to these species. The federal government is revising and updating the current rules applied to the use of nonhuman primates in research.

2. Significant changes are anticipated in the requirements for primate facilities. See the Department of Agriculture, Animal and Plant Inspection Service, FR-9-CFR-Part 3, *Animal Welfare Rules*, August 15, 1990, for further information.

3. There is some divergence of opinion at medical centers as to whether experimentation involving animals should be done in the researchers' laboratory (requiring transport of the animal to the laboratory) or confined within the animal facilities.

4. Some institutions do not permit animals to remain overnight in the laboratory and require that they be returned to the animal facilities at the end of the day. Many researchers object that such policies are restrictive. Certain experiments may require several days of work with the animals and that they should not be moved. In some instances the animal cannot be moved because of the physical nature of the experiment, monitoring devices used, and so on. Prohibiting the use of animals in the researchers' laboratory (outside the animal facility) implies that some duplication may have to be accomplished in facilities and equipment.

The programming phase provides the opportunity to develop criteria that can be translated into generic animal spaces and associated laboratories, and to provide flexible shared-use service and support spaces. A significant advantage to accrue from the use of generic or modular spaces is standardization of the structural and building systems, resulting in economies of design and reduction in overall facility costs. Another advantage is the integration of animal housing, laboratories, administration, and service and support spaces into a functional and aesthetically pleasing facility. The modular concept can permit a measure of design alternatives to accommodate specialized activities, and to maintain sanitation and control of vermin, insects, and so on, within the facility.

Special requirements for specific projects should be identified during the detailed programming phases. The generic spaces then would be modified to accommodate the specific requirements within the design capabilities of the facility. Accessibility requirements to accommodate disabled staff researchers may modify generic and other space configurations.

The services corridor concept has several advantages for animal facilities. It may be adapted to accommodate a double corridor or "clean and dirty corridor" scheme. The service corridor may be used as the dirty corridor. Interstitial space may be adaptable for animal facilities. Animal facilities integrated within the research building may not require a different services system concept. The building systems for the animal facilities must be separate from other functions and activities proposed for the building.

MECHANICAL SYSTEMS

Mechanical systems should be designed to accommodate different environmental requirements for each animal species expected to be housed in the facility. Building systems *must* be designed for continuous 24-hour operations, with controls to operate at reduced levels. Emergency power *must* be provided to maintain the operations of building systems in the event of a power outage. Redundant mechanical and electrical systems *must* be provided in all animal holding areas. These spaces require air in sufficient quantity, quality, and flow and must be controlled to prevent cross contamination among other animals and humans.

Air distribution and diffusion devices for animal rooms should be designed to minimize temperature differentials within the space and avoid mixing air that has been in contact with the animals. The objective is to provide a relatively draft-free environment. Temperature and relative humidity of the animal facility should be maintained at 72°F (dry bulb), 50% RH. The temperature and relative humidity of animal holding spaces should be maintained within a quadrangle established by the four points of a standard psychometric chart:

- 72°F dry bulb (DB) and 63°F wet bulb (WB)
- 72°F DB and 60°F WB
- 78°F DB and 63°F WB
- 78°F DB and 68°F WB

Refer to the *Brochure on Psychrometry* of the American Society of Heating, Refrigerating, and Air-Conditioning Engineers (ASHRAE) for additional data.

General space temperature and humidity criteria for common laboratory animals is listed in Table 5.1. Refer to the National Institutes of Health, *Guide for the Care and Use of Laboratory Animals* (NIH-8623) and *Institutional Administrator's Manual for Laboratory Animal Care and Use* (NIH-88-2959). Refer also to Appendix C for additional information and data sources.

Temperature, humidity, and pressure indicating and recording devices, audio and visual warning systems to indicate abnormal conditions, and control devices for each animal room, including holding, quarantine, feed storage, surgery, recovery, and carcass holding must be provided to monitor the environment of the spaces. The instrumentation should be located in an area that is continually staffed and occupied. The system should be interconnected to the main security office. It must also be on the emergency power system.

RELATIVE AIRFLOW AND PRESSURE CONSIDERATIONS

Control of the airflow supply to the animal rooms should be managed by moving the air through a series of pressure gradients from the clean areas to the dirty areas of the facility. Building systems design must provide redundant supply air and exhaust air systems with redundant duct systems and filter banks to assure continuous service and operations in the event of the loss of outside electrical power. Supply and exhaust fans should be interlocked to operate in unison. Supply air fans

TABLE 5.1 Space Temperature and Humidity Criteria

| Animal | RH (%) | Dry-Bulb Temperature | |
		°C	°F
Mouse	40–70	18–26	64.4–78.8
Rat	40–70	18–26	64.4–78.8
Hamster	40–70	18–26	64.4–78.8
Guinea pig	40–70	18–26	64.4–78.8
Rabbit	40–60	16–21	60.8–69.8
Cat	30–70	18–29	64.4–84.2

should be slaved to the exhaust air fans to maintain a continuous positive air supply and exhaust, and to maintain the designed and required airflow patterns.

Some sources suggest that air may be recirculated if it is filtered with HEPA and charcoal filters. Most authorities recommend against recirculating *any* air from the animal facilities. The risk of contaminated air from a saturated or loaded filter being recirculated and creating severe consequences for the animals and human occupants is not worth the presumed savings in building systems design, energy, or operations. Airflow should be directed from clean to dirty areas. The airflow should be controlled with dampers to prevent reversal or backflow. A minimum airflow of 95 to 115 cfm from clean to dirty spaces should maintain a stable negative pressure relative to animal rooms.

Animal room exhausts should be sidewall type, mounted near the floor in the corners of the room. Filters must be installed in the exhaust ducts to capture animal hair, dander, and other airborne solids from being exhausted to the exterior. Install airflow monitoring and control devices in the supply and exhaust ducts to synchronize and maintain the proper supply and exhaust air quantities that are required for each animal room. Balancing dampers and flow measuring and control devices should be installed on all air supply and exhaust ducts to monitor the status of the duct airflow and pressure.

Room pressure differentials may be an important consideration in animal quarantine holding areas for animals being introduced into the facility. Animals may have to be separated to avoid interspecies disease transmission or because of their source or microbiological status. Animals may have to be isolated from others because of the requirements and protocols of the research project, diagnosis of physiological status, treatment, and control or surveillance, because of a suspicion of some problem or disease.

SUPPLY AIR CONSIDERATIONS

The supply air equipment for the system should be designed to provide a sufficient volume of 100% outside air for adequate ventilation, temperature, and humidity control of the animal rooms. The outside air may have to be treated (filtered, scrubbed, tempered, etc.) based on the local or regional environmental and seasonal conditions.

Supply air quantities should be based on estimated or actual heat loads, minimum dilution and ventilation requirements, and makeup air for exhaust systems. Air changes may range between 12 to 14 and 16 to 18 per hour (or more). Additional fan capacity should be considered to maintain the proper airflow and pressure in the exhaust duct system to overcome the pressure drop that may occur when additional filters may be required or if filters become clogged. Maintenance and service program protocols *must* be followed with due diligence. Detailed building systems maintenance and service *must* be maintained.

Supply air for animal areas should be directed through a prefilter bank, including a 95% A.D./NBS filter at the central air supply intake unit. Sufficient space should be provided in the duct run to permit the addition of a charcoal filter upstream from the 95% A.D./NBS filter, if required. Specific filtration criteria are based on animal species occupancy. Animal cooling Btu load may be calculated on the basis of 45 to 55 Btu and to 75 to 90 Btu per net square foot of animal room space or actual Btu load provided, whichever may be the larger figure and depending on the animal species.

Animal holding facilities require special attention to the air quality provided and control of the airflow to prevent cross-contamination between individual spaces and other species. Generally, unless there are specific requirements, animal rooms should be maintained at negative pressure relative to the clean spaces and clean corridors. However, in certain instances, the relative pressure may have to be maintained at equal or slightly positive pressure to prevent contamination from being carried into the animal room from adjoining spaces.

Air distribution devices should be carefully planned and located within a modular framework. This permits a measure of flexible planning (location of cage racks, casework, equipment, etc.) within the space while maintaining the desired air movement for maximum comfort of the animals. Most animal species are very sensitive to drafts and airflow. All utilities and services, including main and branch duct layouts, pipes and conduit runs, and the like, should be carefully planned and organized in a logical and orderly pattern. This will facilitate renovations as they occur.

REDUNDANT SYSTEMS

Redundant air supply and exhaust systems, and filter banks must be provided to assure continuous service and operation in the animal facility. Supply and exhaust fans must be interlocked to act in unison to provide continuous positive supply and exhaust to maintain stipulated airflow patterns. If the animal facility is part of the research laboratory complex, a separate emergency power system is required to maintain system operations during power interruptions or failures.

Air supply and exhaust systems must provide the necessary isolation capability without compromising the integrity of an area barrier system. This facilitates decontamination procedures in any animal room while adjacent rooms remain in use. Controls for isolation dampers should be easily accessible from outside the animal room. Individual systems control to each animal room is critical. All other utilities, services, shutoff valves, and so on, must be clearly marked and labeled to permit easy and accurate identification and access during renovations. This is especially important in the event of an emergency. The utilities services concept should not prevent the logical and convenient arrangement of services to permit easy and safe access for any purpose.

ACOUSTICAL CONSIDERATIONS

The normal movement of cage racks, cages, feeding trays, and so on, results in metal-to-metal contact, producing many of the irritating noises in the spaces. These loud, sharp noises can be extremely damaging to animals, both psychologically and physiologically. There is more than enough trauma associated with being caged without the introduction of additional sources.

The necessity to use hot water to clean spaces and to provide materials resistant to a wide variety of chemicals and surfaces that withstand abusive treatment requires that interior finishes be hard, rigid, smooth, and chemically resistant. This environment totally negates chances to reduce sound reverberation time within a space. The hard surfaces reflect virtually all the sound energy that strikes the surface. As the reflected sound waves cross each other, the resultant sound may be increased by several times the source energy level. Almost all of the acoustical materials available are soft and porous. Such materials absorb moisture and water, losing their acoustical properties. The moist materials also become ideal environments for the growth of bacteria, fungi, and other organisms.

What is the solution? At this time, virtually nothing can be done until materials with both acoustical properties *and* the desired resistance to water, cleaning, chemicals, and so on, become available. Noise control usually becomes an administrative and operational protocol relative to the movement of cages and use of cleaning equipment and therefore becomes a function of the care and thoughtfulness of the personnel in the execution of their daily chores.

Heavy, dense masonry partitions, if extended to the underside of the structural slab and sealed at all floor, wall, and ceiling joints, will minimize sound transmission between spaces. This is particularly important in animal facilities with large populations of dogs and nonhuman primates, to contain the loud choruses of animals barking.

GENERAL ANIMAL ROOM CRITERIA

General criteria for animal room facilities are listed below. All floor, wall, and ceiling penetrations, including outlet boxes, light switch boxes, and so on, must be sealed to prevent insect and vermin infestation and air leakage. All systems must be designed for 24-hour operations.

- Air supply filtered to remove dust and exhaust air filtered to remove hair and dander, room at negative pressure relative to corridor, nonanimal, and nonlaboratory spaces (offices, etc.).
- Cage rack bumpers to protect wall finishes and reduce equipment noise; reinforced wall mounted.
- Ceiling height at 9'-0" minimum; Keene's cement or gypsum board sealed, with sealed joints and epoxy paint finish to withstand hot water washdown.
- Corridors at 8'-0" clear minimum.
- Day/night automatic lighting controls with manual override, timers, and alarm systems.
- Doors minimum 3'-6" wide with seals, glass panel or sidelight, self-closing, and system to cover glass from light in corridor.

- Floor loading at 125 to 150 psf minimum.
- Individual room thermostat and humidity controls; temperature and humidity will depend on animal species to be housed in each animal room; include sensors to monitor temperature, humidity, and room pressure; sensors and alarms should be connected to control panel centrally located in the animal facility to be monitored by the staff on continuous duty and by the institution's main security office.
- Knock-out panels (minimum of two per animal room) at ceiling for flexible duct connections to accommodate ventilated animal cages; area required varies with species and size of cage racks.
- Lighting fixtures should be waterproof, surface or pendant type; recessed type may be difficult to seal against infiltration of insects and vermin, provide controls for diurnal lighting cycle.
- Lighting illumination levels for small animals range between 60 to 80 fc, depending on the species.
- Masonry partitions in animal holding rooms, cage wash areas, shipping and receiving, feed process and storage, surgery, preparation, and recovery, with sealed troweled epoxy finish to withstand hot water washdown.
- Minimum of two 120-V outlets, waterproof, with ground-fault interrupters (GFIs).
- Noise level controlled at 65 to 75 dB maximum.
- Seamless floor (sheet vinyl or sealed concrete with troweled epoxy finish to withstand hot water washdown), integral base.
- Smoke and flame detectors and alarms.
- Standard hose bib with threaded hose connection.
- Two-way intercom system between offices, all animal rooms, and work areas, with privacy switches at speakers.
- 6"-diameter-minimum floor drain with strainer, solids trap, disposal unit, and threaded cover, and 6"-diameter-minimum drain pipe, slope floor to drain; trap installed to prevent backflow into room. Floor drains not required for rodent rooms (can wet vacuum or mop).
- 36"- to 37"-high stainless steel work counter and frame, 6' long, 30" deep, with integral deep double utility sink, with hot and cold water, plastic faucet, two adjustable stainless

steel wall shelves above work counter, 15″ deep × 72″ long, in each animal holding room.

GENERAL FINISHES

Wall, floor, and ceiling finishes in the animal facility areas, including animal holding rooms, surgery, preparation, recovery, necropsy, feed process and storage, and shipping and receiving, should be smooth, hard, impervious, seamless, and capable of withstanding frequent hot water or steam wash downs. Cleaning solutions containing detergents are used for routine cleaning. Special solutions and other chemicals are used in cleaning for decontamination purposes. The finishes should also be resistant to acids, alkalis, petroleum products (oil, grease, etc.), and solvents. Holding and storage tanks may be required for fluids washed down from animal rooms. This waste may have to be treated or processed before release into the sanitary sewer system. Other classifications of waste may have to be removed and disposed of by other methods (e.g., tank trucks, etc.).

- Floors should be concrete, trowel, or brush finished with specified sealers and hardeners in animal rooms and cage wash and feed storage areas.
- Seamless vinyl (chemical or thermal welded seams) is satisfactory for other areas, including laboratories and service and support spaces. Floors slabs in multistory animal facilities should be constructed with waterproof membrane underlayment.
- Masonry (concrete) blocks are perhaps the most durable and effective material to be used for partitions in animal rooms and cage wash and feed storage areas. Blocks should be solid or filled to prevent infiltration of insects or vermin. Block face should be sealed and smooth epoxy finish applied. Base should be integral with the floor and wall, forming an impervious jointless finish.
- Ceilings should be constructed from hard and impervious materials. Waterproofed gypsum board with sealed joints and epoxy finish, and hard plaster or Keene's cement may also be used. Exposed concrete (underside of structural

slab) is also satisfactory if the finish is smooth. Exposed pipes and fixtures are not acceptable because they provide a surface for dust accumulation, and other problems.

WASTE MANAGEMENT

Waste solutions from the cage wash areas (machines and steam cleaners) must not drain directly into the sanitary sewer system. All fluid wastes from the animal spaces must be directed to holding tanks for processing. Processing may include pH balancing, dilution of various chemicals (acids, etc.), and processing with heat or other chemicals to render the waste biologically safe before release into the sanitary system. Some of the fluid waste may have to be removed physically and transported to designated disposal sites, or be incinerated.

Vented-hood bedding disposal cabinets should be used to contain the dust and aerosolized waste particles created when cleaning and emptying animal cages and trays. The soiled bedding materials are placed directly into a storage container that can be autoclaved, if required, and disposed of safely and properly, minimizing hazards to personnel.

Use of hazardous materials (biologic, radioactive, etc.) with animals adds an additional level of concern. The hazardous substances when mixed with food can become aerosolized and ingested by other animals or personnel. When mixed with food, the hazardous substances can be passed in animal urine or feces and contaminate the bedding. Soiled bedding must be handled and disposed of properly. Injecting the animal may eliminate the former problem but does not change the latter problem.

Bedding and animal waste may have to be autoclaved prior to disposal. If the animals are used in research involving radioactive materials, the waste may have to be held until half-life decay is within safe limits (if low-level or short-half-life isotopes are used). Other radioactive waste may have to be disposed of in accordance with regulations from the U.S. Nuclear Regulatory Commission (NRC), National Council on Radiation Protection and Measurement (NCRP), Department of Energy (DOE), and Department of Transportation (DOT). Many institutions contract with licensed waste management firms to manage and dispose of hazardous waste materials. The penalties and fines are becoming more severe for violations regarding the processing, handling, and disposal of hazardous waste materials. Penalties can include loss of grant monies and prison terms for the individual researcher and administrative personnel.

SPACE CONSIDERATIONS

Table 5.2 is summarized from the *Guide for the Care and Use of Laboratory Animals*, NIH Publication 86-23, Revised 1985. *It is emphasized that the recommendations for the space (volume) allocated each species is a minimum figure.* Recent studies indicate that both height and area are important factors in the welfare of the animals. The objective is to provide as much space as practical.

In their natural habitat, animals frequently stand to survey their surroundings. This ability is equally important in captivity. It is suggested that the minimum floor area be increased between 25 and 50%, and height between 50 and 100%. Although data are not included, space for large animals (cats, dogs, pigs, ducks, etc.), particularly nonhuman primates, should be increased accordingly.

ANIMAL HOUSING SYSTEMS

As indicated in Table 5.2, the cages used to house animals have increased in size over time. Some cage racks have increased in size; others are similar in size but hold fewer cages and animals. Cage rack systems supported or hung from walls are generally not recommended. They are difficult to place on the wail or remove. After a period of time wall hanger systems begin to fail. The most efficient system appears to be cage racks on wheels. The wheels should be at least 6″ in diameter to make transport and traveling over thresholds relatively easy. Wheels should be of durable composition materials to minimize noise when rolling. Materials for the racks should be light, noncorrosive, and easily cleaned.

Most cage racks for small animals vary in size from 24″ deep × 36″ wide × 60″ high to 32″ deep × 60″ wide × 72″ high. Adequate bumpers should be placed on the walls in all areas to receive the cage racks. Wheel locks should be provided to prevent the racks from rolling. Wheel stops may be to be mounted on the floors in animal rooms; however, they can become

TABLE 5.2 Space Recommendations: Small Laboratory Animals

Animals	Weight (g)	Type of Housing	Floor Area per Animal		Height	
			in.^{2}	cm^2	in.	cm
Mice	<10	Cage	6.0	38.71	5	12.70
	10–15	Cage	8.0	51.62	5	12.70
	15–25	Cage	12.0	77.42	5	12.70
	<25	Cage	15.0	96.78	5	12.70
Rats	<100	Cage	17.0	109.68	7	17.78
	100–200	Cage	23.0	148.40	7	17.78
	200–300	Cage	29.0	187.11	7	17.78
	300–400	Cage	40.0	258.08	7	17.78
	400–500	Cage	60.0	387.12	7	17.78
	>500	Cage	70.0	451.64	7	17.78
Hamsters	<60	Cage	10.0	64.52	6	15.24
	60–80	Cage	13.0	83.88	6	15.24
	80–100	Cage	16.0	103.23	6	15.24
	>100	Cage	19.0	122.59	6	15.24
Guinea pigs	<350	Cage	60.0	387.12	7	17.78
	>350	Cage	101.0	651.65	7	17.78
	Kg		ft^2	m^2		
Rabbits	<2	Cage	1.5	0.14	14	35.56
	2–4	Cage	3.0	0.28	14	35.56
	4–5.4	Cage	4.0	0.37	14	35.56
	5.4	Cage	5.0	0.46	14	35.56

obstacles when moving cage racks, create a tripping hazard and eventually working loose no matter what method is used to anchor them to the floor.

Ventilated cages are being used more frequently. Since they are in essence individual environments, more than one species may be housed in the same animal room. They may contribute to energy savings by reducing the number of air changes required in animal rooms. They may also provide a higher-quality environment for the animals because of the immediate removal of ammonia fumes from the cages. These fumes and other gases can cause metabolic and physiological problems for the animals and produce faulty experimental results. Careful consideration must be given to the various animal housing systems to meet the program criteria and research protocols.

There is considerable difference of opinion regarding the proper number of air changes per hour that should be provided for animal rooms. Some sources state that a higher number of air changes are energy inefficient and costly and do not contribute significantly to improving the animal room environment. Reducing air changes certainly will provide energy cost savings but may compound and create other problems, negating the presumed energy cost savings. Experience tends to support the higher rate of air changes per hour because of all the variables involved, including the lack of adequate and frequent maintenance to the building and animal facility air supply and exhaust systems. The lack of proper maintenance of the systems is usually cited as the primary reason to provide the higher air change rates.

TRANSGENIC FACILITY SYSTEMS

Recent developments using animals as carriers of human genes has produced experimental techniques to model various human characteristics for medical purposes. The animals used have become accurate models for a wide range of gene research. Human genes are injected into the animals to produce the desired effect. These animals transmit the gene characteristics to their offspring, producing a unique *transgenic* line of animals. The animals are, however, subject to cross-contamination and the usual maladies that may infect any breed. Special microisolator cage systems have been developed to house these animals. The cage systems provide a high level of protection and permit the animal to be transported to other laboratory areas for research and experimentation.

The microisolator cage provides a barrier at the cage level, protecting the animal from contamination. The cage rack provides HEPA-filtered air to the cages, a self-watering feature, and other attributes. The spent air may be emitted into the cage room and exhausted or connected to a duct for exhaust directly to the exterior. The bedding may be changed every 2 to 3 weeks to reduce the ammonia buildup from animal waste. The animal is transferred to another sterilized microisolator cage in a clean room or biosafety cabinet environment. The animal may be exposed in a biosafety cabinet or worked on in a class 100 special procedures room.

A clean/soiled double-corridor concept may not be very cost-effective. The new microisolator animal cage technology does not require a separate, and double-corridor animal facility concept. The basic plan, may, however, use a clean corridor to restrict access by investigators and others to animal holding areas, (clean rooms, etc.) and procedure rooms (preparation, surgery, recovery, etc.) for work on the animals (inject gene material, perform surgery, etc.). The procedure must be accomplished on a "survival" basis. Investigators must use sterile protocols before surgery (dress, scrub, etc.). New regulations require procedures that are equal to or more restrictive than human surgical procedures.

Cage-rack processing may use tunnel wash and similar systems. (In cage sterilization, the cage and its contents, including bedding, are terminal sterilized and assembled on racks for reuse.) Support and service areas (feed, bedding, waste holding, etc.) can be located convenient to the animal holding and procedure rooms. The system allows a measure of flexibility relative to arrangement of the required facilities. Entry is generally through an isolation double-room plan to permit changing into clean clothes before entering the animal areas. Each room should be designed for conversion to other activities in the future, as functions may change. Security and access to the animal facilities must be controlled. Contamination of the transgenic colony could effectively destroy the colony. The American Association for Accreditation of Laboratory Animal Care (AAALAC) regulations must be followed. Although these regulations are voluntary, nonconformance can result in loss of funding or other penalties.

ILLUMINATION LEVELS

Illumination levels for animal rooms are not known precisely. There are indications for certain species of animals that the higher light levels traditionally provided (75 to 100 fc) may cause retinal damage in some species (albino rats, etc.). Table 3.1 indicates a range between 60 and 80 fc. These figures should be qualified to apply generally to service and support areas in the facility. Lighting levels (at the floor) between 30 and 50 fc are perhaps more acceptable in animal holding areas. It may be prudent to provide multilevel lighting to provide the additional brightness required when cleaning or decontaminating an animal room after the cages have been moved to another room.

FEED AND BEDDING

Feed and clean bedding materials should be stored on racks off the floor. All cracks, openings, and so on, must be sealed to prevent penetration of insects and vermin. Doors should be provided with seals. Air changes should be between 12 and 14 per hour. Temperature and humidity should be controlled at 70°F (±2°F) and 30 to 50% RH. Supply air registers should be located high (ceiling) and return air vents located close to the floor to create a downflow air movement. In most animal spaces, air spaces should flow in this manner. Adequate cold storage (refrigerators and freezers) must be provided for such food perishables as meats, vegetables, and fruits.

Feed mixing and grinding equipment may be required to prepare special diets for certain research protocols. An autoclave may also be required to sterilize diets for the same special purposes. Certain diets may be prepared prior to use and may require refrigeration or freezing. A microwave or electric oven may also be required to thaw frozen diets or prepare certain diets.

SHARED USE SPACES

One of the primary objectives of the design of any research facility is to provide a reasonable level of flexibility in the building systems to accommodate changes in programs without incurring excessive costs. Animal facilities may specialized to the degree that flexibility for accommodating changes may appear to be limited. Cage wash areas, feed processing and storage, and animal rooms may not require frequent changes. However, many of the service and support spaces, including laboratories may require change from time to time to accommodate new programs. A space system based on the module and services system developed for the research laboratories can provide the same relative level of flexibility for the animal facilities.

The following lists of shared-use rooms and spaces and animal facility specific spaces illustrate this potential. Virtually all the spaces listed can be accommodated within the proposed 12' × 24' module or multiples of the module.

Administrative Areas

- Coffee bar
- Conference/seminar room

- Copy/work areas
- Files/records/supply storage facilities
- Mail/work area
- Reception/waiting room
- Researchers' offices
- Secretarial/clerical areas
- Security/safety office
- Technicians' workstations
- Veterinarian offices

Service and Support Areas

- Controlled temperature
- Biosafety levels 2, 3, 4
- Electron microscope
- General storage
- Glassware processing
- Hazardous spill equipment
- Hazardous waste/autoclaving
- Instrument and equipment
- Media preparation
- Photography laboratory
- Preparation and holding
- Waste marshaling/processing

ANIMAL FACILITY SPECIFIC SPACES

The general animal room criteria listed earlier also apply to the following spaces.

1. *Animal Clinic Facilities* (treatment, holding, observation, recovery). To perform minor procedures or to treat animals as required. This facility may not be required if the animals are smaller than rabbits. However, the space may also be used for physiological monitoring. Should be included if using dogs or cats and larger animals. Stainless steel work counter with double sink, hot and cold water, distilled water, plastic faucets, stainless steel base and wall storage cabinets, one-third work counters at 36″ standing height, and one-third at 30″ sitting height with knee-hole spaces, and one-third "free" wall space for animal cage racks and equipment, 6′-wide biological safety cabinet (class II, type B2, 100% exhaust), miscellaneous stainless steel instrument and utility carts, mobile monitoring equipment, refrigerator, scale, autoclave, mobile light stand, adjustable stool(s) with casters, portable oxygen tank, and trash containers for various classes of waste.

2. *Animal Quarantine and Holding Facility* (similar to the modular animal holding rooms or multipurpose animal rooms). Primarily to hold new animals to determine if they may be integrated with existing animals, and observation of animals suspected of having health or other problems. HVAC systems must provide positive isolation from all spaces in the facility. Equipped similar to space 1 above.

3. *Cage Washing, Processing, Holding, Staging, and Repair.* Receiving and holding area for dirty cages, bedding removal from cages, vented-hood bedding disposal cabinets, 36″-high stainless steel work counters with double sink, hot and cold water, plastic faucets, base and wall storage cabinets, 30″-high stainless steel mobile work tables, utility carts, cage wash and glass wash machines, trash containers, autoclaves, storage for bedding holding bags and boxes, hose bib, hose wheel rack, trash containers for various classes of waste, floor drain with solids strainer and trap, floor, all area walls and ceiling have impervious epoxy finishes, and partitions should be masonry filled or solid, with integral base. Cage washing area would be physically part of the dirty cage receiving area, automatic cage washers (throughput to clean cage area), hot water and steam cleaning cage-rack booth or room with exhaust vent, floor drain, solids strainer, trap, wash water temperature 180°F minimum, canopy exhaust hood over doors to cage wash machines. Clean cage marshaling area at output side of cage washers, separate from dirty cage receiving area, 36″-high stainless steel work counters with double sink, hot and cold water, plastic faucets, base and wall storage cabinets, 30″-high stainless steel mobile work tables and utility carts, minor cage rack repair work area.

4. *Diet Preparation* (prepare daily and special diets). "Mini" feed processing, mixing, and storage facility. Air should flow in downflow direction to protect personnel from aerosolized particles produced from the feed products. Refrigerator and freezer, scales, mixer, grinder, feed storage racks and bins, 36″-high work counter with double sink, hot and cold water, plastic faucets, base and wall storage cabinets, 30″-high stainless steel mobile work tables and utility carts, autoclave, adjustable stool with casters, and trash containers for various classes of waste.

5. *Film Processing, and Reading, and Film Files.* If dry processor used, may be in viewing area (depends on volume of procedures). If wet processor, should be separate room for film processing and for film viewing. Film processor, silver recovery unit, film files, film view boxes or automated film illuminators, developer tanks, 36"-high stainless steel work counters with double sink, hot and cold water, plastic faucets, mixing valves, base and wall storage cabinets, 30"-sitting-height work counter with knee-hole spaces (film view boxes above), utility cart, adjustable stool(s) with casters, and trash containers.

6. *Multipurpose Animal Rooms* (same generic size laboratory module, single or multiples). Mobile cage racks for small animals, wall-mounted cage rack bumpers, 36"-high stainless steel work counter with double sink, hot and cold water, stainless steel adjustable shelves above, distilled water, plastic faucets, hose bib (hose should not be stored in animal room), ceiling knock-out panels for duct connections to ventilated animal cages, 6"-diameter-minimum floor drain with solids strainer (large trap with threaded cover, 6"-diameter-minimum waste line).

7. *Necropsy* (similar to an autopsy facility). Stainless steel work counter with double sink, hot and cold water, distilled water, plastic faucets, stainless steel base and wall storage cabinets, stainless steel work tables (30" and 36" high, tissue grinders, tissue and carcass storage (refrigerator and freezer), 6'-wide chemical fume with corrosives and solvents vented storage cabinets under hood, 6'-wide biological safety cabinet (class II, type B2, 100% exhaust), utility carts, wall-mounted x-ray film view box, mobile light stand, adjustable stool(s) with casters, tissue processing and staining work area, and trash containers for various classes of waste.

8. *Radio/Fluorographic Facility.* Consideration must be given to machine point loads: can be as much as 1500 psf, and ceiling-mounted equipment may weigh as much as 1000 lb. Floor cable tray or trench may be required. It is important to know the exact machine to be used before planning services and space. Radio/fluoro machine space, imaging table, 36"-high work counter with sink, base and wall storage cabinets, control booth, protective apron and gloves storage racks, wall-mounted x-ray film view box, mobile transparent x-ray radiation shield, utility cart, mobile light stand, adjustable stool with casters, trash containers, transformer space (may be suspended from ceiling), radiation shielding in walls. Storage cart or cabinet with safety shielding items (gloves, glasses, goggles, collars, body part shields, full face shield, etc.) should be located outside the machine room.

9. *Shipping/Receiving Area* (loading dock facility). If the animal facility is planned as part of the research laboratory facility, the loading dock area may have to be "separated" from other building loading dock facilities. Animal feed, bedding, and waste products should not be mixed with other materials (biologics, supplies, etc.) received at the loading dock. The central security office may be located in this area. Protected loading dock to accommodate tractor-trailer delivery trucks, dock leveler, receiving and storage for supplies and equipment, autoclaves, separate areas for feed and bedding storage, dock scale, refrigerator and freezer (walk-in and chest type), trash dumpster(s), holding areas for hazardous waste materials, forklift equipment, hand trucks, delivery vehicle parking, office and work areas for shipping and receiving personnel, gas cylinder distribution and storage area (a separate outside facility may be required for hazardous gas cylinder storage).

10. *Small Animal Surgery* (dedicated space not required for performing surgery on rodents; however, such surgery must be performed using aseptic procedures. The general practice in medical centers is to arrange sit-down workstations with double-headed microscopes for residents and surgeons to practice microsurgery techniques). Stainless steel adjustable operating/work table, 36"-high stainless steel work counter with double sink, hot and cold water, distilled water, plastic faucets, stainless steel base and wall storage cabinets, overhead single surgery light, instrument, supply and utility carts, 6'-wide biological safety cabinet (class II, type B2, 100% exhaust), wall-mounted x-ray film view box, mobile light stand, explosion-proof fixtures, outlets and switches, adjustable stool(s) with casters, portable oxygen tanks or central system, anesthesia gas cylinders, trash containers for various classes of waste, positive pressure downflow exhaust to remove anesthesia gases. Preparation (substerile) area may be part of the surgery area or planned as a separate space directly accessible from the surgery area: scrub sinks, autoclave, instrument and supplies storage cabinets, pharmaceuticals security cabinet, linens, packs, preparation work space with 36"-high stainless steel work counter with double sink, hot and cold water, distilled water, plastic faucets, stainless steel base and wall storage cabinets, soiled linens holding, and trash containers for various classes of waste.

11. *Staff and Animal Caretaker Facilities* [lockers, change areas, decontamination, toilets and showers (male and female), break and rest areas). It is becoming a requirement (and may be a necessity for certain research protocols employing hazardous reagents) that all personnel entering and working in the animal facility enter the change area, remove street clothing, and dress in protective clothing. The process is reversed when leaving the facility, including showering before leaving in street clothing. Should be arranged functionally so that all personnel entering the animal facility working areas must pass through this area. The break and rest area should be a separate space with natural light (windows), if possible.

WATER SUPPLIES

The animals must be provided with an adequate, fresh, and safe potable water supply. The water should be analyzed and tested for pH content, minerals (hardness), and microbial and chemical contamination. Equipment may be required to treat the water to eliminate the contaminants. Water of a specified purity or other chemical content depends on the specific research protocol. The facilities and equipment for testing, analyzing, and treating the water, as required, may be developed as part of the specific functional laboratory program elements.

VERMIN AND INSECT CONTROL

The design details for the construction of the facility (floor, wall, ceiling systems; building systems; etc.) can have a significant impact on vermin and insect control. Hollow materials, spaces between walls and floors, and so on, become ideal environments for insects and vermin. The architect and engineer should be aware that building details (wall sections, etc.) should be given considerable thought to minimize such spaces. Methods and techniques during construction must also be observed to minimize conditions that may contribute to the intrusion of vermin and insects. Special fine-mesh window screens, double-door-entry airlocks, and similar features may have to be integrated into the design to minimize these problems. Rodents from the animal population within the facility that may escape pose additional concerns and problems. Methods to eliminate vermin and insects should not endanger the existing animal population.

6 LABORATORY CORE SERVICE AND SUPPORT FACILITIES

The concept of laboratory core facilities or core service and support facilities remains a controversial topic among administrators, academicians, researchers, and clinicians. This discussion is usually most vocal in medical center and medical school environments. There are advantages and disadvantages to the concept. Certain research programs and protocols may require duplication of specific equipment and staff to maintain the integrity and continuity of the research objectives, protocols, and grant requirements. Such items may include controlled-temperature work or storage areas, balances and test equipment, refrigerators, freezers, centrifuges, library and reference areas, animal facilities, imaging equipment (e.g., electron microscopes, magnetic resonance spectroscopy, etc.), and technical and administrative support staff.

Perhaps the most persuasive argument against the core facilities concept is the difficulty in establishing the responsibility for the administrative, management, operations, and maintenance of the facility and its equipment. Also, how does one decide on what equipment will be assigned to the core facility? Is the responsibility for the facility assigned to one of the clinical or basic sciences departments? Is a separate department established to administrative the facility? Other questions remain and must be resolved. The concept is valid, has merit, and should be explored in the context of the nature of the programs that may be planned for the proposed research facility. The concept must have the support of the user.

The concept of the core service facility also parallels that of the generic or standard laboratory module or work area, in principle. The core service facility is organized and operated to optimize the use of equipment and services. The generic or standard laboratory is planned and equipped to present a typical laboratory work area, including certain equipment to accommodate a wide variety of activities with little or no change in the layout of the space. Some institutions have attempted to develop several of these typical standard laboratory layouts to accommodate a wider variety of activities. When a new researcher requires space, he or she is presented with the menu or list of the standard laboratories for selection.

The core service and support facilities concept is perhaps more frequently used in private industry and production laboratory facilities. The core facilities concept is becoming more common and in many institutions has become the "driver" in establishing the plan concept and space assignment and allocation policy for the laboratory facility.

FACILITIES CRITERIA

Facilities requirements, restrictions, and budget limitations, including capital, equipment, and operations, may dictate centralization of infrequently used equipment or technical and clerical staff support (secretary and clerical pool). Core facilities can result in conflicts regarding the use of shared items or staff. A controlled-temperature workroom, special hood, centrifuge, electron microscope, or other equipment may be needed by a researcher immediately or with very short notice and within a very short period of time. However, the item may be engaged by another researcher for an extended period of time and there may not be one available in time to maintain the continuity of the research activity. Administrative control and maintenance of the facilities and equipment can be sources of controversy and conflict.

Each concept must be discussed thoroughly and *decisions made during the initial programming phase*. The decisions must be made so that the planning and design criteria can be developed to permit the facilities to be organized in the most practical and efficient manner.

CORE OR SHARED SPACES LIST

Although 15 functions and activities are listed below as core service and support facilities, the list is by no means complete.

The administration of each institution should determine and select the functions that can be classified as core facilities and be managed appropriately. The list may also change over time as the program activities change.

1. Electron microscope (EM) suite
2. Controlled-environment work and storage rooms
3. Waste containment, collection, processing, holding, transport, and disposal facilities
4. Imaging facilities
5. Instrument and equipment rooms
6. Biomedical engineering facilities
7. Computer facilities
8. Materials management and handling facilities
9. Glassware processing facilities
10. Special gas-handling facilities
11. Clean workrooms
12. Library, conference, classroom, seminar, and meeting spaces
13. Animal facilities
14. Staff facilities
15. Media preparation facilities

CORE LABORATORY SERVICE AND SUPPORT FUNCTIONS

The following functions and activities may be considered for inclusion in a laboratory core service and support facility. Selection may be based on department organization, budgets, and scope of research grants; equipment purchase policies; financial and budget allocations; grant stipulations; staff resources available; utilization of equipment and services; and basic costs of facilities and equipment allocated to research, clinical, or production programs.

Electron Microscope Suite

An EM suite includes preparation and work areas and photographic processing and storage space. The EM may require a vibration-free work area (an air table may be required), chilled water for cooling the power supply, clean electrical service, and windowless rooms to avoid glare (darkroom environment with light lock, etc.). Dimmer room light switches are required.

Large work surface areas should be provided. Location in the facility can affect the performance of the EM (e.g., EMF generators such as motors can distort the EM image). An electrical and magnetic field test and analysis of the site proposed for the EM should be conducted to determine its suitability. Ergonomic design considerations should be utilized, as technicians may sit at the EM for long periods of time. Consider a separate electrical circuit for the EM to minimize "noise" from other equipment on the same circuit.

Relative humidity of 50% or less is required to minimize growth of fungi; 10 to 12 air changes per hour minimum are required. Room temperature should be at 72°F (±1 to 2°F). An EM may generate more than 10,000 Btu. Adequate service space surrounding the EM is required to permit servicing of the machine and support equipment. Service tool kits may weigh up to 200 lb.

Controlled-Environment Work and Storage Rooms

Controlled-environment facilities may be built-in or assembled from prefabricated units. The built-in room may require a depressed slab and cannot easily be expanded or relocated. The size, nature of the procedures to be conducted, and other factors may justify built-in facilities. Prefabricated units generally can be assembled in most configurations and sizes, and can be expanded or relocated relatively easily. Space may have to be provided for a ramp at the door to overcome differences in building floor and unit. Walk-in constant-temperature storage rooms (refrigerators, freezers) may be required for specimens, reagents, and biologicals. Animal carcasses may have to be stored prior to incineration. Such units may also be required for long-term storage of certain specimens for legal or research purposes.

Waste Containment, Collection, Processing, Holding, Transport, and Disposal Facilities

The scope of waste management for the waste materials and products produced, including nonhazardous material and radioactive (low and high level, short and long half-life), chemically hazardous, or biohazardous material is no longer an individual problem. Regulations are proliferating and complex, requiring full-time qualified and trained staff to manage the entire process. The facilities and operations may be the responsibility of the materials-handling and management department or under the supervision of the institution safety officer. Some institutions have engaged outside or independent contractors to manage the waste stream from collection at the source to its final disposal.

Facilities may consist of space within the facility or in a separate building to hold and store waste materials for transport by outside waste treatment and disposal services. Space and equipment (forklifts, drums, racks, pits, holding tanks, etc.) may be required to transfer certain materials being held in laboratory waste containers into proper holding and storage containers for transport out of the facility to the final processing and disposal site. Certain waste materials may have to be processed in the institution before being transported out of the facility. Biohazardous and pathological materials may have to be autoclaved and sterilized prior to removal to a disposal site. Incineration may be required for selected biohazardous, pathological or other solid waste materials. On-site incineration may be considered or a shared off-site facility.

Certain radioactive materials may have to be stored in a shielded container for a period of time to permit decay to a safe radioactive level. Special facilities may also be required for processing other waste materials. These facilities may consist of a room for personnel to change into protective clothing, with entry through an airlock (anteroom) to the processing work space, and return through the airlock or anteroom for decontamination, showering and dressing in street or work clothing.

Imaging Facilities

Facilities for radiographic (x-ray), ultrasound, and magnetic resonance imaging (clinical, spectrographic analysis, etc.) include provisions for film processing and storage, computer control, and cryogenic liquids receiving, storage, and distribution. Some MRI units no longer require the very restrictive environments of special electromagnetic isolation and shielding, nonmagnetic building materials, and other requirements. However, many of these items of equipment require very clean sources of electrical power service; restrictive security, control, and access; and other special requirements.

Instrument and Equipment Rooms

Rooms are needed to provide space for and access to centrifuges, ovens, incubators, refrigerators, freezers, balances, and other test and processing equipment. Caution must be taken when grouping such items of equipment. Floor loading (equipment weight), heat generation, and electrical service (capacity, phase, frequency, quality, emergency power, etc.) must all be considered. Centrifuges and other equipment can cause vibrations that create sympathetic frequency vibrations in the structural frame and be transmitted to other areas of the building. These frequencies and vibrations can create problems with sensitive equipment. Noise generated may create interference and distort readings by sensitive instruments. The noise levels may also exceed safe levels for personnel.

Biomedical Engineering Facilities

Biomedical engineering requires space for electronic equipment fabrication and repair, machine and carpentry shops, painting and welding, and special equipment design and fabrication, special glass and plastics items, and working models of equipment or processes. Such machine and fabrication shops are a vital necessity for service and support research activities. A glass-blowing facility is also a necessity.

However, due to the nature of the equipment—size, weight, height, power requirements, noise and vibration produced— and storage for stock items of wood, steel, metal wire, plastics, glass, and plaster of paris these items of equipment and materials are usually nonmodular and do not function or fit efficiently within an established laboratory work area module. It is more efficient and cost-effective to consider providing a separate facility (e.g., a freestanding building or at-grade area adjacent to the loading dock area) for these activities, convenient to the researcher in a shirtsleeve environment.

Consideration must be given to control temperature and humidity within the shop areas. Sensitive electronic test equipment will malfunction if temperatures exceed about 76 to 78°F. Rust will occur on metal stock and machine surfaces if the humidity exceeds 30 to 40%. However, too-low humidity will increase the problem of static electricity generation.

The following indicates items and equipment that may be considered for a biomedical engineering shop. Many machines may be similar to machines in the physical plant maintenance shops. However, the biomedical engineering shop should be a separate facility as it provides services that differ from those of maintenance shops.

Carpentry and Machine Shop

- Blasting abrasive equipment (sand, glass beads, aluminum oxide, plastic media, steel shot, and grit)
- Compressed air, portable, central service (100 psi minimum)
- Containers for waste materials, carts, hand trucks
- Electrical outlets (120 V, 208 V, 440 V, single- and three-phase), emergency power, portable and central
- Electric cutting machine with clear holding space for long stock, rolling stock support stands
- Emergency shower, eye wash; storage for protective eye, face, ear, and head equipment, aprons, gloves, coveralls, fire blanket, fire extinguishers (ABC types)
- Flammable storage cabinets for paints, solvents, fuels, etc.
- Hand shear and press brake
- Hydraulic punch, screw, arbor presses (1000 to 2000 lb. and above
- Materials and equipment storage area (utility carts, ladders, electric lifts, scale, workhorses, platforms, portable fans, hydraulic and screw jacks, portable hoist frame, parts cabinets, etc.)
- Materials, supplies, equipment receiving area; may share building loading dock area
- Milling and boring machines (1000 to 2000 lb and above)
- Office facilities: desk, chairs, drafting board, CADD system, plotter, plan and drawing files, letter files, catalog (supplies, materials, equipment) files, copy machine, FAX machine, telephones, data outlets, office supplies storage
- Portable lights, extension cords
- Storage racks for wood (stock, sheets, panels, etc.) and metal (steel, aluminum, brass, copper, etc.; bars, rods, tubes, angles, strips, pipes, wire, I-beams, sheets, perforated; plastic and glass stock, etc.), bins for scrap stock
- Spray painting booth and drying room, canopy exhaust, compressed air and electric paint sprayer, separate room best, protective spray masks

- Surface and edge grinders; disk and belt sanders
- Table, radial arm, and band saws
- Tables and benches (sinks, hose bibs, hose rack, assembly area, work area, equipment testing, computers, etc.)
- Tool cabinets (fixed and mobile)
- Welding work area with exhaust canopy; space for electric arc welder, oxyacetylene welder, helium-arc welder, gas cylinders, gas cylinder cart, forge, anvil
- Wheel, belt grinders, and buffers (workbench mounted)
- Wood and metal lathes (1000 to 2000 lb and above)

Electronics Shop

- Oscilloscopes, calibrators, power supply units, counters, signal tracers and generators, noise generators, video alignment generators, function and pulse generators, dip meter, high-frequency wattmeter, and so on
- Antennas (broadband, microwave), rooftop or at grade
- Clean power supply, ground-fault interrupters, busbar to building ground grid
- Work tables and benches, with sinks
- Storage for supplies, parts, and so on

Glass Blowing and Fabrication Shop

- Work counters (sit-down at 30″, stand-up at 36″), sinks, base and wall cabinet storage units, worktables, glass cutting area
- Grinders, polishers, glass washer, dryer, miscellaneous tool storage
- Storage for glass tubing, rods, sheets, and similar supplies
- Natural gas, glass gas welder, oven, furnace
- Eye and face protectors
- Trash receptacles for broken glass

Computer facilities

Computer facilities include central mainframe facilities, PCs, terminals, networks, printing, and data and word processing. May require raised floor system, special clean power requirements, fire extinguisher systems, special lighting, temperature and humidity controls, etc.

Materials Management and Handling Systems Facilities

Materials management and handling systems facilities, often called central warehouse facilities, provide space for ordering, receiving, storage, and distribution of supplies (consumables, reusables, etc.), equipment, chemicals and reagents (production and preparation), and so on. Loading dock facilities may be extensive and should not be located close to any of the building air intake areas, to minimize ingestion of truck exhausts and the like. Materials management systems can save an institution many thousands of dollars by controlling lost materials and supplies and reducing overall inventory storage space requirements. A materials management system should include the ordering, purchasing, receiving, control, storage, distribution, and movement of all materials, supplies, and equipment for an institution. The movement of patients in health care facilities (to and from the patient bedroom for diagnostic and treatment procedures, surgery, etc.) should be included as an element of the materials management system.

Glassware Processing Facilities

Glassware facilities provide for cleaning, washing, autoclaving, repairing, manufacturing, storage, and distribution of all glassware items. The scope and complexity of the facility will be determined by the nature of the research processes, policy of reusables vs. disposables, and other factors. Glassware fabrication may require an extensive glass blowing and fabrication area. Energy requirements and heat produced may dictate location with bioengineering and electronics machine shop facilities.

Special Gasses

Special gas-handling areas provide storage and distribution facilities, including recovery of gases (helium, etc.), dewars and gas cylinders, and external tanks (gaseous, liquid). The consumption rates of gases used to support research activities will determine the need for central gas storage vs. gas cylinders. Hazard classifications will also determine management protocols and facilities required for certain gases.

Clean Workrooms

Clean workrooms may be required for the containment, processing, and production of hazardous biologicals, critical electronic components, and the like. The nature of the hazard and the cleanliness required will determine the complexity of systems to provide the proper environments. Most tissue culture, media preparation, and so on, can usually be accommodated within the module(s) established for the laboratory work areas. However, certain classifications (P1, P2, P3 or BSL-2, BSL-3, and BSL-4 isolation laboratories; class 10, class 100 to 10,000 and higher) might be housed more economically and efficiently in specially designed facilities. The program criteria and the nature and scope of the research activities will determine the economics of integrating these spaces within the generic modules or provide separate free-standing facilities. Clean room requirements can also be satisfied with prefabricated units available from several commercial sources.

Library, Conference, Classroom, Seminar, and Meeting Spaces

Areas dedicated to educational uses include classrooms, demonstration areas; lecture halls; auditoriums; TV studios (CCTV, etc.); radio stations; spaces for audiovisual, graphics, illustration, and medical illustration slide (microscopic, photographic), and printout preparation; areas for mailing, clerical, copying, filing, and recording (active, inactive, tape, disks, microfilm processing and viewing), uses; informal brainstorming spaces; and TV conferencing, and multimedia centers. Some of these spaces may also be considered as interactive or brainstorming spaces (conference/classroom, etc.), to attract researchers and investigators to impromptu discussions.

Animal Facilities

Animal facilities can be very expensive, requiring complex building and security systems. The growing influence of animal rights groups is affecting the use of animals in research programs. Policies and protocols may dictate that animals be used in the laboratories only during the day and returned to the animal facilities at night. New regulations being prepared governing the use of primates in research virtually mandates centralized facilities, including laboratory and service and support facilities where all experimental work is accomplished. Depending on the scale and scope of the program and research needs, separate animal facilities are generally the most efficient solution. It is usually difficult (and costly in a single building) to design HVAC systems to meet the demanding and restrictive requirements for the animal holding areas and still prevent odors from permeating the entire facility.

Staff Facilities

Staff facilities include kitchens and cafeterias, coffee shops, snack bars, break areas, vending machine areas, lounge rooms; locker and change rooms, showers and toilets, personal security storage (purse lockers). Some of these facilities are required by code, OSHA, and so on. Most are optional and can have significant impact on the morale, performance, productivity, and efficiency of the staff and personnel of the facility.

The psychological nature of most people will cause a negative reaction: for example, staff will create their own facilities if a coffee bar is not permitted. Coffee pots and other paraphernalia will appear on windowsills, desk drawers, file cabinet tops, and so on. Certain locations can create hazards. All these demonstrations of individual initiative reduce efficiency and waste time.

OSHA is considering requiring staff to change from street clothes to protective clothing when entering certain laboratory facilities. A person would not be allowed to leave without reversing the gowning process. These regulations will mandate changing, lockers, and toilet and shower facilities for such functions and activities.

Media Preparation Facilities

Media requirements and consumption can be significant in biomedical research facilities and may justify in-house central preparation facilities instead of relying on outside suppliers. Operations can become a source of income, supplying institutions in the area. Special media requirements can be prepared in individual laboratories.

7 LABORATORY WORK AREAS: STANDARD PLANS AND DETAILS

Casework standards cited as examples in this book are based generally on Kewaunee Scientific Corporation, P.O. Pox 5400, Statesville, NC 29677, modular and fixed laboratory casework and furniture. All dimensions indicated are nominal.

CASEWORK STANDARDS

Laboratory counter heights are indicated as 36″ for standing activities and 30″ for sit-down activities. Dimensions of the specific casework manufacturer selected may vary. The counter top thickness may vary also. The intent is not to customize a selected manufacturer's casework to fit dimensions that are indicated in illustrations, diagrams, or plans. Aisle widths should not be less than 5′. An aisle width of 5′ permits a person to pass between two seated persons at opposite work counters. Some sources consider an aisle width between 5′-6″ and 6′-0″ to be a minimum. Requirements to accommodate the disabled may change these dimensions.

Mobile equipment, carts, and so on, should not be permitted to reduce the aisle width to less than 3′-6″. Accessibility standards must also be reviewed and incorporated in the selection of clearances in the laboratory work areas (e.g., between work counters, work counters and equipment, and work counters and fume hoods, etc.). Modifications of standard counter heights, ranges of reach, and so on, may have to be made to casework to permit its use by disabled staff in laboratory work areas. An estimate of the length and location of laboratory casework that may be required in a proposed facility can be determined from the laboratory standard plans.

Layouts, sequence of casework, and equipment may vary depending on the scientific discipline to be accommodated. The architect-of-record may consider preparing laboratory standard plans based on the program requirements to test the typical laboratory module concept developed.

COMMENTS

1. Significant cost savings can be achieved by selecting counter materials carefully. The tendency is to specify a monolithic or composition-type acid-resistant material for all countertops. This is unnecessary because corrosive reagents are not used at all workstations. Corrosive reagents may never be used in equipment, instrument, and other service and support areas. A similar analysis should be made for the selection and location of acid sinks and drains.

2. Laboratory-grade laminated-plastic-top materials will provide satisfactory service in most laboratory work areas. This material is less expensive and relatives easy to repair or replace if damaged. The top material most resistant to more chemicals than many manufactured composite top materials is hard-rock maple. It is also more resilient (softer), reducing glassware breakage.

3. Damage to the wood top caused by reagent spills and burns can be repaired by sanding, filling, and refinishing. The wood top is also easily worked with common tools. Unfortunately, hard-rock maple is expensive.

4. As the laboratory criteria and functional relationships evolve, certain selected laboratory work areas should be equipped with the more chemically resistant composite top materials.

5. The tendency is to plan, design, and indicate casework wall to wall on the drawings. Construction tolerances may vary as much as $\pm\frac{1}{4}''$ to several inches. This creates a difficult situation and somewhat of a dilemma for the casework supplier when preparing the shop drawings. The actual field-measured dimension may vary at times, requiring substitutions or changes to the casework elevations on the architect-of-record's drawings. These ele-

vations may also have been based on user-approved design development documents.

6. It is suggested that casework elements be developed consisting of several assorted types of base and wall cabinets, including shelves. As an example, if a wall dimension is 18', the linear feet of casework should be planned at 15'. This allows the casework element to be placed at the right or left corner wall, providing a 3' space on the left or right end. This space can be used to place various items of equipment, such as refrigerators, centrifuges, cryostats, gas cylinders, and waste receptacles. The primary advantage of such an arrangement is that the casework element can be set in place with virtually no custom fitting. This simplifies and reduces the time of installation. A series of these casework elements can be developed and specified by a key or identifying number. These casework elements can also be selected by the user in a mix-or-match fashion.

7. Consider placing a clear plastic sheet of plastic (Lexan, etc.) down the center of an island or peninsula casework unit.

8. The clear plastic allows for visual contact but acts as a shield for the person on the other side if an accident or spill occurs.

WORKSTATION PLANNING CRITERIA

Consider installing several peninsula or island work units with a 6'-0"-wide counter top. This will permit use of equipment that is deeper than 2'-6" and eliminate equipment overhang. The standard work counter width for this configuration is 5'-0". The 6'-0" width can be created without modification of standard casework. However, consideration must also be given to difficulties that will occur when attempting to reach to the center of a 6'-0"-wide counter.

Mobile tables and work carts with wheels or casters (4" to 6" in diameter) instead of traditional fixed or modular casework can provide significant flexibility in the laboratory. The mobile work units should be used for electronic test and analysis equipment that requires service access to the sides and rear. The mobile units are available in various working heights, materials (wood and stainless steel), widths, and lengths to suit a wide range of workstation requirements. These units are also less expensive than comparable fixed or modular casework.

Storage of consumable supplies at the workstation area is a necessity and must be considered. However, workstation storage space should not become a substitute for adequate storage facilities controlled through a materials management system. The casework type should be selected carefully to suit workstation storage requirements. Custom casework designed specifically for autoanalyzers and test equipment should be considered to maximize the productivity and efficiency of the automated equipment.

Depending on the workstation activity and the output of the equipment, consumables (kits, etc.) might require one to several days of storage at the workstation. The practice of "squirreling" supplies and reagents at a workstation can be expensive and counterproductive. Unnecessary volumes of materials and reagents can also create hazardous conditions. A properly managed materials handling system can achieve efficient, economical, and safe laboratory operations.

Workstation planning and layout for various automated equipment may require special attention. Test kits or modules may be used for single tests or for a series of tests to be processed by the machine. The machine and its peripherals may not be accommodated easily within the established typical laboratory module. The functional work space configuration may be in the shape of a U or an L. Adequate space must be allocated for:

- Bulletin (tack) board or chalk (white) board for printouts, notices, and machine procedures.
- Space for waste containers to hold trash, broken glass, fluids, and hazardous waste, and space for a specimen cart.
- Space for a computer terminal and keyboard (machine control or laboratory information system input), printer, and paper supplies. The terminal and keyboard can be mounted on a commercially available movable arm supporting it above the work counter.
- Standing or seated operating position for the technician (must not forget knee space).
- Storage for safety or emergency equipment.
- Storage space for the kits, supplies, and operational manu-

als (consider using the vertical space above the work counter or machine for storage).

- Utilities and services (electrical, water, drain, gas cylinders, telephone and data outlets, etc.), including access to the top, sides, or rear of the equipment for maintenance, and special lighting requirements.

- Work counter space to arrange kits and specimens that have been processed (specimens may require additional testing at another workstation, disposal, or storage for future reference).

- Work counter space to arrange, load, or stage the kits and specimens to be processed.

CASEWORK SPECIFICATIONS OUTLINE

The following outlines and highlights the important items to consider for a laboratory casework specification:

General Requirements

1. General
2. Intent of the casework and equipment specifications
3. Qualifications of the bidders
4. Casework and equipment manufacturer's warranty
5. Samples of the casework

Scope of the Work

1. General
2. Work to be furnished, delivered, and installed by the casework and equipment manufacturer
3. Work not to be furnished, delivered, or installed by the casework and equipment manufacturer
4. Shop drawings submittal requirements

Mechanical Service Fittings

1. General
2. Laboratory-grade service fittings
3. Water, distilled water, and steam
4. Ground key valve hose cocks

5. Needle valve hose cocks
6. Gooseneck outlets
7. Remote control valves
8. Tank nipples
9. Service indexes
10. Electrical fittings
11. Waste lines and traps
12. Sink outlets
13. Crumb cup strainers
14. Vacuum breakers
15. Aerator outlets
16. Plastic-coated finishes
17. Finish performance test criteria for service fittings
18. Maximum line pressures for gas, air, water, and steam

Work Tops and Surfaces

1. General
2. Composite materials
3. Natural stone
4. Resin-bonded fiberboard
5. Molded epoxy resin
6. Hardwoods
7. Laminated plastic materials
8. Stainless steel
9. Physical properties and performance tests for the top materials

Sinks and Drain Troughs

1. General
2. Materials

Metal Furniture

1. General
2. Materials
3. Sheet metal
4. Finishes
5. Glass

Hardware and Trim

1. General
2. Drawer and door pulls
3. Flush pulls
4. Hinges
5. Locks
6. Friction catches
7. Elbow catches
8. Magnetic catches
9. Adjustable shelf clips
10. Base molding
11. Support rods, upright rod assemblies, rod sockets
12. Label holders
13. Number plates
14. Up-and-down bolts
15. Sink supports
16. Support struts

Metal Base Unit Construction

1. General
2. Sheet metal gauges
3. Base units
    a. End uprights
    b. Top horizontal rail
    c. Intermediate rails
    d. Intermediate vertical uprights
    e. Case bottom and rail
    f. Toe space rail
    g. Reinforcements
    h. Adjustable shelves
    i. Drawer assembly
    j. Door assembly
    k. Drawer and door assemblies
    l. Drawer suspension assembly
    m. Knee-space panels
    n. Performance test criteria

Special-Purpose Storage Cabinets

1. General
2. Acid storage cabinets
3. Corrosives storage cabinets
4. Solvent storage cabinets

Metal Sliding-Door Upper Case Construction

1. General
2. End uprights
3. Case tops
4. Case bottoms
5. Case backs
6. Adjustable shelves
7. Glazed sliding doors
8. Solid panel sliding doors
9. Sliding plate glass doors

Metal Swinging-Door Upper Case Construction

1. General
2. End uprights
3. Case tops
4. Case Bottoms
5. Case Backs
6. Adjustable Shelves
7. Glazed Swinging Doors
8. Door Assembly

Metal Sliding-Door Full-Height Case Construction

1. General
2. End uprights
3. Case tops
4. Case bottoms
5. Case backs
6. Toe space rails
7. Adjustable shelves
8. Glazed swinging doors

9. Solid panel swinging doors

10. Door assembly

Metal-Freestanding Table Construction

1. General
2. Apron division rails
3. Table apron rails
4. Table legs
5. Apron corner reinforcements
6. Spreaders
7. Table tops
8. Wheels and casters

Metal Paint System Finish and Performance Specification

1. General
2. Metal paint system finish
3. Performance test criteria
4. Performance test results
   a. Bending
   b. Adhesion
   c. Hardness

COMMENTS

1. Detailed specifications may be secured from the casework and equipment manufacturer to meet a wide range of conditions. The architect-of-record and the facilities manager will also have various specification requirements to be incorporated into the fabrication of the casework and equipment.

2. The specifications should then reflect the institutional furnishings and equipment standards and requirements to suit the specific research program criteria. The institution and architect-of-record should not overlook the capabilities of the plant maintenance shops to fabricate the laboratory casework.

STANDARD LABORATORY WORK AREA PLANS

The standard laboratory work area plans shown in Figures 7.1 to 7.8 are a series of Generic plans to establish several laboratory work area casework and functional arrangements indicating:

- Casework selection, type, work counter heights, etc.
- Equipment selection and density (hoods, refrigerators, centrifuges, etc.)
- Utilities and services density (electrical outlets, gases, sinks (tub: single, double, cup, etc.)
- Offices furnishings, assignment, and allocation
- Laboratory work areas, partition and door densities
- Emergency showers, smoke detectors, dimensions, etc.

The laboratory work area modules are based on generic interpretations of program functions, activities, and space allocations. Casework, fixtures, and services densities may not change significantly as specific laboratory plans are developed to satisfy program requirements. Fixed or modular casework systems should be determined and selected, and casework finishes, top materials, fixtures, sinks, and so on, should be determined early in the planning and design process.

Factors that affect selection criteria include:

- Scientific disciplines assigned to the laboratory work areas
- Nature of the experimentation to be conducted
- Types of reagents to be used
- Grant application criteria
- Budget limitations, life-cycle costs

Although the laboratory work area plans reflect a service corridor concept, the plans are valid for other services systems concepts (e.g., interstitial, ceiling, or floor with laboratory modules back to back, or a combination of utility service concepts). The office support spaces are indicated as "across the hall" only for the purpose of the diagrammatic layout of the illustrations.

The location of the offices and other support spaces will depend on the primary functional relationships indicated in

"Standard Casework Units" should be developed. Manufacturers can bid on "packages" or units of casework assemblies consisting of groups of casework. The casework elevations indicated are a limited selection for planning purposes. The facilities manager and architect-of-record should determine if the institution's casework standards are to be used or whether to develop alternative standards.

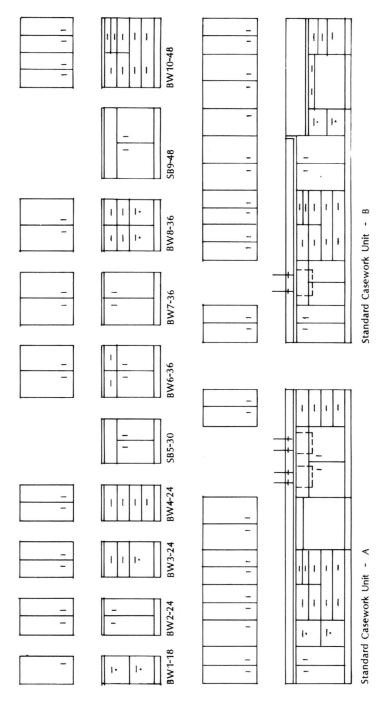

Cabinet widths limited to 18", 24", 30", 36" and 48". Counter heights @ 30" (sit-down) and 36" (stand-up). Units BW1-18, BW3-24 and BW8-36 (w/locks) provided in each laboratory work area. Not all base cabinets available in 30" height. Pencil drawers or aprons available for knee spaces.

No Scale

Figure 7.1 Standard casework units (generic elevation types).

All dimensions are "nominal". The intent is not to "customize" available casework systems, but to indicate generic details, clearances and space required.

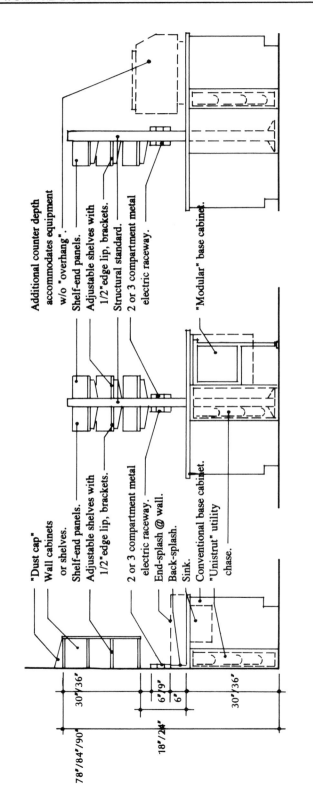

"Dust cap"
Wall cabinets or shelves.
Shelf-end panels.
Adjustable shelves with 1/2" edge lip, brackets.
2 or 3 compartment metal electric raceway.
End-splash @ wall.
Back-splash.
Sink.
Conventional base cabinet.
"Unistrut" utility chase.

Additional counter depth accommodates equipment w/o "overhang".
Shelf-end panels.
Adjustable shelves with 1/2" edge lip, brackets.
Structural standard.
2 or 3 compartment metal electric raceway.

"Modular" base cabinet.

78"/84"/90'
30"/36'
18"/24"
6'/9'
6'
30"/36'

TYPICAL SECTION @ WALL

Scale 3/8" = 1'-0"

TYPICAL SECTION @ 5' WIDE ISLAND or PENINSULA

TYPICAL SECTION @ 6' WIDE ISLAND or PENINSULA

Figure 7.2 Standard casework details (generic sections).

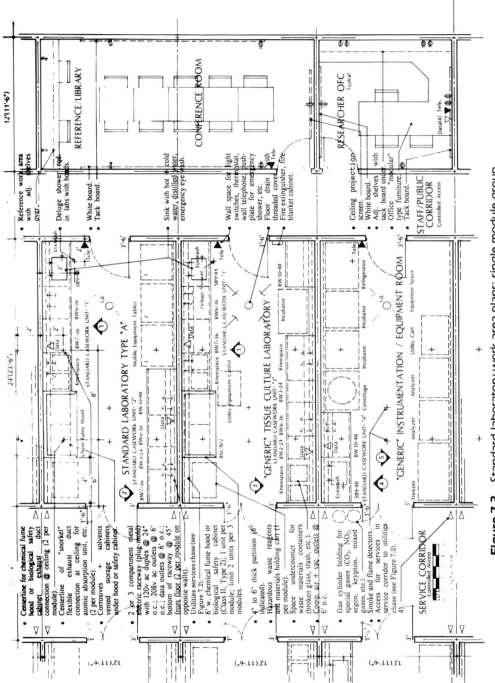

Figure 7.3 Standard laboratory work area plans: single module group.

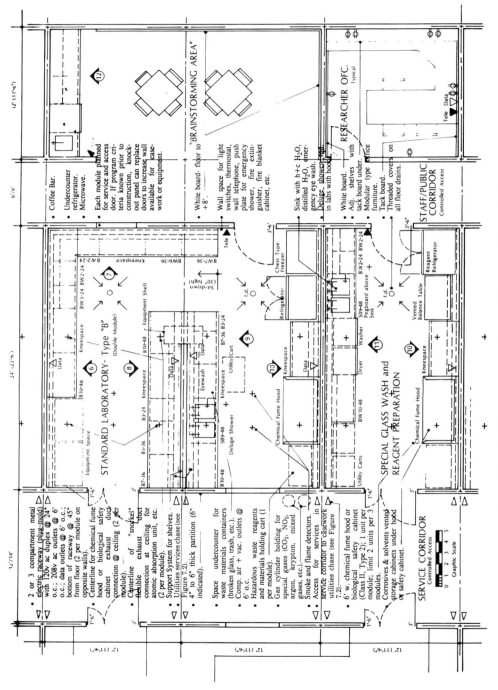

Figure 7.4 Standard laboratory work area plans: multiple module group.

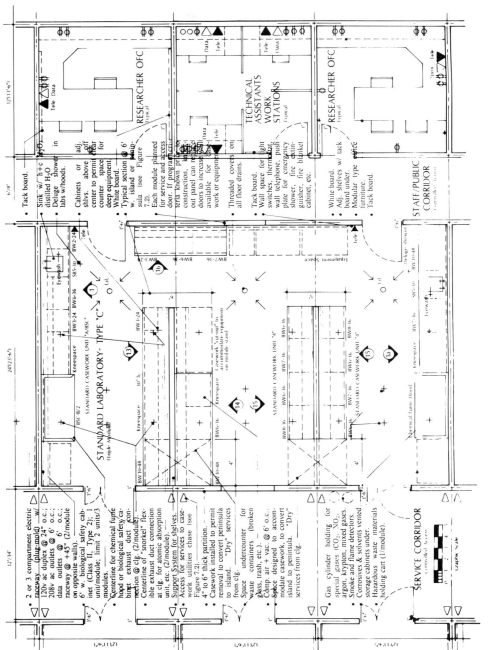

Figure 7.5 Standard laboratory work area plans: work island group.

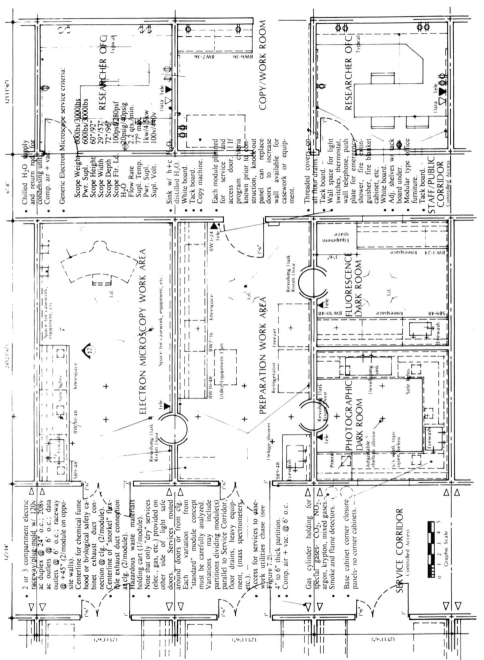

Figure 7.6 Standard laboratory work area plans: specific example group.

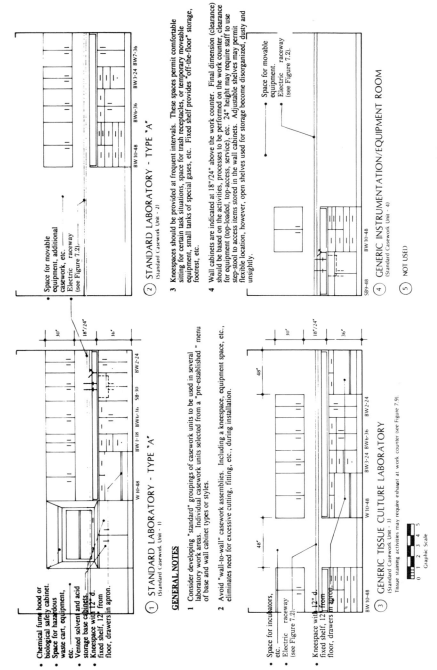

Figure 7.7 Standard laboratory work area casework elevations: single module group.

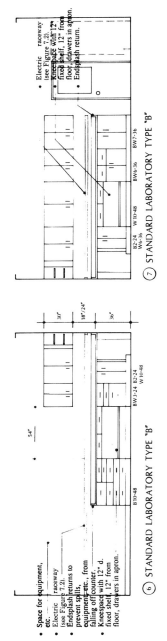

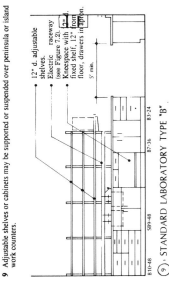

⑥ STANDARD LABORATORY TYPE "B"

⑦ STANDARD LABORATORY TYPE "B"

⑧ STANDARD LABORATORY TYPE "B"

⑨ STANDARD LABORATORY TYPE "B"

- Space for equipment, etc.
- Electric raceway (see Figure 7.2).
- Endsplash returns to prevent spills.
- Kneespace with 12" d. fixed shelf, 12" from floor, drawers in apron.

- Electric raceway (see Figure 7.2).
- Kneespace with 12" fixed shelf, 12" from floor, drawers in apron.
- Endsplash return.

- 12" d. adjustable shelves.
- Electric raceway (see Figure 7.2).
- Kneespace with 12" d. fixed shelf, 12" from floor, drawers in apron.
- Services chase.

- 12" d. adjustable shelves.
- Electric raceway (see Figure 7.2).
- Kneespace with fixed shelf, 12" from floor, drawers in apron.

5 The 48" wide wall cabinet may be 2-24" cabinets -- depends on casework manufacturer. If the institution's Carpentry Shop is large enough and equipped, consideration should be given to fabricating the casework in-house.

6 Equipment dimensions, specimen(s) to be analyzed, service access, control panel, peripherals, hinged panels, etc., must be carefully analyzed before work counter height is established. Top loaded equipment may be difficult to access safely if placed on a 36" high counter. If rear access to equipment is required, consider mounting unit on mobile work stand.

7 Although "traditional" fixed type casework is indicated in these Illustrations, fixed and "modular" casework units manufactured by several companies are "interchangeable".

8 Work counter height is indicated at 36" except as noted or required by program or equipment criteria.

9 Adjustable shelves or cabinets may be supported or suspended over peninsula or island work counters.

Graphics Scale
0 1 2 3 4 5

Figure 7.8 Standard laboratory work area casework elevations: multiple module group.

the program and how these relationships are translated into the architectural design floor plan (floor shape, area, column bay size, etc.). It is again emphasized that office work spaces should not be included within the laboratory work areas. Offices that are adjacent to laboratory work areas should be accessed from the staff (public) corridor, not through the laboratory work areas. Doors between laboratory work areas should only be permitted based on program criteria. A door takes up approximately 8 linear feet of work counter (casework) or equipment space. Building systems (HVAC, etc.) for the office spaces must also be separate from the laboratory work area building systems.

The standard laboratory work area casework elevations shown in Figures 7.9 to 7.11 represent standard casework units. The intent of these units is to permit installation in any laboratory work area and not to be confined only to the standard laboratory type first indicated. These casework units may be mixed or matched to suit program criteria and individual researcher requirements or preferences. The combination of the standard laboratory types and standard casework units increases the number of possible selections or combinations of standard laboratory types available without compromising the basic concept of standardization of these important building elements.

Casework systems or types (fixed and modular) must be analyzed carefully prior to selection. Flexibility or adaptability to movement or change of modular casework in most instances is limited to the vertical dimension. However, in combination with fixed or traditional casework units, accommodations for disabled persons may be made more easily and practically.

General Notes

1. The intent is to develop a series of standard casework units that would be common to a number of different laboratory disciplines. These standard units would consist of a selection of base and/or wall cabinet units; for example:

   a. Island work counter

   b. Peninsula work counter

   c. Wall with chemical fume hood

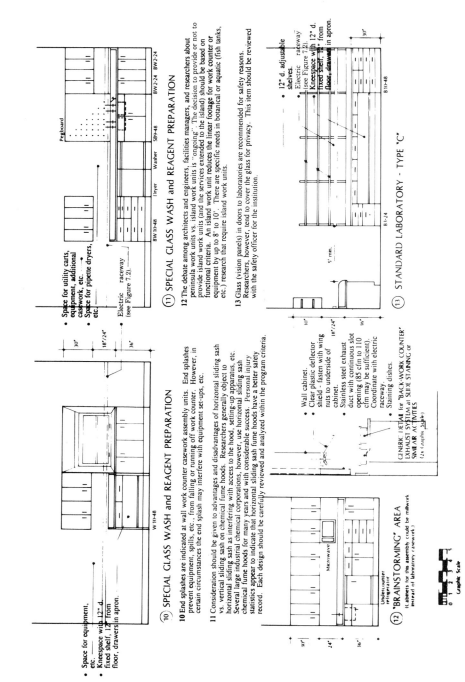

- Space for equipment, etc.
- Kneespace with 12" d. fixed shelf, 12" from floor, drawers in apron.

(10) SPECIAL GLASS WASH and REAGENT PREPARATION

10 End splashes are indicated at wall work counter casework assembly units. End splashes prevent equipment, spills, etc., from falling or running off of work counter. However, in certain circumstances the end splash may interfere with equipment set-ups, etc.

11 Consideration should be given to advantages and disadvantages of horizontal sliding sash vs. vertical sliding sash on chemical fume hoods. Researchers generally object to horizontal sliding sash as interfering with access to the hood, setting-up apparatus, etc. Several large industrial chemical corporations, however, use horizontal sliding sash chemical fume hoods for many years and with considerable success. Personal injury statistics appear to indicate that horizontal sliding sash fume hoods have a better safety record. Each design should be carefully reviewed and analyzed within the program criteria.

- Space for utility carts, equipment, additional casework, etc.
- Space for pipette dryers, etc.

Electric raceway (see Figure 7.2).

(11) SPECIAL GLASS WASH and REAGENT PREPARATION

12 The debate among architects and engineers, facilities managers, and researchers about peninsula work units vs. island work units is "ongoing". The decision to provide or not to provide island work units (and the services extended to the island) should be based on functional criteria. An island work unit reduces the linear footage for work counter or equipment by up to 8' to 10'. There are specific needs in botanical or aquatic (fish tanks, etc.) research that require island work units.

13 Glass (vision panels) in doors to laboratories are recommended for safety reasons. Researchers, however, tend to cover the glass for privacy. This item should be reviewed with the safety officer for the institution.

- Wall cabinet.
- Clear plastic deflector shield - fasten with wing nuts to underside of cabinet.
- Stainless steel exhaust duct with continuous slot opening (85 cfm to 110 cfm may be sufficient). Coordinate with electric raceway.
- Staining dishes.

GENERIC DETAIL for "BACK-WORK COUNTER" EXHAUST SYSTEM at SLIDE STAINING or SIMILAR ACTIVITIES
(2x Graphic Scale)

(12) "BRAINSTORMING" AREA
(Cabinets for this assembly could be millwork instead of laboratory casework.)

- 12" d. adjustable shelves.
- Electric raceway (see Figure 7.2).
- Kneespace with 12" d. fixed shelf, 12" from floor, drawers in apron.

(13) STANDARD LABORATORY - TYPE "C"

Figure 7.9 Standard laboratory work area casework elevations: multiple module group.

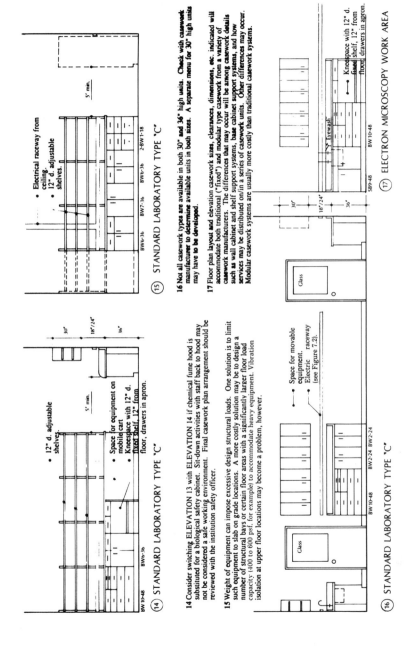

14 Consider switching ELEVATION 13 with ELEVATION 14 if chemical fume hood is substituted for a biological safety cabinet. Sit-down activities with staff back to hood may not be considered a safe working environment. Final casework plan arrangement should be reviewed with the institution safety officer.

15 Weight of equipment can impose excessive design structural loads. One solution is to limit such equipment to slab on grade locations. A more costly solution may be to design a number of structural bays or certain floor areas with a significantly larger floor load capacity (400 to 600 psf, for example) to accommodate heavy equipment. Vibration isolation at upper floor locations may become a problem, however.

16 Not all casework types are available in both 30" and 36" high units. Check with casework manufacturer to determine available units in both sizes. A separate menu for 30" high units may have to be developed.

17 Floor plan layout and elevation casework sizes, clearances, dimensions, etc. indicated will accommodate both traditional ("fixed") and modular type casework from a variety of casework manufacturers. The differences that may occur will be among casework details such as wall cabinet and shelf support systems, base cabinet support systems, and how services may be distributed on/in a series of casework units. Other differences may occur. Modular casework systems are usually more costly than traditional casework systems.

Figure 7.10 Standard laboratory work area casework elevations: work island group.

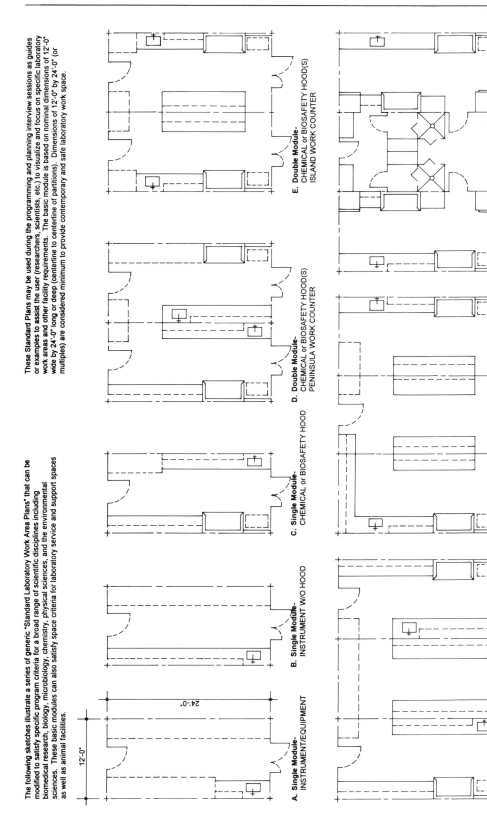

The following sketches illustrate a series of generic "Standard Laboratory Work Area Plans" that can be modified to satisfy specific program criteria for a broad range of scientific disciplines including biomedical research, biology, microbiology, chemistry, physical sciences, and the environmental sciences. These basic modules can also satisfy space criteria for laboratory service and support spaces as well as animal facilities.

These Standard Plans may be used during the programming and planning interview sessions as guides or examples to assist the user (researchers, scientists, etc.) to visualize and focus on specific laboratory work areas and other facility requirements. The basic module is based on nominal dimensions of 12'-0" wide by 24'-0" long or deep (centerline to centerline of partitions). Dimensions of 12'-0" by 24'-0" (or multiples) are considered minimum to provide contemporary and safe laboratory work space.

A. Single Module- INSTRUMENT/EQUIPMENT
B. Single Module- INSTRUMENT W/O HOOD
C. Single Module- CHEMICAL or BIOSAFETY HOOD
D. Double Module- CHEMICAL or BIOSAFETY HOOD(S) PENINSULA WORK COUNTER
E. Double Module- CHEMICAL or BIOSAFETY HOOD(S) ISLAND WORK COUNTER
F. Triple Module- CHEMICAL or BIOSAFETY HOOD(S) PENINSULA WORK COUNTERS
G. Triple Module- CHEMICAL or BIOSAFETY HOOD(S) ISLAND WORK COUNTERS
H. Triple Module- CHEMICAL or BIOSAFETY HOOD(S) EXAMPLE HAZARDS CONTAINMENT AREA

Figure 7.11 Standard laboratory work area plans—generic example layouts multiple module group.

   d. Wall with biological safety cabinet (BSC)

   e. Wall without chemical fume hood or BSC

   f. Base and/or wall storage units

2. knee spaces should be provided at frequent intervals. Use at least one (3' to 4' wide minimum)—two is better—in a single laboratory module (12' × 24'). The knee space provides required proper seating at the work counter whether seated at a 27"- to 29" (30")-high work counter, or a standing 36" (37")-high work counter. The knee space may also be used as parking areas for trash containers, small gas cylinders associated with a particular process or equipment, portable air compressor or vacuum pump, and so on. However, such items of equipment should be considered on a temporary basis because of the high noise coefficient.

3. A 15"-deep fixed shelf mounted 12" from the floor should be installed in the knee space. This provides a foot rest [at a 36" (37")-high work counter] or a shelf for premixed reagent cartons or drain bottles associated with certain processes or automated equipment. Joint Commission regulations forbid such items to be located directly on the floor or in the aisle.

4. Wall cabinets are indicated at 24" above the work counter. Some sources recommend 18". The cabinet height above the work counter should not be an arbitrary or generic number. The height should be determined by the specific activities anticipated to provide adequate clearance for the work to be performed and the equipment used. Equipment with side or front access generally may be located under cabinets that are set at 18" above the work counter. Equipment that require top access or are hinged for top opening generally require 24" (or more) cabinet clearance. Certain equipment may require clear access to the top, precluding cabinets or shelves above. Adjustable shelves may be the preferred selection over all counters instead of wall cabinets. Adjustable shelves may be removed easily to accommodate and provide clearance for countertop equipment.

5. Adjustable shelves may appear to provide the measure of flexibility to accommodate a wide range of equipment and processes. The shelves can be adjusted up or

down. Additional shelves can be added to accommodate items without stacking one on top of each other. This can improve technologist and technician performance by providing convenient access to kits and other supplies and consumables that may be required for various autoanalyzer equipment.

6. Adjustable shelves also provide convenient placement for certain peripherals (monitors, printers, recorders, etc.) that may be associated with various types of equipment (e.g., autoanalyzers, etc.). Placing peripherals on shelves at eye level and within easy reach makes for efficient use of the work space and provides for a much safer workstation. Unfortunately, items stored on shelves are exposed to dust, may become unsightly and disorganized may fall off the shelf, possibly creating a hazardous accident. Security is nonexistent, of course. Shelf standards may be difficult and expensive to attach to the wall, depending on the partition system. Consider mounting CRTs on adjustable arms. Such equipment accessories are available through computer equipment and furniture catalogs.

7. The tendency, often, is to spread out horizontally, resulting in crowding and creating the false perception that additional floor space is needed to satisfy workstation requirements. Applying basic production engineering techniques (process flow, utilization of workstation volume, including the vertical space as well as the horizontal space and ergonomic principles) can significantly improve laboratory staff production, resulting in increased efficiency and safety, and reduce operational costs. Equally important, this operational design approach to workstation utilization may have the added benefit of mitigating the "need" for additional space.

8. Each casework system (open cabinets or shelves, doors on base and wall cabinets; hinged, sliding, glass, solid, lockable, etc.) has inherent advantages and disadvantages. Establishing standard modular layouts, casework systems and types, and so on, may appear to be logical, efficient, and cost-effective during the initial phases of a project. However, considerable care and experienced judgment must be applied during the programming phase to ensure that whatever concept or system is

adopted, it will in fact meet the requirements of the disciplines anticipated to be accommodated within the facility.

9. Most building services systems that may be developed for a modular laboratory space concept can usually accommodate the environmental criteria required for a series of scientific disciplines. However, it will almost always happen that during the programming phase (usually after occupancy) one or more of the presumed-compatible disciplines will require a space that is not easily accommodated within the designed system.

10. The effects of Murphy's law are *always* present. Such extraordinary subspecialty facilities may include nuclear magnetic resonance spectrographic analyses, electromagnetic-shielded test workrooms, ultraclean workrooms, and areas for high-energy gamma radiation shielding.

11. There are several ways to accommodate these anomalies:

    a. Remodel and renovate after occupancy, as required, and pay the price.

    b. Anticipate the anomaly during the programming and planning phases, if possible, and design-in systems to minimize disruption and reduce future remodeling and renovation costs.

    c. Allocate or designate a certain percentage of each floor as shell space to be filled in as special programs or processes develop after occupancy. This option is hardly ever practical because demands for space by researchers and investigators usually exceed the space available.

12. Although a designation of shell space may be the most logical or practical option, institutional policies and certain grant requirements may specifically preclude allocation of shell space and, further, prohibit including unfinished space within the proposed building.

13. Almost all jurisdictions that require a Certificate of Need (CON) for proposed health care facilities design and construction projects specifically prohibit the designation of shell spaces as part of the program.

COMMENTS

1. There are no universally generic facility and building services systems that will accommodate all scientific disciplines efficiently and in a cost-effective and safe manner. This is not to imply that such a system cannot be designed and constructed—however, the costs are usually prohibitive.

2. Each variation from or compromise with the established standard module building services systems design concept will produce a series of conflicts with the standard systems. These changes must be analyzed in context to determine the impact on program criteria, design, and construction costs.

3. The importance of the programming and planning process is emphasized again. This process permits the evolution and evaluation of the facility and building services system design concept to accommodate the criteria of the scientific and technical research programs in an efficient, safe, and cost-effective manner.

A CHECKLISTS

The following checklists provide convenient summaries of programming, planning, and design considerations relating to laboratory facilities. They are not presented as all-inclusive but will provide the facility planner and designer with criteria applicable to a spectrum of laboratory requirements.

- Checklist 1: Generic Laboratory Services and Utilities Considerations

- Checklist 2: Safety Programming Considerations

- Checklist 3: Building Systems Design Considerations

- Checklist 4: Facility Programming Interview Process Summaries

  - 4a: Generic List of Medical Center Functions and Activities

  - 4b: Generic Project Schedule

  - 4c: Generic Interviewee List

  - 4d: Generic Programming Interview Questionnaire Summary

  - 4e: Example Research Laboratory Programming Questions

  - 4f: Example Functional, Space, Staff Program Summary Chart

- Checklist 5: Space Programming Parameters

- Checklist 6: Physical Facilities Survey Guide

- Checklist 7: Items Affecting Costs

- Checklist 8: Generic Program Document Outline

CHECKLIST 1: GENERIC LABORATORY SERVICES AND UTILITIES CONSIDERATIONS

Services and utilities requirements should be evaluated and determined during the programming and planning phases. Selection should be based on the proposed functions and activities to be conducted in the laboratory work areas. The following list indicates general criteria, services, utilities, and fittings that should be considered and made available at each module line (single or multiple modules) for use in laboratory work areas. Although the list is perhaps representative of biomedical laboratories, many of the same services and utilities will be required in other types of laboratories [e.g., environmental, engineering (testing), physical sciences (physics, etc.), and production laboratories]. It should be noted that any or all of the values indicated may vary considerably from those developed for a specific laboratory facility. The figures are intended to provide a generic framework for initial planning purposes.

Heating, Ventilation, and Air Conditioning

■ All laboratory work areas should be maintained at negative pressure relative to corridors and adjacent spaces. Special laboratory environments may have an equal- or positve-pressure relationship as determined by program requirements.

■ Individual thermostat controls should be provided for all laboratory work areas.

■ Minimum of 12 to 16 air changes per hour for all laboratory work areas, depending on internal heat loads, fume hood, and biosafety cabinet supply and exhaust air requirements (face velocity), type of research to be conducted, degree of hazard, etc.

■ Supply air filtered for dust only except in special laboratory work areas. This criterion may have to be modified, depending on outside air quality.

■ The HVAC system should be designed to permit supplemental cooling by fan coil units in laboratory modules that may require special equipment, develop high heat loads, etc.

■ 100% fresh air intake from and 100% exhaust to the outside for all laboratory work areas, service and support spaces, and animal facilities. Location of fresh air intakes relative to the exhaust stacks is a critical item.

Electrical

■ Ceiling fluorescent light fixtures, pendant, surface, or recessed type, two or four tubes, square or rectangular fixture, plain or parabolic lenses; 50, 60, 70, or 100 fc (based on activity) at standing work counter height (36″ to 37″) supplemented with task lighting. Similar illumination may be required for tasks in sit-down work (27″ to 30″) areas.

■ Connected load design capacity should be between 60 and 100 VA/nsf in laboratory work areas only. May be considerably higher (several hundred VA/nsf) in electronics and production laboratory work areas. Equivalent of 50 W/nsf minimum in laboratory work areas only.

■ Each laboratory work area should have provision for an electrical panel package to distribute electrical power. Standard electrical service should be a bus duct system, 120 V/208 V panelboard, single- and three-phase, four-wire, 60-hertz current, with 25 to 35% excess capacity.

■ Explosion-proof light fixtures, switches, and receptacles available in laboratories and fume hoods using highly reactive, volatile, or explosive reagents.

■ Flush-counter top-mounted electric hotplates, 240 V, single-phase, 2000 to 3500 W capacity (varies).

■ Bus grounding bar connected to a special building ground grid system in each laboratory module for instruments and equipment requiring an absolute ground.

■ Minimum 1- to 120-V emergency electrical power outlet on each side of the laboratory work area module line or partition centerline, 1200 to 1500 W capacity. Certain laboratory functions and activities may require multiple redundant electrical systems (e.g., hazardous processes, animal facilities, etc.). The emergency electrical power requirements may become a significant cost factor in such facilities.

■ Smoke and flame detectors in each laboratory work area and in service and support areas.

■ One 208-V single-phase three-wire polarized grounded

outlet per 6 to 8 lf average at laboratory work counters, 20 A minimum capacity.

- Two 120-V three-wire polarized grounding duplex outlets per 2 to 3 lf average at laboratory work counters, metal multiple-channel raceway (plugmold type) or individual receptacles (flush or recessed); and quadruplexes, etc. Pedestal (deck-mounted) outlets generally not satisfactory in research or clinical laboratories; pedestal becomes an obstacle when mounted on the deck. Generally satisfactory for teaching laboratories, 15 A capacity minimum.

- 20-A ground-fault-circuit interrupters for each two to four 120-V duplex receptacles, with adjacent receptacles on different circuits.

- 208-V, three-phase, 480-V polarized grounded outlets as required for special equipment (installed when equipment delivered).

Plumbing

- Acid waste from designated sinks should be diverted to a neutralizing basin or holding tank for dilution, pH adjustment, and disposal. Biohazard liquid waste may have to be diverted to holding and processing tanks before being released in the sanitary sewer system or removed for alternative disposal process. A two-tank system may have to be installed (one to process waste and one to hold waste awaiting processing or removal).

- Carbon dioxide, nitrogen, oxygen, helium, or other special or mixed gases may be supplied from portable gas cylinders mounted/restrained in the laboratory work areas, central gas cylinder room, service corridor, etc., with manifold and distribution system. Gases may also be supplied in liquid form from special containers (dewars) or large tanks located outside the building. Locating gas cylinders in the laboratory work area can pose a safety hazard and is not recommended. Centralized gas cylinder holding and distribution areas are preferable. Recovery systems for helium salvage and recycling may be cost-effective, depending on application and volumes used.

- Central compressed air supplied at 40 to 60 to 150 psi (pressure regulators may be installed in the service corridor, etc.), filtered, dry, and oil-free. Consider portable air compressors to provide compressed air as needed. Machine noise may pose a problem if the unit is located in the laboratory work area.

■ Central natural or propane gas, propane gas supplied from tanks, liquid or gaseous form.

■ Breathing-quality air may be required at selected locations throughout the laboratory work areas for safety and emergency rescue protocols. Quick-connect/disconnect fixtures required.

■ Central nitrous oxide and oxygen supplied to animal surgery areas.

■ Central vacuum supplied at 18" to 22" (ordinary) to 28.5" (high) of mercury. Fixtures at 6' to 8' on-center at the laboratory work counter. Central vacuum may have to be filtered when installed in high-hazard laboratories.

■ Cup drains or cup sinks, one per 8 to 10 lf of laboratory work counter, acid resistant (stainless steel, glass, or composite). Types available include oval, rectangular, and hemispherical. Single (cold water only) rigid or vacuum-breaker gooseneck faucet with straight serrated hose connector. Deck, curb, or panel mounted. Use of cup sinks is diminishing (source of odors, sewer gases, etc.).

■ Drain troughs, 6" to 8" wide × 4" to 6" to 8" deep (function of length) × 18'-0" to 20'-0" long, acid-resistant composite material. Use of drain troughs is diminishing.

■ Emergency deluge shower head and eye wash in laboratory work areas with chemical fume hoods. Emergency shower capped above or at ceiling line in laboratory work areas without fume hoods. Consider floor drains to control water when deluge shower activated. Requirement that shower (in case of emergency, accidental release) can generate large volumes of water.

■ Hot (120 to 140°F) and cold water at each laboratory utility sink, mixing rigid or vacuum-breaker gooseneck faucet with straight serrated hose connector. Deck, curb or panel mounted. Faucets may be actuated by arm handles, wrist blades, knee action, or foot controls or automatic devices. Water manifolds available. Certain laboratories may require distilled or deionized water at the utility sink(s), with separate faucet supply.

■ Plastic drain materials should remain rigid and not soften when carrying liquids at 212°F. Interiors of plastic pipe materials tend to flake over time. These particles may cause problems or hazards.

■ Single-bowl-tub utility sink, acid resistant (stainless steel or composite materials), one per laboratory work area (single module) minimum. Sizes and locations of drains vary. Types available include cylindrical, wall table end sinks, center table end sinks, and double bowls, special sizes available, integral bowl and drain work counter, with or without drain board or pegboard.

■ Water and steam baths, electrical and steam heated, individual or multiple units, combination steam vapor and hot water bath available. Approximate electrical power consumption varies between 1500 and 4500 W. Approximate steam consumption (at 15 psi maximum) varies between 5 and 15 lb/hr. Electric and steam consumption rates a function of the number of bath openings.

■ Wet fire sprinkler system; carbon dioxide or Halon optional. Halon may be neither permitted nor available in the near future because of alleged environmental problems with the ozone layer.)

Data and Communications

■ One telephone outlet minimum for each laboratory single module. Additional telephone and data outlets may be required for modems, FAX machines, etc.

■ Two to four or more data terminals and closed-circuit TV outlets per laboratory work area.

COMMENTS

1. Traditional design practice provided the typical gas–air–vacuum cluster of service fixtures at x number of feet on-centers on work countertops. This practice can be wasteful and costly. Many laboratories no longer require these services at all work counters. Fuel gas can be provided from cylinders; compressed air from portable compressors or gas cylinders, and vacuum from portable vacuum pumps. These items of equipment may also be located in the service corridor or the interstitial services space.

2. Portable air compressors and vacuum pumps con-

tribute to the equipment noise in the laboratory and surrounding areas. Problems may develop from vibrations generated by the motors and compressors of the portable equipment. However, portable equipment provides individualized control and is less costly than central systems. Quality, purity, and control of contaminants can be strictly monitored. The demand for electrical outlets, however, has increased rapids. Ceiling baffles (acoustical "clouds"), movable acoustic screens, and noise-attenuating foam are possible methods of controlling noise in laboratory work areas.

3. The concept of separate buildings to accommodate diverse functions has been discussed briefly. Variations include organizing (locating) functions that have similar service and utility requirements (including functions from different scientific disciplines) within defined areas of the building. This physical organization can permit the grouping of various services and utilities specific to these functions in chases arranged either horizontally (designated floor) or vertically (similar functions stacked one above the other).

4. Grouping different scientific disciplines that have similar services and utilities requirements has other significant academic benefits. The proximity of researchers, physicians, and other personnel permits interchange and communication on a multidisciplinary basis not frequently possible in traditionally organized laboratory facilities. It is somewhat similar to the organizational structure of an institute for the study and treatment of a particular disease vs. a center for the study of a particular activity.

CHECKLIST 2: SAFETY PROGRAMMING CONSIDERATIONS

The following items relative to safety issues must be considered for inclusion in laboratory work areas or immediately convenient and available to the laboratory work areas. Service and support (core, shared areas) should include similar items. Many of these items are mandated by OSHA, EPA, NIOSH, NIH, and other regulatory agencies.

TABLE A.1   Liquid Flammables and
            Combustibles Classifications

	Class	Flash Point (°F)	Boiling Point (°F)
Flammables	IA	<73	<100
	IB	<73	≥100
	IC	≥100 and <100	—
Combustibles	II	≥100 and <140	—
	IIIA	≥140 and <200	—
	IIIB	≥200	—

Note:
■ Classification may change if liquid becomes contaminated.
■ Classifications do not apply to mixtures.
■ Volatility of liquids increases with heating, creating more serious explosions and fire hazards.

■ Vented safety storage cabinets for acids, solvents, flammable liquids, and corrosives can be the base cabinet for the fume hoods in laboratory work areas. Vents for the cabinets may be into the fume hood or into the exhaust duct directly. Hazardous waste storage cabinets, drums, and other containers, and safety containers for storage and disposal of reagents and hazardous waste must also be considered, as must what is being stored, the volume of material to be stored, and the cabinet construction material. Large volumes of flammables may be stored outdoors in approved storage units. Tables A.1 and A.2 were derived from OSHA 29 CFR 1910.106(a)(18); OSHA 29 CFR 1910.106(d)(3); and NFPA 30, Section 4-3.1.

TABLE A.2   Maximum Storage Quantities
            for Cabinets

Liquid Classificaiton	Maximum Storage Capacity (gal)
Flammable, class I	60
Combustible, class II	60
Combustible, class III	120
Combination of classes	120[a]

Note: No more than three cabinets may be located in a single fire area. See NFPA 30, Section 4-3.1.
[a] No more than 60 gal may be class I and class II liquids, nor may more than 120 gal of class III liquids be stored in a storage cabinet.

- Metal safety cabinet requirements may be found in OSHA 29 CFR 1910.106(d)(3) and NFPA 30, Chapter 4, Sections 4-3.2 and 4-3.2.1. The Uniform Fire Code 79.202 requires the same specifications as OSHA 29 CFR 1910.106 and NFPA 30. UFC also requires that self-closing doors be added to the cabinets.

- Wood safety cabinet requirements may be found in OSHA 29 CFR 1910.106(d)(3) and NFPA 30, Chapter 4, Sections 4-3.2 and 4-3.2.2. The Uniform Fire Code 79.202 lists similar requirements for wood safety cabinets.

- Bench cabinets are available to store small amounts of flammables and corrosives under the laboratory workbench. Mobile safety cabinets are also available in compliance with OSHA 29 CFR 1910.106 and NFPA 30 regulations.

- Type I and type II safety cans must comply with Department of Transportation (DOT) 19L and UN 1A1/Y/100/ 92 requirements for storage and use of hazardous and flammable liquids in the laboratory. They may be made of stainless steel, terne plate steel, polyethylene, and other materials. OSHA 29 CFR 1910.106(e)(6)(ii) list regulations for bonding and grounding wire requirements of class I liquids during transfer.

- Assorted containers are required for nonhazardous trash, broken glass, liquid waste, and hazardous waste, including infectious, radioactive, and pathological waste. Consider a "parking space" for the hazardous waste materials utility cart in the laboratory work area; helps to promote safe practices protocols relative to hazardous waste holding for disposal. Separate containers are required for the various classifications of hazardous and nonhazardous waste materials.

- Breathing and respirator apparatus, including portable-SCBA (NFPA compliant apparatus) and supplied-air units, storage for breathing air compressors and tanks, hoses, regulators, cartridges, and filters, must also be considered, as must powered air-purifying respirators (portable/battery, compliant airline system, etc.); OSHA compliant air system requirements for IDLH conditions (immediate danger to life and health); NIOSH-approved pump and hose requirements; storage cabinets; etc.

- New OSHA Standard 29 CFR 1910.146 requires the establishment of a comprehensive permit system controlling entry authorizations, procedures, and training of personnel associated with confined space operations. Storage space for confined space rescue equipment carts and stretchers, will be required. OSHA defines a permit-required confined space as one that presents, or has the potential to present, one or more of the following hazards:

— An atmospheric hazard

— A configuration hazard

— An engulfment hazard

— "Another" recognized hazard [quotation marks added]

COMMENTS

1. There is absolutely no doubt (in the opinion of the author) that OSHA Standard 29 CFR 1910.146 applies (or will be applied) to service corridors and interstitial spaces. The facility manager, safety officer, laboratory workers, and the architect and engineer must review the building services concepts and the planning of these spaces to ascertain whether any hazardous conditions may arise from the building service systems concept selected. Access to service corridors by laboratory staff assumes ominous liability implications in the context of this OSHA Standard. More than $7 million in fines was assessed institutions in 1992 for violating this standard. This does not include the monetary awards made to injured workers as a result of suits brought against institutions.

2. OSHA Standard 29 CFR 1910.146 also requires that teaching, education, and training programs be established for staff relative to this and virtually all other OSHA standards. These programs are not one-shot deals; they must be conducted periodically. This may have a significant impact on conference/classroom spaces. Test equipment must be supplied staff to test and monitor defined and dangerous conditions. This will affect storage and calibration facilities for such instrumentation. An office space may be required for the safety instructor, as well.

- Gas mask storage cabinets are required in laboratory work areas that may generate organic vapors, dusts, fumes, smoke, and mists from chlorine, acid gases, hydrogen cyanide, ethylene oxide, ammonia, and so on. Quick-connect/disconnect outlets should be provided a strategic locations throughout laboratory work areas for portable emergency resuscitation equipment and storage cabinets for fit-test materials and devices (tents, etc.). OSHA regulations require that fit tests be performed for each wearer at least once a year.

- Chemical spill response containment materials and clean-up equipment, including tools, utensils, and spill-response materials and equipment carts, must be provided. May require alcove and closet storage spaces.

- Also required are emergency deluge or drench shower stations (floor, wall, ceiling, counter mounted, pull chain, lever, push plate, or treadle activated):
    - *Indoor*: flow pressures between 5 and 50 psi, flow rates at 20 to 135 gpm
    - *Outdoor*: flow pressure between 10 and 40 psi, flow rates at 25 to 70 gpm, may have to be protected from freezing temperatures
    - Drench hoses and multiple-spray shower booths also available
    - Combination shower and eye wash units available

- Emergency eye, combination eye and face washers (floor, wall, counter mounted, hand or foot activated):
    - Minimum flow pressure at 20 psi, 125 psi maximum static pressure, water temperature range at 60° to 95°F, and flow rate between 2.5 and 12 gpm
    - Portable eye wash units available
    - Alarm systems available to indicate if emergency shower or eye wash activated

NOTE

All deluge shower, eye, and face wash stations must be barrier-free to accommodate disabled persons.

- Fire blanket and fire cover storage cabinets.
- Fire extinguishers (ABC class, dry and liquid).

NOTE

An emergency shower and eye wash station (OSHA 29 CFR 1910.133), fire extinguishers (OSHA 29 CFR 1910.157), and fire blankets are required in all laboratory work areas. OSHA Standard 29 CFR 1910.106 defines fire extinguishers and distance from flammables stored in the laboratory.

- First-aid supply cabinets, emergency equipment carts.
- Flammable materials refrigerators, freezers (plug-in type); and explosion-proof refrigerators, freezers (hardwired type).
- Gas cylinder brackets, retainers, holders, stands, and manifold distribution systems.
- Hazards publications, manuals, communication materials, and notices (holders, bulletin and chalk boards, shelves, wall and floor mounted) to conform to OSHA Hazards Communication Standard 29 CFR 1910.1200 and OSHA Standard for Occupational Exposure to Hazardous Chemicals in Laboratories 29 CFR 1910.1450:
  — Material safety data sheets (MSDS) notebooks
  — Training programs for right-to-know (RTK) laws
  — Wall charts, signs, posters, and other graphics
- Hearing protectors, including earplugs, bands, earmuffs, etc.
- Ladders and step stools, and adjustable work platforms to reach high storage (wall cabinets, shelves, etc.) units; build, assemble, and service equipment used in experiments.
- Smoke and flame detectors and alarms, and portable alarm, warning, and monitoring systems.
- Portable fans, air movement, and ventilation equipment.
- Protective safety eyeware, goggles and face shields, eyeware storage cabinets, and cleaning stations. Eyeware pro-

tection for spills, splashing, sprays, high-intensity light flashes, laser generators, explosions, grinding, welding, dust particles, etc.

NOTE

OSHA Bloodborne Pathogen Standard 1910.130 requires that shields (bench and face types), gloves, masks, and protective clothing be worn by staff when working with such hazardous specimens, reagents, etc. OSHA 29 CFR 1910.134 Standard for Respiratory Protection also applies. Space convenient to workstations is required to store such safety protective items. NCCLS Document M29-T2, Vol. 11, No. 14, *Protection of Laboratory Workers from Infectious Disease Transmitted by Blood, Body Fluids, and Tissue*, 2nd Ed. (Tentative Guideline, Sept. 1991) is consistent with OSHA and CDC standards.

- Protective suits and clothing, coveralls, foot and head gear, boots, hard hats, gloves, storage areas and containers for used and soiled protective gear, and special storage for contaminated protective gear. Clean gear storage, protective creams, barrier creams, skin conditioners and hand cleaners, change areas, decontamination showers, and toilet facilities) may be required.

- Back, wrist, elbow, knee, ankle supports, and pads; ergonomic chairs, stools, etc. Computer operator VDT and keyboard equipment, including antiglare screens, footrests, document holders, adjustable monitor and keyboard holders, wrist rests, etc.

- Storage for special wheelchairs for the evacuation of disabled or injured persons (similar to those used by the airlines to transport disabled persons in and out of aircraft). Chairs of this type are manufactured by EVAC+CHAIR Corporation, 17 East 67th Street, New York, NY 10021.

- Emergency stair, corridor, etc., lighting units (battery powered, fixed and portable) in addition to lighting that may be on the emergency power generator system (fire code requirements).

- ADA Requirements (28 CFR Part 36) for disabled persons must be integrated into and implemented as part of an

institution's safety and disaster program. OSHA Standard
29 CFR 1910.145 specifies that accident prevention signs
and tags must be provided in the workplace. Such devices
must be "visible and/or audible and/or discernible" to
disabled persons. Audible signs and devices must be included for those who cannot read. The architect and electrical engineer must be cognizant of these requirements
when designing and selecting building systems components.

- Safety runners, cushioned mats, etc., may be required to
elevate staff above wet floors, eliminate static electricity
discharge, etc.
- Ceiling- and wall-mounted mirrors at corridor corners,
intersections, etc., are required for safety and security
protocols.
- The designer must include the exterior of the building
site, incorporation of ramps, parking spaces for the disabled, lighting and security systems, etc.

COMMENTS

1. Extreme caution must be exercised when designing
the water piping systems that supply the emergency
shower and eye wash fixtures. Shutoff valves must be
placed and identified to prevent shutoff of water to
emergency fixtures in laboratory work areas that may
continue in use while adjoining spaces are being
remodeled or renovated.

2. The pros and cons of providing floor drains, curbs,
depressed slabs, etc., under (or near) deluge emergency showers are many. Proponents have persuasive reasons, including the need to contain and
dispose of large volumes of water expended in an
emergency or accidental release. Protocols may require drenching for 20 minutes, producing 400 to
500 gal to more than 2500 gal of water per use. This
volume of water can create serious electrical hazards, damage to ceilings and activities in spaces below, etc.

3. The argument that floor drains can dry out, creating a
source of odors and gases to permeate a space, is
valid. This problem, however, is a manifestation of
the lack of well-managed building operations and
maintenance policies and protocols to check and

replenish/recharge the drains with water. Location of the floor drains within the laboratory work area is an important design consideration. Drains should not be located in areas where they may be covered (hidden) from view by equipment, casework, etc.

4. All pipes, conduits, ducts, etc., should be labeled with industry standard graphics to identify the contents and direction of flow. Access panels, cleanout panels (particularly at the bottom of chemical fume hood exhaust duct risers), inspection panels, etc., should contain a small view port to permit a visual check before opening the access panel. Refer to ANSI A13.1-1981 standards for identification and labeling of building systems elements. Larger institutions will require a dedicated graphics department and staff to comply with the requirements of the various regulations under OSHA, EPA, DOT, etc., for the signs and labels required to identify hazardous, radioactive, pathogenic, biologic, and nonhazardous materials used in laboratory facilities. The designer must integrate these required graphics into the architectural features of the building.

5. Safety lockout/tagout units must be located at strategic intervals in service corridors, interstitial spaces, etc., in accordance with OSHA 29 CFR 1910.147 and Instruction STD 1-7.3 regulations. These units must be used when maintenance, servicing, and changes are being made to the utilities supplying laboratory work areas. Lockouts prevent unexpected energization or startup of machines or equipment, or release of stored energy (e.g., steam, water, gas, electrical capacitor discharge, etc.).

6. Excellent sources for a myriad of safety equipment, references, etc., are catalogs available from Lab Safety Supply Inc., P.O. Box 1368, Janesville, WI 53547-1368, (1-800-356-2855).

7. Although not specifically addressed by current statutes or regulations, certain workstations where repetitive tasks are performed (word processing, computer input, etc.) should be equipped with ergonomically designed furnishings (chairs, desks, etc.) to reduce the incidence of carpel tunnel syndrome and other physical problems. The American Conference of Governmental Industrial Hygienists (ACGIH) publishes recommendations for employee work areas. See Ap-

pendix C for the address of ACGIH. Studies indicate that employees using ergonomically designed chairs, desks, etc., improve their work efficiency substantially. The degree of efficiency improvement is related to the specific tasks performed (e.g., how long the person sits or stands, etc.). These factors and requirements are implied in many industry standards and guidelines, including those of the Joint Commission for the Accreditation of Health Organizations (JCAHO PA.2 Standard).

8. Computer printer (laser, etc.) and copy machine work areas should be well ventilated to exhaust fumes and gases (ozone, etc.) produced by the copying process.

9. Sufficient air exhaust hoods should be provided at tissue fixative processor and slide staining work areas and tissue grossing work areas to remove the toxic fumes from formaldehyde, xylene, and other reagent fixatives. An exhaust hood airflow of 75 to 115 fpm is generally suggested. A chemical fume hood or biological safety cabinet may be a more prudent and safe solution for such workstations.

10. OSHA 29 CFR 1910.1200, 1450 refers to Standards for Exposure to Hazardous Chemicals in Laboratories. The Proposed Performance Standards for Laboratories Using Toxic Substances are outlined in 51 FR 26660. Standards for working with carcinogens (hoods, etc.) are also listed in Subpart Z. OSHA also encourages employers to follow CDC guidelines for engineering controls for ventilation, local exhaust, etc.

11. OSHA has revised the permissible exposure limit (PEL) for formaldehyde from 1.0 per million parts of air (ppm) to 0.75 ppm on an 8-hour time-weighted average (TWA) basis. Respiratory protection must now be offered to employees exposed above the new PEL. Engineering and work practice controls must be in place. If tests indicate concentrations over the limits, the facilities must be modified to reduce the levels. Air quality tests should be performed by a professional engineer. OSHA 29 CFR 1910.1000-1500 standards limit employee exposure by inhalation to various agents. See proposed OSHA 29 CFR 1910.1450.

CHECKLIST 3: BUILDING SYSTEMS
DESIGN CONSIDERATIONS

The following items highlight criteria to be considered during the programming and planning process. As criteria develop and are identified and established, the facility design evolves to respond to the criteria.

- *Architectural/Structural:* vibration ("stiffness"), wind loads, acoustics, bay sizes, floor-to-floor heights, floor loadings, walls, floors, ceilings, roof, insulation, asbestos treatment, lead paint, finishes, hardware, materials, colors, textures, future expansion, flexibility and adaptability, remodeling and renovation vs. replacement, building maintenance and operations, intermittent or continuous, degree of obsolescence, systems serviceability to meet current and future programs, vertical and horizontal transport systems, elevators (size, speed, loading, etc.), corridors, stairs, disabled requirements, materials, equipment, supplies handling systems, etc.

- *Mechanical (HVAC):* ductwork, duct materials, air supply, return, exhaust emissions, air changes per hour, rates, adjacent space pressure differentials, air quality of the interior building environment, ventilation, filters, treatment, cooling, heating, insulation, humidity, interstitial vs. service corridor, computer controls, energy conversion, reclamation, solar, fuel storage, operational downtime, energy services costs, etc.

- *Electrical:* lighting quality, intensity, incandescent or fluorescent, power distribution, communications (telephone, intercom, paging, audiovisual, computer networks, microwave, television, data transmission, facsimile, etc.), emergency power equipment, lightning protection, building systems and safety; shielding for electrical, radio-frequency, and magnetic fields; redundant systems; security monitoring systems, etc.

- *Plumbing:* piping materials (cast iron, glass, plastic, copper), fixtures, sinks, staff facilities, sewage, domestic hot water, steam; water and its quality and purity, flow, pressure, temperature; liquid waste and its acidity (pH), toxicity, corrosibleness; liquid waste holding and treatment; special gases, decontamination, dilution, cryogenics (liquid nitrogen, helium, etc.), compressed air, vacuum, distribution, etc.; solid waste, trash, garbage, pathological waste, toxic, biohazardous, radioactivity, carcinogenic, collection, handling precautions, processing, transport, containers, storage, and disposal.

- *Casework, Equipment, and Furnishings:* fixed vs. modular, common vs. individual equipment (core/shared areas); location of fume, exhaust, and biohazard hoods; lasers, refrigerators, centrifuges, incubators, microscopes, gas cylinders, balances, stills, analyzers; consumables vs. reusables, impact on storage, reprocessing, etc.; service and equipment carts; autoclaves; radiographic units; glass washers and dryers; biosafety cabinets; surgical lights, tables and anesthesia systems; office furnishings, records and equipment storage, etc.

- *Facility Codes and Safety Requirements:* AAALAC, AAALAS, ADA, ASHRAE, ASTM, BOCA, CDC, DOE, DOL, EPA, FDA, JCAHO, NEC, NFPA, NIEHS, NIH, NIOSH, NAS, OSHA, UL, and other federal and state regulations, life safety, smoke and flame detectors, alarms, exiting, evacuation, breathing apparatus, emergency deluge showers, decontamination, protective clothing, fire blankets, emergency eye and face wash, door swings and widths; flame, smoke, fumes, dust, and explosion hazards; high-hazard areas, extinguishers, hydrants, standpipes, sprinklers, carbon dioxide and Halon; safety equipment and procedures, etc.

- *Site Considerations:* traffic, parking (surface, decks, pay, free, etc.), security, lighting, pedestrian walks and spaces, crosswalks, circulation, landscaping, public transportation, zoning, adjoining site uses, future expansion capabilities, building setback, height, FARs, access to utilities, roads, easements, contours, shape, size; usable vs. nonusable; drainage, flooding, erosion, orientation, sun control; noise from autos, trains, aircraft; prevailing winds, impact and airflow of hood exhaust gases on adjacent surroundings, stack height, treatment of exhaust gases (scrubbers), etc.

CHECKLIST 4: FACILITY PROGRAMMING INTERVIEW PROCESS SUMMARIES

A facility programming interview questionnaire should be organized to assist in the data-gathering process. The questionnaire can be used to verify, modify, update, or, add to any pertinent information that may be available. Interviewees should be requested to compile pertinent department or section data indicated on the questionnaire prior to the scheduled interviews. The intent is to distribute the data to the interviewer (consultant, architect, etc.) prior to each scheduled meeting, *if possible.*

Interviewers/Interviewees who may not have participated in the facilities programming and planning process should review the manual published by the College of American Pathologists (CAP), *Medical Laboratory Planning and Design*, and other references listed in Appendix C. Master planning and programming interviews should be conducted in a comfortable, neutral-ground conference room outside the interviewee's home base of operations. Adequate writing (white board) and tack board space with a projection screen is preferable. The interview space should be relaxing and provide the opportunity for the interviewee to communicate and share his or her views openly and freely. A project kickoff meeting should be conducted, attended by the interviewees and other key staff. This provides an opportunity to explain the project and answer questions about the process, objectives, and other details. The kickoff meeting also provides the opportunity to dispel any rumors about the project within the academic, corporate, or government environment.

Checklist 4a: Generic List of Medical Center Functions and Activities

The following generic list of Medical Center Functions and Activities includes the school of medicine, research laboratories, the teaching hospital, and service and support activities. The list may be used as a guide to assist in selecting participants for the programming and planning interview sessions.

A. MEDICAL CENTER ADMINISTRATION

1. Director of the medical center
   - Alumni affairs and development
   - Board of trustees
   - Facilities management/planning/construction
   - Information and publications
   - Parking
2. Medical center computer center services
3. Employee health facilities

B. SCHOOL OF MEDICINE

1. Dean of the School of Medicine
   - Student services
   - Faculty development
2. Administrative services
   - Bank/ATM
   - Bookstore/education supplies
   - Environmental services/housekeeping
   - Materials management
     - Purchasing/receiving/distribution
     - General/special storage
   - Personnel/human resources
   - Physical plant
     - Buildings and grounds
     - Graphics/signage
   - Post office/mailroom
   - Print shop
   - Resource management/accounting/finance office
3. Continuing education
   - Faculty
   - Graduate students
   - Others
4. Research development/grants
   - Government (federal/state)
   - Private/corporate
5. Basic sciences
   - Anatomy
   - Biochemistry
   - Comparative medicine/animal facilities
   - Microbiology/immunology
   - Pathology
   - Pharmacology
   - Physiology
6. Clinical science department
   - Anesthesia
   - Community medicine

- Dentistry
- Family medicine/family practice
- Medicine
  - Allergy
  - Cardiology
  - Dermatology
  - Endocrinology
  - Gastroenterology
  - General medicine
  - Hematology
  - Immunology-rheumatology
  - Infectious diseases
  - Nephrology
  - Oncology
  - Pulmonary medicine
- Neurology
  - Neuropsychology
  - Pediatric neurology
- Obstetrics/gynecology
- Oncology research center
- Pediatrics
  - Medical genetics
- Psychiatry
- Diagnostic imaging/radiology
- Surgery
  - Cardiothoracic surgery
  - Emergency medical services
  - General surgery
  - Neurosurgery
  - Ophthalmology
  - Orthopedics
  - Otolaryngology
  - Plastic/reconstructive
  - Urology

7. Support departments
   - Clinical research/clinical research unit

- Medical student teaching/nursing/paramedical/ laboratory technology
- Medical social science and marital health
- Reference/research library/editorial

8. Service departments
   - Audiovisual resources
   - Communications
   - Biomedical engineering/fabrication
   - Core laboratory service/support
   - Health physics/safety officer/infection control
   - Student teaching laboratories
   - Waste management
     — Collection/processing/incineration
     — Holding/recycling/disposal

9. Patient services
   - Department of clinics
     — Admitting/registration/scheduling
     — Business office
     — Clinic areas
       — Allergy
       — Dermatology
       — Gastroenterology
       — Medicine
       — Nephrology
       — Neurology
       — Neurosurgery
       — Obstetrics/gynecology
       — Oncology
       — Ophthalmology
       — Orthopedics
       — Otolaryngology
       — Pediatrics
       — Psychiatry
       — Surgery
       — Urology

C. TEACHING HOSPITAL

1. President and CEO of hospital
   - Assistants/associates
   - Development/fund raising
   - Public relations
   - Parking
2. Denominational relations
3. Internal audit
4. Pastoral care/chaplain
5. Patient relations/ombudsman
6. Human resources/personnel
7. Safety/security
8. Administrative services
   - Admitting/registration/scheduling
   - CFO/financial management division
   - Computer center/data processing
   - Patient financial services division
9. Professional services
   - Cardiology/heart station
   - Chemotherapy/hematology
   - Clinical laboratories/pathology/autopsy/morgue
   - Community education
   - Diagnostic imaging
     — Magnetic resonance imaging
     — Nuclear medicine
     — Radiation biology
     — Radiology
     — Radiotherapy
     — Special diagnostic radiology
       — Cardiac catheterization
       — CT scan
       — PET scan
   - Diagnostic neurology
   - EEG/EKG
     — Electrodiagnostics

       — Neurology diagnostics
       — Neurophysiology
    ■ Hearing and speech
    ■ Cardiology/heart station
    ■ Hemodialysis (chronic)
    ■ Medical library
    ■ Medical records
    ■ Multidisciplinary clinical sonic lab
    ■ Occupational therapy
    ■ On-call accommodations
    ■ Pharmacy
    ■ Physical therapy/fitness
    ■ Prosthetics/orthotics
    ■ Pulmonary function test lab
    ■ Respiratory therapy
    ■ Social services

10. Patient care services
    ■ Ambulatory care facilities
       — Ambulatory surgical services
       — Multidisciplinary clinics
       — POB/MOB
    ■ Central sterile services/SPD
    ■ Emergency medical services/trauma center
    ■ Inpatient care facilities
       — Acute care
          — Gynecology
          — Medical/surgical
          — Nursery/wellborn
          — Obstetrics/maternity/labor/delivery
          — Orthopedics
          — Pediatrics
          — Psychiatry
       — Critical care
          — Acute dialysis/nephrology
          — Burn/special wound unit
          — Coronary care

- — Medical/surgical ICU
- — Neonatal ICU
- — Extended/long-term care
- — Geriatrics
- — Hospice care
- — Intermediate care
- — Oncology
- — Progressive care
- — Rehabilitation/physical medicine
- — Substance abuse
- ■ Nursing service administration
  - — Infection control
  - — Nursing education/inservice
  - — Quality assurance/control
  - — Tumor registry
  - — Utilization review
- ■ Surgery suite/general/special/recovery

11. General services
    - ■ Central employee facilities
    - ■ Communications—audiovisual
    - ■ Environmental services/housekeeping
    - ■ Food/nutrition services
    - ■ Laundry/linens/sewing
    - ■ Materials management
      - — Patient transport
      - — General/special storage
      - — Purchasing/receiving/distribution
    - ■ Plant engineering and maintenance
    - ■ Printing/graphics/signage
    - ■ Public lobby/information
    - ■ Snack bar/vending
    - ■ Waste management
      - — Collection/processing/incineration
      - — Holding/recycling/disposal

12. Miscellaneous/special services
    - ■ Medical mall

— Bank/ATM
— Barber/beauty shop
— Concessions
— Cafeteria/restaurant
— Gift shop/flowers
— Movie/entertainment/education
— Optician/eyeglasses
— Pharmacy/appliances
— Retail establishments

Checklist 4b: Generic Project Schedule

The following generic project schedule illustrates how programming and planning tasks may be represented over time. A specific schedule would be prepared for each project.

- Project Start
— Notice to Proceed
— Administrative Meeting

Schedules for the following phases would be developed as the decision is made to proceed with a specific facilities project:

- Schematic design
- Design development
- Construction documents
- Bidding/negotiation
- Construction
- Occupancy
- Operations/maintenance programs

Checklist 4c: Generic Interviewee List

The following is a representative staff interviewee list. Functions and activities may be combined and require more or less interview time to secure the required design criteria. The list illustrates staff functions and activities that may be selected for interviews. Each institution may have different titles, and organization of functions, activities, and individual staff responsibilities.

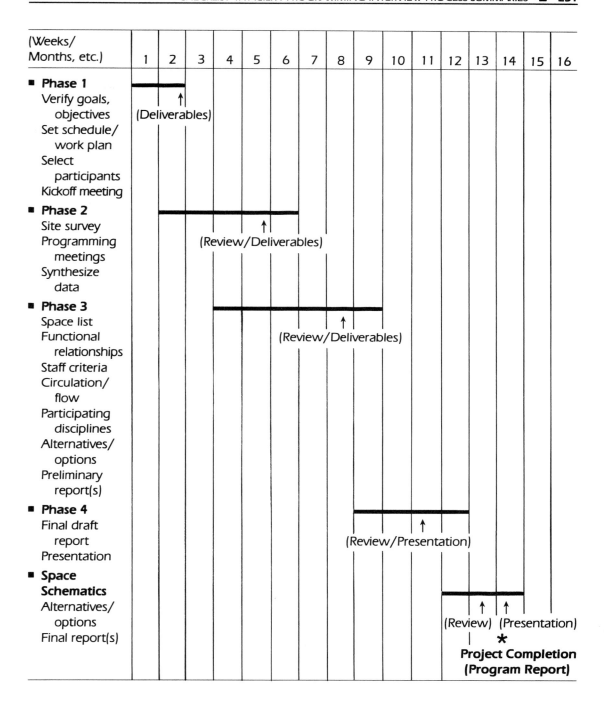

(Weeks/ Months, etc.)	1	2	3	4	5	6	7	8	9	10	11	12	13	14	15	16

■ Phase 1
  Verify goals,
    objectives
  Set schedule/
    work plan
  Select
    participants
  Kickoff meeting

(Deliverables)

■ Phase 2
  Site survey
  Programming
    meetings
  Synthesize
    data

(Review/Deliverables)

■ Phase 3
  Space list
  Functional
    relationships
  Staff criteria
  Circulation/
    flow
  Participating
    disciplines
  Alternatives/
    options
  Preliminary
    report(s)

(Review/Deliverables)

■ Phase 4
  Final draft
    report
  Presentation

(Review/Presentation)

■ Space
Schematics
  Alternatives/
    options
  Final report(s)

(Review) (Presentation)
★
Project Completion
(Program Report)

A kickoff meeting should be scheduled to include participating key staff representatives. The meeting provides an opportunity to explain project methodology, process, and answer questions. The programming interview questionnaire should be distributed prior to the kickoff meeting. Checklists 4d, 4e, and 4f will also assist during the programming interview and data-gathering process. Interviews should be scheduled and conducted with administrative, researchers, principal investigators, and other key staff. Interviews may be conducted at the rate of five to seven per day. Time required may be approximately 0.5 hour to 1.5 and 2 hours for each interviewee.

The sequence of meetings is not critical, although some deans, department heads, etc., may wish to be scheduled first or last (their choice). Additional meetings may be scheduled to permit input from other key individuals and to provide the opportunity for review of the programming and planning criteria as they are developed.

- Laboratory administration
  — Director
  — Laboratory administrator
  — Principal investigator
  — Assistant lab administrator(s)
  — Laboratory manager(s)
  — Secretary/clerical
- Scientific disciplines
  — Physical sciences
  — Basic sciences
  — Biomedical sciences
  — Clinical science
  — Other disciplines
- Environmental services, waste management
- Equipment/instrument services
- Materials management, receiving, storage, distribution
- Core services and support
- Teaching/education
- Physical plant/grounds
- Quality assurance, utilization
- Reception/waiting/public
- Safety/security programs
- Special technologies
  — MRI spectroscopy

— Electron microscopy

— Others

■ Staff lounge, lockers, showers, toilets, etc.

■ Other functions and activities

— Facilities planning

— Administration—president, CEO, CFO, COO, VPs, etc.

— Selected key institutional staff, etc.

■ Public/government

Checklist 4d: Generic Programming Interview Questionnaire Summary

The following is a partial list of subjects that may be discussed during the programming and planning interviews:

Functional Criteria

■ Definition, goals, objectives, mission, services, functions performed, to whom delivered—extent, type, duration of research, protocols, policies, etc.—staff, visitors, etc.

■ Attach statistical data, utilization rates, workloads, procedures, etc., for the past 4 to 5 years.

General Staffing Data

■ Full-time and part-time personnel (maximum number of staff on duty at any given time).

Spaces (Existing and Required)

■ Offices, clerical, transcription, files, records, equipment, supplies and equipment storage, reception, public waiting, lockers, toilets and lounges, receiving, processing, service and support, scientific disciplines, etc.

■ It is not necessary to determine or assign square feet (unless known) to the spaces at this time. Consider intra-functional and interdepartmental relationships, optimum location for the function or activity, staff, visitor, materials, supplies circulation and flow, etc.

■ Space and area deficiencies (e.g., spaces with insufficient area to perform functions efficiently and safely, etc.)

Provisions for Expansion

- Is the department or division expanding or adding services and staff because of planned or future research programs, etc.; additional or new equipment; changes in services methodology?

Shared Services and Staff

- Interaction and dependencies (e.g., materials and supplies provided by a central materials management department may require supply cart staging or holding spaces, etc.). If not, should such systems or shared services, etc., be considered ("core" areas)?

Equipment

- Major items of equipment requiring floor space (e.g., refrigerators, incubators, waste containers, freezers, sterilizers, carts, MRI units, centrifuges, etc.) are important to identify to test assigned and projected square feet. It is not necessary to provide specifications of equipment.
- Detailed equipment data will be requested during subsequent planning phases. It is important to discuss if acquisition of major items of equipment is being considered.

Additional Items and Subjects

- Architectural, structural, mechanical, electrical, plumbing, and other environmental factors [e.g., finishes (floor, wall, ceiling), lighting, temperature, air quality and changes, exhaust, humidity, computers, telecommunications, safety and security, hazadous waste protocols, etc.] will be reviewed.
- Apparent life safety, code violations (e.g., dead-end corridors, safe refuge, inadequate exiting, nonconforming workstations, lack of functional work spaces, etc.). Impact on design of federal, state, and local code requirements (ADA, BOCA, CDC, CLIA, NFPA, NIH, NIOSH, OSHA, etc.).

Checklist 4e: Example Research Laboratory Programming Questions

Checklist 4e illustrates examples of a composite listing of items, questions to be used, and so on, that may be considered when developing a specific interviewee programming questionnaire for use during the master planning, programming, and planning process. Other questions may have to be developed in response to specific research functions and activities that may be proposed, if known.

1. What are the functions and activities to be accommodated within the laboratory work areas?
   (a) Scientific disciplines to be assigned (e.g., biology, physics, chemistry, etc.)
   (b) Processes
      - Hazardous/nonhazardous (solid, liquid, gaseous, fire, explosive, etc.).
      - Will an incinerator be required (pathological, biohazards, solid/liquid waste, etc.)? This process may not be allowed in certain jurisdictions subject to EPA and the Clean Air Act provisions.
      - Chemical, petroleum, etc.
      - Biological (animals required?).
      - Physical (nuclear, electronic, metallurgical, etc.).
      - Engineering/testing (mechanical, electrical, structural).
      - Pharmaceuticals (research/production/manufacturing).
   (c) Relationship with/to other functions/activities (at the departmental level)
   (d) Major items of equipment (movable, built-in, floor/counter mounted)
   (e) Other items/considerations

2. What administrative protocols, scientific research protocols (use of hazardous reagents, animals, etc.)?

3. Definition of goals, objectives, mission, services, etc. Is current planning for interim, short, or long term? Three, five, or seven years? Does the institution have a strategic plan? A master facilities plan? For the department, etc.? If so, how recent? Last update? What type of research planned? Theoretical? Applied? Clinical? Other?

4. List general staffing data, full-time (FTEs), part-time, shifts, 8-, 12-, 24-hour operations, etc.?
   (a) Professional

    (b) Technical

    (c) Administrative

    (d) Support/service

    (e) Other (visiting faculty, etc.)

5. List spaces (existing and required)

    (a) Existing: Provide an inventory of the existing spaces; include area (net square feet) if known.

    (b) Required: List those spaces considered necessary for the proposed program.

    (c) List space/area deficiencies (e.g., x-ray, spectrography laboratory work areas too small, insufficient mechanical/electrical/plumbing services, storage, etc.).

6. Are intra- and interfunctional relationships of all functions and activities convenient, eficient? (e.g., reagent preparation should be located adjacent to reagent storage, etc.) Is flow/circulation of materials, equipment, staff, visitors, etc., efficient? (room-to-room)

7. Is the department, division, etc., expanding? Adding staff and services, new/additional equipment?

8. What functions/activities can be accomplished/supported within a "core" or common work/equipment area (e.g., electron microscopy, NMR imaging, photography, incubation, animal facilities, supplies, glass wash, etc.)?

9. Have space standards/guidelines been established for offices, laboratory work areas, equipment storage, conference/seminar, etc. (e.g., 160 nsf for principal investigator's office, assigned laboratory work areas to investigators at 1200 nsf, etc.)?

10. What safety and security requirements and deficiencies can be identified? Any safety or security conflicts? What types of safety/security protocols are required for personnel, laboratory access, equipment, reagent handling/storage, waste products, etc.?

    (a) Special locks

    (b) Protective clothing

    (c) Protective face/eye/hand/body appliances

    (d) Breathing devices (SCBA, portable, fixed, etc.)

    (e) Anterooms

    (f) Airlocks/change areas

    (g) Decontamination showers

    (h) Emergency treatment

    (i) Other (portable/fixed shielding, ultraviolet light, etc.)

11. Should staff offices/support spaces be within, adjacent to, convenient to laboratory work areas. Why?

12. What functions and activities require 24-hour operations/services, etc.?

    (a) Controlled-temperature work rooms

    (b) Chemical fume hoods, biological safety cabinets, exhaust hoods

    (c) Computers (UPS, controllers, FAX machines, etc.)

    (d) Research processes, etc.

    (e) Production areas

    (f) Clean rooms

    (g) Controlled-temperature storage areas

    (h) Other

13. How and where will equipment be serviced, calibrated, etc.? In the laboratory work area? In the engineering work/fabrication shop? With in-house staff? Manufacturers' representatives? If, by manufacturers' representatives, is work area required for on-site service? Spare parts inventory/holding?

14. What is the policy for storage of electronic media (tapes, disks, etc.)—off-site, on-site (security/access), files, records (hard-copy), printouts, etc.? Active vs. inactive (dead/archives)?

15. List personnel—status (professional, technical, support, etc.), space requirements (enclosed office, open office/workspace, etc.).

16. List major items of equipment requiring floor space (MRI, spectroscopy, atomic absorption, refrigerators, freezers, centrifuges, incubators, etc.)?

17. Identify special services [e.g., clean power, high voltage (440 V, etc.), ac. dc]?

18. Water quality and type, potable, chemically pure (type I, IIA, IIB, III, special purpose), temperature/pressure control for emergency showers, eye washers, etc.?

19. Special casework (modular, traditional, movable), casework and counter-work-top materials (metal, wood, stone, plastic, composition), colors, cabinets, shelves, door (hinged/sliding, solid/glass), sitting/standing workstations with knee spaces, adjustable workstations for disabled staff.

20. Hood types
    (a) Chemical (explosion-proof, non-)
    (b) Radioisotope
    (c) Counter/task/workstation
    (d) Floor/walk-in
    (e) Biological safety cabinet (Class IIA, IIB, IIB2)
    (f) Laminar flow
    (g) Canopy (exhaust type over work areas, equipment, etc.) to remove excessive heat, odors, etc.
    (h) Perchloric
    (i) "Elephant trunk," "snorkel"
    (j) Other

21. Identify/highlight special regulatory requirements related to a specific research activity, if known [e.g., Nuclear Regulatory Commission (management of radio nuclides, etc.), CDC (hazardous materials, etc.), NIH (research protocols, etc.), etc.]

22. List special spaces
    (a) BSL-1, 2, 3, 4
    (b) Clean rooms
    (c) Controlled temperature, humidity, pressure, etc.
    (d) EMS/RF, magnetic, gamma shielding, etc.
    (e) Animal facilities
    (f) Other

23. Communications/data/alarms/sensor systems, etc. (computers, FAXs, telephone, intercom, voice activated, paging, etc.).

24. What special materials for laboratory work areas, sinks, drains (e.g., epoxy, plastic, seamless, chemical resistance, etc., for floor, walls, ceiling)?

25. Interior design treatment, graphics, lighting, image, textures, ADA requirements relative to signs, controls, etc.

26. Laboratory service system developed based on program requirements or preferences (interstitial, services corridor, ceiling, floor, wall, behind casework, hidden, exposed, etc.). Services required at the workstation (water, gas, air, vacuum, electric, emergency power, special gases, etc.).

27. Other items affecting programs, processing, operations, etc., considered important to an individual investigator's laboratory work area.

28. What emergency or disaster plan(s) are required? What types of equipment and materials may be required to support such plans? Spill containment carts, special protective clothing, masks, breathing devices, fire extinguishers, etc.? Is storage space required?

29. What type of materials management plan will be in place to service and supply the laboratory facility?

30. What waste management plan will be required? Is it an in-house managed plan or outside contract plan? Do laboratory staff perform initial decontamination process? If so, what facilities required?

Checklist 4e: Example Functional, Space, Staff Program Summary Chart

The following chart illustrates how the basic statistical data and projections may be presented.

Functions and Activities	199__ Existing NSF	199__ Existing Staff	199__ Projected NSF Midrange (3/5/7 Years)	199__ Projected NSF Low-Range (3/5/7 Years)	199__ Projected Staff Required (3/5/7 Years)
A. Administration Areas					
1. Laboratory director					
Director's office					
Administrative assistant's office					
Investigator's offices					
Reception/waiting					
2. Support/service					
Conference/seminar					
Coffee/snack					

(continued)

Functions and Activities	199__ Existing NSF	199__ Existing Staff	199__ Projected NSF Midrange (3/5/7 Years)	199__ Projected NSF Low-Range (3/5/7 Years)	199__ Projected Staff Required (3/5/7 Years)
Secretary/clerical					
Transcriptionists					
Tape tanks/printers					
Copier/paper storage					
Records/files/slides					
Supplies/cart storage					
Courier/mail/reports					
Staff toilets					
Men					
Women					
3. Etc.					

Similar space detail listings would be developed as above for all functions and activities, including:

B. Research laboratory work areas
C. Procedure/production areas
D. Core/shared equipment areas
E. Special technologies
F. Service and support areas
G. Conference/teaching areas
H. Other functions and activities

Subtotal Department nsf
  Intracirculation/partitions
  (gross area factor)

Subtotal Department gsf
  Intercirculation, stairs,
  elevators, structure, etc.
  (gross area factor)

Total building gsf

CHECKLIST 5: SPACE PROGRAMMING PARAMETERS

The following are general programming criteria and parameters that may be utilized to develop space requirements (net square feet and gross square feet).

■ What are the functions, activities, processes, etc., to be accommodated within the space?

- What are the maximum number of persons to be accommodated within the space? At any given time? Shift? Includes visitors, students, and others participating in the performance of the functions and activities within the space. Some people may not be staff members of the department or section.

- What are the major items of space-occupying equipment and work counters (linear feet of work surface—some sources use equivalent linear feet of work space) required to support the requirements of the functions and activities? Includes refrigerators, freezers, centrifuges, autoanalyzers, hoods, incubators, computers, printers, etc.; and items often overlooked [e.g., trash, glass, and hazardous waste containers; supply and utility carts; movable work tables and furnishings (desks, chairs, bookcases, file cabinets, copy machines, file and storage cabinets for slides, paraffin blocks, records, etc.)].

- Other factors that must be considered during the development of space (square feet) are the givens and intangibles, including agency regulations (NIH, NIOSH, EPA, JCAHO, OSHA, etc.), institutional standards, policy, or guidelines (e.g., "investigator offices shall be 180 nsf; technician offices shall be 80 nsf, etc.").

- Additional factors include workloads, utilization rates, and productivity (units per paid hour); ratio between enclosed spaces and open space planning; initial budget limitations and projections of estimated costs; and the ability of the institution to afford a given amount of space regardless of functional space requirements to support a particular program.

- Perhaps the most complex and difficult item to resolve is a person's psychological or behavioral perception of space (size, volume: ceiling height, windows vs. windowless; configuration: square, rectangle, etc.).

CHECKLIST 6: PHYSICAL FACILITIES SURVEY GUIDE

The physical facilities survey guide may be used during the master plan existing facilities survey phase. The checklist is not all-inclusive. It is presented as a guide for the physical facilities survey process and to assist with the following:

- Identify existing physical facilities problems, deficiencies, etc., which may affect efficient building operations and maintenance costs, decisions whether to remodel and renovate vs. building new space, etc.

■ Determine facilities characteristics, including corridor widths, corridor dead-end conditions, stairs (size, condition, access, exit), direction of door swings, elevators, building relationships; proximity and number of hydrants, standpipes, etc., that may be nonconforming to codes and standards (JCAHO, Life Safety Code, local and national building codes, etc.); and impact on safety, comfort, and convenience of personnel, public, visitors, etc.

■ Develop estimates for the extent of obsolescence for existing facilities (age, conditions, materials, structural, mechanical, electrical, plumbing systems, etc.).

■ Assessment of facilities capabilities to meet existing and future program goals, objectives, mission, etc.

■ Recommendations for plans of action or planning alternatives:

— Rehabilitation and modernization (remodel and renovation)

— Expansion with additions, new buildings

— Consideration of worth/value of existing facilities

— Razing/demolition/removal

— Replacement or retention of existing building for alternative use

Physical Facilities Survey Guide

1. Secure Copies of Existing Documents and Drawings

■ Applicable codes, zoning decisions at time of design and construction

■ Budget, budget limitations financial feasibility studies

■ Environmental impact studies

■ Historical meteorological records

■ Master facility programs, long-range expansion plans

■ Operational, maintenance, machine failure downtime engineering reports, power outage rate caused by storms

■ Project manuals, specifications

- Site, architectural, structural, mechanical, electrical, plumbing drawings
- Soils, boring, geotechnical reports
- Space, equipment inventory
- Strategic plans (goals, objectives, mission), future programs
- Title, index, contents
- Utility bills, invoices
- Utility rights-of-way

2. Site Characteristics

- Easements, zoning, restrictions, requirements
- Graphics and signage: pedestrian, vehicular
- Noise (trains, trucks, autos, aircraft, quarries, manufacturing facilities)
- Odors, pollution (gases, smoke, particulates from neighboring buildings, manufacturing facilities, etc.)
- Parking (public, private, controlled): surface, deck, open, free, charge, assigned by position or car size, bicycles, motorcycles, electric carts, safety and security, condition, age, layout (ramp, helix, etc.), lighting, number relative to code requirements, needs
- Regional, community, neighborhood access, proximity to interstate, major roads, thoroughfares, etc.
- Size, shape, development possibilities, neighbors, acquisition of adjacent property
- Storm and sewage drainage systems
- Streets, roads, sidewalks, crosswalks, barriers, islands, traffic controls
- Topography: slope, contours, usable vs. nonusable land (steep slopes, rock outcrops, swamp, river, pond, marsh, wetland, floodplain), view and orientation, drainage, erosion, flooding, vegetation covering (trees, bushes, grasses)
- Weather (prevailing winds, frequency of storms, tornadoes, hurricanes)

3. Facilities Characteristics and Condition

- Architectural barriers, disability access problems, stairs, elevators, toilets, lack of ramps, lifts, etc.

- Architectural finishes and systems: types of materials, condition, walls, floors, ceilings, roof, insulation, partitions (fixed/movable, masonry, gypsum wallboard and studs)
- Building orientation, sun control
- Construction dates: original, additions (vertical, horizontal, remodeling and renovations
- Mechanical, electrical, plumbing: type system, age, capacity, flexibility, expansion capability
- Structural: type of frame and system, load, stressing, shape (round, rectangular, square, other), floor-to-floor heights, bay sizes, capabilities for expansion, additions (upset spandrels at exterior walls, etc.), seismic and wind design

4. Codes, Regulations, Fire Safety

- Building classification(s), upgrade requirements relative to nature and scope of proposed remodeling and renovations
- Contaminated waste holding, process, and disposal: biological, nuclear, solvents, acid, corrosives, flammables, explosives storage
- Egress and exits: adequacy, construction, location, widths, designation, direction of door swings, architectural barriers, corridor widths
- Fire alarm, extinguishing, suppressing systems: bells, lights, central, remote service, sprinklers (wet, dry), hoses, extinguishers, standpipes
- Fire doors: hinged, sliding, vertical
- Fire resistivity: corridor, walls, doors, glass panels
- Hazard areas: kitchen, laundry, laboratories, maintenance shops, trash holding, processing, and disposal
- Interior finishes: type and condition, smoke and fire rating, toxic by-products created during burning
- Smoke barriers, safety zones, smoke and fire partitions
- Utility shafts and chases (mechanical, electrical, plumbing), elevators and lifts (emergency controls), chutes (trash, linen), etc.

5. Plumbing Systems

- Age, type, adequacy, capacity, capability for expansion
- Fixtures (toilets, lavatories, showers, faucets)

- Pipe materials (cast iron, copper, plastic, glass, composition, concrete, chemical resistance)
- Steam (primary, secondary, pressure, temperature)
- Treatment facilities, on-site sewage plant, holding pond, liquid hazardous waste holding tanks
- Water source and supply (well, municipal), distribution, capacity, treatment, filters, water softeners, domestic hot water, special water (distilled, etc.)

6. Medical Gas Systems

- Control and alarm systems (on site, remote), valves, manifolds, venting (quench phenomena)
- Gas supply, storage, distribution systems: bulk, liquid, high-pressure vessels, tanks, cylinders, dewars, piping systems and materials
- Hazards, violations, safety systems
- Oxygen, nitrogen, nitrous oxide, mixed gases, other
- Vacuum (central, portable units)

7. Heating, Ventilation, and Air Conditioning (HVAC)

- Environmental controls [thermostats, temperature, humidity, pressure (positive, negative, equal)]
- Computer-controlled building systems
- Age, type, capacity, adequacy, capability for upgrade, expansion, accessories
- Energy conservation, reclamation, cogeneration, insulation, glazing, shades, screens, natural foliage
- Emergency systems, redundant systems and controls
- Duct filtration for biohazard materials
- Acoustical insulation
- Quality of supply air for ventilation
- Air conditioning, heating
- Air exchange rates, exhaust system(s)
- Chemical fume hoods, biological safety cabinets (duct materials, lighting, face velocity, filtration)
- Energy systems: oil, coal, gas, combination
- Fuel storage: bins, tanks (above and below ground), size, materials, condition, age

8. Electrical Systems

- Age, capacity, adequacy, distribution (underground, surface), transmission lines, towers, poles, transformers, substations, source, quality, capability for upgrade and expansion, systems reliability
- Electrical power outlets (type, number, location)
- Emergency electrical power generators, controls, automatic "throw-over," etc.
- Communication systems: telephone, paging, television (closed circuit, public, patient, security), physician registry, computer and data, information, audiovisual, TV conferencing, dictating, bed status, nurse call, microwave transmission, other
- Lighting (site, parking, interior), quality, color and frequency of light, illumination levels in work areas (fluorescent, incandescent, halide, other)
- Lightning protection, ground systems
- Safety and security systems

9. Transportation Systems

- Elevators, escalators, dumbwaiters (age, platform size, type, speed, loading capacity, capabilities for upgrade, door width)
- Linen and trash chutes and tubes (pneumatic, gravity), etc.
- Materials handling systems (pneumatic tube, carriers and conveyors, automatic cart systems, cart exchange, dumbwaiters)
- Personnel (auto, bicycles, electric vehicles); patients, visitors, public (buses, vans, trains)

10. Disposal Systems

- Manual, automatic, contract
- Collection, storage, holding, processing, disposal compaction, baling, pulping
- Classification (biohazard, radioactive, chemical, explosive, nonhazardous, recyclable)
- Transportation (carts, trucks, tanks)
- Incinerators (trash, biological, pathological)

CHECKLIST 7: ITEMS AFFECTING COSTS

Consideration should be given very early during the programming and planning process to alternative solutions for design and building systems. These may be alternative floor/wall/ceiling systems, finishes (sheet vinyl vs. composition tile), service and utility systems, building energy and reclamation systems, and so on. The systems can be rated as "best," "satisfactory," and "last resort but acceptable." As the project evolves and develops, choices (substitutes) may be made if estimates begin to exceed budgets. This may be considered part of a value engineering methodology to maintain control of costs vs. systems and still meet program criteria and requirements. The various items may also be organized as alternative bid packages (add-on or deducts).

The following list of cost items are those items, materials, systems, and so on, that have an impact on design, construction, operations, and maintenance costs.

1. Access for equipment, supplies, service(s), maintenance, operations
2. Acid sinks, drains, etc.: glass (seals rot, leaks, allows gases to escape); plastic (softens, chemicals leach/erode inside surface), metal (steel, cast iron, zinc or tin lined, copper), lead solder joints dangerous
3. Acoustical control: equipment noise, vehicular traffic, etc. (massive/dense materials, foam/fiber blankets, clouds, baffles, acoustic screens, perforated/irregular surfaces)
4. Air requirements: positive, negative, equal pressure (pressure, door seals, controls, air changes, 100% fresh, recycle)
5. Animal facilities: feed receiving/storage, bedding, waste storage, handling, processing, decontamination, disposal; isolation, cross-contamination, size of cage room drains, animal carts, cage washing, sterilization, surgery, necropsy
6. Building: ease of adaptability, expansion, renovation, retrofit, life-cycle costs
7. Central vs. decentralized gas systems (cylinders, tanks, liquid vs. gaseous, fire, explosion hazard, blow-out panels, reclamation)

8. Central vs. individual vacuum, compressed air systems (filtration requirements)

9. Central special water system vs. cartridge systems (distilled, deionized, ultrafiltration, etc.), one type of special water as feed source to produce another special water

10. Clocks: battery vs. plug-in, coordinated/synchronous systems

11. Telecommunications, data systems, computers, networks, peripherals, modems, satellite systems, audiovisual, CCTV (educational, security), FAX, coaxial, fiber optics, etc.

12. Concrete vs. steel frame systems vs. combination, isolation and vibration pads at grade

13. Conditions of grants: program changes (once started, cannot stop, etc.), safety violations in laboratory layouts (location of hoods by exit door)

14. Consumables (require more storage space) vs. reusables (require processing areas, equipment, service staff, etc.), materials handling systems (were space allocations based on a materials handling system?)

15. Core (shared) service/support spaces: electron microscopes, glass wash, controlled-temperature rooms, centrifuges, etc. (pros–cons–controversial policy)

16. Cup sinks, tub sinks, troughs (single, double, deep, shallow, type material), hand-wash sinks, accessories

17. Definition and cost of "built-in flexibility or adaptability": extent of accommodating changes, estimates of future needs (strategic and master planning), etc.

18. Demand/diversity factors: how many laboratory modules, equipment, hoods, etc. in operation at any given time; impact on building systems, operations, differences between research, production, and teaching laboratories

19. Disabled persons accommodations: wheelchair, crutches, braces, blind, sight and hearing impaired, etc., require additional space, materials, colors, textures, lighting, visual/audible alarms (American with Disabilities Act)

20. Electrical service capacity: watts, amperes per square foot (20, 30, 60, 100, etc.), emergency power, UPS

21. Emergency and disaster plans: spills, contamination,

fire, explosions, gas, fluids, alarms (emergency equipment, breathing apparatus—portable vs. fixed, etc.)

22. Emergency showers, eye wash, fire blanket, etc. (cabinet type, located in laboratory, in corridor outside laboratory, floor drain, controls, water temperature and pressure, testing, bacterial growth, standing water in fixtures/drains, etc.)

23. Engineering, fabrication, maintenance, repair shops, painting (noise, vibration, ceiling height, size and weight of equipment, materials storage)

24. First costs vs. life cycle costs vs. budgets, etc. (what items included and excluded from the construction cost?)

25. Fixed (traditional floor mounted) vs. modular (expensive, does not stand up) vs. mobile casework (how are services routed to fixtures on work counters?), work counter material(s), chemical/thermal resistance

26. Floor loads: uniform, random, selected areas design, vibration coefficient

27. Floor, wall, ceiling systems: finishes (gypsum board on studs—wood, metal), movable, masonry, sheet vinyl vs. composition tile, exposed, applied, acoustical tile, Keene's cement, etc.)

28. Functions and activities not always compatible: office vs. laboratory vs. production vs. storage vs. maintenance, etc.; requirements for different ceiling heights, floor loadings, structural bay/column clearances, different environmental conditions, etc. (problems to accommodate different specific requirements for each activity in same building envelope)

29. Heat reclamation from hood exhaust, equipment, etc. (mixing air, biohazards, explosion, etc.)

30. Hoods: types, sizes, number, controls, alarms, air face velocity (chemical fume, biological safety, laminar flow, glove boxes, canopy, etc.)

31. Impact of robotics: "Elmers" (require additional space), autoanalyzers (space for kits, etc.), conveyors, horizontal, vertical

32. Impact on and by adjacent buildings: fume hood exhaust stack height, scrubbers, number of stacks, shape, location, aerodynamics, prevailing winds, fan motor/

belt noise, etc. (stack exhaust velocity at 4000 to 6000 fpm minimum, 8000 to 12,000 fpm better)

33. Individual laboratory environmental controls (temperature, humidity, pressure), impact of person's psychological perceptions of comfort zones

34. In-laboratory storage (cabinets, drawers) vs. central storage (materials management system), operational storage requirements for autoanalyzers (kits, etc.), relates to materials management policy

35. Laboratories in-board vs. out-board (windows vs. non-windows), windows reduce work and storage area, questionable advantages with windows, glare, oxidation

36. Laboratory partition systems: movable, demountable, gypsum board on studs, masonry, etc. (durability, chemical and moisture resistance, joint seals, rigidity, structural capability to support cabinets, equipment, etc.)

37. Laboratory standards: varies with institutions, space allocations, square feet per researcher, technician, faculty, etc.

38. Level of excess services capacities: 10%, 15%, 25% (or more) estimated and provided for future programs, costs

39. Lighting: direct, indirect, fluorescent vs. incandescent, task vs. overhead and fixed, illumination levels, color, etc. (light sensitivity, glare)

40. Limitations of casework types (drawers, doors, glass, solid, hinges vs. sliding, etc.): limit selection to six or eight base and wall cabinet types for future inventory needs

41. Location and number of service valves (shutoff) at each or multiple laboratory module(s) for alterations, repairs, emergencies, identification, etc.

42. Location of refrigerators, freezes, etc. (clustered or within functional work areas) with canopy exhaust hoods to capture heat

43. Location of room air supply, returns: high or low, lighter or heavier than air gases, fumes, powders, particles, droplets; toxic vs. nontoxic, air changes per hour, airflow (laminar, random), dilution controversy

44. Location of special-purpose laboratories: explosion, biohazard, etc., in separate areas of building or separate free-standing buildings

45. Mix of laboratory functions, disciplines, etc. (too many services/utilities, may not be used or needed, duplication, redundancy, costs)

46. Special equipment (MRI, mass spectroscopy, etc.), size, clearances, weight of equipment, isolation pad, radio-frequency and gamma-ray shielding

47. Office space designed for conversion to laboratory work spaces (impact on building systems, structural design, first costs)

48. Power requirements: quality, UPS for computers, emergency, phase, dc, ac, isolation transformer, grounding grid systems, etc.

49. Program verification to assist in cost control, value engineering, alternative systems

50. Quality of air, number of air changes per hour, type of filters, airflow, scrubbers (location of supply and exhaust registers in laboratories)

51. Raised floor: unlimited access vs. cost (vermin, rodent, insect hideouts)

52. Reagent transport, storage, preparation, and disposal hazards

53. Redundant systems: electrical, mechanical, etc.

54. Seamless floor vs. tile vs. concrete vs. epoxy, carpet, etc.

55. Security systems: personnel, data, supplies, equipment

56. Separate office work spaces for researchers, vs. in-laboratory office and work spaces (office-type work spaces in the laboratory dangerous, not recommended)

57. Service systems: interstitial space(s), walls, through floor, ceiling, service corridor, combination, etc.

58. Service and utility systems access, clearances, convenience for replacement of equipment, changing filters, maintenance, confined space hazards (OSHA standards), etc.

59. Single or multiple exhaust systems (ducts) for fume hoods, manifold systems (danger in mixing chemical fumes, gases, vapors, dust that could explode, start fires,

etc.), type of duct materials (stainless steel, galvanized steel, plastic)

60. Space between counters: circulation, clearance, equipment transport (5' vs. 6' or more), accessibility for the disabled

61. Stressing foundations and structure for future expansion (vertical or horizontal), only one-third of buildings stressed for vertical addition completed

62. Structural bay size(s), floor-to-floor heights, penetrations

63. Suspended ceiling vs. exposed (materials, finishes, acoustical problems), acoustical baffles, flaking/snow hazards

64. Work countertop materials: plastic laminate, composite, phenolic resin, epoxy, ceramic, stone, wood, etc.

65. 24-hour operations, system shutdowns, brown-outs, power outages

66. Vibration: building, traffic, equipment, trees, etc.

67. Walk-in refrigerators and freezers vs. reach-in type (built-ins vs. prefabricated)

68. Waste management: handling, process, storage, disposal, transport, recyclables

69. Width of counter worktops (island, peninsula): 5' or 6', reach limits of staff

70. Animals brought to laboratory work areas vs. investigators working in animal facilities

71. Windows: size, type, sill height, orientation, fixed vs. operable

72. Zones for special uses and hazardous activities, savings in stacking similar functions and activities requiring similar services

CHECKLIST 8: GENERIC PROGRAM DOCUMENT OUTLINE

Following is an outline for the document, report, or study that is usually prepared at the completion of the programming and planning process. This document may be quite extensive, including lengthy narrative, detailed statistical analyses, diagrams and sketches, and scaled drawings of the proposed project. The document may be referred to by several names, including:

- *Program of Requirements (POR)*. This is the title assigned by many federal government agencies.
- *Advanced Planning Report, Preplanning Study, and Feasibility Study.* These names are used by many state agencies.
- *Functional Narrative and Space Program.* These names are used by many private institutions.

Program Outline

PREFACE

The program document's objective is to develop and list basic facility requirements for design and construction of the proposed laboratory facility. The document will indicate the scope of the proposed facility with sufficient detail to permit the architect and engineering team to develop and prepare design, construction, and specification documents, including predesign and postdesign documents, as required.

CONTENTS

I.   Executive Summary

Concise narrative summary of the principal elements of the document's findings, recommendations, criteria, etc., for the proposed facility.

II.   Functional Narrative

A. Introduction

Defines the functions and activities of the components that are part of the proposed project. Summary of historical background of the component(s), including goals, objectives, mission, and basic responsibilities. Components may include, but are not limited to, administrative areas, laboratories, service and support, core areas, architectural and structural elements, mechanical and electrical criteria, etc.

B. Organizational structure

Defines the components and the overall relationship(s) within the institution, departments, branch(es), and division(s), including existing and proposed line of responsibilities of the components. An organizational chart(s) of the component(s) is/are included.

III. Design Criteria
    A. General requirements
    B. Site
        1. General remarks
        2. Description
        3. Design work
        4. Constraints
        5. Roads/walkways
        6. Orientation
        7. Neighbors
        8. Prevailing winds/weather
        9. Zoning
      10. Vegetation
      11. Potential for expansion
      12. Subsurface conditions
    C. Architectural
        1. General remarks
        2. Flexibility/adaptability/modular design
        3. Structure/vibration/noise
        4. Floor/walls/partitions/ceiling
        5. Sanitation/sterility
        6. Safety
        7. Security
        8. Equipment/furnishings
            (a) General remarks
            (b) Contractor installed
            (c) Owner installed
            (d) New/existing
            (e) Personal
        9. Interior finishes (floors, walls, ceilings)
            (a) General remarks
            (b) Corridors/stairs

        (c) General areas (lobbies, etc.)

        (d) General labs/support spaces

        (e) Special laboratories

        (f) Reagents/solvents storage (hazardous nonhazardous)

        (g) Lockers/change/toilets/showers

        (h) Animal/lab support facilities

  10. Doors, frames, hardware (all areas)

  11. Animal and animal support requirements

        (a) General remarks

        (b) Conventional/exotic species

        (c) Large/small animals

        (d) Specialized animal facilities

        (e) Quarantine facilities

        (f) Special requirements

          — Runs

          — Pasture

          — Barns, etc.

        (g) Codes (AAALAC, NIH, etc.)

        (h) Service and support areas

D. Mechanical

  1. HVAC

        (a) General remarks

        (b) Administrative

        (c) Laboratory

        (d) Service/support

        (e) Special/extraordinary

        (f) Animal facilities

  2. Internal utilities

        (a) General remarks

        (b) Fire protection

        (c) Backflow preventers

        (d) Plumbing

        (e) Laboratory waste (solid, liquid, gaseous)

        (f) Animal waste

              (g) Steam (high/low pressure)

              (h) Laboratory gases (pressurized, cryogenics, liquid)

              (i) Cylinder/bottled gases

                 — Mixed/special

                 — Hazardous/nonhazardous

              (j) Laboratory compressed air

              (k) Laboratory vacuum

              (l) Emergency showers/eye washers

              (m) Breathing apparatus/SCBA

              (n) Spill containment equipment

              (o) Fire blankets/stretchers/first-aid kits

              (p) Distilled/deionized water

              (q) Monitoring/control stations

       E. Electrical

            1. General remarks

            2. Primary distribution

            3. Secondary distribution

            4. Illumination/quality/color/natural/artificial

            5. Emergency power (standard generator, UPS)

            6. Shielding/grounding (EMF, magnetic)

            7. Power quality

            8. Lightning protection

            9. Computer/media/data

            10. Communication systems (telephone, etc.)

            11. Other systems

     F. Fire protection and safety

     G. Site utilities

           1. General remarks

           2. Heating plant

           3. Refrigeration plant

           4. Storm/sanitary sewer

           5. Water

           6. Natural gas

7. Fuel/energy source
8. Electrical distribution system
9. Fire protection/access/lanes/hydrants
10. Signal/monitoring system
11. Cathodic protection

H. Traffic/circulation/parking/public transportation
I. Landscaping/existing/conservation
J. Hazardous materials management/storage
K. Building transport/elevator systems
L. Energy conservation/reclamation/generation
M. Value engineering/cost control and analysis
N. Security considerations/systems
   1. Perimeter/building construction
      (a) General remarks
      (b) Walls/windows
      (c) Roof
      (d) Roof door(s)/escape hatch(es)
      (e) Soffits
      (f) Lighting
      (g) Parking/traffic control
      (h) Doors
      (i) Fire doors
      (j) Landscaping/natural vegetation
      (k) Shipping/receiving
   2. Utilities (underground/surface/above ground)
   3. Adjoining modules/spaces, etc.
   4. Interior security
   5. Intrusion alarm
   6. Guard service (human, animal)
   7. Perimeter/property line/fencing
   8. Security coordination
O. Sanitation (public, holding, processing)
P. Disabled persons accommodations
   1. General remarks
   2. ADA

3. Agency requirements

4. ANSI-A117.1 (FS 795-1)

Q. Codes, standards, guidelines, protocols

    1. General remarks

    2. Architectural

    3. Structural

    4. Mechanical/HVAC

    5. Electrical

    6. Plumbing

    7. Fire protection/safety

    8. Environmental

R. Operations and maintenance manuals

IV. Space Criteria/Directives

A. Allowable area allocations

B. Standards/guidelines/derivation

C. Hierarchy/status/title

D. Definitions

    1. General remarks

    2. Net area usable/assignable

    3. Net to gross area ratios

    4. Gross area factors

V. Specific Design Criteria

A. Description of project requirements within the context of specific research criteria. The architect and engineer may provide alternatives, recommendations, etc., for consideration.

B. Room/control data sheets for each space/room/ areas indicating detailed plan and elevation(s) of casework, equipment, furnishings, services locations, etc.

VI. Scope of Professional Services (Some institutions/ agencies may request such information if the architect/ engineer also prepares the program document.)

A. Introduction

B. General project description

C. Statement of work (scope)

    1. Basic A/E services

           (a) Predesign phase (programming/planning)

           (b) Schematic design

           (c) Design development

           (d) Construction documents

           (e) Bidding/negotiation

           (f) Construction administration

       2. Optional A/E services

       3. Special studies, etc.

       4. Other(s)

    D. Services/data furnished by the owner/client

    E. Instructions/definitions

    F. Owner/architect agreement methodology

    G. A/E services compensation negotiation

VII. Appendices

B CASE STUDIES

Appendix B contains two case studies that present different methodologies for the programming, planning, and design of research laboratory facilities:

Case Study 1   Overview Master Plan Report for the Medical Center at the University of South Alabama, Mobile

Case Study 2   New Research Laboratories for the National Institute for Occupational Safety and Health (NIOSH) of the Centers for Disease Control (CDC), Morgantown, West Virginia

CASE STUDY 1

The following *overview master facilities plan* for a university school of medicine development is presented as a planning case study. The case study indicates how perceived research facilities needs should be planned and integrated within the clinical, educational, or corporate program goals and objectives of an institution, from a strategic and long-range development plan perspective.

The example presented is the overview master facilities plan prepared by the author for the University of South Alabama at Mobile. Although the plan may be several years old, the planning principles are nonetheless valid. The plan has been updated by the author to reflect the evolution in medical education that has occurred within the medical community during the past several years. Much of the evolution can be attributed to institutional responses to changes in health care delivery modes (e.g., emphasis shifting from inpatient care to outpatient care, new tests and technologies, etc.). Third-party payer and government rules and regulations (ADA, CLIA, EPA, NIOSH, OSHA, etc.) also have considerable impact on the facilities, organization, and operations of a medical center and research laboratories.

Readers may question the presentation of a master plan that is more than a decade old. However, the author discussed this point with several associates who are involved in programming and planning, and also with several administrators, researchers, and other practitioners. They all agreed that the master plan presents an excellent classic example of the overall programming and planning process. The principles and framework employed are directly applicable to contemporary planning problems and decisions faced by the medical community in today's environment.

Although any two institutions may be similar, they certainly are not identical. Goals, objectives, and missions differ. Scientific research disciplines and education program emphasis vary. Planning factors for estimating space, staff, faculty, building systems requirements, and so on, can be extracted and developed from the statistics and data presented. To be applied at other institutions, facility planning factors derived from these data would have to be modified and tested.

The application of a given set of factors and criteria used at one institution to another institution may produce distorted values. One institution may emphasize clinical activities above research. Education programs may emphasize certain medical or surgical specialties above others. Emphasis on research may focus on theory or the accumulation of basic scientific knowledge. Another institution may focus on the direct application of scientific discoveries in the clinical arena. Whether the institution organizes functions and activities as an "institute" vs. a "center" will also influence facility planning factors. The corporate or industrial sector usually considers direct application to pharmaceuticals, consumer products, and so on.

The varying institutional or corporate strategic goals, objectives, and missions will generate different factors and criteria that are applicable to planning and design of the physical facilities for housing the clinical, educational, research, and production programs being considered. It is also interesting to note that many institutions generate more return in dollars from investment in research facilities than from any other activity on campus.

The author was ably assisted during the preparation and development of the master plan by the following firms:

- Middleton McMillan Architects, Charlotte, North Carolina
- Mueller Associates, Inc., Consulting Engineers, Baltimore, Maryland

The following addressed to Arthur J. Donovan, vice president of health affairs, comments are by Arvin E. Robinson, associate dean for planning and development and chairman of the planning committee. The comments were delivered upon completion of the original overview master plan report.

This Workbook [Overview Master Plan Report] represents a concentrated effort toward an analysis of the present state of development in Health Affairs at the University of South Alabama with recommended guidelines for future growth. While many of the needs are of an urgent nature and perhaps overdue, the development of this plan has proceeded in an orderly manner. The College of Medicine, College of Nursing and Division of Allied Health Professions have now reached a stable state of administrative structure and community standing whereby direction and scope of existing and new programs can be fully defined.

With this in mind, and with the urgent need for ambulatory care facilities, the College of Medicine Planning Committee almost one year ago began the process of defining the present structure and future potential of the Medical Center Campus. A nationwide search was conducted for consultant services in academic health planning and Mr. Leonard Mayer, an independent planning architect, was chosen. He came highly recommended with many years of service in major health planning and offered the unique ability to gather and analyze data for development of a personalized program most suitable for the University of South Alabama and its surrounding environs.

It was soon evident that the scope of the project needed expansion. The Medical Center Campus could not be planned without consideration of all College of Medicine activities. Likewise, College of Medicine development could not progress exclusive and independent of other related University Health Care and Academic Programs.

The background material and program listed as Scheme 1 was presented to the Planning Committee on schedule in June,

1977. The program outlined full development of the Medical Center Campus in a Stage manner to accommodate immediate needs in rapid expansion. Further growth over longer periods of time would involve relocation and expansion of all Health Affairs activities into areas contiguous with the present Medical Center Campus Site.

While the background material and future projections appeared accurate and realistic, possible locations became a question of discussion. Mr. Mayer was therefore asked to present an alternate proposal (Scheme 2) which would allow Health Affairs development on the original University Campus Site. In late July, Scheme 2 for University campus development with Interim Accommodations for immediate needs at the Medical Center Campus was presented and favored. Continued close affiliation with the University Campus Programs was felt crucial for further academic development and should offer added strength to all University activities. The temporary separation of clinical activities would be workable and tolerable with appropriate Interim Accommodations.

It is important to recognize that this proposal considers the minimal requirements necessary to meet the educational objectives of our teaching programs and the estimated health care activities of a high quality Medical Center. No demographic surveys or financial feasibility studies were performed at this stage of development. Since the proposal offers adequate room for expansion and flexibility in the timetable of development, these studies can be addressed in future considerations.

The Planning Committee, with active representation from all aspects of Health Affairs, favors this proposal and urges prompt consideration. Initial accommodations need to be completed as rapidly as possible and future growth of all Health Affairs activities be allowed to proceed in an orderly manner. The marked overcrowding of our teaching, clinical, and research activities has led to beginning stagnation of our academic progress. We are anxious to proceed with expansion in order to take full advantage of our future potential and accomplish the goals we have always perceived for our new school.

The following are comments from Arthur J. Donovan to Frederick P. Whiddon, president of the university. These comments were delivered upon completion of the original overview master plan report.

The attached report represents the results of the efforts of Mr. Leonard Mayer and his associates and the Planning Committee over the past several months. This effort has been to identify the scope of facilities needed over at least the next ten years for the projected educational programs in the Health Sciences. As you are aware, the Planning Committee has recommended that major development in the future be on the University Campus, but the proposals included in this report conceptualize two major geographic components of facilities. These would be at the present site on Fillingim Street (Fillingim Site) and on the new site on the University Campus. Specific proposals are identified for both sites, with immediate needs at the Fillingim Street site. The importance of maintenance of adequate facilities at the Fillingim Street Site deserves emphasis. Development of a meaningful component of physical facilities on Campus will take three to five years. The Fillingim Site will be a vital component of facilities for education in the Health Sciences at the University of South Alabama during that time and far into the future.

In considering this Master Plan, I believe that is worthwhile to recognize that the University, in educational programs, will deliver patient care at the primary, secondary and tertiary level. the Fillingim Street Site as projected would seem to provide an appropriate Site for emphasis on delivery of the major components of primary care, including emergency facilities. Secondary care, depending on program location, would occur at both the Fillingim Site and at the University. Tertiary Care would be almost exclusively located at the University Site.

A review of this Master Plan by the University administration and the Board of Trustees is eagerly anticipated.

Contents

1 Introduction

The term *medical center* as used in this case study is defined to mean that facility (institution) or grouping of facilities including:

- The school (or college) of medicine, with administrative and faculty staff; medical undergraduate, graduate, postgraduate, and continuing education programs; basic medical sciences; research and medical teaching laboratories; animal facilities (comparative anatomy); core or shared facilities; and service and support activities
- The teaching hospital, with complete clinical, teaching, administrative, and service and support activities
- School of nursing programs
- Allied health care and paramedical programs
- Motel/hotel/continuing education/conferencing facilities
- Surface and structured parking
- Heliport
- Physical plant utility services including heating, ventilating, air conditioning, maintenance, service, primary and emergency electrical services, telecommunications; cogeneration facilities
- Environmental and waste management programs

A medical center planning committee should be established to direct, participate, and monitor the master planning process. (The planning committee for this project was established by the dean of the college of medicine.) Membership should include members from the medical center administration, college of medicine, and the teaching hospital. Representatives from the board(s) of trustees should also be included. Subcommittees, task forces, and so on, can be organized for ongoing or specific ad hoc matters.

The planning committee for this project recognized that the physical space needs of the medical center were rapidly becoming fully occupied. This lack of space was jeopardizing many programs and precluding the development and implementation of new programs, recruitment of first-class staff, and most important, compromising the level and quality of patient health care within certain programs.

Based on these basic needs, the administration of the university made the decision to have an *overview master plan* prepared that would present programming and planning data related to needs and requirements. The master plan could then be utilized in the total planning process to determine growth and expansion established in 3- to 5-year and 7- to 10-year increments related to physical facilities.

Possible land acquisition adjacent to the existing hospital site would provide an adequate area for growth and expansion of the physical plant. These and related factors are addressed in this case study.

The *mission* of the medical center is to:

- Contribute to the education and development of compassionate physicians.
- Provide excellence in teaching and other scholarly endeavors and training of the highest quality to produce physicians, health scientists, and allied health professionals of excellence.
- Contribute to knowledge and skill in the health sciences through basic and clinical research.
- Promote the organization and delivery of the highest-quality health care services through research, teaching, and demonstration in educational programs.
- Provide excellent primary, secondary, and tertiary health care, and since the hospital's primary mission is to serve the community and region through the development of

facilities and staff, to provide an optimum level of service to patients.

- Recognize that the hospital serves as an educational resource to others within the health sciences, and that there is a continuing commitment to provide an environment that is conducive to the educational process. It is further believed that although service and education are synonymous and the goal of the medical center is to place each in proper perspective to ensure that both patient and educational needs are met, the hospital's primary focus must remain on the patient and the delivery of adequate and efficient health care services to *all* patients. Educational and research programs cannot succeed unless the hospital is providing the highest-quality services. The service needs must be viewed as *prerequisites* for educational and research programs.

- Provide services and meet the requirements of educational and research programs. The hospital must also be allowed to exercise sound control over its fiscal operations. If operations are to be subsidized to provide more educational and research material, the funding of the subsidization must be identified and fully developed.

- The hospital must also establish and maintain a comprehensive staff development program for *all* its employees. The hospital's most neglected need to date is employee relations. Requiring employees to staff a 24-hour/day 7-day/week operation adds considerable complexity and pressure to the working conditions at the hospital.

- Provide a hospital environment capable of delivering the highest-quality medical care to both inpatients and ambulatory patients.

The *goals* of the medical center are to:

- Provide for the health care needs of the community.
- Serve as a regional and state resource of tertiary care services to the extent permitted by the funding for these services.
- Provide an environment in which educational and research programs are possible.
- Establish and maintain the medical center as one of the leading medical centers in the state, region, and nation.

- Provide and maintain an environment within which students can achieve their maximum potential.
- Nurture an attitude of scientific inquiry into all areas that relate to human biology and those social forces that affect human health.
- Maintain both adaptability and preparedness to enable timely response to societal requests for seeking an understanding of and solution to those problems of health and health care that may from time to time be accorded the highest priority by the community.
- Engage in direct provision of individual or community health service only when this may be necessary to fulfill specific academic objectives and if there are no other alternatives that are readily available.
- Provide a high-quality one-class system of patient care, delivering the full spectrum of the medical center health services to all patients at every socioeconomic level.

The *objectives* placed on the medical center by the state, region, and nation, which reflect the current perceived demands, are to:

- Provide an educational opportunity for capable students.
- Provide students with a foundation in medical sciences that will equip them to enter the practice of their profession and will enable them to pursue a career in research and/or teaching.
- Provide internship and residency education and training in a variety of medical specialties and other health professionals and to encourage areas of specialization most needed by our population.
- Provide emergency facilities 24 hours/day for all those in need of such care.
- Provide responsible management conducive to the hospital's growth, fiscal health, and personnel advancement.
- Maintain an adequate scholarly inquiry and research essential for maintenance of an environment of learning.
- Work with the community of institutions and practicing physicians and other health professions to maximize their contributions to and participation in the educational and research process.
- Strive for the highest quality of performance in those

patient and community health care services undertaken by the university and to encourage a similar standard in any of those patient care settings with which we may affiliate, including cooperation with the university's graduate school.

■ Produce scientists whose major contributions are related to human health.

The planning process has involved more than 50 representatives from the administration, the college of medicine, the university hospital and the school of nursing and allied health. The data gathered were utilized to develop projection factors to establish the general magnitude and scope of requirements relative to physical space needs and related constructed costs.

The overview master plan report presents the data in a basic workbook graphic format to assist with the decision-making process relative to needs, priorities, directions for growth, and budget cost considerations. The consultant team recommended strongly that the overview master plan be utilized as a dynamic working and planning tool, and that it be updated periodically (at least annually) to reflect changes that inevitably occur with the passage of time.

Although this case study focuses on a scheme indicating development of the medical center at the existing Fillingim site, the basic data collected and the conceptual functional relationships presented may be utilized and applied to develop a scheme for medical center development at a comparable site.

PLANNING TEAM ORGANIZATION

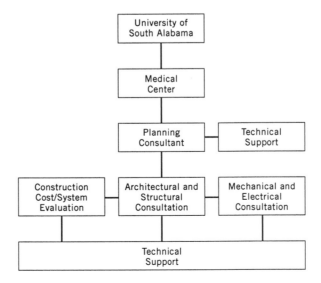

2   Location Maps

STATE/REGION

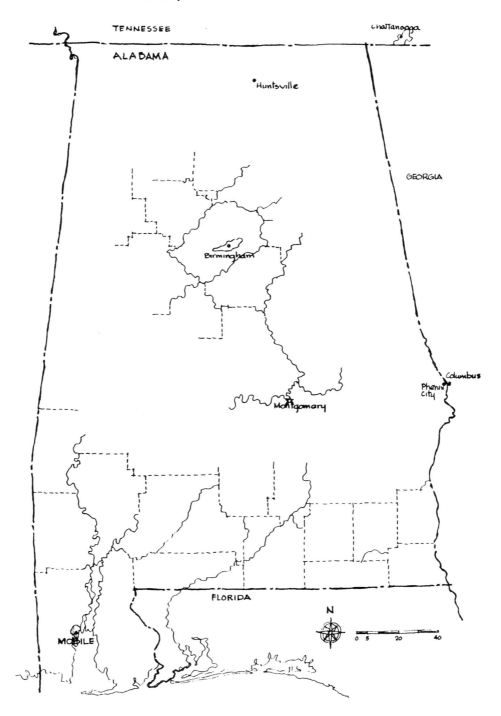

CITY/LOCAL

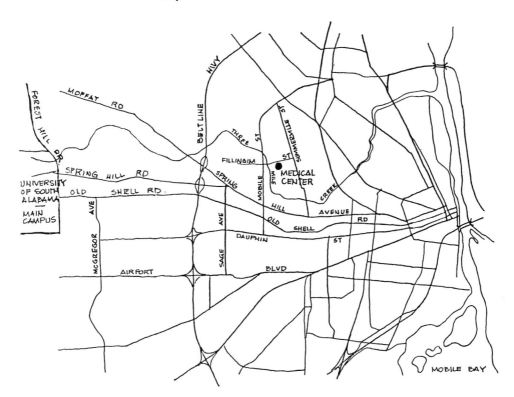

3 Executive Summary

The Overview Master Facilities Plan Report was prepared to assist the administration of the medical center and the University of South Alabama to:

- Assess the mission, goals, and objectives of the medical center, from both an immediate and interim-term perspective (3/5/7 years) and a long-range perspective (5/7/10 years).

- *Determine* and *project* basic faculty, staff, space, and facilities requirements relative to the established immediate, interim, and long-range needs.

- Determine growth and expansion development capabilities at the existing Fillingim site (Scheme 1), and at the main university campus site (Scheme 2).

Data were gathered from medical center, university, and local and regional sources to develop programming and planning criteria. The criteria was utilized to develop Schemes 1 and 2.

SCHEME 1: EXISTING FILLINGIM SITE DEVELOPMENT

- The analysis indicates that with additional site acquisition(s), the existing facilities can be expanded to accommodate the projected medical center program within certain limitations.

- Due to restrictive site acquisition factors for the long term, development at the Fillingim site would probably fulfill medical center needs only for the immediate and interim periods.

- Additional site acquisition is not a certainty and could be very difficult, expensive, and time consuming if property was not acquired in relatively large blocks and within a reasonable time to accomplish required facility expansion needs.

- Converting an existing hospital facility originally designed as a community general hospital with somewhat outdated functional concepts usually results in many physical plan compromises that are relatively inefficient for a teaching hospital.

- Separation of the Fillingim site from the main university campus academic environment raises several important philosophical and academic issues, one of which is the lack of easy access and interchange among members of the medical and nonmedical faculty, students, and administration. This interchange and interaction is particularly important because the lines defining traditional scientific and academic specialties are all but disappearing.

STAGE 1—1987. The programming/planning conceptual cost budget is established at $38,750,000 to $45,000,000. The final amount will relate to defined needs, program data assessment and evaluation, and priorities. The most important determining factor is always the availability of funds based on the state legislature's budgeting and appropriations cycle.

General Conclusion: Scheme 1

Medical center growth and expansion at the Fillingim site is feasible—recognizing certain inherent problems and disadvantages associated with adjacent site acquisition, limitation of future expansion, and compromises to overall medical and education programs necessary in adapting an existing facility to meet strategic and long-range goals and objectives. It became evident early in the planning process that many difficulties were prevalent at the Fillingim site. However, it was more evident that the existing hospital could (and should be planned as such) became an important and integral element of the evolving university medical center health system.

SCHEME 2: MAIN UNIVERSITY CAMPUS AND FILLINGIM SITE DEVELOPMENT

Utilizing the basic data as applied to the preparation of Scheme 1, the main university campus site was studied to determine development possibilities for a new medical center on campus:

- Adequate site area is available for immediate, interim, and long-range medical center development needs. One hundred acres has been dedicated for medical center development on the main university campus.
- Provides excellent functional and intellectual relationships among all the medical and nonmedical academic endeavors.
- Provides a unique opportunity to develop more efficient and functional plan relationships that would not be handicapped, limited, or compromised by existing facilities.
- The Fillingim site facilities can be fully integrated into the overall university medical center health system of primary, secondary, and tertiary health care delivery systems. The Fillingim site facilities could be developed as a neighborhood and regional primary care health center and become an "entry point" into the proposed university medical center health system.
- Permits development of the total medical center as a concurrent plan to minimize disruption of existing activities.
- The Stage 1—1987 programming and planning conceptual cost budget is similar to Scheme 1.

General Conclusion: Scheme 2

The university campus site for the core or university medical center health system development has numerous advantages and attractions relative to elimination of site acquisition cost penalties and permits development of more ideal medical clinical, education, research program, and facility relationships.

4 Organization Chart

The organization chart reflects the basic administrative relationships of the various functions and activities at the medical center. The chart is a general representation of the functional relationships among these administrative elements. However, the facilities planner is cautioned that specific functional relationships (related to facilities) may not always follow the administrative relationships indicated in the chart. For example, the administrative element "Plant Operations and Maintenance" has a direct administrative relationship to "Executive Director of Development and Operations." The physical location for the plant operations manager, however, would probably be in the building housing the building systems and engineering equipment (the central plant). The facilities planner is also advised that as the planning and design proceeds, the administrative and functional relationships should be reviewed as organization changes may occur.

5 Existing Site Plan/Characteristics

TOPOGRAPHY AND LANDMARKS

The existing university medical center hospital site (the Fillingim site) area has an extent of approximately 28.75 acres. The site is located in the northwest quadrant of the city of Mobile, approximately 5 miles east of the main university academic campus.

The site is generally level without large changes in elevation. The high water table throughout the area generally precludes construction below grade (basements). Average rainfall in the Mobile area is approximately 63″ annually. Temperatures range between 59 and 70°F in winter and 79 and 82°F in summer.

The existing hospital (12 levels) is centrally located on the site. The Mastin building (seven levels) is currently used for faculty/administrative and teaching/classroom activities. The Moorer clinical sciences and research facility buildings (one

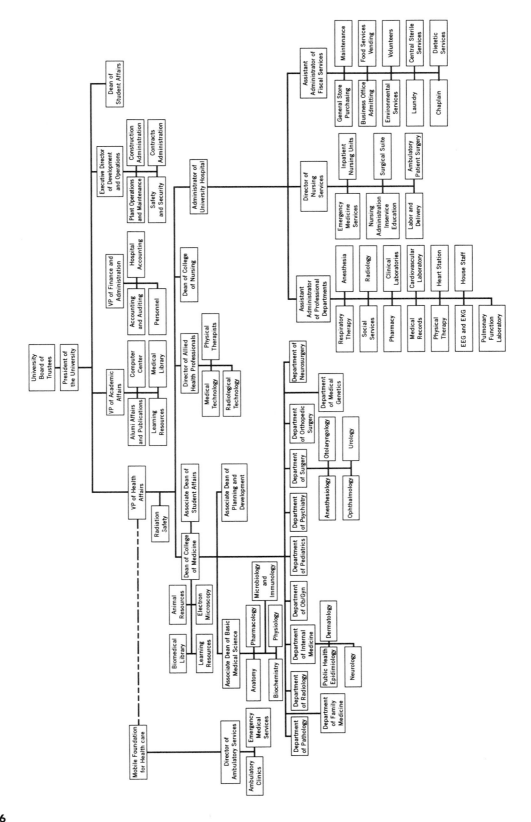

level each) are the remaining structures on the site. Most of the remaining site is utilized in surface parking lots.

The site is bordered on the north by Fillingim Street; on the east by Stanton Road and the Detention Center; on the south by Mobile Mental Health Center, Gordon Smith Rehabilitation Center, and Goodwill Industries; and on the west by Three Mile Creek. A portion of the site to the south is wooded.

ZONING

The site is located within and is largely surrounded by residential neighborhoods varying from low to high-middle income levels. Some commercial activities are located within the area. The property is zoned B-1 (business).

Since much of the adjoining property is residential and some commercial, it is not anticipated that any substantial difficulty would occur in having such acquired property rezoned, as may be required, for projected growth and expansion. However, because many of the residents in the area may be considered low-income wage earners, acquisition/displacement/relocation of residents may become problematic. It may not be necessary, even at this early stage of the planning, to acquire significant adjoining property because of changes occurring in the directions and options available to the evolving goals and objectives of the proposed university medical center health system.

LAND OWNERSHIP

The site is owned by the University of South Alabama (state system). Additional property may be acquired to the west and south.

PARKING

Approximately 889 parking spaces are available for the medical center at this time. Two major parking areas are located north and south of the hospital building. Smaller parking areas adjoin the Mastin building.

Parking spaces vary from a few steps from the hospital building to over 600' distant. Some of the parking areas are not paved, are difficult to control, and become water soaked during the heavy rains that are frequent in the region. Existing parking is generally inadequate for patients, visitors, staff, faculty, and students.

PEDESTRIAN ACCESS

The southwestern entry at the basement of the hospital has been designated as the employee entrance. Other entrances are also used by employees, adding to the confusion of circulation patterns, occurring mostly at change of shifts during the working day. Most employees drive or are driven to work by car.

Visitors and patients generally use the main entrance (except emergency patients) and park in the area north of the hospital building. The admissions area and the clinics are located convenient to the main entrance. Most visitors and patients drive or are driven to the hospital by car.

Physicians (including the faculty) generally park in the area south of the hospital building. Students use this area also. Most of the physician/faculty members and students drive between the hospital and the basic medical sciences and allied health facilities on the main university campus (approximately 5 miles distant).

VEHICULAR ACCESS

The existing site is not served by any major thoroughfares. Most vehicular access to the site is from Mobile and Fillingim Streets. These are of two-lane residential type and often become very congested, particularly during early morning and evening hours.

6 Existing Buildings Area Chart

Floor	University Medical Center Hospital	Mastin Building	Moorer Clinical Sciences	Research Facility	Basic Medical Sciences	Biomedical Library Floor	Fairhope Family Practice Clinic	Sanger Theater Building	Medical Center Total gsf
Basement	67,959	—	—	—	—	—	—	—[a]	67,959
1st	74,169	12,754	30,958	15,336	53,541	—	5,805	—	192,553
2nd	38,967	7,024	—	—	54,505	—	—	—	100,496
3rd	29,310	7,024	—	—	52,435	9,278	—	—	98,047
4th	20,554	7,024	—	—	—	—	—	—	27,578
5th	20,554	7,024	—	—	—	—	—	—	27,578
6th	20,554	7,024	—	—	—	—	—	—	27,578
7th	20,554	7,024	—	—	—	—	—	—	27,578
8th	20,554	—	—	—	—	—	—	—	20,554
9th	20,554	—	—	—	—	—	—	—	20,554
10th	20,554	—	—	—	—	—	—	—	20,554
11th	20,554	—	—	—	—	—	—	—	20,554
Penthouse	1,325	—	—	—	—	—	—	—	1,325
Total gsf	376,162	54,898	30,958	15,336	160,481	9,278	5,805	—	652,918

[a] Area not available (not considered significant for existing area statistical analyses).

COMMENTS

For proponents and users of the "gross square foot per bed rule-of-thumb" criterion, dividing 376,162 gsf by 393 beds equals slightly more than 957 gsf per bed. Using contemporary standards for community general hospitals, this ratio is perhaps moderate to low. However, compared to general standards for teaching hospitals, this ratio is in the low range of gsf/bed for teaching hospitals and may be considered inadequate. A teaching hospital may require between 1200 and 1400 gsf/bed (and as much as 1600 gsf/bed) to support the associated activities for a teaching hospital. The variations that occur are based on the clinical, medical education, and research programs being considered. The author wishes to note that he does not disparage the gsf/bed criterion. This standard has proven itself as a useful tool during the initial space analysis process when applied by an experienced programmer.

7 Existing Buildings Status

Category	University Medical Center Hospital	Mastin Building	Moorer Clinical Sciences	Research Facility	Basic Medical Sciences	Biomedical Library Floor	Fairhope Family Practice Clinic	Sanger Theatre Building
Date built	1964/1966	1968	1972	1977	1974	1972	1977	—
Condition	Good	Good	Good	N/A[a]	N/A	N/A	N/A	—
Gross area	376,162	54,898	30,958	15,336	162,009	9,278	5,805	—
Class of construction	Reinforced poured concrete columns + slabs	Steel frame + poured concrete slabs	Pre-fabricated, steel frame	Pre-fabricated, steel frame	Steel frame + poured concrete slabs	Poured concrete columns, steel frame, precast	Masonry + wood frame	—
Number of beds	406[b]	N/A	N/A	N/A	N/A	N/A	N/A	—
Projected life[c]	50 yr	50 yr	50 yr	50 yr	50 yr	50 yr	50 yr	—
Cost to date ($) as of June 1977	10,429,860	1,600,000	770,000	672,000[d]	6,400,000	2,310,000[e]	212,000[d]	—
Depreciation reserve ($) as of June 1977	1,574,268	N/A	N/A	N/A	N/A	N/A	N/A	—
Unrecovered cost ($) as of June 1977	8,855,591[c]	N/A	N/A	N/A	N/A	N/A	N/A	—
Program status	Various remodel/renovate projects in progress	Renovated	Completed	Under construction	Being completed	Completed	Construction began in 1977	Rented[f]

[a] Not applicable.
[b] Levels 10 + 11 unfinished—space available for 120± additional beds (planned to be used for temporary location of non-inpatient care activities).
[c] Estimated by the university.
[d] Estimated construction cost.
[e] Cost of entire building—biomedical library occupies one floor.
[f] Used for various hospital business office activities.

8 Medical Center Programs

The mission, goals, and objectives of the medical center are outlined in Section 1. They form the basis for the existence of the medical center and the numerous educational, clinical, and research programs: current, planned, and proposed.

The college of medicine and the medical center hospital were established in 1970 and the first medical student class began with 25 students in 1973. Since the medical center is relatively young, the opportunity exists to develop innovative programs uninhibited by previous traditional constraints, and to develop a master plan framework not only for physical facilities but for those educational, clinical, and research programs that form the basic criteria used to develop the physical facility requirements.

Numerous programs have been established by the college of medicine, medical center hospital, and schools of nursing and allied health. Many of the requirements under the mission, goals, and objectives may be attained by expansion, improvement, or reorganization of current programs. These programs relate to the education of medical students and allied health professionals; continuing education programs for practitioners; clinical care for both inpatients and ambulatory patients in a humane and dignified manner, and research (basic and clinical) to develop new and improve existing methods of delivering health and health-related care. Such programs and must be structured to develop the medical center into a major regional and national medical institution.

Programs have been developed with several local institutions to assist in providing additional learning experiences for students, graduates, and practitioners. These programs will continue to be refined to take full advantage of such resources. New programs should be carefully planned and developed to fulfill the requirements under the mission, goals, and objectives statements when current programs cannot be modified or changed to meet such requirements. Additional programs in community health (public and patient health education) need to be expanded to foster closer ties not only with local communities but with state and regional groups as well regarding health care needs. Current programs in the various medical specialties will have to be expanded and new ones developed to continue to improve the medical center's capability and capacity as a major referral and tertiary health care center.

Administration and faculty generally agree that growth and expansion require careful planning and guidance so that the size of medical student classes remains small, as consistent with the mission, goals, and objectives. Comprehensive programs should be offered in selected areas of allied health education and affiliation with other institutions considered for the addition of further programs, all in balance with existing clinical, research, and continuing education programs. Many of the mission, goals, and objectives statements may be attained through current programs with perhaps relatively few changes. Where new programs are established, they should parallel current programs and be complementary to them and the stated mission, goals, and objectives.

Consideration should be given to the establishment of an office of education and education research under the office of the dean of the college of medicine. Thought should also be given to the development of an honors program for medical students and a research center for the study of health care delivery systems. There is a definite need for the development of a primary medical care program for medical students, resident staff, faculty, allied health professionals, and employees. This program for primary medical care should be available to the entire university population, including family members. Perhaps a prepayment plan might be advantageous or some other methodology or system employed. Such a university-wide health care program, if deemed feasible and appropriate, could become part of the medical education program.

A task force could be appointed to consider the system that might prove most advantageous for the medical center and the university. Inclusion or affiliation with local institutions might also be advantageous. Regardless of the plan adopted, consideration must be given to existing community services.

The basic medical science departments appear to be interested in establishing central or core laboratory facilities (under a independent director) to maintain and manage special equipment (electron microscopes, spectroscopy, tissue culture, etc.). This equipment would be available to researchers and clinicians at the medical center. Such facilities could provide continuing organization, services, space, and expertise in specialized areas available to individuals or groups and for research or teaching. These facilities would assist in minimizing (and possibly eliminating) duplication of expensive equipment, space, and personnel, and in reducing energy consumption, grant resources, and costs.

The core facility concept also has disadvantages. If control is placed under an established department (as part of the department organization), there could develop a tendency for that department to monopolize the facilities for its own purposes and benefit. A central organization containing many specialized laboratories may not be able to secure personnel with the expertise required in the many specialties. This shortcoming may result in failure to provide high-quality service. The facility organization and administration may also become cumbersome and self-serving.

As a start for an institution of this size, such facilities could be placed under the organization of one of the basic medical science departments, with general surveillance by someone on the administration staff or the associate dean or director for research development.

There are many advantages to the development of a learning resources center. Such a center would bring together and closely coordinate the resources of the biomedical library, audiovisual department, medical illustration department, computer center, and medical records department. Inclusion of medical records within such a center is a relatively new concept and has not been discussed fully. The concept, however, does suggest advantages that would benefit physicians, faculty, epidemiologist, and students, particularly those involved in research. The entire concept of a learning resources center is generally innovative and advantageous and should be explored to determine its eventual establishment at the medical center. Establishing controls relative to security and privacy of patient records would be significant in minimizing liability risks.

Many programs in the medical specialties that are not now represented at the medical center need development and implementation. Many college of medicine departments need additional faculty and supporting staff. The same needs and requirements may be stated for the various departments at the hospital. Additional facilities would have to be constructed to accommodate these programs and attendant staff.

Increases in the numbers of faculty are necessary to meet current and projected increases in the size of the medical student class, inpatient care beds, and current and planned educational, clinical research and medical research programs. The entering medical student class is projected to be 85 students by 1987 and to increase to 96 sometime after 1987. Inpatient care beds are projected to increase to 758 by 1987 and to reach 900 sometime after 1987.

Using the two basic planning criteria of medical students and beds, programming can be developed to indicate the general scope of gross area requirements to satisfy these and other anticipated and foreseeable program requirements, particularly those related to clinical and research programs. The medical center desires to maintain low student to faculty ratios to continue the close, almost individual faculty and student relationships that are so critical to producing highly qualified, motivated, and dedicated graduates.

Considerable expansion to continuing education programs is required to provide the practitioner with the latest knowledge relative to changing technology, methods, and systems of health care delivery. Programs for medical resident certification requirements imposed by the specialties and governing authorities will have to be developed, established, and maintained on a continuing basis. A number of these programs can be provided or developed as "joint ventures" with other local institutions.

Expansion to programs in allied health education should be developed under careful planning and in concert with the stated mission, goals, and objectives. Programs should take advantage of other university programs and those of local institutions to utilize resources effectively and efficiently. The university and the medical center should be the leader in this most important area of the development of the members of the health care delivery team.

Residency and graduate programs should be developed with the individual departments and the medical center as a total entity. Consideration must be given to the obligations and other commitments of the institution. Local, state, and national needs require review relative to such programs. Graduate programs must be carefully coordinated to coincide with anticipated growth of individual departments, availability of funding, and local, state, and national needs to make full use of available resources. Perhaps a joint task force could be appointed to review departmental graduate programs periodically .

The development, establishment, and implementation of many medical center programs are not possible at present. This is not due to the lack of availability of personnel (although this is not meant to imply that this is not a problem), but the acute lack of space available to house personnel and equipment under such programs has reached critical portions. Laboratory space has been converted to office space for faculty and support personnel. Unfinished space designed for inpatient care activities is being converted to use for other purposes. Authorized faculty positions cannot be recruited for or filled because of lack of space to house faculty and support personnel and equipment. This lack of adequate physical space that is convenient or contiguous to each activity within functional relationship criteria is an urgent and immediate problem that requires the proper decisions and investment of resources to overcome.

If the medical center is to achieve its stated mission, goals, and objectives, it cannot hope to fulfill such statements without the necessary commitment to bring about the centralization of all related activities at one contiguous location. To support less than this commitment will virtually relegate the medical center to a secondary position as a medical center in the true and accepted sense of the phrase.

9 Data Summary and Projection Charts

The following data summary and projection charts were developed from data collected during he programming and planning interviews by approximately 64 representatives from the university administration, college of medicine, and university hospital, including deans, associate deans, administrators, faculty, physicians, nurses, researchers, basic scientists, laboratorians, directors, and department managers:

Section 10	Faculty Complement
Section 11	Student Complement
Section 12	Medical Center Employees
Section 13	Bed Complement by Specialty/Service
Section 14	Parking Program
Section 14a	Parking Program (Alternative Example)
Section 15	Program Area Summary Chart Worksheet

The author and his planning team members, using past and current experience from the medical center, national standards and guidelines, and experience and judgment factors, developed the overview master plan report.

10 Faculty Complement

Department	Authorized	Existing Appointment	Shortage/ Overage	Stage 1 1982	Stage 2 1987	Beyond 1987
1. Medical sciences	(33)	(30)	(−3)	(60)	(100)	(100)
Anatomy	7	7	0	12	20	20
Biochemistry	6	6	0	12	20	20
Microbiology/immunology	6	4	−2	12	20	20
Physiology	7	6	−1	12	20	20
Pharmacology	7	7	0	12	20	20
2. Clinical sciences	(71.25)	(42.5)	(−28.75)	(150)	(176)	(267)
Anesthesiology	1	1	0	3	4	5
Family practice	5	4.5	−0.5	15	20	25
Internal medicine	14.75	9.75	−5	30	40	50
Medical genetics	4	3	−1	8	10	12
Neurosurgery	2	1	−1	4	5	6
Neurology	3.25	0.25	−3	3	5	6
Ob/gyn	5	3	−2	14	19	20
Ophthalmology	1	0	−1	2	3	4
Orthopedic surgery	3	0	−3	4	5	6
Otolaryngology	0	0	0	2	3	4
Pathology	9	7	−2	20	35	50
Pediatrics	8.25	5.25	−3	15	30	35
Psychiatry	8	4	−4	21	28	35
Public health + epidemiology	1	0	−1	2	4	6
Radiology	9	6.5	−2.5	16	24	32
Surgery	5	3	−2	8	12	16
Urology	1	0.25	−0.75	3	4	5
3. School of nursing	—	—	—	(30)	(45)	(55)
4. Allied health	—	—	—	(12)	(22)	(34)
5. VA clinic	—	—	—	(5)	(7)	(8)
Total faculty	113.25[a]	78.5	−34.75	276[b]	385[b]	514[b]

[a] State authorized and supported (except for those positions to be designated and funded from restricted accounts and grants).

[b] These figures reflect department head estimates and experience factors (e.g., faculty/student, physician/patient, clinical specialties, research program ratios, etc.) relative to data gathered. These figures also include estimates for state-supported positions and positions generated through grants, professional accounts, etc. These positions will be required to permit continuation of current programs and development and implementation of new programs.

11 Student Complement

Category	Existing	Existing Appointment[a]	Shortage/ Overage[a]	Stage 1 1982	Stage 2 1987	Beyond 1987
1. Medical students	(338)			(562)	(726)	(891)
1st year	69			72	85	96
2nd year	59			72	85	96
3rd year	60			64	72	96
4th year	61			64	72	96
Interns/residents	79			150	190	240
Postdoctoral	10			45	87	105
Fellows	0			60	85	100
Other	0			35	50	62
2. Paramedical	(628)			(1188)	(1410)	(1769)
Nurse anesthetist[b]	20			26	34	42
Inhalation therapist	0			3	5	8
Medical technologist	95			115	145	170
Cytotechnologist	4			6	8	12
Physical therapist	93			110	125	140
Radiology technician	15			22	30	36
Nuclear medical technician	0			2	4	6
Emergency medical trainee	60			72	86	100
Radiation therapist technician	0			2	2	2
Ultrasonography technician	5			10	15	25
Nurse (RNs)	295[c]			780[c]	920[c]	1200[c]
Undecided	37			30	20	10
Histology technician	4			6	10	12
Blood flow technician	—			4	6	6
Subtotal	966			1750[d]	2136[d]	2660[d]
3. Continuing education[e]	(14)			(400)	(800)	(1020)
Physician	—			300	600	750
Paramedical + lay groups	14			100	200	270
Total students	980			2150	2936	3680

[a] Not applicable.
[b] Currently not a university program.
[a] Does not include approximately 300 part-time nursing students.
[d] These figures are projected from existing/proposed programs and will be utilized to determine gross area requirements.
[e] Numbers vary depending on programs offered.

12 Medical Center Employees

Category	Authorized	Existing Number Appointment	Shortage/ Overage	Stage 1 1982	Stage 2 1987	Beyond 1987
1. Hospital	(1294.9)	(1159.5)	(−135.4)	(1650)	(2480)	(3270)
Admin./mgt.	38	34	−4	61	94	120
Professional	423	333	−90	515	685	907
Technical	218	201	−17	300	465	720
Clerical	232.9	219.9	−13.4	322	494	675
Crafts/trades	27	24	−3	42	62	98
Service	356	348	−8	410	680	750
Part-time staff	—	—	—	—	—	—
2. School of medicine	(142.75)	(126.25)	15 (−16)	(285)	(525)	(695)
Admin. assist.	12.25	12.25	0	45	80	95
Secretary/clerical	67	56	−11	125	210	270
Technician	28.5	23.5	−5	60	120	170
Research technician	31	31	0	55	115	160
Part-time staff	4	—	—	—	—	—
3. School of nursing	—	—	—	(15)	(22)	(36)
4. Allied health	—	—	—	(12)	(18)	(28)
5. VA clinic	—	—	—	(35)	(42)	(48)
Total medical center	1437.65	1286.25	−151.4	1997[a]	3087[a]	4077[a]

[a] Projections based on general data collected and on experience factors to reflect increases in inpatient care beds, student class sizes, various programs, etc. Distribution within the various categories will depend on specific criteria and programs to be developed at the medical center.

13 Bed Complement by Specialty/Service

Specialty/Service	Existing	Immediate Need	Shortage/Overage	Stage 1 1982	Stage 2 1987	Beyond 1987
1. Special care	(37)	(56)	(−19)	(72)	(78)	(96)
Burn unit	5	8	−3	10	10	12
Cadiac ICU	8	14	−6	8	8	10
Coronary care	8	8	0	10	12	15
Medical ICU	8	8	0	16	20	24
Pediatric ICU	0	4	−4	8	8	10
Surgical ICU	8	14	−6	20	20	25
2. Routine care	(356)	(391)	(−35)	(556)	(680)	(810)
Medical	106	126	−20	166	200	230
Ob/gyn	52	47	+5	90	120	140
Pediatrics	54	44	+10	60	75	100
Psychiatry	38	38	0	50	55	70
Surgical	106	136	−30	190	230	270
3. Bassinets[a]	(60)	(35)	(−9)	(86)	(100)	(108)
Neonatal ICU	16	20	−4	25	30	30
Intermediate care	10	15	−5	17	20	23
Newborn	34	0	0	44	50	55
4. Recovery, emergency, admit unit	(16)	(0)	(0)	(28)[b]	(36)[b]	(42)[b]
Total beds	393	447	−54	628[c]	758[c]	906[c]
Δ (change)	—	—	—	+235	+130	+148

[a] Not included in total beds.

[b] Does not include beds for ambulatory surgery.

[c] Includes beds that might be assigned for radiation therapy, urology, neurosurgery, orthopedics, and other specialties. These totals will be used to develop gross area requirements.

14 Parking Program

Category	Existing	Immediate Need	Shortage/Overage	Stage 1 1982	Stage 2 1987	Beyond 1987
1. Physician/faculty	94			210	305	490
2. Administrative/employees	295			1050	1214	1305
3. Students, interns, residents, postdoctoral, fellows, continuing education	237			285	360	490
4. Ambulatory patients	205			250	360	470
5. Inpatient/visitors	—			420	460	570
6. Emergency	18			15	20	25
7. Service/delivery	40			15	20	25
8. Peak load factor	—			75	150	180
Total spaces	889	1250	−361	2320	2895	3560
Area required[a] (acres)	6.84	9.62	2.78	17.85	22.27	27.39

[a] Area requirements based on 130 to 135 cars/acre. The projected "total spaces" figures are considered to be reasonable based on data collected, but as detailed planning progresses, such requirements will have to be reviewed. For example, staggered employee shifts will affect the total spaces required. Also, each "category" estimate may have to be reevaluated/reallocated within the "total spaces" as detailed planning progresses.

14a Parking Program (Alternative Example)

The parking program described below was developed by the author for another major medical center. It presents a detailed analysis and methodology for determining parking needs.

Chart 1 utilizes data developed in the medical center parking study prepared by the director of management engineering. This study projected parking needs for medical center personnel only. This study also indicated that the rate of increase for medical center personnel parking needs is decreasing. Thus previous estimates for medical center personnel parking needs may be too large. The parking requirements indicated on Chart 1 include those for medical center personnel, visitors/patients, service vehicles, and disabled persons. Other criteria, such as utilization factors (experience factors), planning factors, and code requirements were employed to determine total medical center parking requirements.

For the purpose of generating costs at this time, it is generally agreed that an addition to the school of medicine parking deck to accommodate 250 cars will provide sufficient parking space beyond 1985. An addition to the hospital parking deck to accommodate 600 cars should also be sufficient beyond 1985. If negotiations with the city to acquire a nearby city parking facility are successful, this will modify the parking deck additions indicated above. The parking space requirements, allocation, and distribution should be reviewed and revised at that time. Both parking deck additions imply that most, if not all, of the cars utilizing the current peripheral surface parking lots would be accommodated in the new decks.

It should also be noted that personnel figures for 1985 and 1990 exceed those developed by medical center staff. The planning consultant added an additional factor which in effect "accelerates" the rate in personnel growth. This is based on past experience at the medical center, demonstrating that estimated personnel projections are always reached or exceeded by as much as three years before anticipated. These accelerated rates of growth beyond those anticipated again reinforces the need to review periodically all base growth indicators, including personnel projections at least on a semi-annual or annual basis. This periodic review of planning data will permit the administration to "act" to meet needs instead of "reacting" to "crisis" situations. Gross square feet area estimates for the parking deck additions were based on 400 gsf per car. Review of the projections (both staff and parking spaces) in 1988 and 1990 (prior to the construction of parking facilities) indicated that the projections were within 1 to 2% ($\pm$) of actual needs.

Chart 1   Parking Status and Parking Needs: 1985 Through 1990

| | January 1981 | | | |
| | | | Spaces Required | |
Personnel/Category	Personnel	Existing Spaces	Planning Factor	Code Rqmts.[a]
Faculty/physicians	439	182	286	294
Nonfaculty staff	1250	496	812	837
Graduates	70	—	45	23
Medical students	432	125	281	142
Physician assistants	100	—	65	33
Disabled persons	—	3	32	26
Service/delivery	—	6	18	15
Peak load provision	—	—	52	—
Total spaces (school of medicine)	2291[c]	812	1591	1370
Administration	50	5	50	—
Residents/interns	346	196	225	277
Hospital employees	2781	1329	1808	1891
Visitors/amb. patients	—	753	472	—
Disabled	—	6	48	53
Service	—	12	18	13
Emergency	—	—	22	—
Peak load provision	—	—	105	—
Beds	—	—	—	697
Total spaces (hospital)	3177	2346	2748	2931
Total spaces (medical center)[e]	5468	3158	4339	4301

Note: The utilization factor, UF (ratio between number of personnel to existing number of parking spaces, or planning factor spaces, or code required spaces, ranges from 0.55 to 0.852 on a total medical center basis. Experience indicates that a medical center requires a UF of 0.72 to establish design parking space requirements.

[a] Existing code/zoning requirements, personnel category requirements subject to interpretation by authorities regarding factors to be applied to calculate required spaces.

The author recommends that all parking facilities be designed to accommodate small buses or electric vehicles similar to those used in airports. These vehicles can be used to transport patients, visitors, and staff from parking areas to the several medical center facilities. So-called "drop-off" and "pickup" areas are not always convenient. Often, the patient is made to wait alone while the driver of the car leaves to park. Adequate space and clearances (in principal circulation corridors) should always be allocated and designed to accommodate such

1983			1985				1990		
	Spaces Required			Spaces Required				Spaces Required	
Personnel	Planning Factor	Code Rqmts.[a]	Personnel	Planning Factor	Code Rqmts.[a]	Estimated Rqmts.[a]	Personnel	Planning Factor	Code Rqmts.[a]
456	296	305	470	305	314	525	513	333	343
1315	854	881	1367	888	916	422	1490	968	998
76	49	25	80	52	26	—	113	75	37
451	293	148	468	304	187	—	511	322	204
112	73	36	115	75	37	—	128	84	41
—	38	32	—	42	36	—	—	48	40
—	22	18	—	24	21	25	—	30	26
—	68	—	—	74	—	50	—	92	—
2410	1693	1445	2500	1764	1537	1022	2757	1962	1689
53	53	—	55	55	—	—	60	60	—
417	271	334	477	310	382	320	477	310	382
3017	1961	2052	3150	2048	2143	808	3450	2243	2347
—	532	—	—	616	—	1070	—	822	—
—	50	55	—	53	58	—	—	58	66
—	20	16	—	23	19	20	—	28	25
—	24	—	—	26	—	25	—	36	—
—	124	—	—	138	—	170	—	161	—
—	—	697	—	—	961[d]	—	—	—	961
3487	3035	3154	3682	3269	3568	2503	3987	3718	3781
5897	4728	4599	6182	5033	5105	3525	6744	5680	5470

[b] Master strategy plan parking program, Stage 3—1985, based on a projected total medical center staff of 4479.
[c] Includes part-time faculty.
[d] Projected completion date for the critical patient care facility (264 beds), January 15, 1987.
[e] Medical center totals may be utilized to determine parking space design criteria; space assignment may then vary to suit medical center requirements.

electric vehicles. Distances between/among the parking areas and various functions and activities at most medical centers can be considerable. To require a patient who may be in pain or infirm to walk such distances is not only inconsiderate, but inhumane as well. Patients who may be in pain and infirm should be treated with consideration, courtesy, and dignity. If anything, such patient/visitor transport systems become an immense public relations item. It also becomes a staff morale builder and time-saver.

15 Program Area Summary Chart Worksheet

Health Sciences and Related Functions/Activities[a]	Existing Beds[b]	Existing nsf	Existing gsf	Desirable gsf[c]	Shortage/ Overage (gsf)
A. University hospital	(393)	(320,093)	(387,443)	(538,225)	(−150,782)
1. Administration	—	(28,510)	(32,946)	(40,460)	(−7,514)
a. Hospital administration	—	(16,703)	(16,703)	(22,640)	(−5,937)
(1) Administrator	—	3,317	3,775	2,890	+885
(2) Main lobby/gift shop	—	2,943	3,600	5,780	−2,180
(3) Reception/ information/ switchboard	—	300	576	1,445	−869
(4) Business office/patient admitting	—	3,697	2,160	2,410	−250
(5) Nursing administration/ in-service education	—	970	763	1,930	−1,167
(6) Meeting spaces	—	1,176	1,288	960	+328
(7) Personnel	—	720	1,020	1,930	−910
(8) Data processing	—	1,115	960	1,445	−485
(9) Accounting	—	1,680	2,352	2,410	−58
(10) Management engineering	—	—	—	480	−480 −751
(11) Media services	—	180	209	960	
b. Medical records	—	2,466	4,612	4,820	−208
c. Volunteers/auxiliary	—	996	608	1,930	−1,322
d. Chaplain/chapel	—	450	180	960	−780
e. Medical education	—	3,527	4,506	960	+3,096
f. House staff/on-call	—	2,576	3,606	4,820	−1,214
g. Health nurse	—	115	168	960	−792
h. Physician affairs	—	492	572	480	+96
i. Attending physician lounge	—	680	772	480	+292
j. Professional recruitment	—	—	—	480	−480
k. Social services	—	1,110	1,665	1,930	−265
2. Patient care services	—	(195,320)	(220,863)	(302,985)	(−82,122)
a. Nursing units	—	(156,078)	(166,861)	(228,765)	(−61,904)
(1) Special care	(37)	(13,392)	(12,056)	(19,065)	(−7,005)
(a) Surgical ICU	8	—	2,618	3,720	−1,102
(b) Cardiac care unit	8	—	2,618	3,720	−1,102
(c) Coronary ICU	8	—	2,618	3,720	−1,102
(d) Medical ICU	8	—	2,618	3,720	−1,102
(e) Burn unit	5	1,801	1,584	2,325	−741
(f) Pediatric ICU	0	—	—	1,860	−1,860
(2) Routine care	(356)	(114,226)	(108,336)	(143,160)	(−34,824)
(a) Surgical	106	40,176	30,396	42,400	−12,004
(a) Medical	106	20,088	30,396	42,400	−12,004
(a) Psychiatry	38	19,464	17,816	15,960	+1,856
(a) Pediatrics	54	15,098	15,512	21,600	−6,088
(a) Ob/gyn	52	19,400	14,216	20,800	−6,584
(3) Unfinished (10th and 11th floors)[d]	(144)	(21,752)	(41,108)	(57,600)	(−16,492)
(4) Bassinets	(60)	(5,636)	(3,700)	(4,600)	(−900)
(a) Neonatal ICU	16	—	—	1,320	−1,320
(b) Intermediate care	10	—	—	900	−900
(c) Newborn	34	—	3,700	2,380	+1,320

Immediate Need[c] (gsf)	Stage 1—1982		Stage 2—1987		Beyond 1987	
	Beds	Projected gsf	Beds	Projected gsf	Beds	Projected gsf
(150,782)	(628)	(657,385)	(758)	(803,835)	(906)	(971,585)
(7,514)	—	(47,850)	—	(65,720)	—	(81,280)
(5,937)	—	(26,230)	—	(35,950)	—	(43,980)
—	—	3,770	—	4,620	—	5,480
—	—	6,280	—	7,580	—	10,705
—	—	1,445	—	2,320	—	2,675
—	—	3,140	—	3,860	—	4,460
—	—	2,100	—	3,080	—	3,670
—	—	960	—	2,400	—	3,600
—	—	2,510	—	3,280	—	3,570
—	—	1,445	—	2,880	—	2,680
—	—	3,140	—	4,280	—	4,460
—	—	480	—	750	—	900
—	—	960	—	1,500	—	1,780
—	—	6,280	—	9,200	—	12,750
—	—	1,930	—	2,240	—	2,950
—	—	960	—	1,200	—	1,600
—	—	1,260	—	1,500	—	1,780
—	—	6,280	—	7,580	—	8,920
—	—	960	—	1,200	—	1,500
—	—	480	—	750	—	950
—	—	480	—	2,250	—	2,650
—	—	480	—	750	—	750
—	—	2,510	—	3,100	—	3,450
(−82,122)	—	(387,005)	—	(473,515)	—	(565,380)
(−61,904)	—	(268,715)	—	(324,985)	—	(386,180)
(−7,005)	(72)	(33,480)	(78)	(36,270)	(96)	(44,640)
−1,102	20	9,300	20	9,300	25	11,625
−1,102	8	3,720	8	3,720	10	4,650
−1,102	10	4,650	12	5,580	15	6,975
−1,102	16	7,440	20	9,300	24	11,160
741	10	4,650	10	4,650	12	5,580
1,860	8	3,720	8	3,720	10	4,650
(34,824)	(556)	(222,400)	(680)	(273,100)	(810)	(324,000)
12,004	190	76,000	230	92,000	270	108,000
12,004	166	66,400	200	80,000	230	92,000
1,856	50	20,000	55	23,100	70	28,000
6,088	60	24,000	75	30,000	100	40,000
6,584	90	36,000	120	48,000	140	56,000
—	—	—	—	—	—	—
(900)	(86)	(7,185)	(100)	(8,900)	(108)	(9,520)
1,320	25	3,000	30	3,600	30	3,600
900	17	1,105	20	1,800	23	2,070
−1,320	44	3,080	50	3,500	55	3,850

15 Program Area Summary Chart Worksheet (*Continued*)

Health Sciences and Related Functions/Activities[a]	Existing Beds[b]	Existing nsf	Existing gsf	Desirable gsf[c]	Shortage/ Overage (gsf)
(5) Recovery/emergency admitting	(16)	(1,072)	(1,661)	(4,340)	(−2,679)
b. Surgery suite	—	9,883	13,902	20,240	−6,338
c. Central sterile services	—	3,489	9,244	7,230	+2,014
d. Labor/delivery	—	7,862	7,768	8,680	−912
e. Emergency medical services	—	5,688	6,600	10,600	−4,000
f. Ambulatory patient care	—	12,100	16,128	21,690	−5,562
g. Ambulatory patient surgery	—	220	360	5,780	−5,420
h. Hemodialysis	—	—	—	—	—
i. Veterans' care unit	—	—	—	—	—
3. Adjunct services	—	(31,386)	(40,471)	(79,130)	(−38,659)
a. Clinical laboratories	—	7,487	8,208	18,320	−10,112
b. Autopsy/morgue	—	1,850	1,834	5,780	−3,946
c. Radiology (clinical)	—	(9,328)	(16,385)	(29,460)	(−13,075)
(1) Diagnostic	—	4,494	12,098	9,640	+2,458
(2) Special procedures	—	1,760	—	3,860	−3,860
(3) Radiation therapy	—	464	—	3,860	−3,860
(4) Nuclear medicine	—	1,488	2,352	3,860	−1,508
(5) Ultrasonography	—	120	432	5,790	−5,358
(6) Administration/ management spaces	—	1,002	1,503	2,450	−947
d. Physical therapy	—	2,440	2,520	5,790	−3,270
e. Respiratory therapy	—	805	968	1,930	−962
f. Occupational therapy	—	—	—	1,450	1,450
g. Pharmacy	—	4,514	4,606	4,340	+266
h. EKG/EEG	—	1,595	1,581	2,410	−829
i. Pulmonary function laboratory	—	440	510	2,410	−1,900
j. Cardiovascular laboratory/ surgery	—	2,161	2,650	2,890	−240
k. Anesthesia	—	326	489	1,450	−961
l. Vascular laboratory	—	440	720	1,450	−730
m. Fiber optics laboratory	—	—	—	1,450	−1,450
4. Service departments	—	(64,877)	(93,163)	(115,650)	(−22,487)
a. Food services/vending	—	17,063	17,195	20,240	−3,045
b. Environmental services/ housekeeping	—	1,108	832	3,860	−3,028
c. Receiving/general stores	—	3,986	6,456	15,420	−8,964
d. Purchasing	—	690	2,579	1,930	+649
e. Plant operations/maintenance	—	22,357	20,793	26,510	−5,717
f. Laundry/linens	—	8,450	5,846	12,050	−6,204
g. Dietetic services	—	288	384	1,930	−1,546
h. Materials management	—	5,156	5,671	7,200	−1,529
i. Employee facilities	—	3,699	5,140	7,230	−2,090
j. Outside agencies	—	1,600	1,800	2,410	−610
k. Safety/security	—	40	55	480	−425
l. Mailroom/print shop	—	440	676	1,930	−1,254
m. Public toilets	—	—	—	2,410	—
n. Stairs, elevators, etc.	—	—	(25,736)[f]	(12,050)[f]	(+11,276)[f]
Hospital gsf subtotals	—	320,093	387,443	538,225	−150,782

Immediate Need[c] (gsf)	Stage 1—1982		Stage 2—1987		Beyond 1987	
	Beds	Projected gsf	Beds	Projected gsf	Beds	Projected gsf
(2,680)	(28)	(5,650)	(36)	(6,715)	(42)	(8,020)
6,338	—	23,240	—	30,320	—	36,850
—	—	9,420	—	9,850	—	12,250
912	—	10,050	—	13,100	—	15,250
—	—	13,200	—	15,160	—	18,350
—	—	34,500	—	42,550	—	48,750
—	—	6,280	—	10,100	—	14,500
—	16	6,400	22	9,450	32	13,250
—	—	15,200	—	18,000	—	20,000
(38,659)	—	(99,555)	—	(121,360)	—	(147,335)
10,112	—	21,980	—	28,250	—	33,895
3,946	—	6,280	—	7,620	—	10,700
13,074	—	(44,655)	—	(50,775)	—	(60,000)
2,458	—	12,560	—	14,680	—	16,300
3,860	—	4,395	—	4,995	—	5,850
3,860	—	14,700	—	14,700	—	16,000
1,508	—	3,860	—	4,650	—	5,850
5,358	—	6,280	—	8,500	—	10,850
947	—	2,860	—	3,250	—	5,150
3,270	—	6,280	—	7,600	—	10,210
962	—	2,230	—	3,050	—	3,570
1,450	—	1,750	—	2,240	—	2,750
266	—	5,020	—	6,065	—	7,850
829	—	2,410	—	3,150	—	3,650
1,900	—	2,410	—	3,200	—	3,870
240	—	2,890	—	3,350	—	3,670
961	—	1,750	—	2,280	—	2,600
730	—	1,450	—	1,960	—	2,320
1,450	—	1,450	—	1,820	—	2,250
(22,487)	—	(122,975)	—	(142,440)	—	(177,590)
3,045	—	23,860	—	26,830	—	34,710
3,028	—	4,395	—	4,980	—	7,140
8,964	—	18,840	—	21,250	—	25,860
649	—	1,930	—	2,240	—	2,780
5,717	—	28,260	—	33,570	—	38,760
6,204	—	13,815	—	14,920	—	18,650
1,546	—	1,930	—	2,270	—	2,850
1,529	—	—	—	—	—	—
2,090	—	8,160	—	8,950	—	11,850
610	—	2,410	—	2,980	—	3,670
425	—	480	—	750	—	920
1,254	—	2,230	—	2,980	—	3,650
—	—	2,850	—	3,170	—	4,450
(11,276)	—	13,850	—	16,650	—	22,300
150,782	628	657,385	758	803,035	906	971,585

15 Program Area Summary Chart Worksheet (*Continued*)

Health Sciences and Related Functions/Activities[a]	Existing Beds[b]	Existing nsf	Existing gsf	Desirable gsf[c]	Shortage/ Overage (gsf)
B. College of medicine	—	(131,685)	(199,199)	(269,615)	(−70,416)
1. Administration	—	(93,709)	(5,564)	(7,690)	(−2,126)
a. Dean/college of medicine	—	2,337	3,505	3,450	+55
b. Research/development/grants management	—	277	416	620	−204
c. Alumni/student affairs	—	1,095	1,643	1,850	−207
d. Human resources/personnel	—	—	—	620	−620
e. Continuing medical education	—	—	—	1,150	−1,150
2. Basic medical sciences	—	(36,766)	(62,584)	(83,385)	(−20,801)
a. Anatomy	—	8,452	18,408	21,045	−2,637
b. Biochemistry	—	4,286	3,592	12,450	−8,858
c. Microbiology/immunology	—	4,420	10,384	14,760	−4,376
d. Physiology	—	4,470	7,488	12,420	−4,932
e. Pharmacology	—	4,216	7,592	7,590	+2
f. Animal health/resources	—	10,922	15,120	15,120	0
3. Pathology	—	(9,097)	(6,928)	(11,420)	(−4,492)
4. Clinical sciences	—	(46,137)	(69,159)	(95,370)	(−26,211)
a. Family practice	—	1,743	2,164	4,720	−2,106
b. Internal medicine	—	6,611	9,963	26,060	−16,097
c. Pediatrics	—	4,117	6,176	8,420	−2,244
d. Medical genetics	—	1,919	2,879	3,960	−1,081
e. Psychiatry	—	4,205	6,307	7,240	−933
f. Surgery	—	5,000	7,500	9,200	−1,700
g. Orthopedic surgery	—	498	747	1,280	−533
h. Neurosurgery	—	996	1,494	1,670	−176
i. Obstetrics/gynecology	—	2,172	3,258	4,270	−1,012
j. Radiology (academic)	—	5,208	7,812	8,850	−1,038
k. Clinical research facility[g]	—	15,168	22,650	22,650	0
5. Service/support	—	(35,976)	(62,776)	(71,750)	(−8,974)
a. Biomedical library	—	13,337	18,720	25,620	−6,900
b. A-V resources	—	2,568	1,904	2,640	−736
c. Medical student teaching laboratories	—	18,526	40,208	40,210	−2
d. Computer center	—	1,505	1,944	3,280	−1,336
College of medicine gsf subtotal	—	(131,685)	(199,199)	(269,615)	(−70,416)
C. School of nursing	—	—	—	—	—
D. Allied health	—	(776)	(1,232)	(22,650)	(−21,418)
E. Related activities	—	—	(97,790)	(115,570)	(−17,780)
1. Long-term care	—	—	—	—	—
2. Progressive care	—	—	—	—	—
3. Rehabilitation	—	—	—	—	—
4. Community mental health	—	—	—	—	—
5. Motel/hotel/seminar	—	—	—	—	—
6. Student housing	—	—	—	—	—
7. Parking facilities	—	—	(97,790)	(115,570)	(−17,780)
Medical center gsf grand totals	393	452,554	685,664	946,060	−260,396

[a] The functions/activities list includes several functions not now in operation at the medical center. It is reasonable to assume, however, that as the medical center develops and expands, these or similar functions will be added to the clinical, educational, and research programs at the medical center. The gross square feet area projections for such activities are based on experience factors within the basic criteria of number of patient beds, students, faculty, etc., projected to Stage 1—1982, Stage 2—1987, and beyond 1987.

[b] See Section 13 for patient bed service distribution.

[c] Since the existing hospital was originally programmed and planned as a general community hospital, the factor utilized for computing the desir-

Immediate Need^c (gsf)	Stage 1—1982		Stage 2—1987		Beyond 1987	
	Beds	Projected gsf	Beds	Projected gsf	Beds	Projected gsf
(70,416)	—	(286,435)	—	(378,500)	—	(441,515)
(2,126)	—	(7,690)	—	(10,515)	—	(13,495)
55	—	3,450	—	4,170	—	4,970
204	—	620	—	850	—	1,250
207	—	1,850	—	2,950	—	3,825
620	—	620	—	875	—	1,125
1,150	—	1,150	—	1,670	—	2,325
(20,801)	—	(83,385)	—	(107,375)	—	(118,655)
2,637	—	21,045	—	21,045	—	21,045
8,858	—	12,450	—	17,950	—	17,950
4,376	—	14,760	—	16,420	—	22,280
4,932	—	12,420	—	15,650	—	17,900
2	—	12,590	—	16,590	—	16,590
0	—	15,120	—	19,720	—	22,530
(4,492)	—	(11,420)	—	(18,750)	—	(16,270)
(26,211)	—	(112,190)	—	(159,380)	—	(199,040)
2,106	—	9,500	—	12,750	—	16,450
16,097	—	27,300	—	38,250	—	46,500
2,244	—	11,250	—	23,280	—	26,850
1,081	—	7,640	—	8,870	—	10,650
933	—	12,450	—	18,100	—	22,420
1,700	—	16,800	—	20,600	—	27,650
533	—	5,680	—	5,680	—	6,400
176	—	2,860	—	4,250	—	6,250
1,012	—	8,860	—	12,400	—	14,620
1,038	—	9,850	—	15,200	—	21,250
0	—	—	—	—	—	—
(8,794)	—	(71,750)	—	(82,480)	—	(94,055)
6,900	—	25,620	—	29,670	—	32,220
736	—	2,640	—	4,270	—	6,600
2	—	40,210	—	43,720	—	48,650
1,336	—	3,280	—	4,820	—	6,585
(70,416)	i —	(286,435)	—	(378,500)	—	(441,515)
—	—	(24,720)	—	(36,420)	—	(59,310)
(21,418)	—	(38,750)	—	(42,550)	—	(51,480)
(17,780)	—	(767,855)	—	(1,030,510)	—	(1,271,930)
—	—	—	(60)	(15,600)	(90)	(23,400)
—	—	—	(90)	(23,400)	(120)	(31,200)
—	—	(6,725)	—	(12,540)	—	(16,450)
—	—	(10,750)	—	(12,650)	—	(15,820)
—	(40)	(21,760)	(40)	(21,760)	(80)	(34,560)
—	—	(24,620)	—	(48,560)	—	(62,500)
(17,780)	—	(704,000)	—	(896,000)	—	(1,088,000)
260,396	628	1,775,145	758	2,291,015	906	2,795,820

able gsf and immediate need reflect areas relative to current operations and projections.
^d Not included in bed totals.
^e Included in receiving/general stores.
^f Includes public toilets and stairs, elevators, etc.
^g Under construction at Fillingim site. Clinical research laboratory work area and service and support spae requirements factored into projections (Stage 1—1982, Stage 2—1987, and beyond 1987) for each activity under clinical sciences.

COMMENTS

1. The General Notes that follow are perhaps more directly applicable to planning current medical center facilities. Several federal legislative acts, with their attendant governing agencies, were not in existence at the time of preparation of the overview master plan report [e.g., Americans with Disabilities Act (ADA)]. Their requirements are therefore not included in the projections and estimates for space and costs.

2. However, the author and his team members are confident that the projections and estimates would be comparable should the programming and planning be accomplished in today's environment, with one caveat. It is the author's opinion that the impact of the ADA requirements relative to facility accommodations for the disabled have not been fully realized within the architectural and engineering professions. The changes in space programming factors have yet to be fully integrated within the planning process. The legal implications will eventually have an enormous impact on our economy. Already, more than 1000 cases have been filed under the ADA requirements, with many more thousands to come.

3. It should also be noted that the program area summary chart worksheet (Section 15) reflects space estimates on a department level, not an individual space or detailed space program level. A detailed space program would be prepared as specific projects were identified (e.g., identification of the ambulatory care center as a specific element of Stage 1 to be selected for construction to satisfy program priorities, budget, etc.).

GENERAL NOTES

1. Regulations from ADA, CDC, CLIA, EPA, JCAHO, NIH, NIEHS, NIOSH, OSHA, and other agencies require considerable administrative accounting and tracking, with attendant forms, correspondence, record file storage, and so on, to maintain and implement laboratory safety policies and procedures. In-service education programs will have to be prepared, organized, and con-

ducted, requiring conference or classroom spaces.

2. A material safety data sheet (MSDS) display and reading area is required. Safety regulations may require staff to wear protective clothing, face masks, and eye shields and to utilize chemical fume hoods or biological safety cabinets for preparation of reagents, tests, procedures, and so on, based on those utilized in the laboratories. A staff laboratory safety officer should be appointed to monitor these programs and requirements. Depending on the nature and size of the laboratory, these responsibilities may require a full-time staff member. This activity should also be coordinated with the medical center safety officer, as required.

3. Additional space is required for laboratory bench workstations and storage for protective gear (gowns, face masks, eye shields, cover-ups, gloves, breathing apparatus, etc.), and in some instances, clothing change spaces are required for the staff. Space will also be required for soiled protective clothing receptacles, carts, hampers, and trash containers for the several categories of waste, such as biohazardous and sharps.

4. Recent concerns about new resistant strains of microorganisms (TB bacilli, etc.) indicate that isolation spaces and techniques for handling and processing such specimens will be required. Guidelines are being developed and are to be released by the CDC and OSHA. Space requirements for these facilities should be included in the program area summary chart and based on the staff program summary charts (Sections 10, 11, and 12, respectively).

5. The Clinical Laboratory Improvement Amendments Act (CLIA, 1988) will impose additional administration, record keeping, proficiency testing (PT), duplication of tests, quality control, and so on, on laboratory operations. Additional administrative and technical staff may be required to implement the new regulations depending on the size of the laboratory. These staff members will require workstations or office space, records file storage, and so on. Additional NSF of 5 to 15% above traditional guidelines in selected areas are considered reasonable increases to accommodate these requirements.

6. ADA, CAP, JCAHO, OSHA, and other regulations frequently do not specify space requirements. Judgment

and interpretation of the regulations must be applied. Interpretations may also vary with the people involved in the planning process.

7. Additional space will be required in laboratory work areas to accommodate the requirements for proficiency testing and other operations. Several workstations in each of the sections will have to be expanded to provide sufficient work space for staff to record/write/report test results on forms, and so on. Space will be needed to store forms and supplies.

8. As the planning process continues into the subsequent planning phases, the consultants recommend that space and staff estimates indicated in the charts be evaluated periodically to monitor the impact on current needs and anticipated programs. Periodic review of the master plan data cannot be overemphasized. This review provides the opportunity to evaluate changes that may occur to medical center programs that will affect laboratory services, programs, staffing, and eventually facility requirements.

9. The Americans with Disabilities Act regulations will also have significant and immediate impact on space requirements for workstations, clearances, corridors, circulation, fire safety and egress requirements, and so on. The intent of the ADA is to eliminate discrimination in the work place due to a person's disability. This affects the requirements for finishes, textures, colors, lighting levels, alarms (audible and visual), and so on.

10. Program space estimates in current planning projects should consider incorporating the requirements of the Uniform Federal Accessibility Standards (UFAS FED-STD-795-1988). These standards are currently acceptable to satisfy ADA requirements. Functions and activities that will have to be increased in size include locker areas; toilets; certain workstations (adjustable height, depth, etc.); corridor and door widths, including hardware type; and controls and clearances at equipment. Conformance to ADA regulations applies to *all* medical center functions and activities.

11. Direct comparison of existing function and activity line items with projected space requirements is generally difficult. Most existing functions and activities contain

several activities in a single workstation or work area that would otherwise be allocated a specific workstation(s).

12. Net square feet (nsf) estimates are generally based on the maximum number of staff in the laboratory work areas, including students; internal circulation within the specific function or activity; and an estimate of equipment space. The gross square feet (gsf) indicated in the program area summary chart worksheet (Section 15) contains a factor to account for various building elements that are usually part of any series of spaces, a department, and so on. These building elements may include partitions, columns, mechanical and electrical spaces, and secondary corridors, among others.

13. Nsf and gsf figures are generally developed to indicate the differences that occur when estimating nsf based on utilization and experience factors, including standards and guidelines (square feet per technical staff, square feet per x procedures, square feet per total number of beds, etc.), and a judgment or experience factor of how large a workstation, space, and so on, should be to perform a particular function or task.

14. The time line of five years between Stages 1 and 2 is considered reasonable to account for the general scale of such institutional projects, time required for project conception, and programming, planning design, and construction. A time line of 3/5/7 years generally becomes the norm for most institution project cycles. It is also an estimate of the time a laboratory (or other facility) will be able to operate within the projected space without consideration for major internal changes or additional space. Changes that may occur during this time are assumed to be accommodated within the projected space. This time line has a range of ± 1 to 2 years.

15. These factors may include discoveries in human physiology, changes in medical technology, demographics of the region affecting health care delivery needs and systems (e.g., increase in elderly patients, etc.), patterns of health care practices, expanding or new health care programs, and new clinical tests derived from new knowledge of human physiology, biomedical technol-

ogy, and legislative requirements. Each factor individually or collectively can have a significant impact on space requirements for both research and clinical laboratories in the near term and future years. These factors emphasize the importance to maintain a dynamic and periodic semiannual or annual review and update of the master plan for the medical center.

16. Caution must be exercised in attempting to apply national standard space program factors because the figure that is selected may not relate to the specific requirements at a specific institution. The nsf and gsf figures indicated in the chart are based on functions, utilization rates and staffing patterns, specific programs, requirements, and so on, at the medical center. These figures are more accurate than those that might be derived using national standards or other guidelines.

16   Statement of Needs

The following list reflects many of the needs expressed by many of the interviewees during the programming and planning sessions. Certain needs, such as additional space for clinical and research laboratories, parking, and vertical circulation inadequacies (people and supplies), are readily apparent and recognized. Other items may require additional input to determine stated versus actual need(s).

The list is not intended to be all-inclusive and an order of priority will almost certainly be determined during latter stages of the planning process. General priorities are indicated in Sections 17, 17a, 19, and 19a.

A.   JOINT NEEDS (Health Sciences)

1. Expand and improve primary and various secondary mechanical systems to upgrade service in several existing areas and to provide for future growth and expansion as planned.

2. Expand parking facilities for faculty, staff, students, employees, patients, and visitors. Parking needs cannot be met with surface parking areas only. Consideration must be given to planning a parking structure of sufficient size to provide safe, convenient, and controllable parking. A parking structure would also conserve site area for other uses.

3. Improve horizontal and vertical circulation for people and material/supplies.

4. Stress to city authorities need to improve vehicular access to the existing Fillingim site. Improvement and widening of Mobile Street from Springhill Avenue to the hospital might be considered as a first step toward improvement of vehicular access.

5. Provide expanded staff health care services, particularly for students. The services should be available to all university staff and students and eventually, to family members.

6. All facilities for the primary and secondary functions and activities of the medical center should be in a physically contiguous location, including medical and basic sciences, hospital facilities, ambulatory care, school of nursing, allied health facilities, research and education, and service and support spaces.

B. COLLEGE OF MEDICINE

1. Faculty administrative offices and support spaces are required to provide adequate and functional space for staff.

2. Expand the research laboratory facilities in the medical and basic sciences to include laboratory work areas and service and support spaces (core areas).

3. Expand teaching and classroom spaces, including laboratories, library, and learning resources facilities.

4. If a decision is made to develop the medical center on the existing Fillingim site, provision must be made to accommodate activities such as basic medical sciences and research contiguous with the teaching hospital facilities.

5. Expand ambulatory patient care programs and develop adequate clinic facilities within a new ambulatory care center.

6. Expand continuing education programs and community health education programs.

C. MEDICAL CENTER HOSPITAL

1. Expansion and modernization of ancillary services is a critical need, including clinical laboratories; a morgue; autopsy, radiology, radiation therapy, pulmonary function, respiratory therapy, and EEG facilities; and catheterization laboratories.

2. Expansion of administrative functions, including accounting, business office and admitting, purchasing, process stores and storeroom, administration offices, medical records (relocate to contiguous location), and social services.

3. Expansion and modernization of emergency medical services.

4. Complete overhaul, repair, and revision of critical mechanical conveyances (lifts, etc.).

5. Food delivery system to patients: central supply trayveyor and dumbwaiter, pneumatic tube system.

6. Complete refinish of 10th and 11th floors for inpatient care—to be used temporarily for various administrative functions.

7. Provide additional service and support spaces for teaching, administrative, and storage activities on the inpatient care units.

8. Expand and modernize (replace equipment) in the laundry, consider relocation because of lack of headroom.

9. Expand house staff facilities.

D. SCHOOL OF NURSING AND ALLIED HEALTH

1. Expansion to administrative, faculty, classrooms, conference, seminar, teaching, and laboratory work areas, including service and support areas.

17 Directions for Growth and Functional Relationships (Fillingim Site)

TOPOGRAPHY, LANDMARKS, AND AESTHETIC VALUES

The existing Fillingim site is generally level, with some changes in elevation, although not major ones that would cause design and construction problems. A wooded tree grove exists on the southwestern area of the site, and Three Mile Creek follows the western border of the existing site. These natural features should be preserved to provide natural enhancement of the existing and proposed development of the site. Development should take advantage of the existing trees everywhere on the site (as practical) and the creek. The creek's course flows to the university campus. Perhaps it should be investigated whether this natural connection could become a link between the two sites.

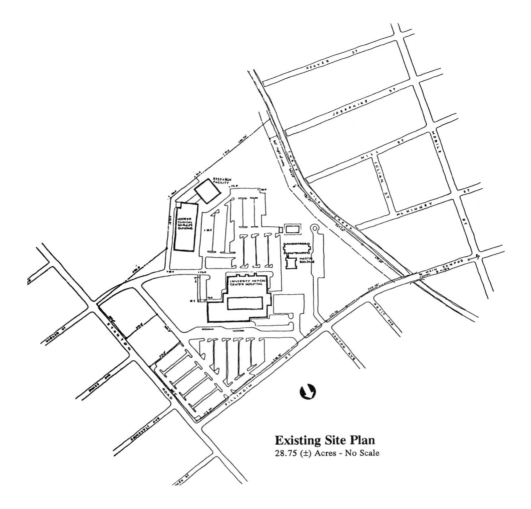

Existing Site Plan
28.75 (±) Acres - No Scale

SITE LOCATION AND LAND ACQUISITION

The property along Stanton Road (the nearest intersection at Fillingim Street) containing the Detention Center (not owned by the medical center) forms a peninsula on the central eastern border of the existing site. The medical center should assign a high priority to eventual acquisition of this property. It is recognized, however, that acquisition may be delayed because of a number of factors. Therefore, development will not include this property as part of the medical center at this time.

Steps have been instituted to acquire approximately 50 to 80 acres of additional property to the west (across Three Mile Creek) and south of the existing site, paralleling both sides of Mobile Street. This total site area will be utilized during the planning process to indicate how growth and expansion may be accomplished for the facilities of the medical center.

Consideration has been given to the possibility that the medical center might be relocated to the university main campus. At present, however, this does not appear to be probable because of the possibility of acquiring the additional property adjoining the current existing site. The planning report will complete the analyses of the Fillingim site development potential (Scheme 1). Consideration for the development of a new medical center at the university campus site (Scheme 2) will begin subsequent to the completion of Scheme 1. The consultant was requested not to pursue relocation of the medical center to the main university campus as a direction for growth at this time. See Sketch 1.

PEDESTRIAN ACCESS

Entrances have been designated for staff and visitors. However, since all parking is in surface lots on the site, pedestrian circulation does not follow simple patterns. The frequent heavy rainfall in the area further complicates pedestrian circulation. Circulation patterns are also difficult within the hospital; however, this is due mainly to the location of employee time clocks to the lack of sufficient space to accommodate this and other activities properly. Improvement in exterior and interior pedestrian circulation is of considerable importance and will be emphasized in the several solutions that will be considered during the planning process.

VEHICULAR ACCESS

One of the major disadvantages of the current location of the medical center is its generally poor vehicular access from the roads serving the site. Major access is currently from Mobile Street to Fillingim Street driveways. Mobile Street is a narrow two-lane residential street and will require widening to improve vehicular access to the site. Indications are that the city is willing to improve Mobile Street from Springhill Avenue to Fillingim Street. Vehicular access to the medical center will be greatly enhanced when this work is accomplished. Fillingim Street should also be widened. Although the main university campus is approximately 5 miles from the Fillingim site, travel time between the two sites is not very convenient, at best.

PARKING AREAS

At present all parking is on surface lots "scattered" throughout the existing site. Existing parking spaces do not meet current

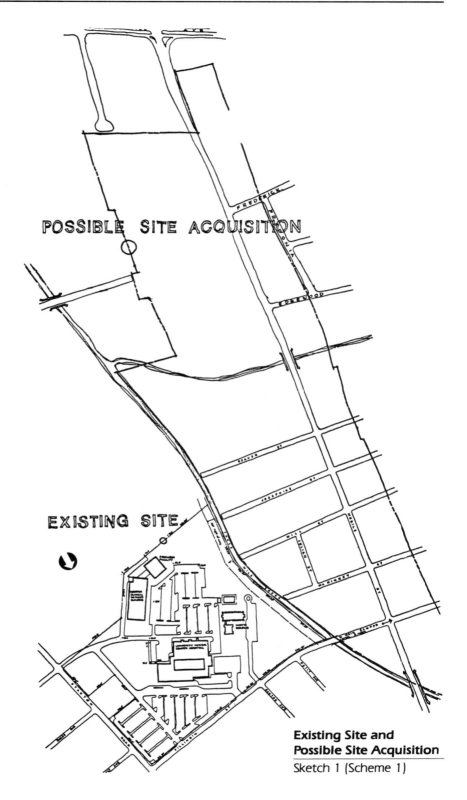

POSSIBLE SITE ACQUISITON

EXISTING SITE

**Existing Site and
Possible Site Acquisition**
Sketch 1 (Scheme 1)

needs. As the physical facilities expand and consume ground area, and consume ground area, more site area will be lost to surface parking. Therefore, as expansion proceeds, parking will have to be accommodated in multilevel parking structures for reasons of economy of site utilization, functional relationships, personnel safety, and convenience. A parking structure would also permit some return on investment through modest parking charges to those using the facility. Parking needs will also have to be accommodated in more than one parking structure because of the projected parking demands and functional relationships.

PROPOSALS FOR GROWTH

The following proposals for growth are not necessarily in order of priority but indicate the several options that are available for study and needs that should be accommodated. Priorities will ultimately have to be determined and take into account needs, functional relationships, and budget considerations:

1. Provide expansion to service and support activities such as clinical laboratories, morgue/autopsy, general and process stores, EEG, pulmonary function, respiratory therapy, business office and admitting, various administration activities, and medical records. Expand and modernize laundry facilities (also consider relocation). Comparison should be made of the costs of developing a new laundry versus contracting for such services. Expand and modernize the emergency medical service facilities. Provide expansion to the central plant to accommodate proposed expansion. This expansion may be at the existing location or relocation should be considered to provide the nucleus of a new central plant that would eventually servie the entire medical center. Final determination of this concept will parallel development and refinement of the various stages of development and expansion to be explored.

2. The space needs discussed above probably could be accommodated in additions to the hospital on its eastern and western sides, including remodeling and renovations to various areas. Additions to the south would be reserved for a possible second Bed Tower plus expansion for needed service and support activities in a base unit of two or three levels. The eastern and western additions would also be on two or three levels.

3. Complete refinishing of the 10th and 11th floors in the hospital for inpatient care service. This space could also be used for various administrative or other activities on an interim basis until other new administrative space became available.

4. Provide an ambulatory care center (ACC) with sufficient facilities to improve and expand the ambulatory care capabilities of the medical center. This new ACC could be in a separate building with direct connection and contain other activities related to ambulatory care. The vacated space in the hospital would provide needed expansion and relocation for several of the activities listed above. The ACC could be located to the west or east of the hospital, preferably the east side.

5. Provide a parking facility for 1200 ($\pm$) cars with capability of adjacent expansion. This facility should be convenient and connected directly to the hospital and the proposed ACC. A possible location would be in the northwestern corner of the site, thus being able to serve the hospital (at the main entry) and the ACC located east of the hospital. Pedestrian access would be through horizontal circulation spines, covered or enclosed. Parking for special purposes (emergency, service, etc.) would be allocated to several surface parking lots.

6. Formalize (with the goal of improvement) both pedestrian and vehicular circulation patterns at the medical center.

7. Provide administrative space for faculty, including support and service spaces for secretarial, clerical, and technical personnel and research laboratory facilities. In general, faculty spaces should be separate from (but convenient to) clinical activities. Such faculty activities could form the nucleus for the medical and basic sciences facility that eventually will have to be developed at the Fillingim site. This facility could be located southwest of the hospital across Three Mile Creek if this property becomes available. The faculty office activities could also be part of an administrative facility housing hospital and college of medicine administrative activities; a learning resources center, including the biomedical library; and audiovisual resources. The facility could "straddle" the creek on site west of the hospital.

8. Organize the existing and proposed facilities into zones or areas to improve access, functional relationships, pedestrian and vehicular circulation, site utilization, and so on. Create, as required, horizontal circulation spines for pedestrians to permit convenient and protected access to and from various facilities on the site— a "shirtsleeve" environment.

9. Consider bridging or relocating Three Mile Creek farther west as the site becomes available and expansion continues in this direction.

10. Consider a centralized building concept (megastructure), housing all medical center facilities under one roof, versus a more decentralized or campus plan.

11. Consider a second parking structure located to the west across the creek to service several of the facilities in this area of the site.

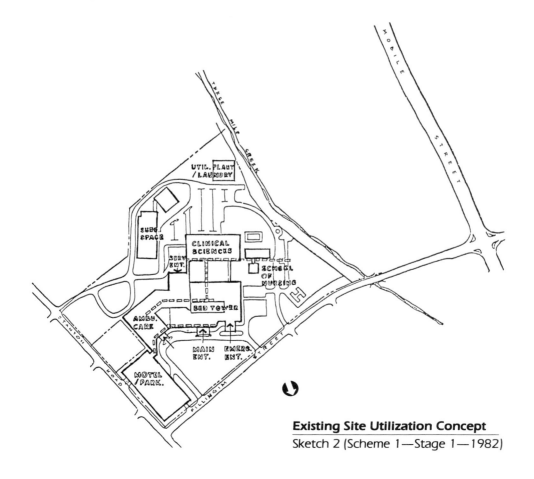

Existing Site Utilization Concept
Sketch 2 (Scheme 1—Stage 1—1982)

12. Preserve existing green spaces as much as possible and create sufficient additional open and green spaces to soften or humanize the scale of the medical center as it develops and expands physically. These spaces could be utilized in various therapy programs or be there simply to enjoy.

Sketches 2 through 6 indicate direction for growth and functional relationships for the proposed development at the Fillingim site.

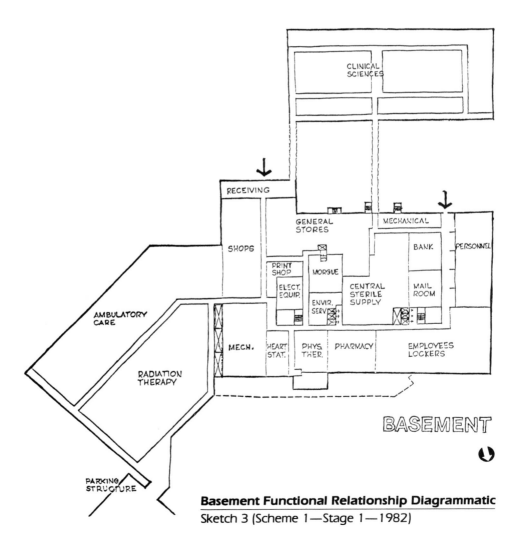

Basement Functional Relationship Diagrammatic
Sketch 3 (Scheme 1—Stage 1—1982)

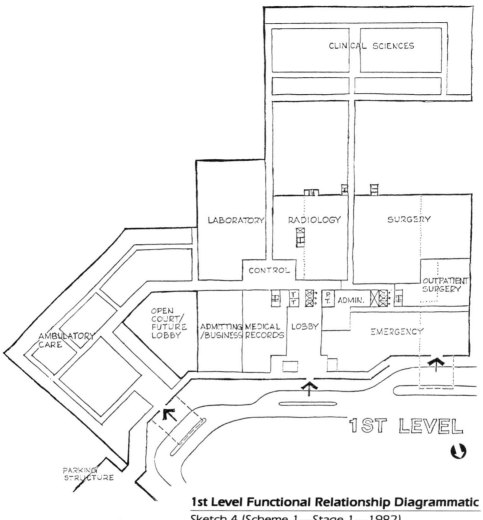

1st Level Functional Relationship Diagrammatic

Sketch 4 (Scheme 1—Stage 1—1982)

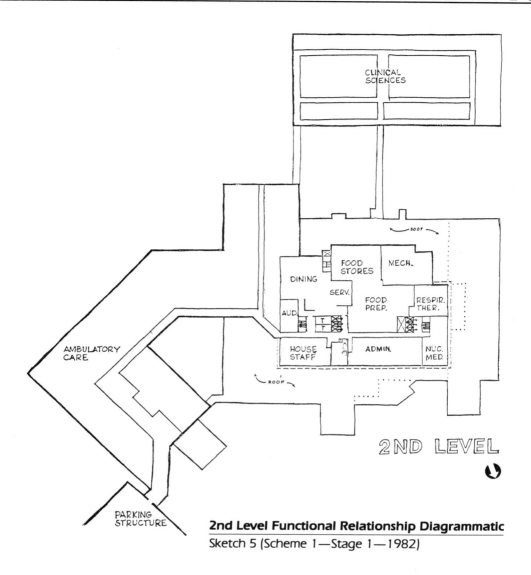

2nd Level Functional Relationship Diagrammatic
Sketch 5 (Scheme 1—Stage 1—1982)

Site Utilization Concept

Sketch 6 (Scheme 1—Stage 1—1987
and Beyond 1987)

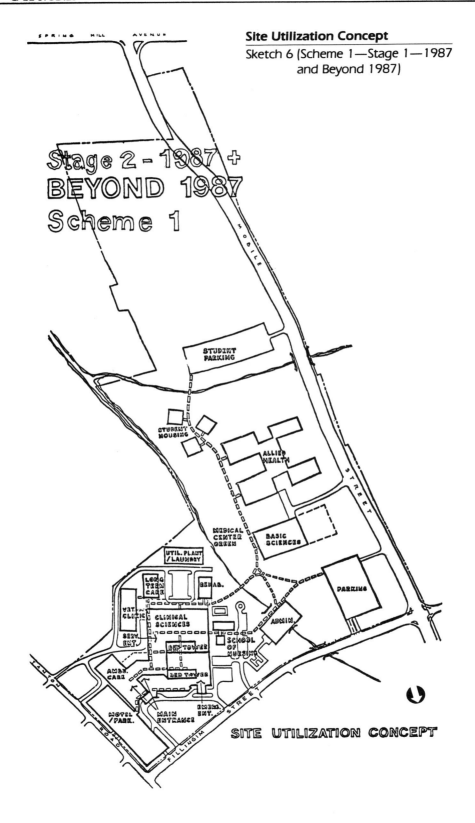

SITE UTILIZATION CONCEPT

17a Directions for Growth and Functional Relationships (University Campus Site)

Shortly before the completion of development of Scheme 1 (medical center program at the existing Filligim site) the university administration directed that Scheme 2 be prepared, exploring the possibilities of relocating and developing the medical center at the University main campus. There are varied reasons for selecting the campus site for development of the main medical center:

1. Philosophically, this would place all the diverse disciplines of medicine in close proximity with the other activities, such as natural sciences, engineering, education (other than medical), administration, business, music and the arts, service and support activities, and so on, permitting convenient intellectual interface on practical and academic matters of mutual concern.

2. Physically, adequate land is available to permit planned, logical growth and expansion of the proposed medical center. One hundred acres have been allocated to the medical center in the campus master plan. There are no existing buildings in this area that would require demolition (or relocation) with the development of a new medical center.

3. Medical center program development is not compromised by existing facilities that may not have been planned originally as a major medical center.

4. Elimination of site acquisition costs and related problems.

5. Excellent and convenient access from virtually all surrounding metropolitan and regional areas.

6. The existing facilities at the Fillingim site do not have to be, *nor should they be, abandoned* at any time. These facilities can become an important adjunct part of and function within the total university medical center health system concept, providing ambulatory care and special services, and become one of the patient entry points into the developing health care system of the region. The Fillingim site facilities can also perform other functions to be determined as the planning develops.

SITE LOCATION

The main campus is approximately 5 miles west of the existing site (see the location maps in Section 2), bounded on the east by University Boulevard, south by Old Shell Road, and on the west and north primarily by residential areas. Some commercial development also borders the campus. The entire campus site consists of more than 640 acres. The main campus location is within one of the most rapidly growing areas in the metropolitan area.

TOPOGRAPHY, LANDMARKS, AND AESTHETIC VALUES

The campus consists of numerous academic, administration, service, and support buildings, including the university administration, life sciences, physical education, music and art studies, engineering, residence halls, central plant utilities, and maintenance services. Medical and basic sciences is also located on the campus. The campus has varied changes in elevation and is heavily wooded. Three Mile Creek meanders through the northern part of the site and with careful planning and development could become an attractive environmental asset and focal point for the entire campus.

The area of the campus selected for the proposed medical center is north of Three Mile Creek. This portion of the campus covers more than 100 acres and is almost entirely wooded. Elevation changes, especially near the creek area, are considerable. The central part of the site does not have large changes in elevation. A portion of this area has already been designated as the site for the future medical school on previous campus master plans.

VEHICULAR ACCESS

The campus is literally minutes away from most areas by way of major improved city thoroughfares from and to I-65, other areas of the city, the airport, and the region. Long-range plans include further improvements to various neighborhood streets and extensions of major highways that will further improve and provide direct and convenient access to the campus from almost anywhere in the area. Internal campus roadways will have to be extended to service the proposed medical center development.

PROPOSALS FOR GROWTH

The basic programming data gathered, developed, and employed for the preparation of Scheme 1 (the Fillingim site) is also utilized for the Scheme 2 (campus site) development. The brief graphic analysis demonstrates that the proposed campus site will permit a major medical center complex, including all basic functional elements. The campus site also includes the principal advantages listed above.

The Scheme 2 Site Development sketches indicate a central location on the site allocated for the medical center. This placement will simplify future expansion in all directions.

Stage 1—1982 (Sketch 7) indicates a scope of development similar to Stage 1—1982 of Scheme 1 (Fillingim site). The basic functional elements are similar, but further detailed planning and programming (with established budgets, priorities, etc.) determining the specifics to be included in Stage 1—1982 development will have to be completed. The basic elements of Stage 1—1982 should be the teaching hospital, clinical sciences, medical center core facility (administration, learning resources, etc.), ambulatory care, student health, and parking facilities.

The existing basic medical sciences building on campus would continue to provide services and support for teaching and research programs. Convenient pedestrian pathways (over Three Mile Creek) connecting the existing campus facilities and the medical center would have to be added. The existing central plant would also have to be expanded and services extended to the medical center. The new laundry could be part of this expansion to the central plant.

Stage 2—1987 beyond 1987 site development (Sketch 8) indicates the medical center at its programmed maximum development, with a teaching hospital of approximately 1000 beds. It is interesting to note that the scale (size) of the proposed medical center is approximately equal to all of the current academic and administrative facilities on the campus. Other elements have been added to the center, including allied health, and nonacute care (extended care, rehabilitation, etc.). Other activities have been expanded and developed further.

Basic medical sciences has been added to the heart of the medical center to locate its activities into proper functional relationships with other medical center activities. The existing building would be reprogrammed to become part of the natural sciences academic programs, thus preserving its function as an part of the overall university education programs. Additional pedestrian walkways and bridges are to be added. Three Mile Creek is to be developed and expanded into one or more lakes or ponds with the shorelines landscaped to provide enhanced environmental amenities to all on campus, including patients.

It should be emphasized that these Scheme 2 sketches indicate that the proposed site is adequate for a major medical center complex. Certain other basic functional relationships can be developed and refined as the planning progresses. Subsequent planning phases are required to refine the concept that will meet basic program requirements and enhance the mission, goals, and objectives of the university. Sketches 7 and 8 indicate the direction for growth and functional relationships for development at the university campus site.

18 Utilities Evaluation (Filligim Site)

INTRODUCTION

The overview master plan, which provides basic data relative to the growth and expansion of the physical plant and the current and future needs of the medical center, must consider the impact of this expansion on the existing utility systems at the Fillingim site. This impact will affect the on-site utilities as well as those commercial and municipal utilities (off-site) that must serve the medical center.

This utilities evaluation is presented to review briefly the existing utilities serving the present physical plant on the existing site and then to project broad planning objectives and directions for growth with estimated quantitative values that would adequately serve the needs projected for Stage 1—1982 and general estimates for Stage 2—1987 and beyond.

MECHANICAL SYSTEMS

The following narrative is a brief review of the existing systems based on site visits, review of existing drawings and other documents of the original project(s), and discussions with university physical plant personnel.

Plumbing, heating, ventilating, and air-conditioning systems are of high quality and represent the latest in the state of the art for hospitals designed and constructed during the late 1950s and early 1960s. The air-conditioning systems are energy inten-

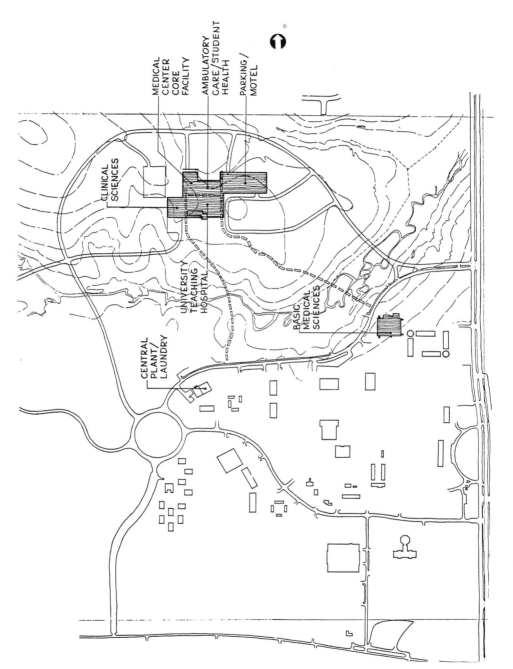

CLINICAL SCIENCES

MEDICAL CENTER CORE FACILITY

AMBULATORY CARE/STUDENT HEALTH

PARKING/MOTEL

UNIVERSITY TEACHING HOSPITAL

BASIC MEDICAL SCIENCES

CENTRAL PLANT/LAUNDRY

Site Utilization Concept
Sketch 7 (Scheme 2—Stage 1—1982)

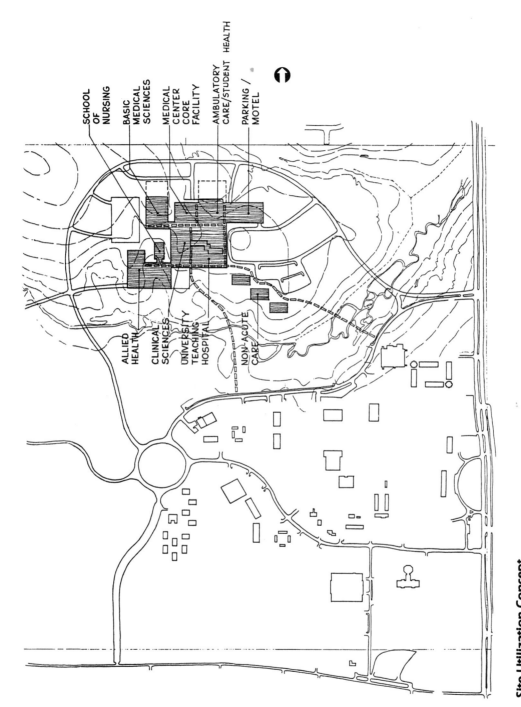

Site Utilization Concept

Sketch 8 (Scheme 2—Stage 2—1987 and Beyond 1987)

sive by present standards but were designed prior to the oil embargo crisis. The air-conditioning system serving the tower patient bedrooms is a high-velocity two-pipe induction unit system utilizing 100% outside air. Interior spaces and areas are serviced with high-velocity double-duct systems, with one system serving the basement and first level and a second system serving the interiors of the inpatient nursing unit levels. Several separate systems each serve the surgical suite, labor/delivery suite, and the food preparation area. A separate air-handling system and a chilled water system mounted on the roof service the ICU areas on the 8th and 9th levels.

Central chilled water is generated by three electrically driven centrifugal chillers with a combined capacity of approximately 800 tons. Two chillers were made by the American Standard Company and one by the Carrier Corporation. The former units are no longer manufactured. All three chillers are required to meet demands for cooling in severe hot weather.

Growth and Expansion

Based on observations relative to the cooling and heating capacities of the existing mechanical facilities, it may be assumed that the existing heating equipment could service a new structure(s) of approximately the same size as the existing building, but the cooling plant does not have capacity beyond completion of the 10th and 11th floors. Energy conservation measures employed in any new structure would almost ensure adequate capacity from the existing heating equipment. Updating the existing hospital with an energy conservation program would also reduce fuel consumption and improve standby capabilities.

Any proposed structure(s) would require a new cooling facility. Its size and location would depend on projected growth and expansion. As indicated in Section 17, a new central plant is suggested to be initiated in Stage 1. Ultimately, this central plant would provide service for the entire medical center development proposed at the Fillingim site.

The proposed growth and expansion program would *add* the estimated heating and cooling requirements shown in Chart 2 to existing loads. Since the existing heating equipment has an aggregate capacity of 30 million Btu/hr, the present equipment could conceivably service the estimated demand through 1982 (28 million Btu/hr). This capacity does not allow for standby capacity, which if deemed necessary, would

**CHART 2 Estimated Heating and Cooling Requirements
(Added to Existing Loads)**

Facility	Heating (floor area, 1000 Btu/hr)	Cooling (tons)
University hospital	12,600	7,900
College of medicine	1,800	110
Motel/hotel	870	60
Parking	0	0
Total additional load	15,270	960
Total existing load	12,800	800
Total estimated load		
Stage 1—1982	28,070	1,760
Stage 2—1987	44,350	2,800

raise the boiler equipment capacity to 42 million Btu/hr, based on three boilers, each at 50% full load (three boilers at 14 million Btu/hr = 42 million Btu/hr).

As indicated above, the existing chilled water plant does not have any spare capacity. Stage 1—1982 estimated expansion indicates a requirement of an additional 960 tons of cooling and (1760 − 800 = 960). Stage 2—1987 programs suggests a total added load of 2000 tons (2800 − 800 = 2000) (see Chart 1).

As indicated in Section 17 for Stage 1—1982 expansion, it is suggested that a central plant be constructed. The new central plant should contain a central chilled water system and possibly space for central boilers at a future date. Central boilers may or may not be required during Stage 1. This would depend on the capacity of the existing heating equipment relative to how growth and expansion occurs during Stage 1. The central plant could be included in the lowest level of a new building, or if economically feasible, be housed in a separate building. Each solution has advantages and disadvantages and should be considered as specific facility designs develop.

The additional population and construction suggested by Stage 2—1987 might have an impact on the domestic water and sanitary sewer availability and capacity in the neighborhood. As detailed planning progresses, an environmental impact statement will have to be prepared to assess the impact upon the surrounding area of any proposed growth and expansion. All services will have to be analyzed in sufficient detail.

For the purposes of conceptual planning in this overview master plan report, it is assumed that proposed growth and expansion would be supplied by the services available in the existing neighborhood. These services may not be of sufficient size or be in the condition to accept the proposed loading on a trouble-free basis for the long-term requirements of the medical center. Stormwater drainage is presumed to present no serious problems in view of the drainage system readily available on site.

It is further suggested that as detailed planning progresses, the program for growth and expansion should include investigation of the feasibility of applying certain emerging technology to the systems at the medical center. Some of these technologies include:

1. Computerized central control for monitoring utility systems
2. Solar-augmented space heating and domestic water heating, especially for laundry operations
3. Solid waste-to-steam conversion (cogeneration systems)

ELECTRICAL SYSTEMS

A detailed examination was not made of the electrical equipment, maintenance, or test records of major electrical systems for this phase of conceptual planning. However, a visual survey of the existing systems indicated that the equipment was in satisfactory condition, consistent for the hospital as originally designed.

The hospital is served by the Alabama Power Company at 4.16 kV from a power company substation to two 2000-kVA transformers located in the hospital. Each transformer serves one side of a double-ended switchboard. The buses are connected with a manual tie switch so that it is possible to supply the entire switchboard from one transformer. Load data from the power company indicate peak load in August 1976 to be 2360 kV (approximately 2600 kVA).

The hospital emergency power system is supplied by two 500-kV Waukeshaw diesel engine generators and appears to have adequate capacity to supply sufficient emergency power to the hospital. The engine generators are not paralleled and the transfer switch arrangement and controls do not meet the current NFPA 76A, Standard for Essential Electrical Systems for

Health Care Facilities. This system should be upgraded to meet current NFPA requirements. The Mastin building and the Moorer clinical sciences building are each served separately by power company secondary services and appear to be functioning appropriately. The total combined electrical service data for the three major buildings on the Fillingim site are shown in Chart 3.

Growth and Expansion

It is apparent that the existing hospital electrical service and distribution system is not adequate to supply any major new expansion or new buildings. The proposed growth and expansion would add the estimated electric loads listed in Chart 4.

It is apparent that the estimated Stage 2—1987 (Chart 4) demand will double the existing electrical load. As noted above, each building on the site is supplied separately by the power company. There would be cost savings if these existing services were combined on a single electric meter as the incremental costs decrease for increased usage, provided that demand is reasonable. It is suggested that Stage 1 expansion include a new large-capacity primary substation to be located near the proposed central plant. This new substation should supply primary service to any major new facilities and backfeed the existing hospital as soon as possible to start consolidating the on-site services on a single electric meter. This suggested scheme would require that all new facilities contain university-owned, university-maintained transformer substations to reduce the primary distribution voltage (either 4.16 or 13 kV) to building utilization (either 208/120 or 480/120 V). The proper voltages would be determined as detailed planning progresses.

CHART 3 Combined Electrical Service Data

Peak demand (kW) (estimated at 3300 kVA)	2800
1976 Consumption (kWh)	14,294,460
1976 Cost	$313,377
Total area served	416,018
Overall average watts per square foot	6
Overall consumption of kilowatts per square foot per year (108,840 Btu per square foot per year)	31.9

CHART 4 Projected Electrical Loads (Added to Existing Loads)

Building/Facility	Kilowatts
University hospital	1800
College of medicine	300
Motel/hotel	100
Parking	700
Total additional load	2900
Existing peak demand	2800
Total estimated load	
Stage 1—1982	5700
Stage 2—1987	9000

The primary distribution system would require a duct-bank system to supply the buildings from the new substation. It is suggested that the system include multiple empty spare ducts and manholes for extending primary service from the primary substation to contiguous adjacent properties now being considered for possible acquisition by the university. The system should include ducts (into separate manhole compartments or separate manholes) for telephone and data system lines. (See the discussion of communications systems below.)

Because of the high cost and limited supply of energy sources, as detailed planning progresses, consideration should be given to the economics of on-site power generation. Possibly, the proposed central plant could include a local solid waste system as fuel for a thermal plant to generate them, chilled water, and electricity. The relatively high load factor and use of steam in a large medical center may make such a system cost-effective.

COMMUNICATION SYSTEMS

Telephone

The existing hospital contains a central PBX system that has certain limitations. It is suggested that a Contsrex system be considered as the medical center expands. Adequate capacity should be provided for the proposed expansion for the medical center beyond 1987. This telephone system will require a duct bank to interconnect the buildings with the main telephone equipment or terminal space. Telephone exchange (switching) equipment can be provided on- or off-site.

Data, Video, and Miscellaneous

A major contemporary medical center makes extensive use of computer, closed-circuit television (CCTV), and other information systems as part of patient care, administrative, education, and research programs. At the present time, coaxial cable systems are the most reliable, cost-effective transmission systems available. An extensive duct bank system to interconnect all buildings should be included in future growth and expansion programs.

In addition to the systems discussed above, facilities should be provided for a central monitoring and control system for building system and energy management. Centralized fire alarm and security systems for monitoring all buildings from one central location to optimize building operation, energy usage, and response to alarm conditions should also be evaluated for inclusion in the medical center facilities.

18a   Utilities Evaluation (University Campus Site)

INTRODUCTION

The overview master plan, which provides basic data relative to the growth and expansion of the physical plant and the current and future needs of the medical center, must consider the impact of this expansion on the existing utility systems at the main campus. This impact will affect the on-site utilities as well as those commercial and municipal utilities that must serve the medical center.

This utilities evaluation is presented to review briefly the existing utilities serving the present academic campus and then to project broad planning objectives and directions for growth with estimated quantitative values that would adequately serve the needs projected for Stage 1—1982 and general estimates for Stage 2—1987 and beyond, with reference to Scheme 2 development.

MECHANICAL SYSTEMS

The following narrative is a brief review of the existing systems based on site visits, review of existing documents, and discussions with university physical plant personnel.

Plumbing, heating, ventilating, and air-conditioning systems are of high quality and represent the latest in the state of the art for each time frame in which the buildings were constructed.

The various academic buildings are served by air-conditioning systems that are energy intensive by present standards but were designed prior to the oil embargo crisis. The air-conditioning systems generally are high-velocity double-duct systems. Separate low-pressure air-handling systems serve miscellaneous special-purpose areas.

Central chilled water is generated by multiple electrically driven centrifugal chillers and an absorption chiller with a combined capacity of approximately 4800 tons. The two older electric chillers (1000 tons capacity each) were originally gas engine driven and made by the Carrier Corporation. The two new chillers (1200 tons each) were made by the York Corp. A fifth chiller, rated at 400 tons, is a Carrier steam absorption type of the same vintage as the two older machines.

Growth and Expansion

Based on observations relative to the cooling and heating capacities of the existing mechanical facilities, it may be assumed that the existing central cooling and heating plant could accommodate a 350,000-gsf (±) medical center facility. This is based on the fact that one boiler now carries the entire load, and it is reported that the two 1000-ton chillers plus the 400-ton absorption chiller carry the entire cooling load, leaving 2400 tons available for additional service needs. It is estimated that a doubling of floor area that can be serviced is possible with the present heating and cooling capacities. However, responding to such service demands would eventually limit the standby capability. Updating the existing buildings with energy conservation programs would improve standby capabilities and save energy without the need to add additional equipment in the central plant.

Chart 5 illustrates the estimated heating and cooling requirements in addition to existing loads imposed by the proposed growth and expansion program. The additional population and construction suggested by Stage 2—1987 and beyond 1987 development might have an impact on the existing domestic water and sanitary sewer capacity on campus. As detailed planning progresses, an environmental impact statement will have to be prepared to assess the impact on the surrounding neighborhoods of any proposed growth and expansion. All services will have to be analyzed in sufficient detail as planning progresses.

CHART 5 Estimated Heating and Cooling Requirements

Facility	Heating (floor area, 1000 Btu/hr)	Cooling (tons)	Floor Area [gsf (±)]
University hospital	8,000	500	200,000
College of medicine	6,000	375	150,000
Motel/hotel	1,000	65	25,000
Parking	0	0	600,000
Total additional load	15,000	950	375,000
Total existing load	40,000	2,500	1,000,000
Total estimated load			
Stage 1—1982	55,000	3,450	1,375,000
Stage 2—1987	71,300	4,400	1,775,000

Note: The values used to estimate service requirements for development on the main campus (Scheme 2) are similar to those utilized for development of the existing Fillingim site (Scheme 1) relative to gross square feet of area. It should also be noted again that the scope (construction dollar estimate) is essentially the same for Schemes 1 and 2. The differences between Schemes 1 and 2 would be in the distribution of area (new vs. remodeled). Further detailed planning would provide additional data to refine these and other estimates. The requirements above are based on a program and budget similar to that estimated for Scheme 1. Mechanical requirements estimates will change as the total program is refined during subsequent phases of planning.

For the purposes of conceptual planning in this overview master plan report, it is assumed that proposed growth and expansion would be supplied from the services available in the existing neighborhood. These services may not be of sufficient capacity or be in adequate condition to accept the proposed loading on a trouble-free basis for the long-term requirements of the medical center. Stormwater drainage is presumed to present no serious problems in view of the drainage system readily available on site. Domestic water is supplied by a large water main running through the campus and appears to be adequate. A secondary feed, affording standby capability for the medical center requirements, should be investigated.

ELECTRICAL SYSTEMS

Following is a brief review of the present electrical systems on campus based upon a site visit, review of existing drawings, and discussions with university physical plant personnel.

The existing primary electrical distribution system serving the campus buildings is a radial underground loop rated 12.4/7.2 kV. Cable size is number 4/0 AWG, 15 kV. The primary loop system is supplied by a radial feeder from an Alabama Power Company primary substation located on the south side of the campus. High voltage of 110 kV is supplied to the 7500 kVA primary substation transformer, which transforms the 110 kV to 12.4/7.2 kV for distribution on the campus. Alabama Power Company owns and maintains the primary substation. The 12.4 kV/7.2 kV primary loop system loops the main campus and is installed in underground duct banks to transformers located in or adjacent to existing buildings. The loop switches are in the transformers or in some cases consist of separate pad-maintained switchgear.

The present academic campus peak demand load is approximately 5300 kVA, with an expected near-term increase to 560 kVA when new load additions are energized. There are currently several planned building additions on campus that will increase this load further. Telephone, television, and miscellaneous data systems are distributed in underground duct banks that interconnect the major buildings on the campus. Some spare capacity exists in the duct bank system.

The overall campus electrical systems and equipment are well planned, flexible, and very suitable for a growing academic (nonmedical) university. However, the existing campus system has some limitations when considering the development of a major medical center that may also be served from the same electrical system. It is apparent that inclusion of a major medical center development was not considered when the original electrical system was planned. However, several alternatives are available that will utilize but add to the present system for a much expanded, highly reliable electrical system for the total campus.

Growth and Expansion

As indicated, the existing primary electrical distribution system has certain limitations when considered to supply a major medical center. A detailed analysis of electrical systems appropriate for a large medical center is beyond the scope of this overview master plan report, but whatever systems are selected, high reliability and flexibility are absolute essentials. The present single-radial-loop system, although offering adequate reliability for academic buildings (classrooms, offices, etc.), is not suitable for a medical center. A medical center requires multiple sources of power, including utility sources, multiple transformer supplies and standby, and emergency power.

Also, the present primary substation and the loop system cable size do not have sufficient capacity to supply the ultimate electrical needs for the proposed medical center. Chart 6 summarizes the electrical loads projected for the proposed medical center.

Any electrical planning for a major campus should include consolidation of electrical services, such as that for the existing academic campus system, to take advantage of a single-meter bulk power rate of the utility company. For the expansion of the existing campus primary distribution system alternative approaches should be considered subject to utility company provisions to meet the alternate total projected campus load requirements and needs for reliability as follows:

System A

1. Expand and modify the existing Alabama Power Company primary substation for the incoming 110-kV feeders and two primary step-down transformers, with capacity to service the entire campus demand of approximately 12,000 kVA. The 12.4/7.2-kV bus should be managed for multiple outgoing feeders with the switches to circuit breakers to interconnect the buses.

CHART 6   Projected Electrical Loads

Building/Facility	Kilowatts
University hospital	1800
College of medicine	300
Motel/hotel	100
Parking	700
Total additional load	2900
Existing peak demand	6000–7000
Total estimated load	
Stage 1—1987	9000
Stage 2—1987	12,000

Note: The electrical loads for the present campus are not included, but the present peak demand of about 5300 kVA plus the planned building additions to the academic (non-medical) campus will probably add 6000 to 7000 kVA to the medical center load for an ultimate projected total campus load of more than 9000 kVA for Stage 1—1982 and 12,000 kVA for Stage 2—1987.

2. Add to and modify the campus duct system to expand two or three express feeder from the 12.4/7.2-kV switch to the medical center substation (each feeder should be from a different transformer bus). Provision should be included for extending additional feeders to the academic campus.

System B

1. Construct a new primary substation on the north side of the campus in the general area of the proposed medical center. Preferably, this new substation should contain two primary 110- to 12.4/7.2-kV step-down transformers, each with the capacity to service the total campus load on an emergency basis.

2. An alternative approach would be to supply a single transformer from a second 110-kV feeder different from the feeder supplying the south campus substation and then interconnect the north and south substation 12.4/7.2-kV switch gear buses. Extend the 12.4/7.2-kV feeder from the north and south substation to the proposed medical center.

Further detailed planning will resolve the preferred primary system. Regardless of which system is selected, secondary substations of multiple transformers with 480/277-V "secondaries" will be provided at the medical center. Duct-bank systems for telephones, television, and data should be extended from the academic campus to the medical center.

COMMUNICATIONS AND MISCELLANEOUS SYSTEMS

A contemporary major medical center makes extensive use of computers, closed-circuit television, and other information systems as part of patient care treatment, educational, and research programs. At the present time, coaxial cable systems are the most cost-effective reliable transmission system available. An extensive duct-bank system to interconnect all buildings should be included in future growth and expansion programs. The future of fiber optic systems also appears promising. A properly designed duct-bank system would accommodate such future systems.

In addition to the systems discussed above, facilities should be provided for a central monitoring and control system for the medical center systems and energy management. Centralized fire alarm and security system alarms for monitoring all buildings from one central location to optimize building operation, energy use, and response to alarm conditions should also be evaluated for inclusion in the medical center. This should be interconnected with the academic (nonmedical) campus system.

Because of the high cost and limited supply of energy sources, as detailed planning progresses, consideration should be given to the economics of on-site power and steam generation (cogeneration systems). The central plant expansion could be designed to include a local solid waste system as a fuel for a thermal plant to generate steam, chilled water, and electricity. A relatively high load factor and steam usage in a large medical center could make such a system cost-effective.

It is further suggested that as detailed planning progresses, the program for growth and expansion should include investigation of the feasibility of applying certain emerging technology to systems at the medical center. Some of these technologies include:

1. Computerized central control for monitoring utility systems
2. Solar-augmented space heating and domestic water heating, especially for laundry operations
3. Solid waste-to-steam conversion

19 Construction Stages and Cost Estimates

Based on data developed to date relative to proposed and projected physical facility needs, the following stages and conceptual cost estimates (Chart 7) are presented to indicate a general magnitude of costs. As the detailed planning phase progresses and the facilities for each stage of development become more specifically defined (in scope and time for construction), costs can be refined further to reflect the additional detail.

The gross areas indicated are derived from the program area summary chart worksheet in Section 15. The elements of the stages reflect of data collected relative to needs and are intended to indicate possible groupings of elements to meet several stated needs. It is reemphasized that the figures indicated are conceptual cost estimates based on general cost experience data for the Mobile area. The figures are for general budget and planning purposes.

CHART 7   Conceptual Cost Estimate: Stage 1—1987

Element	Gross Square Feet	$ Cost, June 1977[a]
1. University hospital	200,000	$12,750,000
■ Commence planning, Jan. 1978		
■ Median occupancy date, 1981[b]		
■ Functions:		
— Administration		
— Patient care services		
— Adjunct services		
— Service departments		
— Mechanical and electrical		
2. College of Medicine	150,000	8,750,000
■ Commence planning, Jan. 1978		
■ Median occupancy date, 1980		
■ Functions:		
— Administration		
— Laboratories		
— Service and support		
Subtotal	(350,000)	($21,500,000)
3. Parking structure (1600 ± spaces)	600,000	3,750,000
■ Commence planning, Jan. 1978		
■ Median occupancy date, June 1979		
4. Motel/hotel (40 rooms)	25,000	875,000
■ Commence planning, Jan. 1979		
■ Median occupancy date, June 1979		
Subtotal	(625,000)	($4,625,000)
Total construction cost	975,000	26,125,000
Total project costs		$32,750,000
■ Includes fees, contingencies, etc., at 25% of construction cost = $6,625,000 (±)		

[a] Construction costs are based on June 1977 average costs. Cost shown should be escalated at the current average of 7%/year (±) from June 1977 to time for actual construction to begin.

[b] Median occupancy date are based on the fact that a series of phases within a stage must be implemented to permit continuation of ongoing operations.

STAGE 1—1982 (Approximate Occupancy)

1. Upgrading and expansion of existing hospital adjunct services and support activities, including administration areas, patient care services, radiology, surgery, clinical laboratories, radiation therapy, pulmonary function, emergency medical services, laundry, related mechanical and electrical systems, and teaching spaces (conference, classroom, seminar, etc.).

2. Addition of ambulatory care center with related administrative, service, and support activities.

3. Addition of clinical medical sciences facilities for college of medicine activities, including administration areas (faculty/physician offices with secretary, support, and service personnel spaces), laboratories with service and support spaces (core areas), and teaching spaces. As these facilities become available for occupancy, the Mastin building would revert to school of nursing activities).

4. Addition of parking structure for approximately 1600 cars.

5. Addition of motel/hotel unit with approximately 40 rooms.

6. Addition of related horizontal circulation spines to provide a "shirtsleeve" environment.

STAGE 2—1987 AND BEYOND 1987

These stages, although not specifically defined, would include facilities for:

1. Basic medical sciences with teaching facilities

2. Hospital adjunct services and support activities with inpatient care beds, additional ambulatory care facilities, and so on

3. Parking structure

4. Allied health facilities

5. Medical center administration facility

6. Progressive care; long-term care, mental health, rehabilitation, and alcoholic treatment facilities; and so on

7. Residential facilities

8. Site acquisition

9. Central plant facilities expansion

Construction costs and time estimates are not indicated for these stages at this time. Cost estimates particularly would have little or no validity projected 5 to 10 years into the future. However, the importance of periodic updating [at least annually (better semiannually) based on 5-year projections to include cost and time estimates] of the data, projections, estimates, and so on, contained in this overview master plan report cannot be overemphasized. Such review and updating will provide the administration of the medical center with a vital planning and control tool with respect to physical facility needs to support continuing and new programs.

19a Construction Stages and Cost Estimates

The data indicated in Section 19 for the Fillingim site are equally applicable to Scheme 2 development, the university campus site. The major differences would be in the program to provide for a measure of immediate needs (interim accommodations phase) for the facilities of the Fillingim site.

There may also be some change in the order of the development and construction of the elements that might be included in Stage 1—1982 development. However, the same conceptual cost budget of $32,750,000.00 is used to establish the scope of the program and plan Scheme 2 development.

It must be emphasized that the medical center development program includes continued use of the facilities existing at the Fillingim site. These facilities will remain a key element in the university medical center health system programs for health care delivery systems, including patient care (clinical activities) and medical and paramedical education and research.

20 Interim Accommodations

Briefly stated, the term *interim accommodations* refers to the proposed development at the existing Fillingim site to provide for certain immediate needs. In general, these needs include:

1. Expansion for ambulatory patient care services
2. Administration service support activities, such as offices and medical records
3. Various inpatient care–related service and support functions, such as radiation therapy, clinical laboratories, and laundry

4. Faculty, physician, and basic scientist office, laboratory work areas, and service and support facilities (core areas)

5. Parking facilities

6. Repair and upgrade of building mechanical, electrical (including communications systems), and plumbing systems and services.

It is estimated that some additional new space will be required [20,000 to 30,000 gsf ±], with most needs accommodated in remodeling and renovation of existing areas and completion of the 10th and 11th floor renovation projects.

Interim Accommodations

Sketch 9—Basement

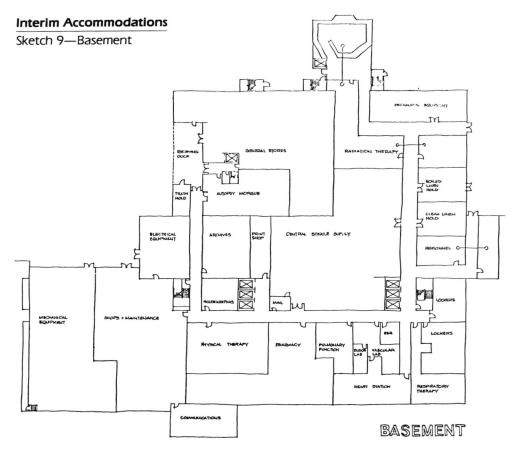

Several of these projects have been authorized and are under way, including emergency department expansion and completion of the 10th and 11th floors. The budget for these items, estimated at $5,000,000, includes monies authorized for projects currently in progress.

It is again emphasized that the existing Fillingim site facilities are planned to continue as part of the total medical center complex and will participate in the overall health, education, and research programs of the new university medical center health system. Sketches 9 to 12 indicate the proposed functional changes to be accomplished during the interim accommodations phase.

Interim Accommodations

Sketch 10—1st Level

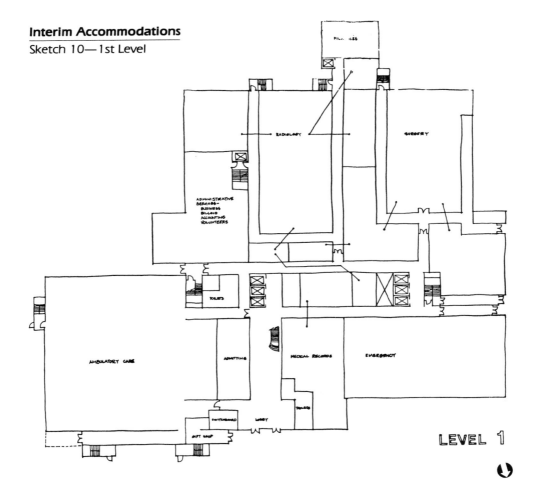

Interim Accommodations
Sketch 11—2nd Level

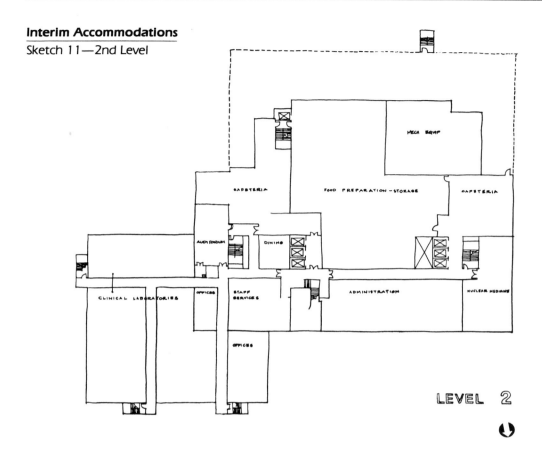

LEVEL 2

Interim Accommodations
Sketch 12—10th & 11th Levels

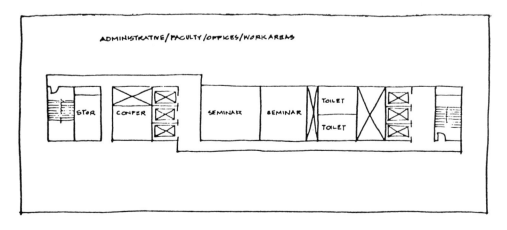

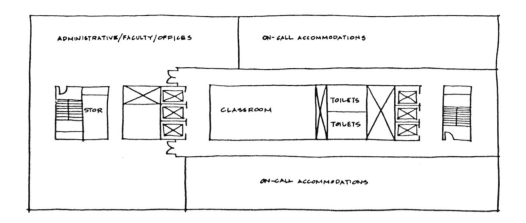

LEVELS 10 ÷ 11

CASE STUDY 2

Case Study 2 presents the new research laboratory and academic facility for the National Institute for Occupational Safety and Health (NIOSH). The facility is under construction, with completion scheduled for early spring 1995. This new facility is located on the University of West Virginia campus in Morgantown, West Virginia. The building owner is the Centers for Disease Control (CDC), Atlanta, Georgia. This case study outlines how the facility design developed to meet specific research laboratory criteria, academic protocols, and building systems requirements.

Cannon, Architects, Engineers and Planners, Washington, DC, one of the nation's leading research and development laboratory design and planning firms was selected as the design architectual/engineering firm for the project. Programming and planning began in September 1990 and continued for approximately two years. Architectural and engineering design began in July 1992. The contract documents (working drawings and specifications) were completed and the contractor selected, and construction was begun in November 1992. Building occupancy is scheduled for early spring 1995.

As in Case Study 1, although all research laboratory facilities may have similar requirements and building systems, they certainly are never identical. Goals, objectives, and missions differ. Scientific research disciplines, protocols, and academic programs emphasis vary. Planning factors for estimating space, staff, faculty, building systems requirements, and so on, can be extracted and developed from the statistics and data presented in this case study. Such factors would have to be modified and tested should they be applied to develop other research laboratory facility programs.

Many thanks are extended to the principals and staff of the Washington, DC office of Cannon for permission granted to use this exemplary project as Case Study 2. The author has utilized much of the programming, planning, and schematic design documentation that was developed by Cannon for this presentation.

Contents

1. Introduction
2. Project Summary
3. Site Criteria
4. Architectural Design Criteria
5. Space Program Summary
6. Mechanical Design Criteria
7. Plumbing Design Criteria
8. Fire Protection Design Criteria
9. Laboratory Piping Design Criteria
10. Electrical Design Criteria
11. Interior Space Design Criteria
12. Probable Construction Cost

1 Introduction

The primary goal and mission of the new research laboratory and academic facility is to provide the scientific work environment to support the investigative research endeavors that will result in knowledge to assist in increasing worldwide understanding of occupational safety and health concerns for the betterment of all who work. Basic objectives are to:

- Develop a world-class research laboratory and academic facility to attract the most talented and imaginative investigators in the field of biomedicine related to occupational safety and health.
- Create the best site use and location for the new facility to merge the design fully with the existing site environmental characteristics.
- Develop a direct physical connection between the new facility and the existing buildings to permit close functional and operational relationships with the Appalachian Laboratory for Occupational Safety and Health (ALOSH) activities.
- Develop a new laboratory facility that is safe, efficient, functional, flexible, and adaptable to accommodate new programs as they develop and technologies that will certainly evolve in the future.
- Design and provide interior spaces that complement and support the daily tasks of individual researchers, technical and administrative staff, and visitors through selection and sensitive use of materials, colors, textures, natural and artificial light, volume (space), and natural features. For example, interior and exterior views and perspectives, selection and placement of plants both indoors and outdoors, moving water/fountains, and so on, can greatly enhance the interior environment.
- Design an environment (site and structure) that provides and fosters positive and attractive scenes on arrival at the site and to enhance movement through the site in a vehicle or as a pedestrian, in the walk from the parking area to the building entrance, including sights and vistas, landscaping, and paths, then entering the building and going to the relevant space.

2 Project Summary

a. PROJECT INFORMATION

Building owner   Centers for Disease Control (CDC), Atlanta, Georgia: new research laboratory and

	academic facility for the National Institute of Occupational Safety and Health (NIOSH)
Owner organization	Federal agency: Department of Health and Human Services
Owner contact	Ms. Jennifer Fabrick Assistant Director of Design and Construction CDC, Atlanta, Georgia
Building location	Morgantown, West Virginia
Project type	New construction
Building functions	Research and testing
Architect/engineer	Cannon (Washington, DC office)
Consultants	Laboratory planning: Earl Walls Associates Civil: MSES Consultants, Inc. Structural: Cannon Mechanical/electrical: Cannon Lighting: Cannon Model builder: Trojan Models Photographer: Eric A. Taylor
Builder	Pray Contracting Company, Morgantown, West Virginia
Tenant/user	NIOSH, Morgantown, West Virginia
Funding	Federal (taxpayer) appropriation

b. PROJECT SCHEDULING

Programming and planning	September 1990
Design	July 1992
Construction	November 1992
Project completion	March 1995
Total design time	26 months

Total construction time	28 months
Construction cost	$29.5 million
Total project cost	$32.0 million
Cost per gross square foot (GSF)	$214.00

c. BUILDING INFORMATION
(Gross Square Feet Space Program)

	Building Area (gsf)
Ground floor	31,300
1st floor	32,500
2nd floor	25,100
3rd floor	26,800
4th floor	26,800
Penthouse	6,400
Total gsf	148,900

d. GENERAL DESIGN REQUIREMENTS

Concepts for site development were based on analysis of existing conditions. The challenge was to select a location to minimize earthwork movement and satisfy all access and visibility requirements. A successful building site that met program objectives was determined and selected.

Solar orientation was a major factor, to take full advantage of natural light for spaces within the building. Protection from the energy effects of solar heat gain was also developed.

Economical solutions were provided for several conflicts that evolved with an existing site utility corridor. The solutions adopted improved the existing site system, satisfied the new building demands, and provided for future growth and expansion.

Final site location also anticipates building expansion to provide additional laboratory, office, and service and support spaces without compromising basic functional relationships. The exterior wall has been designed with removable panels to facilitate the construction and connection of future additions.

e. METHODOLOGY AND PROCESS

A special committee of research scientists was established to evaluate program trends and current and proposed research processes, techniques, and protocols. The committee developed and recommended a series of adaptable, modular laboratory work, service and support areas. The committee's work was closely monitored and coordinated with the Cannon programming, planning, architectural, and engineering team members. This planning process ensured integration of research criteria demands with building systems design requirements and capabilities.

Several alternative concepts were developed, studied, reviewed, and revised. The concept that best included all the program requirements was selected.

f. CONCEPTS AND SOLUTIONS

The building systems and plan layout promotes the development of creative solutions that can accommodate program changes and new technologies. It is anticipated that the design solution will also permit adaptation to accommodate scientific research protocols not yet defined. The design of the building, with its creative and innovative environment, provides the spaces for advanced technology research, examination, and analysis while providing for the spectrum of dynamic human concerns of those who occupy and work within the building, including visitors.

Several plans were developed and analyzed. The final concept became a modified L-shaped plan or "footprint," consisting of:

- A centralized main visitor and staff entrance providing security control and convenient access to the administrative office core areas, and to the laboratory work, service and support areas.
- Administration offices and service and support (mail, work, conference, seminar, library/reference, classrooms, etc.) core areas.
- Staff amenities include spaces such as:
  — Exercise/weight room
  — Aerobics
  — Employee health
  — Dining/cafeteria/patio
  — Convenient parking
- Modular, adaptable laboratory work areas located on the exterior of the building, permitting windows for natural light.

- Laboratory service and support core spaces are directly across a staff/service corridor from the laboratory work areas. This core service and support areas concept can reduce duplication of specialized equipment items that may be used occasionally by researchers. The core concept can reduce equipment, services, energy consumption, and space costs. The core areas include activities such as:
  — Tissue culture
  — Equipment space
  — Electron microscopy and photography
  — Glassware washing and processing
  — Fluorescent microscopy
  — Isotope counting
- Principal laboratory work areas accommodate such scientific research and testing functions and activities as:
  — Thermal stress laboratory
  — Respiratory stress laboratory
  — Respiratory research
  — Aerosol laboratory
  — Gas vapor laboratory
  — Aerosol chamber
  — Cellular biochemistry
  — Nuclear magnetic resonance imaging (MRI)
  — Pathology laboratory
  — Pharmacology laboratory
  — Cellular physiology
  — Pulmonary toxicology
  — Analytical chemistry
  — Clinical immunology
  — Mycology lab

g. STRUCTURAL SYSTEM

Architectural, structural, mechanical, electrical and communications, plumbing, and fire protection building systems have been designed and selected to provide a building life of approximately 60 years with minimum maintenance and replacement of major components. The structural system is poured-in-place reinforced concrete with a concrete pan and joist floor system. Selected floor loadings are as follows:

Room/Area	Load (psf)
Laboratory work areas	125
Library stack areas	150
Archive record storage	125
Industrial shops	125
All other areas	100
Mechanical spaces (as required)	150 (min.)

h. MECHANICAL SYSTEMS

Laboratory supply and air handling systems consist of:

- A variable-air-volume (VAV) system was designed for laboratory supply and exhaust requirements. It is anticipated that a 30 to 50% energy cost savings will be achieved over a constant-volume system. The air-handling units include a run-around heat recovery coil.

- Temporary redundancy is achieved through bypass ducts with automatic dampers between each supply air duct system. This system will support periodic service and maintenance protocols and any breakdowns that may occur.

- Laboratory exhaust requirements are 1500 cfm per double laboratory module for one 6'-wide fume hood (1200 cfm) and two exhaust snorkels (150 cfm each).

- Three central exhaust units located in the penthouse provide service for each laboratory floor (2nd, 3rd, and 4th floors). Exhaust ducts are 304 stainless steel round/oval with welded joints. Main manifold exhaust ducts provide an air velocity of 3,000 fpm at maximum flow.

- Laboratory work areas are maintained at a static pressure negative to the corridors, to prevent fumes escaping from the laboratory.

- Dedicated exhaust systems are provided for biological safety cabinets, perchloric acid hoods, and other locations requiring special exhaust.

- Two variable-air-volume (VAV) recirculating air-handling systems service the administrative office areas, corridors, and other nonlaboratory or service and support spaces.

- Two domestic water systems supply potable cold water and nonpotable (laboratory) cold water. Two hot water systems provide hot water (110°F) for the two requirements.
- Deionized water is provided locally within the laboratory work or core areas using cartridge water processing systems.
- Vacuum and compressed air is provide through central systems piped to the laboratories and core areas.
- The entire building is protected by a wet pipe sprinkler system, three zones per floor.
- Natural gas is available in all laboratories. Special gases, gas mixtures, and so on, will be provided in cylinders. Low-temperature liquid gases will be supplied from mobile dewars.

i. ELECTRICAL SYSTEMS: BLOCK LOADS FOR ELECTRICAL POWER

Load Densities: Lighting and Receptacles (Watts/SF)

Room or Area	Lighting Connected[a]	Receptacles Connected
Electrical, telephone, mechanical rooms	1.5	3.0
Laboratories	3.0	N/A[b]
Laboratory/support	3.0	N/A
Lobby	6.0	3.0
Food service	2.0	3.0
Computer center	3.0	3.0
Research support	2.0	3.0
Office areas	1.5	0.25
Service areas, corridors + stairways	1.5	0.25
Storage rooms	1.5	N/A
Utility rooms	1.5	3.0

[a] The minimum lighting feeder and panel capacity are designed on the basis of 4.5 W/sf, in accordance with the *National Electrical Code*, Article 220-3.
[b] N/A, not applicable.

Load Densities: Heating, Ventilation, and Air-Conditioning Equipment (Watts/SF)

Room/Area	Connected
Laboratory work areas	12
Laboratory service/support	12
Laboratory office	10
Research support	10
Computer center	10
Food service center	17
Facility support	19

Load Densities: Special Equipment (Watts/SF)

Room/Area	Connected
Laboratory work areas	50
Laboratory service/support	50
Laboratory office	1
Research support	3
Computer center	20
Food service center	3
Facility support	3

Demand/diversity factors are generally not applied to an individual laboratory module since virtually all the equipment within the space could be in operation at the same

Architectural Rendering of the New Research Laboratory and Academic Facility under construction for the National Institute for Occupational Safety and Health of the Centers for Disease Control.

Photograph of Scale Model—Main Entry and Courtyard View

Photograph of Scale Model—View of East Elevation

time. Following is a representative example of selected demand/diversity factors for laboratory facilities:

$$1 \text{ module} \rightarrow 100$$
$$2 \text{ to } 10 \text{ modules} \rightarrow 100 \text{ to } 80\%$$

$$10 \text{ to } 40 \rightarrow 80 \text{ to } 50\%$$
$$\text{Over } 40 \text{ modules} \rightarrow 50\%$$

Distribution design is arranged to serve large groups of laboratories in order to take advantage of the lower factors in sizing distribution equipment and feeders. Spare capacity, however, is designed into the power distribution system.

3. Site Criteria

a. GENERAL DESIGN REQUIREMENTS

The site development concepts were based on the analysis of existing conditions, the program of requirements, and anticipated future needs. Site visits and discussions with the CDC/NIOSH project team identified advantages and disadvantages of site characteristics that were considered during the schematic design phase. The effort emphasized the need to develop a state-of-the-art research laboratory and academic facility to project a high-quality image. The analysis and review of the site issues indicated that a location in the southeastern quadrant of the site, with its prominent orientation to Willowdale Road, was a prime location for the proposed facility.

The contours (topography) of the existing site provided the most challenging element of the site features. The design challenge was to develop a solution to include all the access requirements for the new building on the existing site and to minimize the volume of earthwork to be moved. The site analysis indicated that the building would consist of multiple levels to take advantage of the several site characteristics. (See U.S. Geological Survey Map.)

Access to the site is from the intersection of Chestnut Ridge Road, Willowdale Road, and Old Chestnut Ridge Road. The traffic analysis indicated that a road should be located adjacent to Willowdale Road. This road will assist in accommodating the additional cars expected as the employee population increases to approximately 500. This solution is intended to improve traffic patterns along Willowdale Road and provide separation between university medical center traffic and NIOSH employee traffic.

b. CIRCULATION AND PARKING

- Primary vehicular access to the site passes through the intersection of Chestnut Ridge Road, Willowdale Road,

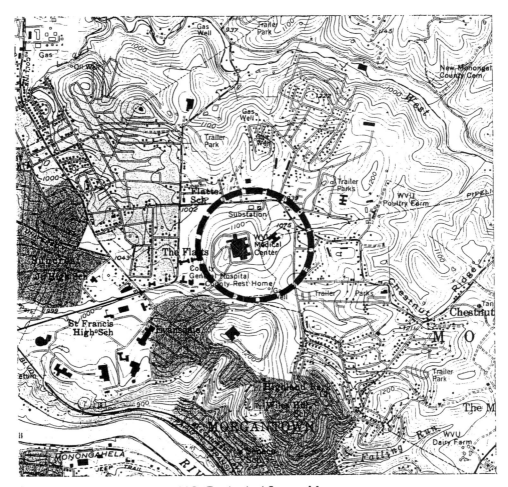

U.S. Geological Survey Map

and Old Chestnut Ridge Road. This intersection is considered somewhat confusing and not without hazard.

- The main entrance to the existing building is not visible from the surrounding thoroughfares or from the principal vehicular entrance. The rear of the building faces the public side of the site.
- Visitors, employees, and service vehicles enter the site from the access road bordering the northern property line. This road also serves the university hospital complex.
- Pedestrian circulation from the parking garage crosses several roadways on the site.
- Existing service roads and access to the loading dock at

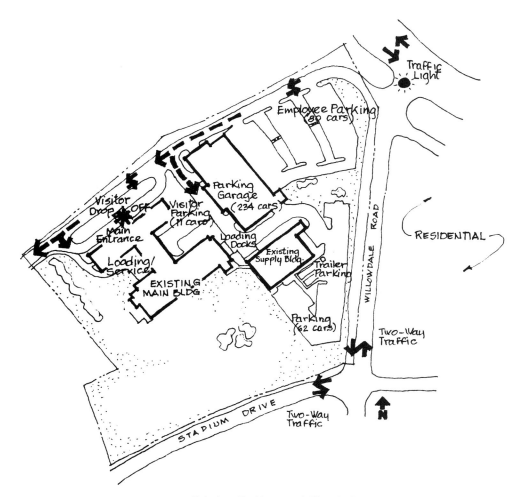

Existing Parking and Circulation

the existing building are located close to the parking garage entrances. This situation is certain to cause some congestion.

■ The existing safety building occupies the most strategic and highly visible location on the site. Since one of the objectives of the new laboratory facility is to provide a high-visibility location, demolition of the existing safety building may have to be considered. Removal of the safety building will also permit more appropriate and efficient use of the site.

■ See "Existing parking and circulation."

c. TOPOGRAPHY

- The northwestern corner of the site is the high point. The site slopes down from this point toward Chestnut Ridge Road, Willowdale Road, and Stadium Drive.
- The slopes along Willowdale Road and Stadium Drive create some difficulties for the development of access roads to the proposed new entrance. Regrading, cutting, and fill will be evaluated in detail for optimum utilization and reuse of existing fill.
- The slope of the present site presents an opportunity for creating partially exposed basement mechanical space and on-grade access for equipment and supplies.

d. SOLAR INCIDENCE

- The solar angles will strike the "clan south" and "plan west" faces of the proposed building. Solar studies will be conducted to take full advantage of natural light and protect from solar gain in the proposed building orientation.
- See "Existing site conditions."

e. ZONING

- The site proposed for the new facility is not located within the city limits of Morgantown.
- The current county land-use regulations will not adversely affect the proposed development at the site.

f. SITE UTILITIES

- All primary site utilities come from Willowdale Road. Access to the site will be studied carefully during the next phase of planning to consider and resolve potential conflicts among proposed roads and development to determine if existing utility lines may have to be relocated. The predesign estimate includes an estimate of costs to relocate the utility lines along the eastern property line.
- See "Existing site utilities."

g. FUTURE SITE DEVELOPMENT

Planning studies were prepared, indicating site access, parking, entrance identification, vehicle circulation, pedestrian cir-

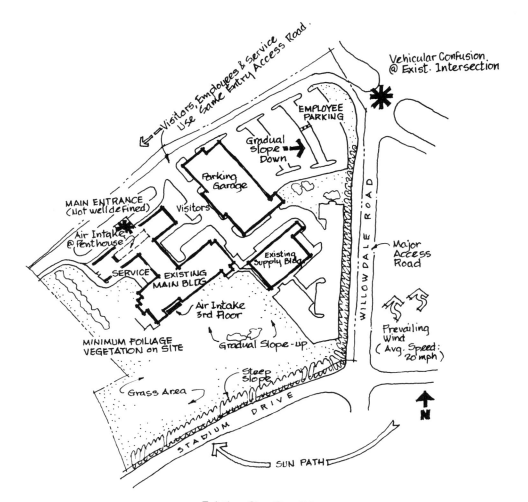

Existing Site Conditions

culation, service, and so on. Based on the program requirements, the recommended preliminary concepts are illustrated in the "preliminary site concept plan. This plan appears to indicate the best development of the site and location for the new facility.

All the planning studies prepared indicated the need to improve vehicular access to the site by eliminating hazardous entry from the intersection of Old Chestnut Ridge Road, Willowdale Road, and Chestnut Ridge Road. Moving the vehicular entrance presents an opportunity to create a new, safe approach for visitors and staff. Service vehicles and university traffic are separated from the main entrance with a new dedicated service drive along the western site boundary.

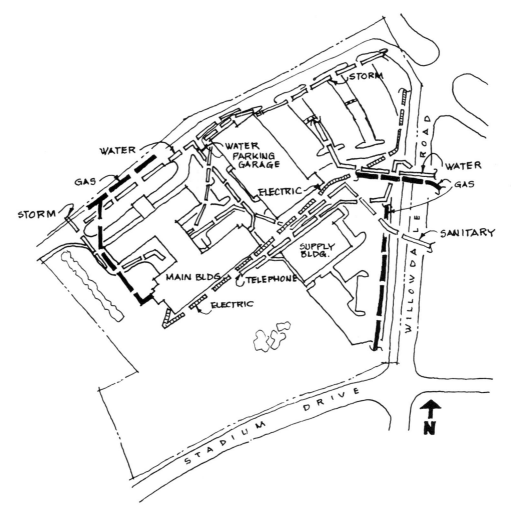

Existing Site Utilities

h. PRELIMINARY SITE CONCEPT

The preliminary site concept plan represents the summary of the analysis performed by the project team of potential site development options. The concept plan became the recommended solution for site development.

- The new main visitor and staff entrance is located at the midpoint of Willowdale Road between Chestnut Ridge Road and Stadium Drive. The strategic location of the main site entrance supports the proposed L-shaped building configuration, reinforcing the location of the front

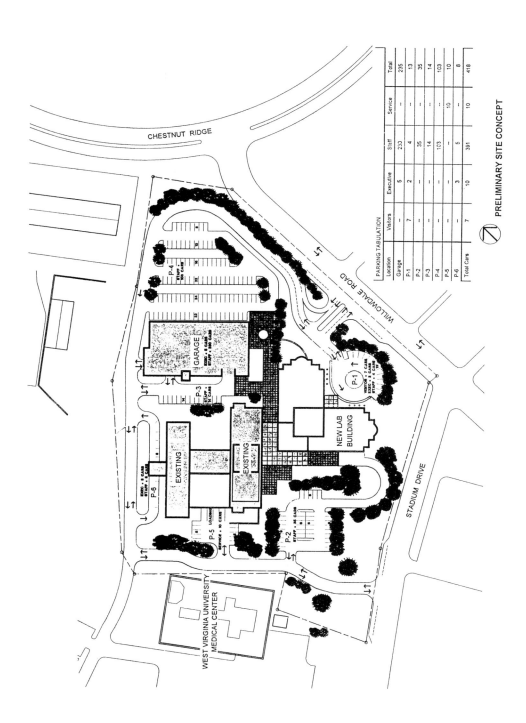

PARKING TABULATION

Location	Visitors	Executive	Staff	Service	Total
Garage	–	5	230	–	235
P-1	7	2	4	–	13
P-2	–	–	35	–	35
P-3	–	–	14	–	14
P-4	–	–	103	–	103
P-5	–	–	–	10	10
P-6	–	3	5	–	8
Total Cars	7	10	391	10	418

PRELIMINARY SITE CONCEPT

door of the new building. Many design opportunities are available in this option for creating formal and informal well-defined approaches to the new building entrance. The building and main entrance are oriented toward the public side of the site. This orientation provides an opportunity to design a building that project a strong, positive, appealing image to the surrounding community.

- The proposed building shape also anticipates several future options. The planning uses the site efficiently, permitting maximum building area with minimum site coverage. The site area immediately to the west remains open for future development—an important planning strategy.

- Developing the entrance from Willowdale Road creates a potential conflict with existing underground site utilities. Relocation of the utilities may be required. Additional study and evaluation will be conducted during the next planning phase. The predesign construction cost estimate includes cost estimates for relocating underground utilities.

- See "Preliminary Site Concept."

i. ALTERNATIVE SITE OPTIONS

- Alternative site options were studied and evaluated. The main visitor and staff entrance was proposed on Stadium Drive. This location would create a much more formal approach directly to the proposed new building with visitor parking arranged in a traditional linear fashion to the rectangular building shape. The simple building shape would be somewhat less expensive to construct, however, its shape and location would not allow for future expansion. The longer internal roadway to the parking garage and the existing laboratory building would be an additional expense with minimum benefit.

- All options proposed a new service/access road along the western boundary of the site, connecting Stadium Drive to the south with the existing access road to the north. This feature was reviewed and approved based on the traffic study report completed in July 1990. The study recommended a main entrance from Willowdale Road. This entrance will permit separation of NIOSH service vehicle circulation from private auto traffic and can also be used by university personnel to access the university hospital complex. This road will relieve traffic congestion and permit access to all areas of the site by service and emergency vehicles.

4 Architectural Design Criteria

a. INTRODUCTION

This section presents the overall design concept of the new building and site and the functional organization of the building interior. This case study outlines the description of the new laboratory building and site development in the form of text, drawings, and a space summary. The plans, sections, and elevations presented are the result of the efforts expended during the schematic design, design development, and construction documents phases. These documents indicate the scope, quantity, and quality of the project.

The new building represents the standards and guidelines established by the CDC engineering services office, and the design challenge stated by the NIOSH planning team. The design also reflects a sense of quality and the sophistication and complexity of the vital work that will be conducted within the laboratories and service and support spaces when the building is completed for occupancy.

As planning progressed, numerous changes created a continuing evolution of design concepts, floor plan layouts, and building architecture. As information was gathered, analyzed, and synthesized, its impact on site access and development, topographical adjustments, utility requirements, program changes, and other existing conditions were assessed and coordinated. The design concepts were altered, changed, and refined to accommodate each new parameter. Changes in program criteria occurred, modifying the requirements for space and the working environment in many functional areas. For example, space needs increased for the library and computer center, laboratories were relocated to other floor levels to improve functional relationships with other activities, and space was reallocated for administrative functions.

The requirement for flexibility and adaptability in all spaces is an integral part of the design theme. Expanding knowledge of safety and health factors, changing technology, and new programs are the principal reasons that will generate modifications requiring reconfiguration of currently planned spaces.

b. DESIGN GOALS

The primary design goal was to create a building that responds to the space and service demands of complex research facilities. The exterior and interior physical characteristics and appearance are representative of sophisticated high-tech facilities.

c. RECRUITMENT

Morgantown is located in the mountains of West Virginia. Its amenities are the natural resources, the peaceful lifestyle, a safe environment to establish families and raise children, and the resources of the University of West Virginia. However, Morgantown does not offer the scope of cultural and technical resources of larger urban centers. The lack of such amenities may be viewed as a potential liability for recruiting top-notch research investigators.

Recruitment of leading scientists and researches is a high priority of NIOSH and the CDC. To assist in the recruitment of leaders in the field of safety and health biomedical research, NIOSH and CDC charged the design team with creating a building that will attract leaders in these disciplines. The New Facility has been designed to be one of the most advanced research laboratory facilities in the country.

d. EXISTING UNIVERSITY CAMPUS

The existing Appalachian Laboratory for Occupational Safety and Health (ALOSH) has been a research partner with the University of West Virginia for many years. This new NIOSH facility will continue this partnership of cooperation and mutual interests. The new reference and research library will be available to all on campus. It is conveniently located adjacent to the lobby on the first floor for use by staff, visitors, and students.

The design concept has been developed carefully to be sensitive and responsible to the existing architectural and natural environment. The new building is an attractive addition to the campus and surrounding community. The site development will improve traffic patterns and access for NIOSH and the West Virginia University Medical Center. A new service road from Stadium Drive to the existing hospital access road bypasses the new main entrance, providing a more direct route to the West Virginia University Medical Center and Chestnut Ridge Hospital.

e. EXISTING CONDITIONS

Since the new building is not completely independent of the existing buildings, the following general conditions were considered:

- The intersection of the existing entry drive with Willowdale Road, Chestnut Ridge Road, and Old Chestnut Ridge Road is congested and potentially hazardous.
- Willowdale Road must be accessible to the main entrance of the new building.
- Access from Willowdale Road to the new parking garage and surface parking lots must be convenient for the staff.
- The new building must connect with all levels of the existing building, including the ground, first, second, and third floors.
- The new building must establish a minimum 15'-0" floor-to-floor height. The existing building has a 14'-0" floor-to-floor height.
- The staff will enter from the pedestrian plaza to the lobby opposite the main entrance.
- The second and third levels of the parking garage and the staff entrance all open onto the pedestrian plaza.
- Secondary access points are the terraces adjacent to the classrooms and dining areas and grade access for the high-bay labs and service entrance.

The challenge to incorporate all of the foregoing requirements into the existing site with a minimum amount of earthwork was satisfied. To accommodate these requirements. the building has been organized to allow access on multiple levels. The primary task was to connect the new building at all levels with the existing building to facilitate convenient access and interchange between NIOSH and ALOSH investigators and staff.

The existing building was developed with its primary orientation away from the community. The main entry faces the existing hospital drive. The lobby of the existing building was not very well planned. The first floor of the new building will create a new main entrance and lobby of sufficient size to serve the entire facility. This will enhance the experience of arriving and establishing orientation with the NIOSH and the ALOSH facilities.

The new building has been designed to facilitate future expansion. Removable panels have been installed in the central areas of the southern facade. They can be removed at all levels to provide access to the new building. The remainder of the exterior precast panels will not have to be disturbed.

f. FLEXIBILITY

The new facility has been designed to accommodate changes and adapt to new technologies. The design will allow creative solutions to be developed to accommodate scientific research and technology that has yet to be defined. The primary challenge is to create innovative solutions and produce an environment that accommodates advanced technology while providing for a wide range of dynamic human concerns for all who occupy the building has also been satisfied.

g. DURABILITY

The projected life of the building has been established at 60 years. High-quality materials have been selected and arranged to meet this objective. The longevity of the building can be achieved through the careful selection of materials including components such as stone, masonry, concrete, and steel. These basic building components will withstand the elements for a long period of time.

h. CONCEPT STUDIES

Concept studies were developed that focused on general massing of the new building, the use of materials, and the general arrangement of the internal organization of the building. In addition, the various division locations were coordinated with studies conducted by the CDC/ESO for proposed renovations to the adjoining existing building.

The site plan, floor plans, elevations and sections presented here are the result of numerous alternatives that were reviewed by the consultants and the NIOSH staff. The general concepts presented are valid. Many modifications and improvements were made before the final plans were developed and accepted.

i. SITE PLAN

- The site plan remains essentially as presented in the preliminary site concept. The location and orientation of the new building have not been changed.

- The new entrance road has been shifted east along Willowdale Road to conform to the existing topography. This creates an 8% rise in the new road from Willowdale Road to the main entrances.

- Refinements to the floor plans reduced the width of the east wing, placing the main entrance in a more prominent position when viewed from Willowdale Road.

- Accessibility for the disabled is provided from the main drive to the main entrance and from the pedestrian plaza to the staff entrance.

- Parking spaces for the disabled have been provided in the surface lots at the new main entrance, between the parking garage and the H building, and surface parking in the southwest zone. The new parking garage was constructed without parking spaces for the disabled. The east parking lot is not accessible because of the topography.

- The new loading dock has been located within the alcove of the H building. Existing topography required that the service drive to the loading dock be moved to the east.

- The position of the main entry was shifted to the midpoint of the slope between the high point of Willowdale Road and the intersection of Chestnut Ridge Road and Willowdale Road. The main entrance matches more closely the elevation of the site with the elevation of Willowdale Road.

- Preliminary analysis of the stormwater runoff caused by the new construction indicated a need for stormwater retention. New stormwater retention ponds were proposed at the eastern zone of the site, near the Chestnut Ridge Road and Willowdale Road intersection, and in the southern zone adjacent to the intersection of Willowdale Road and Stadium Drive.

- Careful integration of the buildings was studied thoroughly to protect the integrity of the existing laboratory building foundations. The southern wall is supported on a perimeter grade beam at approximately 31'-0" below grade. Coverage was maintained to prevent exposure of the foundations to the frost line.

- The preliminary topographic plan indicated sharp grades surrounding the new parking garage. A staircase was designed and constructed to accommodate the difference in

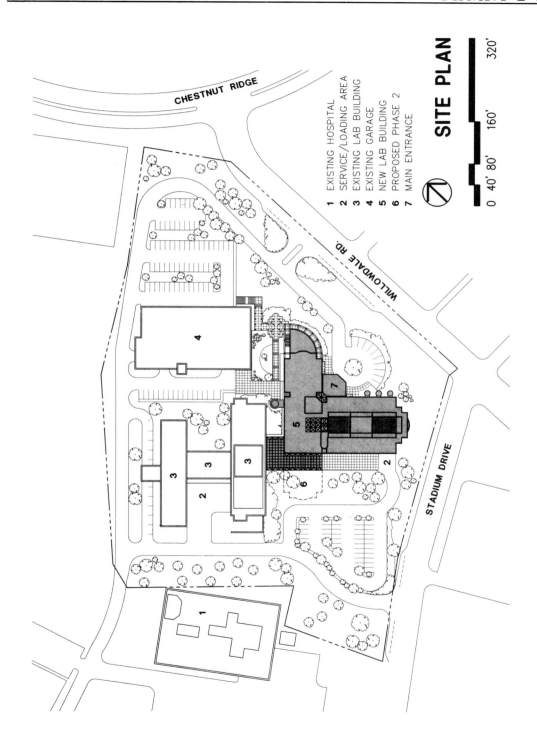

SITE PLAN

0 40' 80'   160'   320'

1 EXISTING HOSPITAL
2 SERVICE/LOADING AREA
3 EXISTING LAB BUILDING
4 EXISTING GARAGE
5 NEW LAB BUILDING
6 PROPOSED PHASE 2
7 MAIN ENTRANCE

CHESTNUT RIDGE

WILLOWDALE RD.

STADIUM DRIVE

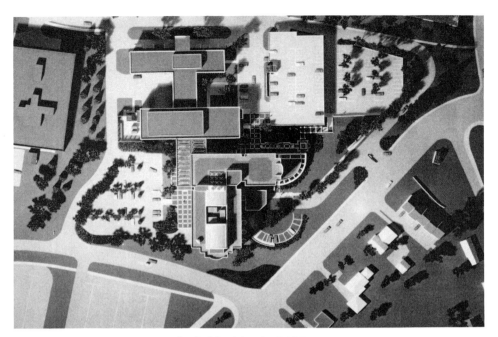

Scale Model—Aerial View

elevation of 20' and to provide access between the pedestrian plaza and the surface parking lot.

See "Site Plan" and "Aerial view."

j. GROUND FLOOR

Access

The loading dock and materials management department have been relocated to the western side of the existing building. The around level of the new building is connected to the ground floor of the existing building, permitting access for materials and supplies distribution.

Building Storage

The main building storage area is located in the ground floor. The space accommodates general and laboratory supplies in designated enclosed lockable rooms. The storage area is placed strategically to permit convenient access from the loading dock in the existing building and from the laboratories on the floors above.

Industrial Fabrication Shops

The fabrication shops are located on the ground floor of the new building to permit convenient access to the research service dock, the high-bay laboratories, and the laboratories on the upper floors. A service elevator is located near the shop areas to permit convenient access to all the laboratories.

High-Bay Laboratories

The high-bay laboratories are located on the ground floor with direct access to the exterior at the service drive. An large overhead door is located in the southernmost bay. The high-bay laboratories are organized as one space in two volumes, with different dimensions of 30' long × 30' wide × 17' high and 30' long × 30' wide × 37.5' high, respectively. The floor elevation of the high-bay laboratories is the same elevation as the ground floor.

Employee Facilities

The employee clinic lifestyle center are located in the east wing of the ground floor adjacent to each other. The passenger elevators provide direct access from the main lobby.

k. FIRST FLOOR

The first floor contains the entry, lobby, administrative offices, library, canteen, and conference centers. All are intended for use by the facility.

Lobby

The new building will function as the main entrance to the entire facility. Visitors, officials, and staff will enter the facility through the new lobby. It is designed to serve both buildings as the primary public and staff entrance. The main entrance will face Willowdale Road, with parking spaces for visitors. The staff entrance provides convenient access to the new parking garage and staff parking areas. The size and space of the lobby will be useful for special events and a general gathering place for informal staff use.

Security Desk

The security desk is located strategically in the lobby to observe both the main visitor entrance in the southeastern corner of the

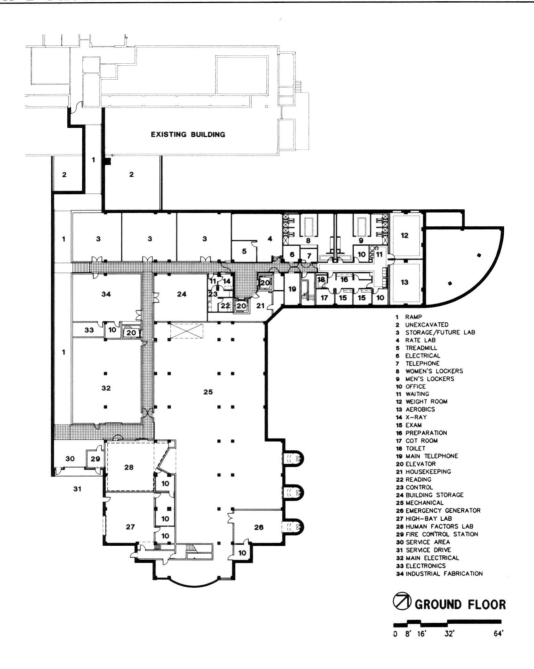

EXISTING BUILDING

1 RAMP
2 UNEXCAVATED
3 STORAGE/FUTURE LAB
4 RATE LAB
5 TREADMILL
6 ELECTRICAL
7 TELEPHONE
8 WOMEN'S LOCKERS
9 MEN'S LOCKERS
10 OFFICE
11 WAITING
12 WEIGHT ROOM
13 AEROBICS
14 X-RAY
15 EXAM
16 PREPARATION
17 COT ROOM
18 TOILET
19 MAIN TELEPHONE
20 ELEVATOR
21 HOUSEKEEPING
22 READING
23 CONTROL
24 BUILDING STORAGE
25 MECHANICAL
26 EMERGENCY GENERATOR
27 HIGH-BAY LAB
28 HUMAN FACTORS LAB
29 FIRE CONTROL STATION
30 SERVICE AREA
31 SERVICE DRIVE
32 MAIN ELECTRICAL
33 ELECTRONICS
34 INDUSTRIAL FABRICATION

⊘ GROUND FLOOR

0 8' 16'   32'   64'

lobby and the staff entrance to the north of the lobby. The function of the security desk is to greet visitors and check identification and be the receptionist for the facility. Additional functions
and elements of the security desk include:

- Coat closet for visitors with space for six to eight garment bags
- Storage for:
— Flags
— Traffic cones
— Visitor ID tags
- Sign-in/sign-out book
- Holding area for small-package pickup and delivery
- Two two-drawer file cabinets
- Two staff positions
- Two telephones
- Card key door monitor
- Two printers
- Five to six monitors for surveillance cameras
- Computer terminal
- Electronic bulletin board (television)

Connecting Link

The connecting link permits primary access between existing and new buildings. The area will also function as an informal gathering and meeting place and is an important integrating element for the two buildings. The single volume creates a dynamic visual break in the transition from one building to the other at all levels. The openness of the space permits natural light to permeate the interior of the new building, provides visual relief with views to the university medical center and Mountaineer Stadium to the west, and along the pedestrian plaza toward Willowdale Road to the East.

Food Service Center

The food service center will be located within the connecting link providing convenient access from the conference center, the new building and direct access from the existing building. The center will include a warming kitchen for catering lunches and receptions, a vending area, and seating for 40 to 50 persons.

Information Center

The information center is adjacent to the main entry of the building and lobby. The entry to the library is located in the building lobby. Glass walls enclosing the library permit high visibility from the entry drive, building entrance, and main lobby. The prominent location displays the library and emphasizes its critical function within the facility. The circulation desk, located at the main entry, will be staffed full time. Space is provided in the lobby for coats. Bags and bookcases will be checked at the circulation desk. A display case is provided in the library lobby.

The front area of the library will be organized in an informal seating area for 8 to 10 people with couch and club chairs. Seating will be adjacent to periodicals and other open shelf areas.

Computer Science Center

The computer science center is located on the first floor to facilitate access for sharing of technologies with the library in the future. The computer room and wire room are adjacent to each other. The wire room is sufficient to support additional staff and associated laboratory space needs. The computer room includes space for file servers, on-lines, controllers, CD-ROM devices, on-line storage, modem pools, database servers, FAXs, printers, tape drives, E-mail servers, and FAX gateways.

Office and storage space have been centralized. Storage for bulk computer paper is located on the ground floor in the general building storage area. Arrangement of the offices allows for staff meetings. Offices are provided for the section chief, LAN CIO, LAN administrator, TC specialist, database administrator, LAN/PC support office auto clerks, mainframe and administrative support, and the computer operator.

Repair of microcomputer hardware, work benches, and so on, will be part of the function of the industrial fabrication shops.

I. SECOND FLOOR

Division of Safety Research

The second floor relates to the larger second floor of the south wing. The laboratories and support areas are located in the south wing. Branch and division administrative offices are located in the east wing. Conference rooms, training centers, and study/break areas for the staff are centrally located. These spaces are designed as a pleasant environment to encourage personal contemplation and conversation with staff and colleagues.

A second break area is provided at the southernmost end of

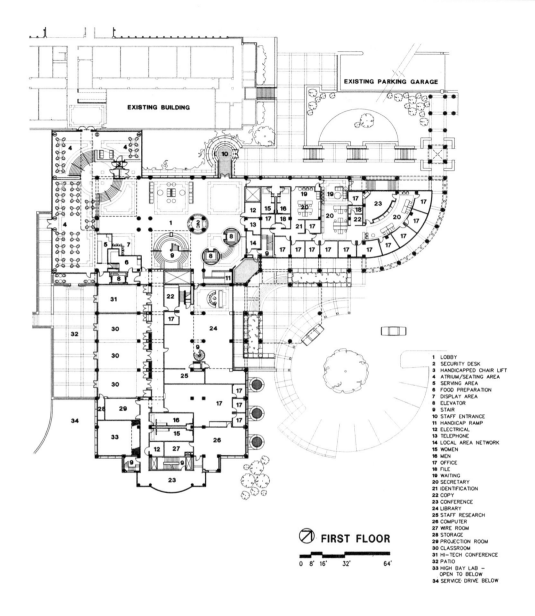

FIRST FLOOR

0 8' 16' 32' 64'

1 LOBBY
2 SECURITY DESK
3 HANDICAPPED CHAIR LIFT
4 ATRIUM/SEATING AREA
5 SERVING AREA
6 FOOD PREPARATION
7 DISPLAY AREA
8 ELEVATOR
9 STAIR
10 STAFF ENTRANCE
11 HANDICAP RAMP
12 ELECTRICAL
13 TELEPHONE
14 LOCAL AREA NETWORK
15 WOMEN
16 MEN
17 OFFICE
18 FILE
19 WAITING
20 SECRETARY
21 IDENTIFICATION
22 COPY
23 CONFERENCE
24 LIBRARY
25 STAFF RESEARCH
26 COMPUTER
27 WIRE ROOM
28 STORAGE
29 PROJECTION ROOM
30 CLASSROOM
31 HI-TECH CONFERENCE
32 PATIO
33 HIGH BAY LAB – OPEN TO BELOW
34 SERVICE DRIVE BELOW

the laboratory wing for more intense conversations and interaction among the researchers. Marker boards, tack surfaces, and so on, including large windows and views to the south, will create an informal work and academic space.

This division is organized in two sections located on the second and ground floors. The high-bay laboratories are located on the ground floor to permit direct access to the exterior and provide for a larger unobstructed volume of space.

The offices for the division are located in the southeastern zone of the laboratory wing. This area has been designed for conversion to laboratory space, as required.

The second floor of the existing building is connected to the new building with a pedestrian bridge. The bridge spans the connecting link, providing convenient access between the buildings without the need to use the elevators or stairs.

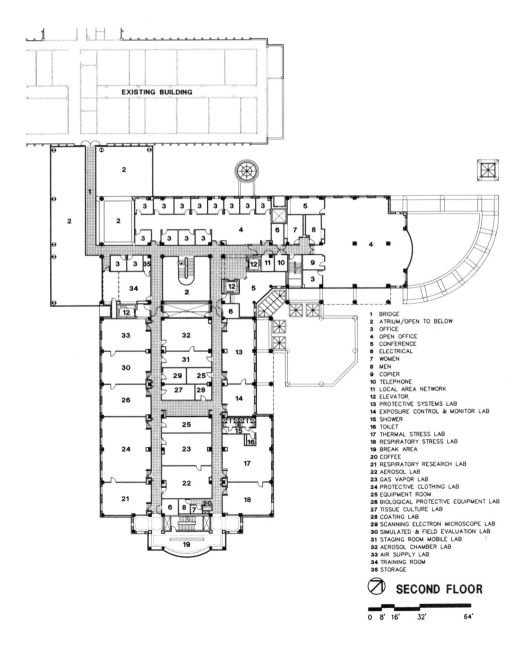

EXISTING BUILDING

1 BRIDGE
2 ATRIUM/OPEN TO BELOW
3 OFFICE
4 OPEN OFFICE
5 CONFERENCE
6 ELECTRICAL
7 WOMEN
8 MEN
9 COPIER
10 TELEPHONE
11 LOCAL AREA NETWORK
12 ELEVATOR
13 PROTECTIVE SYSTEMS LAB
14 EXPOSURE CONTROL & MONITOR LAB
15 SHOWER
16 TOILET
17 THERMAL STRESS LAB
18 RESPIRATORY STRESS LAB
19 BREAK AREA
20 COFFEE
21 RESPIRATORY RESEARCH LAB
22 AEROSOL LAB
23 GAS VAPOR LAB
24 PROTECTIVE CLOTHING LAB
25 EQUIPMENT ROOM
26 BIOLOGICAL PROTECTIVE EQUIPMENT LAB
27 TISSUE CULTURE LAB
28 COATING LAB
29 SCANNING ELECTRON MICROSCOPE LAB
30 SIMULATED & FIELD EVALUATION LAB
31 STAGING ROOM MOBILE LAB
32 AEROSOL CHAMBER LAB
33 AIR SUPPLY LAB
34 TRAINING ROOM
35 STORAGE

SECOND FLOOR

0 8' 16'   32'   64'

Break Areas are strategically located to encourage interaction among the researchers. These areas provide important refuge and relief for the research staff to meet and discuss ideas with others or just relax. Private spaces are available for one-on-one conversations or individual quiet concentration.

Creating pleasant spaces for short breaks from the routine of concentrated research activities is one of the means used to respond to the need for recruiting tools. Recruitment of new staff is a continuous endeavor. These physical elements and amenities designed into the building play an important part toward attracting new staff.

A feature of the building design has been to arrange the functions and activities in different configurations to test the adaptability and flexibility of the spaces and systems. The building can be remodeled relatively easily to accommodate different programs without changing the basic building systems design concept.

m. THIRD FLOOR

Division of Respiratory Disease Studies

The third floor is organized similar to the second floor except that all division programs are located on the third floor. Larger floor area is provided to respond to the space program requirements in the laboratory wing. Laboratories, support, conference, break areas, and administration spaces are in the same location and orientation as those functions on the second floor.

n. FOURTH FLOOR

Division of Molecular Biochemistry

Refer to the comments for the second and third floors. Since the fourth floor is one story higher than the existing building there is no connecting bridge.

o. PENTHOUSE/ROOF PLAN

Major mechanical equipment, air-handling units, exhaust fans for the laboratory hoods, cooling towers, and elevator equipment rooms are located in the penthouse. Access will be restricted to maintenance staff and authorized personnel. The configuration of the penthouse and the location of the ventilation equipment (supply and exhaust) was determined by prevailing winds to prevent recirculation of exhaust air into fresh

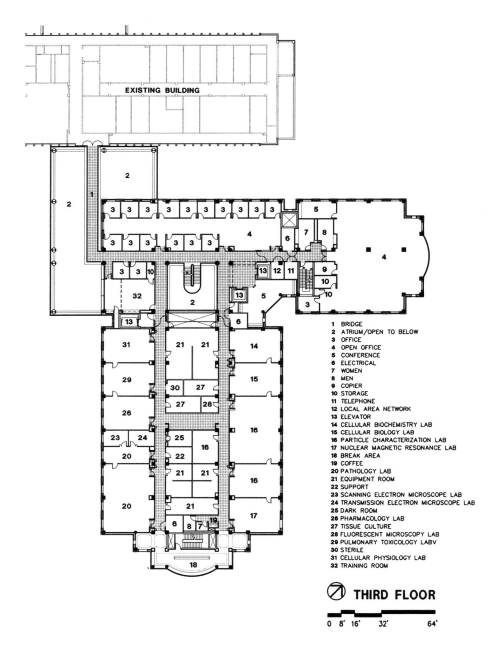

1 BRIDGE
2 ATRIUM/OPEN TO BELOW
3 OFFICE
4 OPEN OFFICE
5 CONFERENCE
6 ELECTRICAL
7 WOMEN
8 MEN
9 COPIER
10 STORAGE
11 TELEPHONE
12 LOCAL AREA NETWORK
13 ELEVATOR
14 CELLULAR BIOCHEMISTRY LAB
15 CELLULAR BIOLOGY LAB
16 PARTICLE CHARACTERIZATION LAB
17 NUCLEAR MAGNETIC RESONANCE LAB
18 BREAK AREA
19 COFFEE
20 PATHOLOGY LAB
21 EQUIPMENT ROOM
22 SUPPORT
23 SCANNING ELECTRON MICROSCOPE LAB
24 TRANSMISSION ELECTRON MICROSCOPE LAB
25 DARK ROOM
26 PHARMACOLOGY LAB
27 TISSUE CULTURE
28 FLUORESCENT MICROSCOPY LAB
29 PULMONARY TOXICOLOGY LABV
30 STERILE
31 CELLULAR PHYSIOLOGY LAB
32 TRAINING ROOM

THIRD FLOOR

0 8' 16'   32'   64'

air intakes. The service elevator will provide access to the penthouse for equipment maintenance and service.

p. BUILDING ELEVATIONS/SECTIONS

Exterior

The exterior of the new building is primarily precast concrete, constructed in modular panels of standard size to provide unit

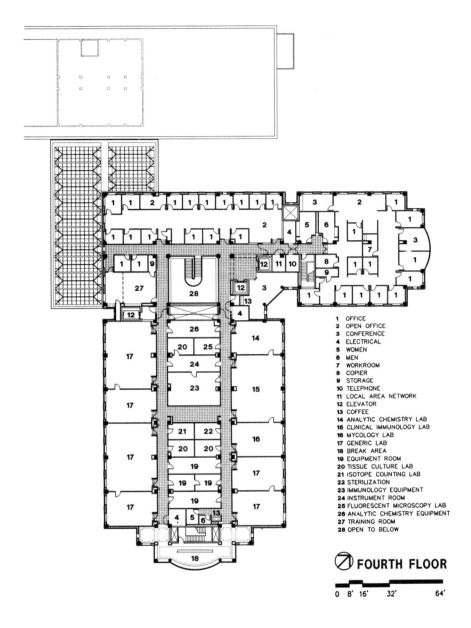

1 OFFICE
2 OPEN OFFICE
3 CONFERENCE
4 ELECTRICAL
5 WOMEN
6 MEN
7 WORKROOM
8 COPIER
9 STORAGE
10 TELEPHONE
11 LOCAL AREA NETWORK
12 ELEVATOR
13 COFFEE
14 ANALYTIC CHEMISTRY LAB
15 CLINICAL IMMUNOLOGY LAB
16 MYCOLOGY LAB
17 GENERIC LAB
18 BREAK AREA
19 EQUIPMENT ROOM
20 TISSUE CULTURE LAB
21 ISOTOPE COUNTING LAB
22 STERILIZATION
23 IMMUNOLOGY EQUIPMENT
24 INSTRUMENT ROOM
25 FLUORESCENT MICROSCOPY LAB
26 ANALYTIC CHEMISTRY EQUIPMENT
27 TRAINING ROOM
28 OPEN TO BELOW

FOURTH FLOOR

0 8' 16'   32'   64'

economy. The first-floor facade consists of window wall units. Fixed punched windows are centered in each precast panel to provide natural light into each space. Glazing will be a low-E tinted glass with aluminum mullions of metallic fluoroponic finish. Due to the slope of the site, the ground floor is partially above grade and partially below grade. The exposed portion above grade is clad with a splitface concrete masonry veneer and a structural masonry backup. The masonry veneer is of con-

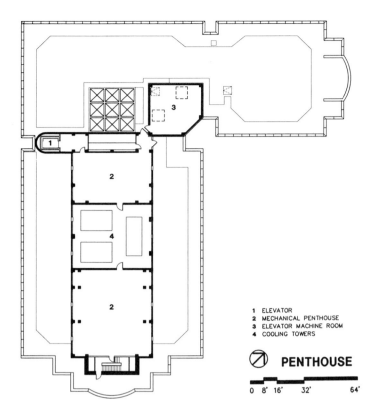

1 ELEVATOR
2 MECHANICAL PENTHOUSE
3 ELEVATOR MACHINE ROOM
4 COOLING TOWERS

PENTHOUSE

0 8' 16'   32'   64'

trasting color to the precast and will serve as a visually strong, rusticated base to the building.

Connecting Link

Integrating the roof of the connecting link with the existing building created a special problem t malntalnthe integrity of the water seal. The solution developed enclosed the connecting link at the top parapet of the existing building, constructing a straight-line flashing detail, avoiding the undulations of the flutes and minimizing the potential for leaks.

Skylight/Glazing System

A series of ridge-type skylights with gabled ends make up the roof of the connector link between the new and existing buildings. This creates a pleasant seating and circulation area for employees to relax and relieve any stresses that may have accumulated. "Thermally broken" metal mullions with low-E, insulated and tinted glass are used in the skylights to provide a well-designed and low-maintenance skylight system.

Curtain Wall

High-span window wall systems are attached to an internal structural tube frame at each floor level with a maximum horizontal spacing of 30' between vertical structural members. Maximum height for window walls is 20' (average 15'). The aluminum mullions are completely thermally broken to minimize the transmission of energy from the exterior during the summer, and heat from the interior of the building to the exterior during the winter. Mullions have a metallic fluoroponic finish. Low-E insulated and tinted glazing is used to control excessive heat gain.

Recommendations

The basic design of the new building significantly changes the appearance of NIOSH's presence on the University of West Virginia campus. The building design and organization was reviewed and endorsed by the members of the client's team. The design team recommendations of the basic design and planning concepts developed and presented in this section were accepted and approved by NIOSH/CDC. Authorization was granted to proceed with the next phase of planning and design.

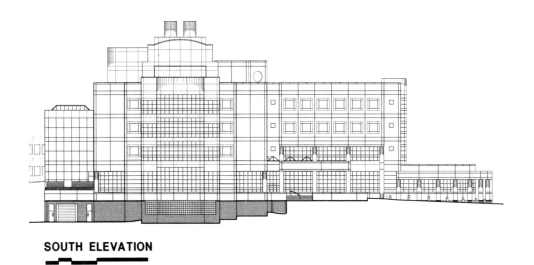

SOUTH ELEVATION

0 8' 16' 32' 64'

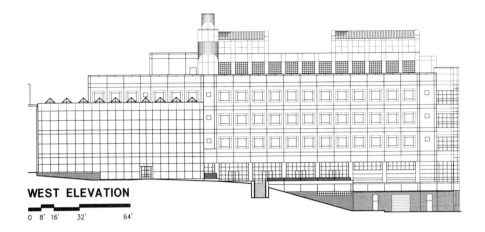

WEST ELEVATION

0 8' 16'   32'   64'

q. ALTERNATIVE CONCEPTS

Laboratory Floor Plan

An alternative layout for the laboratories, placing laboratories in both wings, was reviewed and evaluated. The offices and administrative support areas were located in the "elbow" of the plan. This alternative proved to be less flexible than the plans eventually accepted and presented in this case study. The alternative has six laboratory planning modules per section of each wing or four laboratory areas with 1980 nsf. This would limit the ability to create laboratories, with many variations of layouts and module combinations.

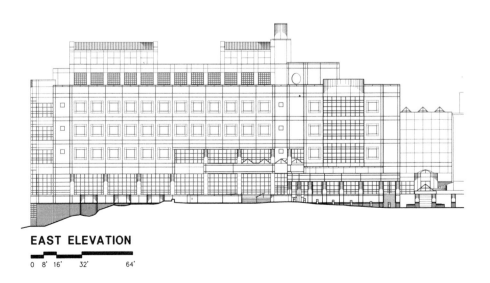

EAST ELEVATION

0 8' 16'   32'   64'

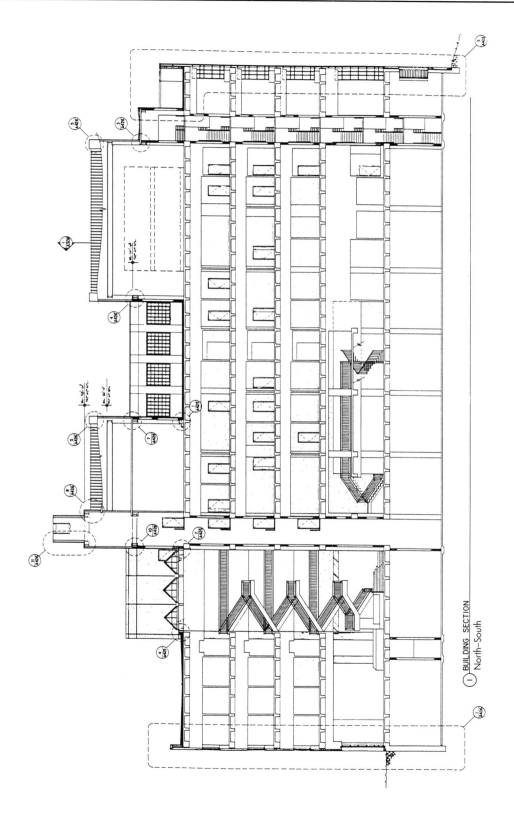

1 BUILDING SECTION
North–South

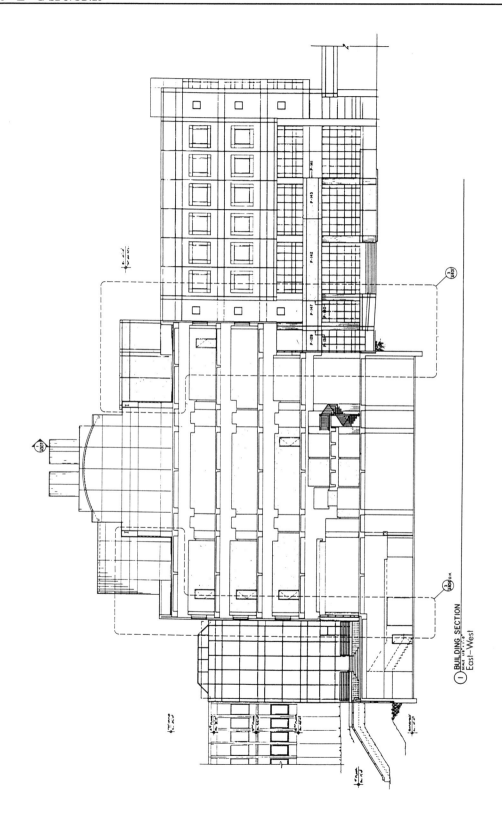

BUILDING SECTION
East—West

The recommended (and accepted) plan layout allocates 24 laboratory modules in one wing, with 12 modules per side, providing 3960 nsf of usable space. This plan provides the most flexibility of floor space for alternations and modifications to the laboratories as required. The accepted configuration permits one 12-module laboratory per side, six two-module laboratories, or a variety of combinations. The alternative plan does not provide the same flexibility to divide laboratories and adapt to meet changing research demands.

The allocation of a laboratory wing and office wing creates a clear division of functions and activities. The alternative layout "sandwiches" the administrative offices between the laboratory work areas in the center of the building. The interaction among the researchers would be limited because the location of the offices creates a barrier between the laboratories in the two wings of the building.

5 Space Program Summary

SPACE PROGRAM ANALYSIS

Floor	Program nsf	Design nsf	Difference
Ground floor	13,874	14,078	204
First floor	18,702	19,150	448
Second floor	17,322	16,888	(2434)
Third floor	20,380	18,942	(1438)
Fourth floor	20,380	18,942	(1438)
Total nsf	90 718[a]	88,000	(2658)

[a] The program net square feet has increased from 85,158 nsf to 90,718 nsf; and 147,323 gsf (as listed in the predesign report) to 157,185 gsf. This is a 6.7% increase in area.

BUILDING GROSS SQUARE FEET

Design net to gross square foot factor =   1.73
Program net to gross square foot factor = 1.73

The net/gross conversion factor of 1.73 is the same as that used in the predesign report.

Floor	Building gsf
Ground floor	32,912
First floor	34,120
Second floor	29,965
Third floor	29,126
Fourth floor	28,520
Penthouse	5,542
Total building gsf	157,185

The change in project area increased the construction cost estimate and project budget. The estimate was reviewed and alternatives were considered. The actual design net square feet presented was a preliminary analysis. A revised space program was issued by CDC/NIOSH, reflecting changes for the administrative and laboratory areas. These changes were incorporated in the final drawings.

SPACE PROGRAM SUMMARY

Function/Activity	Number of Spaces	Unit Area	Program nsf	Design nsf	Change
Ground Floor					
East Wing					
Lifestyle center					
Exercise room	1	1,700	1,700	1,622	−78
Locker room	2	550	1,100	1,204	104
Office/storage	1	200	200	212	12
Subtotal			3,000	3,038	38
Employee clinic					
Reception/waiting	1	200	200	—	—
Prep. Lab.	1	120	10	—	—
Exam rooms	3	80	240	—	—
Resting area	1	80	80	—	—
Office	1	120	120	—	—
Storage	1	140	140	—	—
Subtotal			900	843	−57
North Wing					
Building and laboratory storage					
Division A	1	990	990	953	−37
Division B	1	990	990	953	−37
Division C	1	990	990	953	−37
General building	1	990	990	1,010	20
Subtotal			3,960	3,869	−91
Central Core					
Service/support					
Photo/darkroom	1	150	150	224	−26
Workroom	1	100	100	—	—
Housekeeping	1	600	600	556	−44
Janitor closet	1	60	60	61	1
Subtotal			910	841	−69
Laboratory support (high-bay lab.)					
Equipment	3	110	330	—	—
Support	3	110	330	—	—
Equipment/special lab.	1	330	330	—	—
Subtotal			990	1,264	274
Industrial fabrication shops					
Metals	1	990	990	—	—
Plastics	1	330	330	—	—
Electronics	1	330	330	—	—
Office storage	1	220	220	—	—
Subtotal			1,870	1,885	15

Space Program Summary (*Continued*)

Function/Activity	Number of Spaces	Unit Area	Program nsf	Design nsf	Change
		South Wing			
High-bay lab.: Division C					
General research lab.	3	660	1,980	2,028	48
Section chief	1	100	100	110	10
Investigator	1	100	100	100	—
Secretary	1	64	64	100	36
Subtotal			2,244	2,338	94
		Ground floor total	13,934	14,078	204
		First Floor			
		East Wing			
Institute director's office/surge space					
Institute director's satellite office	1	200	200	232	32
Director	1	200	200	232	32
Assistant director	1	150	150	150	0
Engineer	1	100	100	101	1
Writer/editor	1	100	100	101	1
Reception	1	100	100	161	61
Visitor's office	2	100	200	208	8
Secretary	4	64	256	239	83
Recruitment coordinator	2	100	200	200	0
Conference	1	400	400	443	43
Graphics	1	120	120	101	−19
Storage	1	120	120	101	−19
Copier	1	100	100	161	61
Subtotal			2,246	2,530	284
Operations officer's suite					
Operations officer	1	400	400	398	−2
Staff	1	120	120	115	−5
Administrative clerk	2	80	160	139	−21
Secretary	3	64	192	145	−47
Graphics	1	120	120	0	−120
Storage	1	120	120	0	−120
Copier	1	100	100	0	−100
Subtotal			1,212	797	−415
Shared operations spaces					
Conference	1	200	200	195	−5
Storage	1	100	100	0	100
Subtotal			300	195	−105
Procurement					
Senior staff	1	120	120	125	5
Staff	3	100	300	291	−9

Space Program Summary (*Continued*)

Function/Activity	Number of Spaces	Unit Area	Program nsf	Design nsf	Change
Administrative Clerks	4	80	320	190	−130
Secretary	1	64	64	115	51
Subtotal			804	721	−83
North Wing/Central Core					
Lobby	1	1,500	1,500	1,500	0
Food service center					
Preparation area	1	200	200	100	−100
Vending	1	200	200	100	−100
Seating (60)	60	15	900	3,326	2,426
Office	1	100	100	111	11
Storage	1	200	200	0	−200
Subtotal			1,600	3,637	2,037
South Wing					
Training and conference					
Divisible classroom	1	3,200	3,200	2,476	−724
High-tech conference	1	800	800	612	12
Preparation	1	300	300	396	96
Equipment storage	1	200	200	140	−60
Subtotal			4,500	3,824	−676
Information center					
Main entry/circulation desk	1	200	200	—	—
Informal	1	500	500	—	—
Study seating	1	800	800	—	—
Stacks	1	1,600	1,600	—	—
Microfiche room	1	250	250	—	—
Copy center	1	100	100	—	—
Staff work area	1	400	400	—	—
Director's office	1	120	120	—	—
Computer work station	1	120	120	—	—
Book storage	1	120	120	—	—
Subtotal			4,210	3,632	−578
Computer science center					
Computer room	1	810	810	904	94
Wire room	1	200	200	156	−44
Satellite units	1	50	50	(50)	−50
Closed office	1	120	120	97	−23
Closed office	2	100	200	182	−18
Open office	1	50	750	742	−8
Storage	1	200	200	233	33
Subtotal			2,330	2,314	−16
First-floor total			18,702	19,150	448

Space Program Summary (*Continued*)

Function/Activity	Number of Spaces	Unit Area	Program nsf	Design nsf	Change
Second Floor: Division C					
East Wing					
Director's office	1	200	200	254	54
Deputy director	1	150	150	160	10
Admin. officer	1	120	120	130	10
Writer/editor	1	100	100	104	4
Science advisor	1	120	120	160	40
Division conference	1	200	200	254	54
Branch conference	1	200	200	207	7
Secretary	4	64	256	396	140
Graphics	1	120	120	92	−28
Storage	1	120	120	22	−98
Copier	1	100	100	100	0
Branch chief's office	3	120	360	397	37
Secretary	3	64	192	297	105
Visitor's office	3	100	300	267	−33
Open office	3	200	600	585	−15
Subtotal			3,138	3,425	287
North Wing					
Section chief	8	100	800	658	−142
Investigator	8	100	800	656	−144
Secretary	8	64	512	807	295
Subtotal			2,112	2,121	9
Central Core					
Section conference	1	200	200	205	5
Training room	1	400	400	412	12
Conference/break	1	200	200	508	58
Coffee alcove	1	50	50	—	—
Study/reading	1	200	200	—	—
Subtotal			1,050	1,125	75
South Wing					
Office	3	120	360	369	9
Office	10	100	1,000	988	−12
Open office area	1	1,600	1,600	1,653	53
Open office area	1	400	400	418	18
Open office area	1	300	300	309	9
Files	1	220	220	204	−16
Computer workroom	1	220	220	222	2
Conference	1	110	110	98	−12
Office supplies	1	102	102	68	−34

Space Program Summary (*Continued*)

Function/Activity	Number of Spaces	Unit Area	Program nsf	Design nsf	Change
Field equipment	1	110	110	—	−110
Subtotal			4,422	4,329	−93
General research lab.	6	660	3,960	3,615	−345
Equipment	6	110	660	553	−107
Support	6	110	660	553	−107
Equip./special lab.	2	330	660	553	−107
Shared lab. support	1	660	660	614	−46
Subtotal			6,600	5,888	−712
Second floor total			17,322	16,888	−434

Third Floor: Division A

East Wing: Third and Four Floors

Office and administration	1	200	200	254	54
Director's office	1	150	150	160	10
Deputy director	1	120	120	104	−16
Administrative officer	1	100	100	104	4
Writer/editor	1	120	120	160	40
Science advisor	1	200	200	254	54
Division conference	1	200	200	207	7
Branch conference	4	64	256	396	140
Secretary	1	120	120	52	−68
Graphics	1	120	120	0	−120
Storage	1	100	100	100	0
Copier	4	120	480	50	40
Branch chief's office	4	64	256	200	−56
Secretary	4	100	400	460	60
Visitor's office	4	200	800	1,054	264
Open office			3,622	4,025	403
Subtotal					

North Wing: Third and Fourth Floors

Section chief	12	100	1,200	974	−226
Investigator	12	100	1,200	905	−295
Secretary	12	64	768	1,143	357
Subtotal			3,168	3,022	−146

Central Core: Third and Fourth Floors

Section conference	1	200	200	205	5
Training room	1	400	400	412	12
Conference/break	1	200	200	473	273
Coffee alcove	1	50	50	—	—
Study/reading	1	200	200	—	—
Subtotal			1,050	1,090	290

Space Program Summary (*Continued*)

Function/Activity	Number of Spaces	Unit Area	Program nsf	Design nsf	Change
South Wing: Third and Fourth Floors					
Laboratories					
General research lab.	12	660	7,920	7,279	−641
Equipment	12	110	1,320	3,526	−1,094
Support	12	110	1,320	—	—
Equip./spec. lab.	4	330	1,320	—	—
Division lab. support	1	660	660	—	—
Subtotal			12,540	10,805	−1,735
		Third floor total	20,380	18,942	−1,438

Fourth Floor: Division B

Function/Activity	Number of Spaces	Unit Area	Program nsf	Design nsf	Change
East Wing: Third and Fourth Floors					
Office and administration					
Director's office	1	200	200	254	54
Deputy director	1	150	150	160	10
Admin. officer	1	120	120	104	−16
Writer/editor	1	100	100	104	4
Science advisor	1	120	120	160	40
Division conference	1	200	200	254	54
Branch conference	1	200	200	207	7
Secretary	4	64	256	396	140
Graphics	1	120	120	52	−68
Storage	1	120	120	—	−120
Copier	1	100	100	100	—
Branch chief's officer	4	120	480	520	40
Secretary	4	64	256	200	−56
Visitor's office	4	100	400	460	60
Open office	4	200	800	1,054	254
Subtotal			3,622	4,025	403
North Wing: Third and Fourth Floors					
Section chief	12	100	1,200	974	−226
Investigator	12	100	1,200	905	−295
Secretary	12	64	768	1,143	357
Subtotal			3,168	3,022	−146
Central Core: Third and Fourth Floors					
Section conference	1	200	200	205	5
Training room	1	400	400	412	12
Conference/break	1	200	200	473	23
Coffee alcove	1	50	50	—	—
Study/reading	1	200	200	—	—
Subtotal			1,050	1,090	40

Space Program Summary (*Continued*)

Function/Activity	Number of Spaces	Unit Area	Program nsf	Design nsf	Change
	South Wing: Third and Fourth Floors				
Laboratories					
General Research Lab.	12	660	7,920	7,279	(641)
Equipment	12	110	1,320	3,526	−1,094
Support	12	110	1,320	—	—
Equip./spec. lab.	4	330	1,320	—	—
Division lab. support	1	660	660	—	—
Subtotal			12,540	10,805	−1,735
	Fourth floor total		20,380	18,942	−1,438

6 Mechanical/Criteria

a. INTRODUCTION

This section presents the general HVAC systems concepts. The data and plans of this case study represent the general results of the schematic design, design development, and construction documents phases, establishing the overall scope, quantity, and quality of the project. The HVAC systems presented are designed to the standards established by the CDC Engineering Services Office (ESO), the NIOSH team, and the Cannon team. The information presented establishing the general system types, configurations, and locations were modified somewhat in the latter phases of the project.

The HVAC system has been designed for maximum adaptability. Changing technology and new programs that result in modifications of spaces can be accommodated by the design. Various system options have been considered while developing the design.

b. CODES

Mechanical systems have been designed in accordance with all current building and design codes applicable to construction in the Morgantown, West Virginia, area. These include:

- *BOCA National Building Code*, 1990 Edition
- National Fire Protection Association (NFPA), *National Fire Codes*, 1991 Edition, all applicable sections
- *National Electrical Code*

c. STANDARDS

Mechanical systems have been designed in accordance with the following standards and guidelines:

- CDC/NIOSH Program of Requirements (POR)
- American Society of Heating, Refrigerating, and Air-Conditioning Engineers (ASHRAE) Standards
- Sheet Metal and Air Conditioning Contractors' National Association, Inc. (SMACNA) Standards
- Institute of Boiler and Radiator Manufacturers (BRM) Standards
- Air Conditioning and Refrigeration Institute (ARI) Standards
- Heat Exchangers Institute (HEI) Standards
- Energy Conservation Voluntary Performance Standards for Commercial and Multifamily High Rise Residential Buildings; Mandatory for New Federal Buildings; Interim Rule, 10 CRF Part 435 (published in the January 30, 1989, *Federal Register*)
- *State of West Virginia Plumbing Code*, current edition
- American Water Works Association (AWWA) Standards
- American Society of Mechanical Engineers (ASME)
- Regulations of the Occupational Safety and Health Administration (OSHA)
- American Conference of Governmental Industrial Hygienists (ACGIH) Standards

d. BASIC MECHANICAL SYSTEM

Energy Source

- Gas and electricity are readily available energy sources for this facility. The cost of gas is calculated to be $0.55/therm (based on 1990 utility bills).
- Under general service schedule D from Monongahela Power Company, electricity is available at approximately $0.043/kWh.
- Gas will produce heat for $6.47 per million Btu at 85% boiler efficiency. Electricity costs $13.47 per million Btu. No. 2 fuel oil, at an anticipated cost of $0.80/gal and 80% boiler efficiency, will produce heat at $7.14 per million Btu.

- Gas was selected as the least expensive energy source for space heating and domestic water heating.

Energy Conservation

- Energy conservation will be accomplished by minimizing supply and exhaust air volumes in laboratory spaces with the installation of variable air volume supply and exhaust systems.
- Supply air and exhaust air volumes in each laboratory will be adjusted based on actual hood ventilation and/or space heat gain requirements. Supply air and exhaust air volumes will also be reduced to minimum levels during unoccupied hours.
- Ventilation amounts will be maintained at a minimum volume to provide 15 cfm/person of actual occupancy.
- Fume hoods have been equipped with automatic controls to maintain face velocity and minimize exhaust air quantities during various operating conditions.
- A glycol runaround heat recovery system was recommended and installed to reclaim heat energy from air exhausted from the laboratories, general building exhaust, and transfer to air-handling system outside air intakes.
- A complete system of direct digital controls (DDCs) has been provided to ensure optimum operation of all HVAC equipment. Various energy management strategies can be incorporated with this system. Flexibility of the DDC system will ensure owner adaptability of all control sequences.

Energy Conservation Measures

Because of the nature of this building, large volumes of outside air are brought into the building and then exhausted. Heating and cooling this air consumes a much greater amount of energy than in a conventional building. To conserve energy, four alternative systems were considered for recovering energy from the exhaust air to precondition the outside air (intake air). The four systems are:

- A glycol runaround loop
- A heat recovery refrigerant coil (Q-Dot)

- A flat plate heat exchanger
- An enthalpy wheel

In comparing each system, the following criteria were considered:

- Ease of installation
- First costs
- Annual energy savings
- Operating costs
- Maintenance
- Reliability
- Payback period

As each criterion was considered, factors emerged indicating that a heat recovery system possibly was not justified. A fifth option was considered.

Laboratory Supply and Air Handling Systems

- A variable-air-volume laboratory air-handling system was recommended and installed to provide maximum adaptability and to accommodate variable laboratory supply and exhaust requirements. These systems also provide substantial energy savings over constant-volume systems. Anticipated reduction in energy cost is between 30 and 50%. This includes savings due to air-volume reductions, during unoccupied hours, and reductions in air volumes due to varying laboratory exhaust requirements.
- Three variable-air-volume nonrecirculating central air handling systems are to be installed for laboratory areas and laboratory support spaces.
- The air handlers are located in the penthouse mechanical room and each serves a laboratory floor. The unit serving the second floor also serves the high-bay laboratory area and the industrial fabrication shop on the ground floor.
- Air-handling units are custom built utilizing 100% outside air and are constructed from 2-inch double-wall panels.
- Each air-handling unit shall comprise the following components:
  - Runaround heat recover coil
  - 30% prefilter

- — Humidifier, steam grid type
- — Cooling coil with stainless steel drain pan
- — Draw-through supply fan with variable-frequency drives and high-efficiency motors
- — Air distribution plate
- — 90% efficient final filters
- — Supply air plenum

- The installation of sound attenuators is not anticipated because of the distance between the supply fan and the first outlet in a laboratory. However, an acoustical analysis will be made after selection of the supply fans to determine if sound attenuators are required.
- Air will be ducted to single-inlet variable-volume terminal units. These terminal units are quipped with heating coils to heat 55°F supply air to maintain space temperatures.
- Supply terminal units will modulate air volumes to make-up air exhausted from the laboratory.
- Supply air volumes will not be reduced below 6 changes of air per hour (ach) (adjustable) during occupied hours and 3 ach (adjustable) during unoccupied hours.
- Control and adjustment of this system will be accomplished through the building automated control system.
- To provide temporary redundancy during breakdown or servicing of an air-handling unit, bypass ducts with automatic dampers are installed between each supply air duct system.
- Air intakes for the fans in the penthouse are located at roof level upstream of the laboratory exhausts relative to prevailing winds. Horizontal distance between laboratory exhaust stacks and intake is approximately 120'. The exhaust stacks discharge 30' above the intake louvers.

Laboratory Exhaust

- The alternative location for the air intakes was at grade level. This location would have required duct shafts to the penthouse.
- Supply ducts are galvanized steel, fabricated and installed in accordance with SMACNA standards for 4 inches of WG positive static pressure. Supply riser ducts are sized for (2500 fpm) at maximum airflow.

- Total air supplied to each laboratory was determined by the maximum of:
  - — Exhaust requirements
  - — Cooling load in space
  - — Minimum ventilation rate
  - — Pressure relationships to adjoining spaces
- Maximum laboratory exhaust requirements determined the size of the air supply and exhaust systems. This was established at 1500 cfm per double laboratory module for one 6'-wide fume hood (1200 cfm) and two exhaust snorkels (150 cfm each).
- Reducing the air exhausted through fume hoods when the sash is closed will reduce the actual volume of air exhausted from each laboratory, reducing energy consumption.
- Alternative systems were examined to accomplish fume hood exhaust-air volume reductions before the final system was selected.
- Exhaust for laboratory spaces will be provided by central exhaust systems. These systems will provide fume hood exhaust and general room exhaust.
- Three central exhaust units have been installed in the penthouse mechanical room. Each serves a laboratory floor and is interlocked with a laboratory supply air handling unit. The unit serving the second floor also serves the high-bay laboratory area and the industrial work shop.
- Units are custom built of 2-inch double-wall steel construction and have the following components:
  - — Intake plenum
  - — Prefilter: 25% efficient
  - — Heat transfer coil
  - — Fan suction plenum
  - — Centrifugal exhaust fans with variable-speed drive
- All unit components that come in contact with the exhaust air are provided with a corrosion-resistant epoxy coating.
- Fume hood, snorkel, and general room exhaust from the laboratories are ducted to these units. All exhaust ductwork will be round or oval, factory fabricated, 304 stainless steel with welded joints.

- Main manifold exhaust ducts will be sized for 3000 fpm air velocity at maximum airflow.

- Exhaust system will be constructed and installed in accordance with SMACNA standards for 4 inches of WG negative static pressure.

- Laboratory rooms containing chemicals or emitting odors and not under special control will be maintained at a static pressure negative to the corridors and sufficient seals to prevent vapor from escaping from the laboratory.

- Dedicated exhaust systems will be provided for exhaust from biological safety cabinets, perchloric acid hoods, and other locations that require special exhaust.

- To provide temporary redundancy during breakdown or servicing of an exhaust unit, bypass ducts with automatic dampers are installed between each exhaust-air duct system.

- Exhaust air will be discharged vertically from stacks above the penthouse roof with a terminal velocity of 2500 to 4000 fpm.

7 Plumbing Design Criteria

a. BASIC PLUMBING SYSTEMS

Domestic Cold Water Service

A 4-inch domestic cold water service will be provided with a shutoff valve and meter assembly. A domestic water booster system will be provided to boost the incoming water to the pressure required. The water service will then be split into two domestic systems:

- Potable domestic cold water
- Nonpotable (Laboratory) domestic cold water

Potable Domestic Cold Water System

A complete potable domestic cold water system is provided with parallel backflow preventers located on the main after the service split. This system serves all nonlaboratory plumbing fixtures and fixtures within the laboratories requiring potable water.

Potable Domestic Hot Water System

A complete potable domestic hot water (110°F) supply and recirculating system is provided. This system is supplied by two gas fired storage-type water heaters and serves all non-laboratory plumbing fixtures.

Nonpotable (Laboratory) Domestic Cold Water

A complete nonpotable domestic cold water system is provided with parallel backflow preventers located on the main after the service split. This system serves all nonpotable plumbing fixtures, equipment in the laboratories, and all mechanical equipment.

Non-Potable (Laboratory) Domestic Hot Water

A complete nonpotable domestic hot water (110°F) and recirculating system is provided. This system is supplied by two gas-fired storage-type water heaters and serves all plumbing fixtures and equipment requiring hot water in the laboratories.

Sanitary, Water, and Vent System

A complete sanitary, waste, and vent system is provided to serve all plumbing fixtures except the laboratory fixtures and drains by gravity to the building sewer.

Acid Waste and Vent System

A complete acid waste and vent system is provided to serve all laboratory fixtures and will drain by gravity to the building sanitary sewer through an acid neutralization tank. All above-grade acid waste piping is glass.

Storm Drainage System

A complete storm drainage system is provided utilizing roof drains to convey the stormwater to interior conductors. The system drains by gravity to the building storm sewer system.

Deionized Water

A central deionized water system will not be installed. Deionized water will be generated in the laboratory work areas using cartridge or other generators.

Vacuum System

A complete vacuum system has been provided to serve terminals (inlets) in the laboratories. The system is supplied by a duplex vacuum pump and receiver assembly located in the ground floor mechanical equipment room.

Compressed Air

A complete compressed air system is provided to serve outlets in the laboratories. The air will be smooth flowing (nonpulsating) and free of dirt, oil, and moisture. The system is supplied by a duplex compressor assembly with filters, including refrigerated air dryers. Compressor assembly is located in the ground floor mechanical equipment room.

Natural Gas System

A complete natural gas system is provided. The system provides fuel for the gas-fired mechanical equipment and outlets in the laboratories. Valve boxes located in the corridor are provided for each laboratory.

b. RECOMMENDATIONS

- New fire hydrant flow test data were obtained to determine accurately the sizing for a domestic water booster system.
- Gas-fired water heaters are recommended for better efficiency and lower energy cost.
- Wall-mounted water closets are recommended to improve sanitation.
- Glass acid waste and venting piping are recommended for lower costs and a state-of-the-art system.
- Include the compressed air and vacuum shutoff valves with the gas valves in the valve cabinet outside the laboratories.

c. ALTERNATIVE CONCEPTS

Water Heaters

- Electric water heaters in lieu of gas-fired water heaters
- Two gas-fired water heaters versus four gas-fired water heaters

- Two electric water heaters versus four electric water heaters
- Small electric water heaters at toilet groups in lieu of central gas-fired water heaters for potable system

Water Closets

- Floor mounted
- Tank type

Acid Waste and Vent Piping

- High-silicon iron hub and spigot piping in lieu of glass piping
- Schedule 40 polypropylene piping in lieu of glass piping
- Deletion of the acid neutralization tank

8   Fire Protection Design Criteria

a. BASIC FIRE PROTECTION SYSTEMS

- An 8″ fire protection water service is provided with a shutoff valve, double-detector check valve, and fire pump. The service serves the three combined sprinkler and fire standpipes and preaction systems.

b. FIRE PUMP

- A 1000-gpm fire pump assembly is provided complete with jockey pump, fire pump test connection, and fire department Siamese connection and controls.

c. COMBINED FIRE SPRINKLER AND STANDPIPE SYSTEM

- A complete combined sprinkler and standpipe system is installed with three standpipes and hose valve connections at each floor capable of providing protection to all areas with a 100′ hose and 30′ water stream.
- The standpipes supply a wet pipe sprinkler system. The system is in three zones per floor. The entire building is protected by a wet pipe sprinkler system, except for the computer room, which is protected by a preaction system.
- The entire system is hydraulically designed.

d. FIRE EXTINGUISHER

- Wall-mounted 10-lb ABC fire extinguishers are provided in all locations as required by code.

e. RECOMMENDATIONS

- New fire hydrant flow test data were obtained to size the fire pump accurately.
- Sprinkler system for the entire building.

f. ALTERNATIVE CONCEPTS

- Fire protection system to use the computer room in lieu of preaction system.
  - Carbon-dioxide system
  - Halon system
- Provide a preaction system in the library.

9 Laboratory Piping Design Criteria

a. GENERAL DESIGN REQUIREMENTS

- Compressed air is required at 15 to 30 psig and 100 psig; both will be instrument grade with a-112°F dew point.
- A vacuum system is required. Filtration will be local.
- The consultant recommends providing natural gas to all laboratories.
- CO_2 to be provided by users (gas cylinders).
- Other special gases to be provided by users (gas cylinders).

b. BASIC LABORATORY PIPING SYSTEM

Distribution of laboratory piping is down the floor on each floor. Local isolation will be provided by means of valve boxes in the corridor for each lab.

10 Electrical Design Criteria

a. INTRODUCTION

- This section presents the overall concepts of the electrical systems. The data and plans represent the completion of the schematic design, design development, and construction documents phases. The documentation establishes the overall scope, quantity, and quality of the project.

■ The electrical systems presented have been designed to the standards established by the CDC engineering services office, the NIOSH Team, and the Cannon team.

■ The information presented establishes the general system types, configurations, and locations. Some changes may occur as the planning progresses.

■ The electrical systems have been designed for reliability and flexibility. Changing technology and new programs that result in modifications of spaces can be accommodated by the design.

■ Various system options have been considered while developing the design. The options are summarized in the discussion below.

b. CODES

The CDC/NIOSH program of requirements and scope of services, laboratory consultant design guidelines, and Cannon's design standards were utilized in conjunction with the following codes and standards were utilized to establish basic project criteria:

■ The BOCA Basic National Building Code, 1990

■ National Electrical Code (NEC)

■ American National Standards Institute (ANSI)

■ Institute of Electrical and Electronic Engineers (IEEE)

■ National Electrical Manufacturers Association (NEMA)

■ National Fire Protection Association (NFPA)

■ Underwriters' Laboratories (UL)

c. BLOCK LOADS FOR ELECTRICAL POWER

Load Densities: Lighting and Receptacles (Watts/SF)

Room/Area	Lighting, Connected[a]	Receptacles, Connected
Electrical, telephone, mechanical, rooms	1.5	3.0
Laboratories	3.0	N/A[b]
Laboratory support	3.0	N/A

Load Densities: Lighting and Receptacles (Watts/SF) (*Continued*)

Room/Area	Lighting, Connected[a]	Receptacles, Connected
Lobby	6.0	3.0
Food service	2.0	3.0
Computer center	3.0	3.0
Research support	2.0	3.0
Office areas	2.0	3.0
Public/staff toilets, service areas, corridors and stairways	1.5	0.25
Storage rooms	1.5	N/A
Utility rooms	1.5	3.0

[a] The minimum lighting feeder and panel capacity is designed on the basis of 4.5 W/sf, in accordance with the *National Electrical Code*, Article 220-3.
[b] N/A, not applicable.

Load Densities: Heating, Ventilation, and Air-Conditioning Equipment (Watts/SF)

Room/Area	Connected
Laboratory	12
Laboratory, support	12
Laboratory, office	10
Research support	10
Computer center	10
Food service center	17
Facility support	19

Load Densities: Special Equipment (Watts/SF)

Room/Area	Connected
Laboratory	50
Laboratory, support	50
Laboratory, office	1
Research support	3
Computer center	20
Food service center	3
Facility support	3

Demand and diversity factors are generally not applied to an individual laboratory module where virtually all the equipment within the space could be in operation at the same time. Following is a representative example of selected demand/diversity function for laboratory facilities:

$$
\begin{aligned}
\text{1 module} &\rightarrow 100\% \\
\text{2 to 10 modules} &\rightarrow 100 \text{ to } 80\% \\
\text{10 to 40 modules} &\rightarrow 80 \text{ to } 50\% \\
\text{Over 40 modules} &\rightarrow 50\%
\end{aligned}
$$

Distribution design has been arranged to serve large groups of laboratories to take advantage of the lower factors in sizing distribution equipment and feeders. Spare capacity is designed into the power distribution system to every extent possible. Approximately 30% over building design loads has been included in accordance with the program of requirements.

d. PRIMARY POWER SERVICE

Existing

- The existing building utilizes a dual-source 12,470-V connected, four-wire distribution network provided by Monongahela Power Company.
- The power company provides service to the property line via two widely separated overhead lines along Willowdale Road. Each service point is fed from a separate power company substation. The building takes service from each of these points with No. 2 wire installed in a common underground duct bank. The building is connected to these services such that one is standby and not carrying any building load. Each service is connected to a 1000-kVA transformer located on the outside of the building which feeds a common switchboard in a secondary selective manner. Power company revenue metering occurs on the primary side of the transformers. The owner owns the entire system from the point of service into the building.
- The underground service conductors are limited in growth potential for any significant expansion and is routed through the sites identified for the new building and road work. Power service alternatives have been explored with the power company.

Primary Service Alternatives

Since the existing service does not have adequate capacity for expansion and also requires relocation due to new construction, three new service alternatives were evaluated.

ALTERNATIVE A. Maintain the existing 12.47-kV dual-service concept and reconduct feeders to existing power company service points for new service to both the existing and new buildings. The new building will be connected to the dual service in a primary selective arrangement and the existing building will be connected as currently configured.

At the request of the power company, each service must carry about 50% of the total load under normal operating conditions. Under emergency conditions the power company has indicated that one service can carry the entire complex. The primary selective arrangement will allow for simple load balancing and transfer in case of an outage. This alternative is reliable and requires little rework at the existing building and essentially maintains the original power service concept currently in place.

ALTERNATIVE B. Obtain 23-kV radial service from the power company to serve both the new and existing buildings. The existing building primary service switchgear and transformers will be replaced and the existing building will be served in simple radial fashion. The power company point of service is approximately 800' from the property line but is currently fed by three different power company substations.

This concept could be designed with dual-source capability from the service point into our site but would come at a substantial cost at this time due to upgrade requirements at the existing building. This scheme would be about 30% more expensive (60% if dual source) and be more reliable than alternative A. There is also a slightly lower COT for power usage associated with this service voltage, but not enough to offset the additional cost over a five-year period.

ALTERNATIVE C. Provide 23-kV radial service to a new 12.47-kV outdoor substation and serve both the existing and new buildings at 12.47 kV. The existing building service equipment and transformers will not be replaced. This could be designed with future dual source capability. This scheme would be about 45% (90% for dual) more expensive than alternative A.

Reliability and power usage cost would be about the same as for alternative B.

e. RECOMMENDATION

Alternative A was recommended for use on this project due to owner state reliability and first-cost considerations. Maintaining service to the existing facility during construction will be studied to minimize power interruptions but does not appear to be significant at this time due to present dual-source configuration.

f. SECONDARY POWER SERVICE

Secondary Service Alternatives

The existing building's distribution system is secondary selective and is not intended to be modified or expanded under this project. The secondary service alternatives within the new building have been evaluated as they relate to the cost and reliability goals of the project. These are:

ALTERNATIVE A. Provide new single-ended switchboards in simple radial fashion, one at 480 and one at 208 V secondary. Each switchboard will be served by a 1500-kVA transformer. This alternative is the least reliable but also the least expensive. Also, if one of the transformers is lost for any reason, one half of the new building would be shut down.

ALTERNATIVE B. Provide new 480- and 208-V double-ended switchboards, each connected in a secondary selective arrangement. Each switchboard section will be served from a 1500-kVA transformer. Each transformer will be designed to carry the full combined load of the switchboards within the double-ended arrangement. This alternative is very reliable but is 23% more expensive than alternative A. Load shifting in the event of transformer loss would be simple to accommodate under this alternative.

ALTERNATIVE C. Provide new double-ended 208- and single-ended 480-V switchboards in the new building. Each switchboard section will be served from a 1,500-kVA transformer. The new 480-V substation will be connected to the existing buildings 480-V system with a normally open tie feed. This alternative is similar to B except on the 480-V side, which requires interfacing with the existing building. Due to the wide separation between the two service points, the cost for B and C would be about the same. Also, the ability to carry the full load of the existing building along with the full 480-V load of the new would not be possible, due to the size of the existing and new transformers, and load shedding would have to take place.

g. RECOMMENDATION

The secondary service alternative B, was recommended for use on this project order to achieve high reliability and to have a distribution system similar in function to the existing and in keeping with owner-stated design goals.

h. SECONDARY DISTRIBUTION

Vertical Distribution

The internal distribution system will be vertical in nature, utilizing plug-in busway risers, installed in a manner to facilitate the overall flexibility goals of this project. Electrical closets will be vertically stacked. Dedicated panelboards, installed flush mounted in the corridor, will be provided for every two laboratory planning modules (660 sf total) with wireway routed from the panel into each module to facilitate branch-circuit reconfiguration. Laboratory floor electrical closets will be sized to accommodate special power supplies, power regulation and conditioning equipment, and so on, to accommodate the most demanding laboratory configuration requirement. This special equipment will not be provided as part of this project.

Distribution Alternatives

Three methods of distributing power on the laboratory floors were evaluated:

ALTERNATIVE A. Provide vertical busway through one electrical closet per laboratory wing, sized for all building laboratory loads. Serve loads from closet utilizing horizontal plug-in busway installed in laboratory corridor.

ALTERNATIVE B. Provide vertical busway through two electrical closets per laboratory wing, each sized for half the laboratory loads. Serve loads from each closet utilizing horizontal plug-in busway with a normally open cross connection. This is about 10% more expensive than alternative A but is far more reliable by allowing each riser to be fed from a different power source, along with the ability of cross connection in the event of an emergency where one source is lost. The cross connection will be designed to prevent two simultaneous sources of power.

ALTERNATIVE C. Provide vertical busway through two electrical closets per laboratory wing. Serve laboratory loads from a power panel in the closet using pipe and wire. Each riser closet would be designed to serve about half of the laboratory loads. This is about 66% less expensive than alternative B and is far more flexible if ceiling space becomes congested but redundancy is lost.

i. RECOMMENDATION

We recommend alternative B for use on this project due to owner-stated flexibility and reliability goals.

j. EMERGENCY POWER

The overall design considered the use of redundant feeders, transformers, and switchgear, to allow laboratory and basic building services to function at a predetermined reduced level along with full specialty system operation in the event of power system failure.

k. LOADS

A standby diesel-fired emergency power generator is provided. The generator is located on the ground floor with the exhaust taken up to the highest roof. The total emergency power capacity for the new building provides for the following:

- Fire alarm
- Security
- Exit and corridor lighting
- Elevator (one only)
- Freezers and special laboratory equipment
- Stairwell lighting and power
- Two outlets in each laboratory module (660 sf)
- Building heating, sump pumps
- Building automation systems
- Smoke exhaust systems

- Various specialty systems
- Computer center equipment
- Special laboratory exhaust systems (12 total)
- Building fire pump
- 35% spare capacity

l. AIR OPTIONS

The general laboratory hood exhaust and supply air systems will not be placed on emergency power except as necessary to support building heating needs. In the event of a power outage, one laboratory exhaust and one laboratory supply fan will operate on emergency power.

m. EMERGENCY POWER ALTERNATIVES

The following alternatives were considered in the design of the emergency power system.

ALTERNATIVE A. Provide a single standby generator with 35% spare capacity (approximately 850 kW) with standard automatic transfer switches.

ALTERNATIVE B. Provide two parallel standby generators each with 35% spare capacity (approximately 450 kW) complete with synchronization and load shedding gear. This is about 60% more expensive than alternative A but is extremely flexible and reliable.

ALTERNATIVE C. Provide bypass isolation automatic transfer switches on critical and life safety power supplies to allow servicing of switch without shutting down power to the load. This feature adds about 200% to the cost of a standard switch but allows maintenance and service without shutting down power.

n. RECOMMENDATION

Alternative A and C were recommended as meeting with owner-stated reliability and design goals of the project.

o. UPS

In addition to the emergency generator system, the following loads within the new building will be connected to an uninterruptible power source (UPS).

- Computer center equipment
- Building automation system
- Fire alarm system

p. EMERGENCY DISTRIBUTION

The emergency power distribution system will be separated into the following branches.

Life Safety

This branch provides continuous (normal or emergency generator) power for lighting and communications/signaling equipment related to the safety of life for all building occupants, such as illumination of means of egress, exit signs, fire alarm systems, and so on.

Critical

This branch provides continuous (normal or emergency generator) power of lighting, selected receptacles, and so on, related to the critical (laboratory, support, etc.) areas, and equipment essential to experimental functions, laboratory bench areas, and equipment designated by the user. This branch will also provide necessary service to an uninterruptible power supply (UPS) and/or power conditioning equipment, as necessitated, and their associated computerized equipment loads.

Equipment

This branch provides continuous (normal or emergency generator) power to equipment loads essential for critical functions, such as sump pumps, fans, boilers, specialty laboratory exhaust fans, and so on.

Elevator

This branch provides (normal or emergency generator) power for elevators. The system will be designed so that under normal power all elevators will operate and under emergency power only one will operate.

Fire Pump

This branch provides continuous (normal or emergency generator) power to the fire pump to maintain power, for pressure, on the sprinkler system.

q. LIGHTING

Interior Lighting

Interior lighting will be primarily fluorescent, with incandescent sources being used only in specially designated areas. In office areas, task lighting will be provided along with indirect general illumination. Occupancy sensors will be installed in selected areas, and rooms not used 24 hours a day. Special dimming systems will be used in selected areas such as conference and training rooms. Electronic ballasts will not be utilized, due to harmonic impact on the building's distribution system.

Exterior Lighting

Exterior lighting will be located along all new access roads, parking lots, and walkways. This lighting will utilize metal halide lamps and will be controlled from the building automation system and/or photocells. The lighting of the existing parking area between the garage and existing facility, the existing northern access road, and the existing building drop-off area is not part of the current scope of work. Design guidelines will be recommended for changing existing site lighting to match the new lighting system.

r. SECURITY SYSTEMS

Security

The security system will tie into the existing building system and provide door monitoring and card key access into the building and into selected areas inside the building. A central monitor will be located at the main reception desk.

Safety

Systems for power shutdown and panic alarm annunciation will be provided within the laboratory areas.

s. SPECIAL ELECTRICAL SYSTEMS

Fire Alarm

A fire alarm system will be installed complete with graphic annunciator panels located at the new main entrance into the building complex. Alarm initiating and indicating devices will be located in the new addition in accordance with applicable codes and standards. This system will interface with the fire alarm system the existing laboratory building.

It was not the intent to upgrade the existing building but to design a system for the new building to be expandable in the future. Three system alternatives were evaluated.

ALTERNATIVE A. Provide a hardwired system in the new building. Maintain the existing building system with code minimum interconnection.

ALTERNATIVE B. Provide a multiplex system in the new building with capacity for future inclusion of the existing facility. Maintain the existing building system with code minimum interconnection. Overall, this system will be about 4% more expensive than alternative A but will be easier to expand and maintain. We may be able to reuse equipment from the safety building demolition for an additional cost saving.

ALTERNATIVE C. Provide an addressable multiplex system similar to that of alternative B. The cost of this system should now be the same as B but we would not be able to reuse existing equipment. This system will add tremendous convenience to maintenance (tracking nuance alarms) and actual firefighting by pinpointing the actual device in the alarm or trouble condition.

t. RECOMMENDATION

Alternative C was recommended from a safety and maintenance standpoint.

u. INTERCOM

Intercom systems will be installed at the loading dock and receiving areas and within the employee clinic.

v. MUSIC/SOUND

Localized music and amplification systems will be included for the lifestyle, training centers, and high-tech conference rooms.

w. LIGHTNING PROTECTION

A lightning protection system is provided on the new building that will interface with the existing laboratory building system in a manner to allow for a complete master labeled system for the entire complex provided that the building existing is currently so labeled. The existing building will not be upgraded as part of this project.

x. TELEVISION

An empty conduit and back box system is provided for future television system wiring. Conduit will be installed from the outlet to the ceiling plenum. Open wiring is anticipated for use within the facility. Specialty systems such as clock, program, and CCTV are not included at this time.

y. TELEPHONE AND DATA SYSTEMS

Telephone and Data

Chesapeake and Potomac Telephone Company (C&P) service is currently provided to the main communications room in the existing laboratory building. Service to the new laboratory building will be taken radially from the existing main communications room located on the ground floor of the existing building to a main communications room located in the new laboratory building. In addition new empty service conduits will be stubbed out of the new room to 5' outside the building for future use. The two new service access roads will also interfere with existing underground communications services into and around the site. These services will require relocation.

Distribution

Two communications closets will be provided on each floor, stacked vertically. These closets will be utilized for all specialty systems and telephone and data systems. A cable tray will be utilized from closet to corridor and run the length of all laboratory modules and other specialty areas. This cable tray will be installed with 12″ clearance for both front and top access. An empty conduit and back box system will be provided for telephone and data system wiring from outlet to tray or closet.

z. RECOMMENDATIONS

The following summarizes the electrical system recommendations derived as a result of Cannon's design efforts and the owner's direction.

Primary Power Service

- 12.47-kV dual source primary selective
- 480- and 208-V double-ended switchboards connected in a secondary selective arrangement.

Secondary Distribution

Secondary distribution will be provided by a vertical busway through two electrical closets per laboratory wing, each sized for half the laboratory load. Dedicated panelboards will be provided for every two laboratory planning modules served from the horizontal busway. A horizontal busway will be provided throughout the laboratory floor and cross connected through a normally open tie, to allow the entire floor to be served from one closet.

Emergency Power

Emergency power will be supplied by one generator with 35% space capacity with bypass isolation automatic transfer switches on both critical and life safety power supplies.

UPS

An uninterruptible power supply will be provided by dedicated systems for the computer center, building automation system, and fire alarm system.

Lighting

primarily fluorescent with occupancy sensors installed in selected rooms and areas not utilized 24 hours a day. Electronic ballasts will not be utilized due to harmonic impact on distribution system.

Light Dimming

Special systems will be utilized in such areas as the training center and high-tech conference room.

Exterior Lighting

Lighting will be located along all new access roads, parking lots, and walkways.

Security Systems

Security will be assured by selected exterior and interior door monitoring and card key access.

Safety

Safety will be provided by emergency power shutdown and panic alarm annunciation within the laboratory areas.

Fire Alarm

The fire alarm will be an addressable multiplex-type system with a graphic annunciator at the main entrance. The system will be suitable for expansion into the existing building but will not be extended as part of this project.

Intercom

Separate systems will be provided within the employee clinic and at the loading dock and receiving areas.

Music and Sound Systems

Localized music and amplification systems will be provided for the lifestyle, training centers, and high-tech conference rooms.

Lightning Protection

A complete system will be provided for the new building suitable for a master label.

Television

An empty conduit and back box system will be provided for future television system wiring.

Telephone and Data Systems

Two communication closets will be provided on each floor. A cable tray will be utilized throughout the building and an empty conduit will be installed from tray to telephone or data outlet.

The existing service into the building will not be reworked. A new empty conduit service will be stubbed 5' outside the new building and capped for future use. The new main communications closet will be interconnected with the existing closet with empty conduit.

11   Interior Space Design Criteria

a. INTRODUCTION

- This section presents the overall interior space concept of the new building and site and the functional organization of the building interior. The plans, sections, and elevations presented are the completion of the design phases, establishing the overall scope quantity, and quality of the project.

- The new building represents the standards set by CDC engineering services office and the interior space challenge stated by the NIOSH team.

- As the project developed, numerous changes created a continuing evolution of the interior space concepts. The interior space concepts have been altered and changed to accommodate each new parameter. In addition, programmatic changes have been made, changing the requirements for space and environment in many areas. For example, space needs have expanded for the library and computer center, laboratories have been relocated to different floors, and space reallocated for administrative functions.

- The requirement for flexibility in all spaces is a principal of the design theme. Changing technology and new programs are the primary reasons why interior alterations and different space needs will be required in the future from those currently planned.

b. GENERA DESIGN REQUIREMENTS

Goals and Objectives

The following project goals and objectives were taken in part from the program of requirements for the NIOSH lab building, Morgantown, West Virginia, prepared by the U.S. Public Health Service, and were in part generated by the planning and design team. The project goals and objectives establish a broad framework for the development of new laboratory facilities on the NIOSH campus. From the project goals and objectives, more detailed planning and design objectives, and ultimately planning and design criteria, are developed that will be used to generate one or more design concepts. The planning and design team and CDC/NIOSH will be responsible for evaluating the project from concept selection through the design development to ensure that the project fulfills the goals and objectives cited here.

- Establish design criteria reflecting the requirements for a safe workplace. Selection of building elements is to emphasize safety and a safe environment.

- Provide additional, high-quality research facilities that

will enable NIOSH to continue to fulfill its mission to ensure a healthier and safer working environment for Americans and will renew NIOSH's role as a leader in occupational safety and health research.

- Enhance the image of NIOSH as a center of the CDC that engages in quality research and is a recognized leader in the field of occupational safety and health research.

- Develop a functional and attractive environment to ensure a high quality of life for scientists and staff working at the NIOSH facility. Create an environment that is conducive to staff interaction while allowing privacy, when desired, for independent research. Create facilities that attract and retain top researchers.

- Develop flexible and adaptable facilities capable of accommodating changing research programs without disruption to the central building infrastructure system and adjacent activities.

- Optimize efficient operation of the NIOSH complex, including existing and new facilities. Minimize maintenance and operational costs of the physical plant, emphasizing life-cycle costs and energy-efficient design.

- Establish a framework of circulation, functional zones, green areas, and expansion zones to support development of the current project and to accommodate future expansion.

- Develop the new NIOSH laboratory facilities in the most expeditious manner and with the least disruption to existing activities.

c. BASIC INTERIOR SPACE DOCUMENTATION

Laboratory Casework

The following is a brief description of the two most probable alternatives: (1) conventional, and (2) suspended cantilever system. Laboratory-top materials will be determined by the functional requirements as well as first-cost considerations.

CONVENTIONAL CASEWORK. This is a floor-mounted system of steel, wood, or plastic laminate construction. In steel construction, each cabinet is generally supplied with four leveling screws and/or attached to adjacent cabinets by four bolts, and fastened to the top material by at least one, generally two, fasteners. Installation requires that all four leveling screws per cabinet be adjusted and then the adjacent cabinets adjusted and the bolts inserted. Where knee openings are to occur, the top is normally supported from an apron drawer unit that attaches two cabinets to either side.

Final connections to underbench piping and electrical systems is accomplished either by delaying the insertion of some casework, working through a removable back, or through use of independently force-supported pipe chases. Conventional wood casework is similar except for the leveling of the units, normally accomplished by the use of a common base under several cabinets, and the leveling is accomplished by the use of wooden wedges. In both the steel and wood configurations, the base of the cabinets is covered with a coved flooring material such as vinyl or rubber to match the floor covering. Any maintenance work on or additions to the mechanical systems under the benches must be accomplished either by removing the cabinets or attempting to work through them. Should it be necessary to remove the cabinets, this work involves removal of the side bolts and cover material.

SUSPENDED CANTILEVER SYSTEMS. In suspended cantilever systems the entire furniture system is suspended within a cantilevered steel frame that supports the individual cabinets and the working surface or benchtop. Generally, the legs of the supporting system are spaced 6 to 7' apart, greatly reducing the necessity of leveling the systems as they are installed. Each cabinet is suspended independently in the frame systems with two fasteners. The cabinets are more easily installed or removed from the framing system than in the conventional system.

No side-bolting or use of base materials is necessary for this system, greatly enhancing the ability to maintain or to change the mechanical or electrical systems under the bench work. Inasmuch as the working surface or benchtop is supported by the framed system, it is not necessary to have the actual cabinets in place until very late in the construction process. This is opposed to the necessity of having the cabinets in the conventional system upon which to support the top.

d. PARTITION LOCATION: LABORATORIES

Conceptually, the laboratory space has been planned on a modular generic basis to establish a uniform building systems distribution network and to enable the development of a flexible, cost-effective approach to casework design. This maximizes the inherent flexibility of the laboratories to respond to changes in research programs and developments in experimental technologies and laboratory instrumentation.

The laboratory space on each floor has been divided into two research blocks located on the perimeters, with support labs in the interior core area between the blocks. This basic layout accomplishes two highly desirable goals: (1) daylighting the perimeter labs where the laboratorians are based and spend most of their time, and placing in interior space support functions for which daylight is either unnecessary or harmful; and (2) providing easily accessible support labs which house special functions and expensive, shared laboratory instrumentation and apparatus.

To establish a basic geometric flexibility in both perimeter and core support labs, the potential partition locations have been designed on a modular basis which is 10'-6" wide by 31'-6" deep for both the perimeter and support labs. This module is based on work-space and instrument requirements in similar laboratories. The perimeter research labs are typically made up of two, three, or four such modules, depending on the anticipated programmatic function. However, the 31'-6" depth in itself a multiple of the 10'-6" width, and therefore research laboratories can be subdivided into smaller units if necessary to accommodate a special function, the minimum unit being 10'-6" × 10'-6". This allows casework to be placed along any of the walls while permitting flexibility in locating the entries. Partitions can be removed to create larger, more open laboratories.

The central support labs are also designed on this modular approach. Because some of these labs will house special instrumentation, several of the spaces will be 1 module lab in area (330 nsf) but partitioned to be 21'-0" wide by 15'-9" deep. In addition, many of these support spaces will be a modular fraction, such as one-third, one-half, or two-thirds, of a lab module.

The HVAC, service piping, and electrical power distribution and valving design will be integrated into the modular approach, thus providing an inherently flexible laboratory partition scheme.

e. PARTITION LOCATION: OFFICES

Drywall and metal stud partitions will be used for the office areas, similar to general commercial office buildings. This type of partition construction is used for economy and ease of remodeling when new space needs are required. Standard office partitions will be constructed with acoustical properties and materials to provide scientists and administrators with acoustically private work spaces. Conference and training rooms will be of similar construction.

f. PROGRAM LAYOUTS AND DESCRIPTION

Perimeter Research Laboratories

The typical biochemical or microbiological lab (DRDS) will be designed to maximize safety and flexibility. The mechanical systems are integrated with the functional zones: The air supply end of the lab is located at technician desks along the daylighted exterior wall; the chemical fume hoods and heat-producing equipment will be located at the end farthest from the desks and associated with the exhaust system. Major sinks will be located on the laboratory benches across from the hood/equipment zones. All perimeter laboratories will have secondary exits to satisfy safety concerns.

The device testing and research laboratories (Division of Safety Research, DSR) will have the same basic design as far as systems integration is concerned. However, the nature of these laboratories requires a design that permits much greater flexibility in location of specialized testing equipment and less dependency on fixed laboratory casework. Perimeter casework with no center islands will be the basic difference between DSR and other labs.

Laboratory Support Core

These support spaces will be of four basic types:

1. *Tissue culture.* It is expected that these labs will house one or two biological safety cabinets with provisions for incubators and refrigerators (provided by the owner). There will be some countertop space for microscopy.

2. *Cold rooms.* These will be 4°C rooms used either for storage or as a working environment. The first will have expanded metal shelving and a utility electrical outlet. The working cold rooms will have 36"-high bench work with storage cabinets below. It is anticipated that a 4' to 5'-low bench, approximately 20" high, with a built-in dis-

tillation rack for chromatography column work, will be provided, depending on researcher preference.

3. *Glasswash.* This shared space will be provided with one large glassware washer, one dryer, and one to two sterilizers, as well as stainless steel counters and large sinks.

4. *Instrumentation labs.* These spaces will house either individual pieces of instrumentation, such as a flow cytometer or immunofluorescent spectrophotometer, or commonly used apparatus such as centrifuges, lyophilizers, or large freezers which, because of their high heat loads and noise, are less suitable for research labs. These laboratories will be provided with a minimum amount of fixed casework to provide as flexible a space as possible.

Program Activities

As discussed above, the laboratories are basically divided into research laboratories and support laboratories and are designed to accommodate the types of activities associated with each. It is anticipated that the research laboratories will be divided into two basic types: (1) bench laboratories, with fume hoods and laboratory casework; and, (2) equipment or device testing laboratories, where casework is largely absent to allow for relatively large-scale testing apparatus to be set up and reconfigured.

The support labs will vary depending on the use of the research labs. However, because piped services and electrical power will be extended into each of these labs as well as full exhaust capability, they will be able to respond to programmatic changes.

12 Probable Construction Cost

a. INTRODUCTION

The schematic design construction cost estimate is based primarily on reevaluation of the predesign cost estimate. The approach evaluated which building systems have changed significantly and reestablish their costs. Those systems that deviate only through changes in the building gross square footage are adjusted accordingly.

In context, the exterior wall system, roof system, structural system, and mechanical and electrical systems were all requantified and repriced. The remaining building systems, the flooring, ceiling, partitions, doors, miscellaneous items, miscellaneous iron, and painting, were adjusted to match the program requirements and the new building gross square footage.

At this stage of the design process, it is not possible or expected that all architectural and engineered systems be fully explored or understood. It is the goal of the estimator to glean detail out of intent to solidify design from assumption. Where system assemblies fail under certain basic standards, our concern over our assumption is not significant. Historical data and experience provide the direction. Where system assemblies are customized and unique to the project, we then focus on details, measure quantities, and costs for accuracy.

b. LIMITS OF CONSTRUCTION

The estimate includes the construction of a new 157,185-bgsf (see Section 5) laboratory building with connections to the existing building through a tunnel at the ground floor and bridges at the second and third floors. Light renovations are included at all four floors of the existing building through a tunnel at the ground floor and bridges at the second and third floors. Light renovations are included at all four floors of the existing H building to accommodate these connections. The tunnel burrows under the H building ground floor slab-on-ground and ties into the ground floor, rather complex and difficult construction with little information on logistics. (This was estimated conceptually without regard for potential rock excavation or program disruption on the ground floor.)

The sitework is limited to the utilities, roadways, and parking related directly to the new facility. There was no consideration for special soil conditions regarding the presence of coal and its potential effect on the substructure construction.

c. PROJECT DELIVERY PROCESS

The contract was awarded through an open bidding process. The construction will be handled by a general contractor who will have all other trades submit bids as subcontractors. The estimated duration of the project is 21 months. Construction was scheduled to begin June 1991 and conclude March 1995.

d. PROBABLE CONSTRUCTION COST

The schematic design construction cost estimate incorporates all architectural, structural, mechanical, electrical, and civil building systems, with the pricing based on regional union labor, local material pricing, and the region's prevailing conditions.

The laboratory equipment and furnishings was estimated by the laboratory consultant. The scope and cost includes all lab equipment, furnishings, plumbing lines and fittings, and electrical requirements (not lighting) from the lab neatline into the labs. The detailed mechanical and electrical estimates provide 100% of the fire protection system and HVAC, of the plumbing lines up to a shutoff valve outside the labs, of the power to a panel outside the laboratories, and of the lighting for the entire building, including the labs.

A sales tax of 6% has been included for materials. The general contractor's overhead and profit have been set at 7% and escalation has been calculated to the midpoint of construction, May 1993, at 3.2% per year.

Probable Construction Cost

System Description	System Cost
Exterior skin	$2,641,648
Roof system	722,704
Floor system	411,816
Ceiling system	289,334
Doors and frames	321,878
Interior partitioins	977,642
Misc. iron and metals	179,655
Paint and surfacces	318,920
Miscellaneous items	540,655
Equipment	35,370
Laboratory equipment	2,642,850
Excavation and backfill	186,209
Foundation and slab on grade	620,029
Structural framing	2,761,573
Conveying sysem	279,440
HVAC system	3,977,532
Plumbing systme	1,446,100
Electrical system	3,115,600
Site utilities	591,937
Site improvements	731,547
General condition	1,388,500
Subtotal	$24,180,950
Material sales tax	821,600
GC overhead and profit	1,500,153
Escalation	1,484,151
Design contingency	1,399,343
Total estimate	$29,386,197

Contingencies

A design contingency of 5% was itemized to allow for changes and adjustments in the project during the design process. When initial predesign and schematic design assumptions are validated, invariably there is an increase in either scope or detail which results in changing costs.

C

CODES, REGULATIONS, STANDARDS, GUIDELINES, AND REFERENCE PUBLICATIONS

The publications listed indicate the scope and complexity of criteria that should be considered by administrators, facilities managers, researchers, faculty, physicians, architects, engineers, etc., during the programming, planning, and design of research and health care facilities. The lists are not complete, however.

Many jurisdictions have developed additional regulations and modifications to existing codes. Federal, state, and local agencies revise existing regulations and develop new ones frequently. The facilities manager and architect must determine the codes and regulations applicable for each project location.

Particular attention must be given to the numerous federal regulations and guidelines published by EPA, NIH, NIOSH, OSHA, and other agencies pertaining to the health and safety of laboratory and health care personnel. These regulations and guidelines may impose more restrictive standards than existing codes. Providing and maintaining a safe working environment for employees, eliminating or reducing exposure to hazardous substances to acceptable levels, establishment of waste disposal protocols and requirements, and facilities for monitoring personnel working in hazardous environments are just a few of the paramount issues and concerns related to planning, designing, operating, and maintaining laboratory facilities.

If an institution is considering remodeling and renovating existing laboratory facilities, it is suggested that a thorough code and federal regulatory review be conducted of the facilities to determine infractions, violations, and so on, that may exist. Such a review may require the assistance of an architect and engineer or code consultant. It is not suggested that representatives from any federal agency be invited to assist until the review is completed and commitments have been made to remedy infractions and violations.

Reagents that until recently were not considered dangerous are now classified as hazardous. These changes may place personnel at risk in many existing laboratory facilities. Health and safety is no longer the sole responsibility of the institution or the employer. The architect and engineer are now required to design facilities to safety standards that were not in existence as little as 3 to 5 years ago.

CHANGES AFFECTING DESIGN

It is not the intent of this book to provide detailed ADA information. However, recent safety and civil rights legislation, including the ADA, have important and significant implications on the planning and design process for all types of facilities. It is no longer sufficient just to provide the typical handicap-accessible toilet stall to satisfy disabled access requirements. The facility design must accommodate not only the wheelchair disabled person but also people using crutches, those with sight and hearing impairment, patients with neurological disorders, and so on. Government representatives are considering the addition of obesity to the list of disabilities. The architect must assume an active role with representatives of the institution to ensure that the facilities designed and constructed are accessible to and safe for *all* persons.

The Department of Justice (DOJ), Department of Labor (DOL), Department of Transportation (DOT), Equal Employment Opportunity Commission, and the Architectural and Transportation Barriers Compliance Board are just a handful of government agencies that are involved with the implementation and interpretation of ADA requirements. Architects are required to certify that the facility designed conforms to the ADA regulations. Expert input during the planning and design process relative to facility requirement for disabled persons accommodations is a *must*. It is also important to be certain about the correct definition of "disabled person." Several useful ADA references are listed in this section.

The introduction of computer technology with its attendant peripherals (monitors and printers) in the workplace has created a new (or renewed) awareness of the design of individual workstations. Video data terminals (VDTs or CRTs) emit radiation. Considerable research has been accomplished on the effects of people sitting in front of VDTs for long periods. Particular concern has been addressed to the effects on pregnant women. More than nine states and the District of Columbia have enacted legislation regulating the use of VDTs. Ten states currently have legislation pending. Other states are in the process of considering introduction of similar legislation.

The city of San Francisco regulations require extensive changes to workstations with VDTs. Ergonomic chairs, adjustable work counters, and increased clearances for people are just part of the requirements for improving workstations and the total work environment.

The costs involved to conform to the regulations can be significant. A business owner with 100 employees estimated that it will cost almost $2000 per employee to modify existing workstations in his facility. The configuration of many existing and older facilities may make remodeling and renovations too costly to justify changes. Estimates of additional net square feet required to satisfy VDT requiremens range from 3 to 5% to as much as 10% more net square feet per individual workstation.

Many companies, however, have provided properly designed workstations. These facilities were planned and constructed years before the regulations were passed. Although the initial costs were somewhat higher than they would have been without ergonomic planning, management representatives have reported increased employee productivity, reduction of time lost from work, and increased employee satisfaction with their individual ergonomic workstations. There is no longer any question that properly designed workstations more than pay for the added cost through improved employee efficiency, productivity, and satisfaction.

A major western telephone company approached the problem from the standpoint of reducing health care costs (almost $2 million annually) and employee time lost due to problems associated with repetitive stress injuries (carpal tunnel syndrome, etc.). Implementation of the new regulations will cost approximately $8 million to upgrade employee workstations during the next 4 to 5 years. However, the upgraded workstations have contributed to an almost immediate reduction of

24% in health care costs. There have been modest gains in employee productivity and reduction in turnovers, and with the health care cost savings, the company expects that costs to upgrade the workstations will probably equal savings during the period of time it will take to upgrade the workstations at all company facilities.

The science of ergonomics has prompted reevaluation of employee workstations of all types. Ergonomics involves materials, lighting, colors, textures, seating, standing, reaching, wrist supports for typing (computer inputting), footrests, and other features of the workplace. Motorized work counters are available that allow personnel to adjust working heights automatically at individual workstations. OSHA regulations restrict the height of shelves to 7'-0". Such height limitations effectively reduce the usable area (volume) in work spaces. Various square feet allocations for certain work spaces may have to be increased to accommodate functional requirements (e.g., storage of consumables, test kits, etc.).

Women comprise more than 50% of the work force. It is estimated that women will makeup 65% of the work force by the mid-1990s. Workstations for women will require significant changes in the design of casework, furniture, and facilities because women are shorter than men and have less reach and physical strength. Since women make up the overwhelming majority of clinical laboratory technologist and technician positions, the following items are extremely important design and safety criteria.

- Work counter height (sit-down and stand-up). The traditional design standard has been 29" to 30" for sit-down, and 36" to 37" for stand-up work counters. Ask any woman what she thinks of the 36" standard for the kitchen work counter height. (The author dares any architect to ask this question.)
- Wall shelf and cabinet heights from the floor (individual reach, etc.).
- Depth of work counter.
- Access to counter equipment from standing or seated position (side, top loading, etc.).

The California Department of Health Services has developed nonbinding guidelines for minimizing human exposure to volatile organic compounds (VOCs). Copies may be secured by contacting Steven B. Hayward, Indoor Air Quality Program, California Department of Health Services, 2151 Berkeley Way, Berkeley, CA 94704-1011 (510-540-3427). It would be extremely interesting to secure a definition of exactly what non-binding means.

What does this mean to the facilities manager and architect? The current wave of environmental concerns and regulations have changed previous space planning standards. Many current space standards may even become illegal. Employee work-stations (and the building envelope) must be designed and constructed in accordance with a variety of new standards, guidelines, and *regulations*. Institutions that recognize these changes and requirements, and assume the initial costs of implementing a well-planned and well-designed work environment, will benefit from immediate gains in employee efficiency and productivity. The institution will also avoid potential future liability costs associated with ergonomic health issues brought about by employee damage suits.

CONSEQUENCES OF REGULATIONS

Many jurisdictions require the architect-of-record to state on the sealed construction documents that the facilities to be constructed from the plans and specifications conform to all applicable laws, regulations, and codes. These certifications, however onerous, have far-reaching legal and financial implications for design professionals.

Facility design requirements indicated in codes and regulations of local, state, and federal agencies *must* be followed because of legal and financial liabilities, and enforcement and penalties. However, the architect should be aware that compliance with codes and regulations may (and can) be considered an inadequate argument and defense by some courts when a person is injured, particularly in the event of a fire or other emergency (chemical spill, toxic gas release, etc.) in the building.

It may be many years after exposure to hazardous substances before symptoms develop in personnel who have worked in a laboratory. It is quite conceivable that the courts may adjudge the design professional responsible for such injuries because of alleged design defects that created the hazardous environment.

Some courts have determined that the architect or contractor can still be held liable for injuries to building occupants even though codes and regional customary practices have been followed. The courts have stated that the architect must recognize, *using common knowledge and ordinary judgment*, that a particular material selection, building detail (floor, wall, and ceiling systems, etc.), and plan configuration may create a dangerous situation in the event of an emergency even though materials have been selected and systems designed in accordance with code requirements. Such liability implications literally *mandate* the involvement of the institution's safety management personnel in the programming and planning process. If an institution has a "disaster response team" (fire department, etc.), representatives should be included in the planning process along with respresentatives from community emergency response organizations and municipal code representatives.

The Clean Air Act, the Clean Water Act, and OSHA Standard 29CFR1910.1450, *Occupational Exposures to Hazardous Chemicals in Laboratories*, and many other regulations, have a significant impact on facilities requirements and costs. Architects and engineers must be aware and knowledgeable of these regulations so that the facilities designed conform to the requirements.

Conformance to regulations for the management of waste products and materials requires spaces, equipment, and personnel that were not necessary in laboratory facilities as recent as 3 to 5 years ago. As an example, regulations applicable to certain radioactive isotope waste products require that the materials be processed and stored on-site until safe to transport to a disposal site.

Standards indicated in several guideline publications listed [e.g., *Guide for the Care and Use of Laboratory Animals* (NIH Publication 85-23)] must also be followed. Various criteria contained in these guidelines may be more restrictive than the requirements contained in the Animal Welfare Act. Grants or funding for research projects may be withdrawn or terminated if certain guidelines and standards are not incorporated in the design of laboratory and animal facilities. The facilities manager and architect may have to contend with the dilemma of compliance with required codes and regulations as well as recommended guidelines and standards from the grant source.

PROFESSIONAL SOCIETY AND ASSOCIATION PUBLICATIONS

1. **Air Movement and Control Association** (AMCA), 30 West University Drive, Arlington Heights, IL 60004

   - *Classification for Spark Resistant Construction*, Publication 99-0401-86

   - *Fan Approval Manual, Part 1*, Publication 201-1990

2. **American Chemical Society** (ACS), 1155 16th Street, NW, Washington, DC 20036

   - *Design Considerations for Toxic Chemical and Explosives Facilities*, Scott and Doemeny, Eds., Chemical Health and Safety Division

   - *Emerging Technologies in Hazardous Waste Management*, D. W. Tedder and F. G. Pohland, Eds., ACS Symposium Series No. 422, 416 pp. (1990), ISBN 0-8412-1747-5

   - *Emerging Technologies in Hazardous Waste Management II*, D. W. Tedder and F. G. Pohland, Eds., ACS Symposium Series No. 468, 446 pp. (1991), ISBN 0-8412-2102-2

   - *Emerging Technologies in Hazardous Waste Management III*, D. W. Tedder and F. G. Pohland, Eds., ACS Symposium Series No. 518, 466 pp. (1993), ISBN 0-8412-2530-3

   - *Environmental Remediation: Removing Organic and Metal Ion Pollutants*, G. F. Vandegrift, D. T. Reed, and I. R. Tasker, Eds., ACS Symposium Series No. 509, 275 pp. (1992), ISBN 0-8412-2479-X

   - *Forum on Hazardous Waste Management at Academic Institutions*, Office of Federal Regulatory Programs, Department of Public Affairs

   - *Good Laboratory Practice Standards: Applications for Field and Laboratory Studies*, W. Y. Garner, M. S. Barge, and J. P. Ussary, Eds., ACS Professional Reference Book, 571 pp. (1992), ISBN 0-8412-2192-8

- *Harnessing Biotechnology for the 21st Century*, M. R. Ladisch and A. Bose, Eds., Conference Proceedings Series No. 494, 612 pp. (1992), ISBN 0-8412-2477-3

- *Hazardous Waste Management*, K. A. Ream

- *Hazardous Waste Site Remediation*, D. Grasso, University of Connecticut, Storrs, 624 pp. (August 1993), ISBN 1-56670-056-6

- *Instrumentation in Analytical Chemistry*, 1988–1991, L. Voress, Ed., 478 pp. (1992), ISBN 0-8412-2202-9

- *Less Is Better: Hazardous Waste Control*

- *Liquid Chromatography/Mass Spectrometry: Applications in Agricultural, Pharmaceutical, and Environmental Chemistry*, M. A. Brown, Ed., ACS Symposium Series No. 420, 312 pp. (1990), ISBN 0-8412-1740-8

- *Pesticide Waste Management: Technology and Regulation*, J. B. Bourke, A. S. Felsot, T. J. Gilding, J. K. Jensen, and J. N. Seiber, Eds., ACS Symposium Series No. 510, 273 pp. (1992), ISBN 0-8412-2480-3

- *Pollution Prevention in Industrial Processes: The Role of Process Analytical Chemistry*, J. J. Breen and M. J. Dellarco, Eds., ACS Symposium Series No. 508, 316 pp. (1992), ISBN 0-8412-2478-1

- *Reagent Chemicals*, 6th ed.

- *Resource Conservation and Recovery Act (RCRA) and Hazardous and Solid Waste Amendments*, Environmental Protection Agency, 401 M Street, SW, Washington, DC 20460

- *Resource Conservation and Recovery Act (RCRA) and Laboratories*, K. A. Ream

- *Safety in the Chemical Laboratory*, Vols. 1–3, N. V. Steere; Ed., Vol. 4, M. M. Renfrew, Ed., Chemical Health and Safety Division

- *Synthesis and Chemistry of Agrochemicals III*, D. R. Baker, J. G. Fenyes, and J. J. Steffens, Eds., ACS Symposium Series No. 504, 468 pp. (1992), ISBN 0-8412-2473-0

3. **American Conference of Governmental Industrial Hygienists** (ACGIH), 6500 Glenway Avenue, Building D-7, Cincinnati, OH 45211-4438

   ■ *A Guide for the Control of Laser Hazards*, Publication 0165

   ■ *A Guide to OSHA Regulations on Storing and Handling Flammable and Combustible Liquids*, Publication 3190

   ■ *Active and Passive Smoking Hazards in the Workplace*, Publication 9139

   ■ *AIDS Policies and Programs for the Workplace*, Publication 9112

   ■ *Air Contaminants: Permissible Exposure Limits* (OSHA PELs), Publication 3130

   ■ *Biohazards Management Handbook*, Publication 9121

   ■ *Biological Effects and Medical Applications of Electromagnetic Energy*, Publication 9185

   ■ *Biological Monitoring of Exposure to Chemicals*, Publication 9002

   ■ *Cancer Causing Chemicals*, Publication 9077

   ■ *Chemical Process Safety: Fundamentals with Applications*, Publication 9156

   ■ *Computers and Visual Stress*, Publication 9193

   ■ *Controlling Indoor Radon: Measurement, Mitigation and Prevention*, Publication 9166

   ■ *Coping with Radiation Accidents*, Publication 9178

   ■ *Design of Industrial Ventilation Systems*, Publication 0440

   ■ *Engineering Design for the Control of Workplace Hazards*, Publication 9040

   ■ *Ergonomics: A Practical Guide*, Publication 9129

   ■ *Essentials of Modern Hospital Safety*, Publication 9155

   ■ *Estimating Costs of Air Pollution Control Equipment*, Publication 9186

- *Exhaust Ventilation System Duct Sizing and Balancing* (MS-DOS Computer Programs), Publications 9910, 9911

- *Guide to Industrial Respiratory Protection*, Publication 3240

- *Guidelines for Assessment of Bioaerosols in the Indoor Environment*, Publication 3180

- *Handbook of Environmental Rate and Exposure Data for Organic Chemicals*, Publication 9087 (Vol. I), Publication 9133 (Vol. II)

- *Handbook of Hazardous Waste Management for Small Quantity Generators*, Publication 9048

- *Hazardous Waste Management Engineering*, Publication 9164

- *Heating, Ventilation, and Air Conditioning Analysis and Design*, 3rd ed., Publication 7070

- *Human Aspects of Occupational Vibration*, Publication 7050

- *Indoor Air Pollution*, Publication 0580

- *Indoor Air Quality Control Techniques*, Publication 9035

- *Industrial Ventilation Manual*, 20th ed., Publication 2080

- *Industrial Ventilation Workbook*, Publication 0428

- *Infectious Waste Management*, Publication 9177

- *Low-Level Radioactive Waste*, Publication 9147

- *Noise Control: A Guide for Workers and Employers*, Publication 9019

- *Occupational Hazards to Health Care Workers*, Publication 0170

- *Occupational Health Guidelines for Chemical Hazards*, Publication 315C

- *Personal Protective Equipment for Hazardous Materials Incidents: A Selection Guide*, Publication 0860

- *Practical Guide to Respirator Usage in Industry*, Publication 5000

- *Radiation Protection*, Publication 9194

- *Recognition of Health Hazards in Industry*, Publication 0500

- *Reproductive Health Hazards in the Workplace*, Publication 9089

- *Right-to-Know Pocket Guide for Laboratory Employers*, Publication 9158

- *Safe Storage of Laboratory Chemicals*, Publication 0750

- *Standard Operating Safety Guides*, Publication 3140

- *The Hazardous Waste Q & A*, Publication 9109

- *The Laboratory Quality Assurance System*, Publication 9107

- *The Risk Assessment of Environmental Hazards*, Publication 9082

- *Threshold Limit Values (TLV) for Chemical Substances and Physical Agents*

- *Underground Storage Systems Leak Detection and Monitoring*, Publication 9105

- *Understanding Radioactive Waste*, Publication 9174

- *Ventilation for Control of the Work Environment*, Publication 9094

- *Worker Protection During Hazardous Waste Remediation*, Publication 9138

4. **American Hospital Association** (AHA), 840 North Lake Shore Drive, Chicago, IL 60611; publications: AHA Services Inc., P.O. Box 99376, Chicago, IL 60693

   - *Design Planning for Freestanding Ambulatory Care Facilities*, Cat. No. C-043181

   - *Design That Cares: Planning Health Facilities for Patients and Visitors*, Cat. No. C-043182

   - *Effective Health Care Facilities Management*, Cat. No. 055975

- *Ethylene Oxide Use in Hospitals: A Manual for Health Care Personnel*, 2nd ed., Cat. No. C-031181

- *Fire Warning and Safety Systems*, Cat. No. C-055203

- *Fitness Facility Planning: Resources and Recommendations*, Cat. No. C-070907

- *Food Service Manual for Health Care Institutions*, Cat. No. 046171

- *Maintenance Management for Health Care Facilities*, Cat. No. C-055852

- *Management of HIV Infection in the Hospital*, 3rd ed., Cat. No. C-094642

- *Managing Health Care Construction Projects, A Practical Guide*, Cat. No. A87-055100

- *Managing Hospital Infection Control for Cost-Effectiveness*, Cat. No. C-094118

- *Materials Management: Policy and Procedure Manual*, 2nd ed., Cat. No. 142100

- *Outpatient Cancer Centers: Implementation and Management*, Cat. No. C-016141

- *Safety Guide for Health Care Institutions*, Cat. No. C-181148

- *Safety Management for Health Care Facilities*, MACS Vol. 5, Cat. No. C-055204

- *Universal Precautions, Policies, Procedures, and Resources*, G. Pugliese, Ed., Cat. No. EO6-094119

- *Working with Health Care Consultants*, Cat. No. C-001114

5. **American Industrial Hygiene Association** (AIHA), 2700 Prosperity Avenue, Suite 250, Fairfax, VA 22031

- *Biohazards Reference Manual*

- *Computers in Health and Safety*

- *Engineering Field Reference Manual*

- *Ergonomics Guide Series*

- *Noise and Hearing Conservation Manual*

- *Nonionizing Radiation Guide Series*

- *Occupational Exposure and Work Practice Guidelines for Formaldehyde*

- *Quality Assurance Manual for Industrial Hygiene Chemistry*

- *Respiratory Protection: A Manual and Guideline*

- *Welding Health and Safety Resource Manual*

- *Workplace Environmental Exposure Level Guide Series*

6. **American National Standards Institute, Inc.** (ANSI), 11 West 42nd Street, New York, NY, 10036

- *Acceptable Concentrations of Carbon Tetrachloride*, ANSI Z37.17

- *Acceptable Concentrations of Formaldehyde (Formalin)*, ANSI Z37.16

- *Acceptable Concentrations of Toluene*, ANSI Z37.12

- *Fundamentals Governing the Design and Operation of Local Exhaust Systems*, ANSI Z9.2-1979(R1991)

- *Hazardous Industrial Chemicals: Precautionary Labeling*, ANSI Z129. 1-1982

- *Immediate Evacuation Signal for Use in Industrial Installations Where Radiation Exposure May Occur*, ANSI N2.3

- *Laboratory Ventilation Standard* (revised, includes fume hood controls), ANSI/AIHA Z9.5-1993

- *Method for Pressure Measurement*, ANSI/ASHRAE 41.3-1989

- *National Plumbing Code*, ANSI A40.8

- *Practice for Occupational and Educational Eye and Face Protection*, ANSI Z87.1

- *Practices for Respiratory Protection*, ANSI Z88.2

- *Providing Accessibility and Usability for Physically Handicapped People*, revisions contained in Federal Standard 795.1-Apr88, ANSI A117.1

- *Safety Code for Compressed Air Machinery*, ANSI B19

- *Safety Level of Electromagnetic Radiation with Respect to Personnel*, ANSI C95.1

- *Scheme for the Identification of Piping Systems*, ANSI A13.1-81

- *Standard Method for Temperature Measurement*, ANSI/ASHRAE 41.1-1986

- *Ventilation for Acceptable Indoor Quality*, ANSI/ASHRAE 62-1989

7. **American Society for Testing and Materials** (ASTM), 1916 Race Street, Philadelphia, PA 19103-1187

- *Atlas of Odor Profiles*, DS 61, PCN 05-061000-36

- *Chemical Thermodynamic Data and Energy Release Computer Program Manual*, DS 51A, PCN 05-051895-15

- *Design of Buildings for Fire Safety*, STP 685, PCN 04-685000-31

- *Flammability and Sensitivity of Materials in Oxygen Enriched Atmospheres*, fourth volume, STP 1040, PCN 04-010400-31

- *Hazardous and Industrial Solid Waste Minimization Practices*, STP 1043, PCN 04-010430-56

- *Inhalation Toxicology of Air Pollution: Clinical Research Considerations*, STP 872, PCN 04-872000-17

- *Measured Air Leakage in Buildings*, STP 904, PCN 04-904000-10

- *Performance of Protective Clothing: Second Symposium*, STP 989, PCN 04-989000-55

- *Specification for Metal Solder*, B-32-83

- *Specifications for Plastic Pipe, Tubing and Fittings, and Building Products*, including acrylonitrile-butadiene-styrene (ABS), chlorinated poly vinyl chloride (CPVC), polybutylene (PB), poly vinyl chloride (PVC), polyethylene (PE), reinforced thermosetting, and styrene-rubber, Vol. 08.04

- *Specification for Polyburylene (PB) Plastic Hot and Cold Water Distribution Systems*, D-3309

- *Specification for Poly (Vinyl Chloride)(PVC) Plastic Pipe*, Schedules 40, 80, and 120, D-1785-83

- *Standard Specifications for Reagent Water*, D1193

- *Susceptibility to Inhaled Pollutants*, STP 1024, PCN 04-010240-17

- *Test for Resistance to Chemicals of Resilient Flooring*, F 925, PCN 01-150490-44

- *Toxic and Hazardous Industrial Chemicals Safety Manual*, PCN 13-119085-24

- *Water (I)*, Vol. 11.01; *Water (II)*, Vol. 11.02; standards, definitions, reagents, laboratory precision, microbiological examination, etc.

8. **American Society of Heating, Refrigeration, and Air-Conditioning Engineers, Inc.** (ASHRAE), 1791 Tullie Circle, NE, Atlanta, GA 30329-2305

Publications

- Air Movement and Control Association (AMCA), *Fan Application Manual*, Code 96510

- *Air Quality Ventilation, Hazardous Gas, and Radon Contaminants*, Code 88006

- *ASHRAE Brochure on Psychrometry*, Code 90160

- *ASHRAE Transactions*, compilation of technical and symposium papers preserved at ASHRAE's annual and winter meetings; call ASHRAE, 404-636-8400

- *Building Systems: Room Air and Air Contaminant Distribution*, Code 90305

- *CFCs: Time of Transition–Alternative Refrigerants, Recycling and Recovery*, Code 90315

- *CFCs: Todays Options–Tomorrow's Solutions*, Code 90325

- *Cool Storage Modeling and Design*, compares thermal storage cooling and gas air-conditioning for a lab building, Code 88150

- *DDC and Building Automation Systems*, control of semi-conductor manufacturing cleanrooms, energy optimization in a hospital, and other topics, Code 88152

- *Directory of State Building Codes and Regulations*, 5th ed., Code 96410

- *Engineering Solutions to Indoor Air Problems*, pollutants, design concepts, and filtration/controls, Code 90062

- *Fire, Smoke and Radiation Damper Installation Guide for HVAC Systems*, Code 96040

- *Handbook: Fundamentals* (inch pound edition, 1989); call ASHRAE, 404-636-8400

- *Handbook: Heating, Ventilation and Air-Conditioning Applications* (inch pound edition, 1991); call ASHRAE, 404-636-8400

- *Handbooks: Fundamentals, Equipment, HVAC Systems and Applications, Refrigeration Systems and Applications*; call ASHRAE, 404-636-8400

- *Heat Recovery*, design of a run-around heat recovery system and other systems, Code 88154

- *Hospital and Operating Room Ventilation*, Code 88090

- *HVAC Duct Construction Standards: Metal and Flexible*, Code 96032

- *HVAC in Nuclear Facilities*, Code 88120

- *HVAC Systems: Duct Design Tables and Charts*, Code 96034

- *Indoor Air Quality*, Code 96048

- *International Daylighting Conference—1986*, various topics including the psychological aspects of daylighting, Code 90320

- *Laboratory Fume Hoods*, Research Project RP-70

- *Managing Indoor Air for Health and Energy Conservation*, indoor environment of offices, building associated diseases, passive smoking implications, formaldehyde, radon, and carbon dioxide levels, practical engineering solutions, Code 90060

- *Mechanical Estimating Guidebook for Building Construction*, 5th ed., Code 96186

- *Practical Control of Indoor Air Problems*, design deficiencies frequently associated with sick buildings, Code 90061

- *Procedural Standards for Certified Testing of Cleanrooms*, Code 96305

- *Rule-of-Thumb Cost Estimates for Building Mechanical Systems*, Code 96187

- *Smoke Control Technology*, stairshafts, elevator safety, etc., Code 88146

- *The Effect of Room Air Challenge on the Efficiency of Laboratory Fume Hoods*, Caplan and Knutson, ASHRAE Trans. 83, Part I, 1977

- *The Energy Directory*, 1989 ed., combined source of technical and administrative energy criteria in building codes and regulations in the United States, Code 96420

- *The Human Equation*, health and comfort, focus on the human effects of indoor air quality, Code 90063

- *T-Method Duct Design*, system condensing, fan selection, and system expansion, Code 88140

- *Ventilation Directory*, 1990 ed., identifies the major U.S. codes and standards on ventilation, Code 96425

- *Ventilation for control of the work environment, Code 96270*

Standards

- *Energy Conservation in Existing Buildings—Institutional*, Standard 100.5-1981, Code 86288

- *Energy Conservation in New Building Design*, Standard 90A, Code 86235

- *Energy Efficient Design of New Buildings*, Standard 90.1-1989; Computer Programs, Codes 86237 and 86238

- *Guideline for Reducing Emission of Fully Halogenated Chlorofluorocarbon (CFC) Refrigerants in Refrigeration and Air-Conditioning Equipment and Applications*, Standard 3-1990, Code 86802

- *Method of Rating Computer and Data Processing*

Room Unitary Air Conditioners, Standard 127-1988, Code 86400

- *Method of Testing Air-Cleaning Devices Used in General Ventilation for Removing Particulate Matter*, Standard 52-1968 (RA76), Code 86140

- *Methods of Testing Performance of Laboratory Fume Hoods*, Standard 110-1985, Code 86335

- *Practices for Measurement, Testing, Adjusting, and Balancing of Building Heating, Ventilation, Air-Conditioning and Refrigeration Systems*, Standard 111-1988, Code 86337

- *Safety Code for Mechanical Refrigeration*, Standard 15-1989, Code 86016

- *Standard Method for Measurement of Flow of Gas*, Standard 41.7-1984

- *Thermal Environmental Conditions for Human Occupancy*, Standard 55-1981, Code 86145

- *Ventilation for Acceptable Indoor Air Quality*, Standard 62-1989, Code 86157

9. **American Society of Mechanical Engineers** (ASME), 345 East 47th Street, New York, NY 10017; Mail orders to ASME, 22 Law Drive, P.O. Box 2300, Fairfield, NJ 07007-2300

- *Building Services Piping*, Order No. AX1688

- *Cast Copper Alloy Solder Joint Fittings for Solvent Drainage Systems*, Standard B16.32-84

- *Clean Rooms*, Order No. 986637

- *Code on Nuclear Air and Gas Treatment*, Order No. AX2288

- *Decommissioning of Major Radioactive Facilities*, Order No. 986602

- *Floor Drains*, Order No. J00040

- *Handbook on A17.1 Safety Code for Elevators and Escalators*, 1987 ed., Order No. A000112

- *Hazardous Waste Incineration: A Resource Document*, Order No. I00266

- *HVAC Systems Design Handbook*, Order No. 693130

- *Low and Intermediate Level Radioactive Waste Management*, Order No. I0292A

- *Mechanical Signature Analysis: Machinery Vibration, Row Induced Vibration, and Acoustic Noise Analysis*, Order No. H00407

- *Part 10—Flue and Exhaust Gas Analyses*, Order No. C00031

- *Quality Assurance Program Requirements for Nuclear Facilities*, Order No. AX0589

- *Recommended Guide for the Prediction of the Dispersion of Airborne Effluents*, 3rd ed., Order No. H00037

- *Safety Standard for Air Compressor Systems*, Order No. AX9785

- *Safety Standard for Conveyors and Related Equipment*, Order No. JX8887

- *Safety Standard for Pressure Vessels for Human Occupancy*, Order No. JX9290

- *Seismic Engineering—1989*, Order No. H00497

- *Seismic, Shock, and Vibration Isolation—1989*, Order No. H00496

- *The Management and Disposal of Intermediate and Low Level Radioactive Waste*, Order No. 986238

- *The Role of Damping in Vibration and Noise Control*, Order No. H00405

10. **American Society of Sanitary Engineering** (ASSE), P.O. Box 40362, Bay Village, OH 44140

- *Backflow Preventers with Intermediate Atmospheric Vent*, Standard 1012-78

- *Hose Connection Vacuum Breakers*, Standard 1011-82

- *Laboratory Faucet Vacuum Breakers*, Standard 1035-84

- *Reduced Pressure Principle Backflow Preventers*, Standard 1013-80

- *Vacuum Breakers, Anti-siphon, Pressure Type*, Standard 1020-82

11. **Building Officials and Code Administrators International, Inc.** (BOCA), 4051 West Flossmoor Road, Country Club Hills, IL 60477-5795

   - *The National Building Code*
   - *The National Mechanical Code*
   - *The National Plumbing Code*

12. **Building Seismic Safety Council** (BSSC), 1015 15th Street, NW, Suite 700, Washington, DC 20005

   - *Abatement of Seismic Hazards to Lifelines: Proceedings of the BSSC Workshop on Development of an Action Plan*, Vols. 1–6, Publications 135, 136, 137, 138, 142, 143
   - *An Action Plan for Reducing Earthquake Hazards of existing Buildings*, 1985, Publication 90
   - *Improving the Seismic Safety of New Buildings*, Publication 99
   - *National Earthquake Hazards Reduction Program (NEHRP), Recommended Provisions for the Development of Seismic Regulations for New Buildings*, 1986, Publications 95, 96, 97
   - *Proceedings: Workshop on Reducing Seismic Hazards of Existing Buildings*, 1985, Publication 91
   - *Seismic Considerations for Design and Construction of Health Care Facilities*, Publication 150

13. **College of American Pathologists** (CAP), Publications Order Department, 325 Waukegan Road, Northfield, IL 60093-2750

   - *Laboratory Accreditation Program*
   - *Laboratory Instrument Verification and Maintenance Manual*
   - *Medical Laboratory Planning and Design Manual*
   - *Reagent Water Specifications by the Commission on Laboratory Inspection and Accreditation*
   - *So You're Going to Collect a Blood Specimen: An Introduction to Phlebotomy*

14. **Compressed Gas Association, Inc.** (CGA), 1235 Jefferson Davis Highway, Arlington, VA 22202-3269

   - *Handbook of Compressed Gases*
   - Publications AV-1, C-2, C-6, C-6.1, C-7, C-14, P-1, P4, P-12, S-1.1, S-1.2, S-1.3

15. **Institute of Environmental Sciences** (IES), 940 East Northwest Highway, Mt. Prospect, IL 60056
    - *Recommended Practice for Laminar Flow Clean Devices, RP-CC-002-86*

16. **International Conference of Building Officials** (ICBO), 5360 South Workman Mill Road, Whittier, CA 90601
    - *Uniform Building Code* (UBC)
    - *Uniform Mechanical Code* (UMC)

17. **International Facilities Management Association** (IFMA), 1 East Greenway Plaza, Suite 1100, Houston, TX 77046-0194
    - *Acoustics in the Open Office Plan*, Proceedings from IFMA '89
    - *Architectural Lighting Design*, No. 46167
    - *Building Air Quality: A Guide for Building*, No. 146154
    - *Building Design and Human Performance*, No. 146156
    - *Building Economics: Theory and Practice*, No. 146173
    - *Construction Inspection Handbook*, No. 146146
    - *Corporate Facility Planning*, No. 146112
    - *Designing the Cost Effective Office*, No. 146175
    - *Environmental Quality in Offices*, No. 146164
    - *Ergonomic Design for People at Work*, Vols. I and II, 146124, No. 146126
    - *Facilities Maintenance Standards*, No. 146159
    - *Facilities Planning Handbook*, No. 146132
    - *Handbook of Facilities Planning: Laboratory Facilities*, No. 146150
    - *Hazardous Material and Hazardous Waste: A Construction Reference Manual*, No. 146157
    - *Health Care Facility Planning & Construction*, No. 146140
    - *Human Factors Essentials: An Ergonomic Guide for Designers, Engineers, Scientists, and Managers*, No. 146170
    - *Improving VDT Work*, No. 146172

- *Interior Design of the Electronic Office: The Comfort and the Productivity Payoff*, No. 146176
- *Managing Indoor Air Quality*, No. 146169
- *Office Space Planning and Management*, No. 146114
- *Open Protocols: Communications Standards for Building Automation Systems*, No. 146148
- *Planning and Designing the Office Environment*, No. 146174
- *Planning and Managing Interior Projects*, No. 146142
- *Post Occupancy Evaluation*, No. 146106
- *Problem Seeking: An Architectural Programming Primer*, No. 146155
- *The Americans with Disabilities Act: A practical Guide to Its Understanding and Cost Effective Implementation*, IFMA Professional Reference Programs, 378 Halstead Avenue, Suite 205, Harrison, NY 10528; 1-800-932-0191
- *The Ergonomics Payoff*, No. 146104
- *The Facilities Manager's Reference*, No. 146145
- *Understanding Building Automation Systems*, No. 146171
- *Using Office Design to Increase Productivity*, No. 146116
- *VDT Health and Safety: Issues and Solutions*, No. 146144

18. **Joint Commission on Accreditation of Healthcare Organizations** (JCAHO), One Renaissance Boulevard, Oakbrook Terrace, IL 60181 (call Customer Service Center at 708-916-5800)

   - *Controlling Occupational Exposures to Tuberculosis*
   - *Designing the Environment of Care*
   - *Hospital Scoring Guidelines*
   - *Hospital Standards*
   - *Medical Equipment Safety: Meeting the Requirements of the Safe Medical Devices Act* (1993)
   - *Plant Technology and Safety Management (PTSM) Series*

19. **National Committee for Clinical Laboratory Standards** (NCCLS), 771 East Lancaster Avenue, Villanova, PA 19085

- *Blood Specimen Processing*, H18
- *CLIA Collection*, SC11
- *Collection, Transport and Preparation of Blood Specimens for Coagulation Testing, etc.*, H21-A
- *General Laboratory Practices and Safety*, SC4
- *Guidelines for Laboratory Safety*, Proposed Guideline (1989), GP17-P
- *Instrument Biohazards*, 117
- *Inventory Control Systems for Laboratory Supplies; Proposed Guideline (1983)*, GP6-P
- *Laboratory Design (1994), GP18-P*
- *Laboratory Waste Management*, Approved Guideline, 1993, GP5-A
- *Power Requirements for Clinical Laboratory Instruments and for Laboratory Power Sources*, ASI-5
- *Preparation and Testing of Reagent Water in the Clinical Laboratory 2nd ed., Approved Guideline (1991)*, C3-A2
- *Preparation of Manuals for Installation, Operation and Repair of Laboratory Instruments*, ASI-1
- *Procedures for the Handling and Transport of Domestic Diagnostic Specimens and Etiologic Agents*, 2nd ed., Approved Standards (1985), H5-A2; see also M29-T2
- *Protection of Laboratory Workers from Infectious Disease Transmitted by Blood, Body Fluids and Tissue, Tentative Guideline*, M29-T2
- *Protection of Laboratory Workers from Instrument Biohazards*, Proposed Guideline, I17-P
- *Quality Control*, C24
- *Slide Preparation and Staining of Blood Films for the Laboratory Diagnosis of Parasitic Diseases*, Tentative Guideline, 1992, M15-T
- *Specimen Collection, SC2*
- *Temperature Monitoring and Recording in Blood Banks*, 116-T
- *Toxicology Containers*, H-31

20. National Fire Protection Association (NFPA), 1 Batterymarch Park, P.O. Box 9101, Quincy, MA 02269-9101

- *Fire Protection Handbook*, 16th ed., A. E. Cote, Ed.
- NFPA 10   *Standard for Portable Fire Extinguishers*
- NFPA 12   *Carbon Dioxide Extinguishing Systems*
- NFPA 12A   *Halon 1301 Fire Extinguishing Systems*
- NFPA 12B   *Halon 1211 Fire Extinguishing Systems*
- NFPA 13   *Standard for the Installation of Sprinkler Systems,* also NFPA 13A
- NFPA 30   *Flammable and Combustible Liquids Code*
- NFPA 43A   *Storage of Liquid and Solid Oxidizers*
- NFPA 43B   *Storage of Organic Peroxide Formulations*
- NFPA 43C   *Storage of Gaseous Oxidizing Materials*
- NFPA 45   *Standards on Fire Protection for Laboratories Using Chemicals* (includes Fume Hood Monitoring)
- NFPA 49   *Hazardous Chemicals Data*
- NFPA 50   *Bulk Oxygen Systems at Consumer Sites*
- NFPA 50A   *Gaseous Hydrogen Systems at Consumer Sites*
- NFPA 50B   *Liquified Hydrogen Systems at Consumer Sites*
- NFPA 53M   *Fire Hazards in Oxygen Enriched Atmospheres*
- NFPA 56C   *Laboratories in Health Related Institutions*
- NFPA 58   *Storage and Handling of Liquified Petroleum Gases*
- NFPA 68   *Deflagration Venting (Guide for Explosion Venting)*

- NFPA 69   *Explosion Prevention Systems*
- NFPA 70   *National Electrical Code*
- NFPA 70B   *Electrical Equipment Maintenance*
- NFPA 70E   *Electrical Safety Requirements for Employee Workplaces*
- NFPA 72   *Installation, Maintenance and Use of Auxiliary Protective Signaling Devices*
- NFPA 72E   *Automatic Fire Detectors*
- NFPA 75   *Standard for the Protection of Electronic Computer/Data Processing Equipment*
- NFPA 77   *Static Electricity*
- NFPA 78   *Lightning Protection Code*
- NFPA 80   *Standards for Fire Doors and Windows*
- NFPA 82   *Incinerators, Waste and Linen Handling Systems and Equipment*
- NFPA 86   *Ovens and Furnaces: Design, Location and Equipment*
- NFPA 88A   *Parking Structures*
- NFPA 90A   *Installation of Air Conditioning and Ventilating Systems*
- NFPA 91   *Blower and Exhaust Systems for Dust, Stock, and Vapor Removal or Conveying*
- NFPA 92A   *Smoke Control Systems*
- NFPA 99   *Standards for Health Care Facilities*
- NFPA 99B   *Hypobaric Facilities*
- NFPA 101   *Life Safety Code*
- NFPA 101M *Alternative Approaches to Life Safety*
- NFPA 110   *Emergency and Standby Power Systems*
- NFPA 110A *Stored Energy Emergency and Standby Power Systems*
- NFPA 171   *Public Firesafety Symbols*
- NFPA 172   *Symbols for Architectural and Engineering Drawings*
- NFPA 204M *Smoke and Heat Venting*

- NFPA 220   *Standard Types of Building Construction*
- NFPA 221   *Standards for Indoor General Storage*
- NFPA 231   *General Storage*
- NFPA 231C *Rack Storage of Materials*
- NFPA 232   *Protection of Records*
- NFPA 321   *Basic Classification of Flammable and Combustible Liquids*
- NFPA 325M *Fire Hazard Properties of Flammable Liquids, Gases and Volatile Solids: Flash Point Index of Trade Name Liquids*
- NFPA 418   *Roof-top Heliport Construction and Practices*
- NFPA 471   *Responding to Hazardous Materials Incidents*
- NFPA 491M *Manual of Hazardous Chemical Reactions*
- NFPA 493   *Standard for Intrinsically Safe Apparatus and Associated Apparatus for Use in Class I, II, III, Division 1* Hazardous Locations
- NFPA 495   *Explosive Materials Code*
- NFPA 497A *Classification of Class I Hazardous Locations for Electrical Installations in Chemical Plants*
- NFPA 497M *Classification of Gases, Vapors and Dusts for Electrical Equipment in Hazardous (Classified) Locations*
- NFPA 704   *Identification of the Fire Hazards of Materials*
- NFPA 801   *Facilities Handling Radioisotope Materials*
- NFPA 802   *Nuclear Research Reactors*
- NFPA 1141 *Planned Building Groups*

21. **National Institute of Building Sciences** (NIBS), 1201 L Street, NW, Washington, DC 20005; write for a complete list of publications on subjects including

- *Asbestos abatement and management*

- *Earthquake hazards*
- *Lead based paint (LBP)*
- *Metric in construction*
- *Moisture control in buildings*
- *Radon reduction methods*
- *Seismic regulations and considerations*

22. **National Sanitation Foundation** (NSF), P.O. Box 1468, 3475 Plymouth Road, Ann Arbor, MI 48105

   - *Class II (Laminar Flow) Biohazard Cabinetry*, Standard 49-1987

23. **Scientific Apparatus Makers Association** (SAMA), 225 Reinekers Lane, Suite 625, Alexandria, VA 22314

   - *Laboratory Fume Hoods*, Standard LF10-1980.

24. **Sheet Metal and Air Conditioning Contractors' National Association** (SMACNA), P.O. Box 70, Merrifield, VA 22116

   - *Architectural Sheet Metal Manual*
   - *Duct System Calculator*
   - *Energy Conservation Guidelines*
   - *Energy Recovery Equipment and Air-to-Air Systems*
   - *Fibrous Glass Duct Construction Standards*
   - *Fire, Smoke and Radiation Damper Guide for HVAC Systems*
   - *Guide for Steel Stack Design and Construction*
   - *HVAC Air Duct Leakage Manual*
   - *HVAC Duct Construction Standards: Metal and Flexible*
   - *HVAC Systems: Testing, Adjusting and Balancing*
   - *Indoor Air Quality*
   - *National Environmental Balancing Bureau*
   - *Procedural Standards for Certified Testing of Clean Rooms*
   - *Procedural Standards for Measuring Sound and Vibration*
   - *Procedural Standards for Testing, Adjusting and Balancing of Environmental Systems*
   - *Round Industrial Duct Construction Standards*
   - *SMACNA Master Index of Technical Publications*

- *Sound and Vibration in Environmental Systems*
- *Thermoplastic Duct (PVC) Construction Manual*

25. Additional publications relating to laboratory and health care facilities planning and design may be secured by writing to the sources listed below. The reader is also referred to the *Encyclopedia of Associations*, published by the **Gale Research Company** and available at local libraries.

- **Adhesive and Sealant Council** (ASC), 1600 Wilson Boulevard, Suite 910, Arlington, VA 22209

- **Air and Waste Management Association** (AWMA), P.O. Box 2861, Pittsburgh, PA 15230

- **Air Conditioning and Refrigeration Institute** (ARI), 1501 Wilson Boulevard., Suite 600, Arlington, VA 22209

- **Air Diffusion Council** (ADC), 230 North Michigan Avenue, Suite 1200, Chicago, IL 60611

- **American Architectural Manufacturers Association** (AAMA), 2700 River Road, Suite 118, Des Plaines, IL 60016

- **American Association of Cost Engineers** (AACE), P.O. Box 1557, Morgantown, WV 26507-1577

- **American Concrete Institute** (ACI), P.O. Box 19150, Detroit, MI 48219

- **American Concrete Pipe Association** (ACPA), 8320 Old Courthouse Road, Vienna, VA 22180

- **American Consulting Engineers Council** (ACEC), 1015 15th Street, NW, Suite 802, Washington, DC 20005

- **American Council of Independent Laboratories** (ACIL), 1725 K Street, NW, Washington, DC 20006

- **American Federation of State, County and Municipal Employees** (AFSCME), 1625 L Street, NW, Washington, DC 20036

- **American Filtration Society** (AFS), P.O. Box 6269, Kingwood, TX 77325

- **American Institute of Architects** (AIA), 1735 New York Avenue, NW, Washington, DC 20006-5292 (202-626-7300); Contract Documents Division, AIA

Book Store, AIA Library, and Staff Executive for AIA Academy of Architecture for Health/Healthcare Facilities

- **American Institute of Chemical Engineers** (AIChE), 345 East 47th Street, New York, NY 10017

- **American Institute of Plant Engineers** (AIPE), 3975 Erie Avenue, Cincinnati, OH 45208-1998

- **American Institute of Steel Construction** (AISC), 400 North Michigan Avenue, 8th Floor, Chicago, IL 60611

- **American Institute of Timber Construction** (AITC), 333 W. Hampden Ave., Englewood, CO 80110

- **American Iron and Steel Institute** (AISI), 1000 16th Street, NW, Washington, DC 20036

- **American Lumber Standards Committee** (ALSC), P.O. Box 210, Germantown, MD 20874

- **American Plywood Association** (APA), P.O. Box 11700, Tacoma, WA 98411

- **American Society for Pharmacology and Experimental Therapeutics** (ASPET), 9650 Rockville, Pike, Bethesda, MD 20814

- **American Society of Landscape Architects** (ASLA), 4401 Connecticut Avenue, NW, 5th Floor, Washington, DC 20008-2302

- **American Society of Plumbing Engineers** (ASPE), 15233 Ventura Boulevard., Suite 811, Sherman Oaks, CA 91403

- **American Society of Safety Engineers** (ASSE), 1800 East Oakton Street, Des Plains, IL 60018-2187

- **American Water Works Association** (AWWA), 6666 West Quincy Avenue, Denver, CO 80235

- **American Welding Society** (AWS), P.O. Box 351040, 550 Le Jeune Road, NW, Miami, FL 33135

- **Architects' First Source for Products**, 4126 Pleasantdale Road, Suite B222, Atlanta, GA 30340

- **Architectural Precast Association** (APA), 1850 Lee Road, Suite 230, Winter Park, FL 32789

- **Association of Consulting Chemists and Chemical Engineers** (ACCCE), 295 Madison Avenue, New York, NY 10017

- **Association of Energy Engineers** (AEE), 4025 Pleasantdale Road, Suite 420, Atlanta, GA 30340

- **Association of Official Analytical Chemists** (AOAC), 2200 Wilson Boulevard, Suite 400, Arlington, VA 22201-3301

- **Biophysical Society** (BS), 9650 Rockville Pike, Bethesda, MD 20814

- **Builders Hardware Manufacturers Association** (BHMA), 60 East 42nd Street, Room 511, New York, NY 10165

- **Canadian Society for Chemical Engineering** (CSCE), 130 Slater Street, Suite 550, Ottawa, Ontario, Canada KIP6E2

- **Canadian Standards Association** (CSA), 178 Rexdale Boulevard, Rexdale (Toronto), Ontario, Canada, M9W1R3

- **Cast Iron Soil Pipe Institute** (CISPI), 1499 Chain Bridge Road, Suite 203, McLean, VA 22101

- **Cogeneration Institute of the Association of Energy Engineers** (AEE), 4025 Pleasantdale Road, Suite 420, Atlanta, GA 30340

- **Concrete Reinforcing Steel Institute** (CRSI), 933 Plum Grove Road, Schaumburg, IL 60195

- **Cooling Tower Institute** (CTI), 530 Wells Fargo Drive, Suite 113, Houston, TX 77090

- **Energy and Environmental Research Center** (EERC), North 23rd Street, Grand Forks, NC 58202

- **Engineering Foundation** (EF), 345 East 47th Street, New York, NY 10017

- **Federal Specifications**, General Services Administration, 7th and D Streets, SW, Washington, DC 20406; copies may be obtained from regional GSA offices, or purchased from the GSA Specifications Unit–WSIS

- **Flat Glass Marketing Association** (FGMA), White Lakes Professional Building, 3310 Harrison, Topeka, KS 66611

- **Hazardous Materials Control Research Institute** (HMCRI), 9300 Columbia Boulevard, Silver Spring, MD 20910-1702

- **Illuminating Engineering Society of North**

America (IESNA), 120 Wall Street, 17th Floor, New York, NY 10005

- **Institute of Business Designers** (IBD), 341 Merchandise Mart, Chicago, IL 60654-1104
- **Institute of Chemical Engineers** (ICE), 165–171 Railway Terrace, Rugby, Warwickshire, CV21 3 HQ, UK
- **Institute of Electrical and Electronic Engineers, Inc.** (IEEE), 345 East 47th Street, New York, NY 10017
- **Institute of Gas Technology** (IGT), 3424 South State Street, Chicago, IL 60616
- **Institute of Industrial Engineers** (IIE), 25 Technology Park, P.O. Box 6150, Norcross, GA 30091-6150
- **Instrument Society of America** (ISA), 67 Alexander Drive, Research Triangle Park, NC 27709
- **Insulating Glass Certification Council** (IGCC), Route 11, Industrial Park, Cortland, NY 13045
- **International Electrophoresis Society** (IES), c/o Barr Enterprises, P.O. Box 279, Walkersville, MD 21793
- **Manufacturers Standardization Society of the Valves and Fittings Industry** (MSS), 127 Park Street, NE, Vienna, VA 22180
- **Materials Handling Industry of America** (MHIA), 8720 Red Oak Boulevard, Suite 201, Charlotte, NC 28217
- **Materials Research Society** (MRS), 9800 McKnight Road, Pittsburgh, PA 15237
- **Mechanical Contractors Association of America** (MCAA), 5530 Wisconsin Avenue, Suite 750, Chevy Chase, MD 20815
- **Metal Lath/Steel Framing Association** (ML/SFA), 221 North LaSalle Street, Chicago, IL 60601
- **MidAtlantic Environmental Hygiene Resource Center**, University City Science Center, 3624 Market Street, Philadelphia, PA 19104 (215-387-2255)
- **National Association of Architectural Metal Manufacturers** (NAAMM), 221 North LaSalle Street, Chicago, IL 60601

- **National Association of Corrosion Engineers** (NACE), 1440 South Creek, Houston, TX 77084

- **National Electrical Contractors Association** (NECA), 7315 Wisconsin Avenue, Bethesda, MD 20814

- **National Electrical Manufacturers Association** (NEMA), 2101 L Street, NW, Washington, DC 20037

- **National Elevator Industry, Inc.** (NEII), 600 Third Avenue, New York, NY 10016

- **National Paint and Coatings Association** (NPCA), 1500 Rhode Island Avenue, NW, Washington, DC 20005

- **National Petroleum Refiners Association** (NPRA), 1899 I Street, NW, Suite 1000, Washington, DC 20036

- **National Roofing Contractors Association** (NRCA), 8600 Bryn Mawr Avenue, Chicago, IL 60631

- **Plastics Institute of America** (PIA), Stevens Institute of Technology, Castle Point, Hoboken, NJ 07030

- **Plumbing and Drainage Institute** (PDI), c/o Austin O. Roche, Jr., 5342 Boulevard Place, Indianapolis, IN 46208

- **Prestressed Concrete Institute** (PCI), 201 North Wells Street, Chicago, IL 60606

- **Resilient Floor Covering Institute** (RFCI), 966 Hungerford Drive, Suite 12-B, Rockville, MD 20805

- **Royal Flemish Society of Engineers** (RFSE), 2018 Antwerpen, Desguinlei 214, Belgium

- **Royal Society of Chemistry** (RSC), Field End House, Bude Close, Neilsea, Bristol, BS19 2FQ, UK

- **Safety Glazing Certification Council** (SGCC), 1640 West 32 Place, Hialeah, FL 33012

- **Society for Automotive Engineers** (SAE), 400 Commonwealth Drive, Warrendale, PA 15096

- **Society for Biomaterials** (SB), 1371 Glacial Parkway, P.O. Box 717, Algonquin IL 60102-0717

- **Society for Mining, Metallurgy and Exploration** (SMME), 6431 South Hoyt Street, Littleton, CO 80162

- **Society for the Advancement of Material and Process Engineering** (SAMPE), P.O. Box 2459, Covina, CA 91722

- **Society of American Registered Architects** (SARA), 1245 South Highland Avenue, Lombard, IL 60148

- **Society of Chemical Industry** (SCI), 14/15 Belgrave Square, London SW1X 8PS, UK

- **Society of Manufacturing Engineers** (SME), One SME Drive, P. O. Box 930, Dearborn, MI 48121-0931

- **Specifications Consultants in Independent Practice** (SCIP), 1145 Oban, Los Angeles, CA 90065

- **Steel Deck Institute** (SDI), P.O. Box 3812, St. Louis, MO 63122

- **Steel Door Institute** (S.D.I.), c/o A. P. Wherry and Associates., Inc., 712 Lakewood Center, North, Cleveland, OH 44107

- **Steel Joist Institute** (SJI), 1703 Parham Road, Suite 204, Richmond, VA 23229

- **Steel Structures Painting Council** (SSPC), 4400 5th Avenue, Pittsburgh, PA 15213

- **Technical Association of the Pulp and Paper Industry** (TAPPI), P.O. Box 105113, Atlanta, GA 30348

- **Textile Research Institute** (TRI), P.O. Box 625, Princeton, NJ 08542

- **The College of Engineering, University of Wisconsin–Madison, Department of Engineering Professional Development**, 432 North Lake Street, Madison, WI 53706 (608-262-2061)

- **The Construction Specifications Institute** (CSI), 601 Madison Street, Alexandria, VA 22314

- **The Electrochemical Society** (TES), 10 South Main Street, Pennington, NJ 08534-2896

- **Tile Council of America** (TCA), P.O. Box 326, Princeton, NJ 08540

- **Toxcon Engineering Co.**, 3334 Richmond Avenue, No. 200, Houston, TX 77098; Information on incineration systems

- **Underwriters' Laboratories** (UL), 333 Pfingsten Road, Northbrook, IL 60062.

GENERAL AND TECHNICAL PUBLICATIONS

26. Handbooks and references available from miscellaneous publishers and other sources

- *A Guide to Laboratory Water Purification*, Labconco Corporation, 8811 Prospect, Kansas City, MO 64232

- *A Guide to the Measurement of Fan-System Performance in the Field*, Air Movement and Control Association, Inc. (AMCAI), 30 West University Drive, Arlington Heights, IL 60004

- *American Institute of Architects/Association of Collegiate Schools of Architecture* (AIA/ACSA) Council on Architectural Research, 1735 New York Avenue, NW, Washington, DC 20006. Write for listing of publications available from:
  - — The Health Facilities Research Program
  - — The Energy Design Research Program
  - — The Natural Hazards Research Program

- *Asbestos in Buildings*, Safe Buildings Alliance Booklet, 655 15th Street, NW, Suite 1200, Washington, DC 20005

- *Building Construction Cost Data 1994*, Product 60011, R.S. Means Company, Inc., 100 Construction Plaza, P.O. Box 800, Kingston, MA 02364-0800

- *Carcinogenic Chemicals Information and Disposal Guide*, The Lab Store, 3888 North Fratney Street, Milwaukee, WI 53212

- *Chemical Hygiene Plan for OSHA Laboratory Standard*, Genium Publishing Corp., DS1A, 1145 Catalyn Street, Schenectady, NY 12303-1836

- *Chemical Technicians' Ready Reference Handbook*, 3rd ed., G. J. Shugar and J. T. Ballinger, McGraw-Hill Book Co., 1221 Avenue of the Americas, New York, NY 10020

- *Chemistry of Hazardous Materials*, 2nd ed., E. Meyer, Prentice Hall, Inc., Englewood Cliffs, NJ 07632

- *Conference Series on Laboratory Fume Hoods* (1990), controls and biological safety cabinets by advance information and Applied Technologies Company, 3619 C Midway Drive, Suite 262, San Diego, CA 92110

- *Criteria for Effective Eyewashes and Safety Showers*, American Society of Safety Engineers (ASSE), 1800 East Oakton Street, Des Plaines, IL 60618

- *Engineering Design for the Control of Workplace Hazards*, R. A. Wadden and P. A. Scheff, 067664-X, McGraw-Hill Publishing Company, P.O. Box 400, Hightstown, NJ 08520-9403

- *Explosion Protection*; for information contact Fike Metal Products, Division Fike Corporation, 704 South 10th Street, P.O. Box 610, Blue Springs, MO 64015

- *Explosives*, 3rd ed., R. Meyer, VCH, Deerfield Beach, FL 33442

- *Foundations of Laboratory Safety*, South Rayborn, Cat. No. L-15052-00, Cole-Palmer International, 7425 North Oak Avenue, Chicago, IL 60648

- *Guide for Safety in the Chemical Laboratory,* Chemical Manufacturers Association (CMA), 1825 Connecticut Avenue, NW, Washington, DC 20009

- *Handbook of Water Purification*, McGraw Hill Book Co., 1221 Avenue of the Americas, New York, NY 10020

- *Hazardous Laboratory Chemicals Disposal Guide*, M. A. Armour, 1991, ISBN 0-8493-0265-X, The Lab Store, 3888 North Fratney Street, Milwaukee, WI 53212

- *HAZWOPER Compliance Manual* (OSHA's Hazardous Waste Operations and Emergency Response Standard), J. J. Keller & Associates, Inc., Specialists in OSHA Plant Safety Compliance, 3003 West Breezewood Lane, P.O. Box 368, Neenah, WI 54957-0368

- *How to Select the Right Fume Hood*, Labconco Corporation, 8811 Prospect, Kansas City, MO 64132

- *Infectious and Medical Waste Management*, Reinhardt and Gordon, 1991, ISBN 0-8737-158-0, The Lab Store, 3888 North Fratney Street, Milwaukee, WI 53212

- *Laboratory Fume Hood Standards*, Environmental Protection Agency, Contract 68-01-4661, for sale by the Superintendent of Documents, U.S. Government Printing Office, Washington, DC 20402

- *Laboratory Health and Safety Measures*, 2nd ed., S.

B. Pal, Ed., Kluwer Academic Publishers, P.O. Box 358, Accord Station, Hingham, MA 02018-0358

- *Laboratory Safety, Principals and Practice*, American Society for Microbiology, 1913 I Street, NW, Washington, DC 20006

- *Material Safety Data Sheet Collection*, Genium Publishing Corp., DS1A, 1145 Catalyn Street, Schenectady, NY 12303-1836

- *Methods and Techniques for Reducing Radon Levels Within New Buildings*, National Institute of Building Sciences (NIBS), 1201 L Street, NW, Suite 400, Washington, DC 20005

- *Odor Thresholds*, American Industrial Hygienists Association (AIHA), 475 Wolf Lodges Parkway, Akron, OH 44311

- *Prudent Practices for Handling Hazardous Chemicals in the Laboratory*, National Academy Press, 2101 Constitution Avenue, NW, Washington, DC 20418

- *Reactive Chemical Hazards*, 4th ed., L. Bretherick, Butterworth, 80 Montvale Avenue, Stoneham, MA 02180

- *Right-to-Know Pocket Guide for Laboratory Employees*, Genium Publishing Corp., Room 724, 1145 Catalyn Street, Schenectady, NY 12303-1836

- *The Pesticide Manual: A World Compendium*, 9th Ed., C. R. Worthing and R. J. Hance, BCPC Publications, Worchestershire, England

- *Ventilation for Containment Control*, 2nd ed., H. J. McDermott, Butterworth, 80 Montvale Avenue, Stoneham, MA 02180

- *Waste Management Guide: Laws, Issues and Solutions*, D. H. Jessup, Order Code 0713, BNA Books Distribution Center, 300 Raritan Center Parkway, P.O. Box 7816, Edison, NJ 08818-7816 (1-800-372-1033)

- *What Every Engineer Should Know About Lasers*, D. Winburn, Marcel Dekker, New York, 1987, ISBN 0-8247-7748-4

27. Handbooks and references available from **Academic Press**, A Division of Harcourt Brace & Company, Order

Fulfillment Department, 6277 Sea Harbor Drive, Orlando, FL 32821-9816 (1-800-321-5068)

- *Biotechnology: A Laboratory Course*, J. M. Becker and G. A. Caldwell, Order No. 084560-1

- *Encyclopedia of Microbiology*, J. Lederberg, Ed.-in-Chief, Order No. 226890-3

- *Immunochemical Techniques Laboratory Manual*, J. Goers, Order No. 287048-4

- *Maintenance of Microorganisms and Cultured Cells: A Manual of Laboratory Methods*, 2nd ed., B. E. Kirsop and A. Doyle, Order No. 410351-0

- *Molecular Biology and Pathology: A Guidebook for Quality Control*, D. H. Farkas, Ed., Order No. 249100-9

- *Recombinant DNA Laboratory Manual, Rev. ed.*, J. W. Zyskind and S. I. Bernstein, Order No. 784401-5

- *RNA Methodologies, A Laboratory Guide for Isolation and Characterization, R. E. Farrell, Jr., Order No. 249700-7*

- *Virology, A Laboratory Manual*, F. G. Burleson, T. M. Chambers and D. L. Wiedbrauk, Order No. 144730-8

28. Handbooks and references available from **Building Operating Management Press**, 2100 West Florist Avenue, Milwaukee, WI 53209 (414-228-7701 x460)

- *Americans with Disabilities Act (ADA) Facilities Compliance Workbook*, Evan Terry Associates, PC, Order No. BWY39

- *Building Air Quality: A Guide for Building Owners and Facility Managers*, published by the Environmental Protection Agency (EPA) and the National Institute for Occupational Health and Safety (NIOSH), Order No. BGV58

- *ComputerAided Facility Management*, E. Teicholz, Order No. BMH47

- *Energy Management Handbook*, W. C. Turner, Order No. BAE57

- *Facilities Evaluation Manual*, K. L. Petrocelly, Order No. BAE32

- *Facilities Maintenance Management*, G. H. Magee, Order No. BRM63

- *Handbook of HVAC Design*, N. R. Grimm and R. C. Rosaler, Order No. BMH06

- *HVAC Controls and Systems*, J. I. Levenhagen and D. H. Spethmann, Order No. BHM64

- *Indoor Air Quality Design Handbook*, M. Meckler, Order No. BAE44

- *Lighting Efficiency Applications*, A. Thumann, CEM, Order No. BAE08

- *Managing Energy Resources in Times of Dynamic Change*, Wm. H. Mashburn, Order No. BAE56

- *Managing Indoor Air Quality*, S. J. Hansen, Order No. BAE10

- *Office Planning and Design Reference*, J. Rappoport, R. Cushman, and K. Daroff, Eds., Order No. BWY49

- *Optimizing HVAC Systems*, A. Thumann, Order No. BAE34

- *Plant Engineers' Handbook of Formulas, Charts and Tables*, D. W. Moffat, Order No. BPH62

- *Strategic Corporate Facilities Management*, S. Binder, Order No. BMH61

- *The Facilities Management Handbook*, D. G. Cotts and M. Lee, Order No. BM59

- *The Facilities Manager's Reference*, H. H. Kaiser, Order No. BRM28

- *The New ADA: Compliance and Costs,* D. S. Kearney, Order No. BRM60

29. Handbooks and references available from **Lab Safety Supply Inc.**, Mail Order Department, P.O. Box 1368, Janesville, WI 53547-1368

   - *Building Air Quality*, by EPA and NIOSH, Order No. WB-22466

   - *Chemical Guide to the OSHA Haz-Com Standard*, 7th ed., K. B. Clancsky, Ed., 1992, Order No. WB-6059

- *Environmental Statutes*, Order No. WB-10355
- *Prudent Laboratory Practices Series*
  - *Disposal of Chemicals from Laboratories*, Order No. WB-2413-2
  - *Handling Hazardous Chemicals in Laboratories*, Order No. WB-2413
  - *Biosafety in the Laboratory*, Order No. WB-12413
- *RCRA Hazardous Wastes Handbook*, Crowell and Moring, Order No. WB-5011
- *SARA Title III: A Guide to Emergency Preparedness and Community RTK*, C. Harris and D. A. Berger, Order No. WB-10443

30. Handbooks and references available from **John Wiley & Sons, Inc.**, P.O. Box 6793, Department 063, Somerset, NJ 08875-9977

- *An Introduction to Laboratory Automation*, Cerda and Ramis
- *Analytical Methods in Toxicology*, H. M. Stahr, 1-85136-1
- *Beyond the Crime Lab: The New Science of Investigation*, J. Zonderman
- *Clean Air Act 1990 Amendments: Law and Practice*, J. M. Stensvaag, 1991, 1-54705-0
- *Cleanroom Design*, W. Whyte, Ed, 1-92814-3
- *Design for Research*, Goodman and Baybrook
- *Destruction of Hazardous Chemicals in the Laboratory*, G. Lunn and E. B. Sansone, 1-51063-7
- *Electronic Light Microscopy*, D. M. Shotton, 1993, 1-56077-4
- *Grounding and Shielding in Facilities*, J. R. Morrison and R. J. Lewis, ISBN 0-471-83807-1
- *Guidelines for Laboratory Design, Health and Safety Considerations*, L. J. DiBerardinis, J. S. Baum, M. W. First, G. T. Gatwood, E. F. Groden, and A. K. Seth, 1-89134-7

- *Handbook of Human Factors*, G. Salvendy, Ed., 1-88015-9
- *Handbook of Occupational Safety and Health*, L. Slote, Ed., 1-81029-0
- *Handling Laboratory Microorganisms*, C. Penn, 1991, 1-93252-3
- *Hazardous Waste Incineration Calculations: Problems and Software*, J. P. Reynolds, R. R. Dupont, and L. Theodore, 1-50782-2
- *Improving Safety in the Chemical Laboratory: A Practical Guide*, 2nd ed., 1991, J. A. Young, Ed., 1-53036-0
- *Incompatible Chemicals in the Storeroom: Identification and Segregation*, L. Bretherick
- *Indoor Air Pollution: Characterization, Prediction and Control*, Wadden and Scheff
- *Industrial Ventilation: Engineering Principals*, R. J. Heinsohn, 1991, 1-63703-3
- *Introduction to Hazardous Waste Incineration*, Theodore and Reynolds
- *Kirk-Othmer, Encyclopedia of Chemical Technology*, Vols. 1–27, H. F. Mark et al., Eds., 0-47152704-1
- *Laboratory Architectural Design*, S. Baybrook, Ed.
- *Laboratory Fume Hoods: A Users' Manual*, G. T. Saunders, 1993, 0471-56935-6
- *Laboratory Health and Safety Handbook: A Guide for the Preparation of a Chemical Hygiene Plan*, R. S. Stricoff and D. B. Walters, 1990, 1-61756-3
- *Leadership in Safety Management*, J. R. Thomen, 1-53326-2
- *Measuring Indoor Air Quality*, J. E. Yocom and S. M. McCarthy, 1991, 1-90728-6
- *Occupational Biomechanics*, 2nd ed., D. B. Chaffin and G. B. J. Anderson, 0-471-60134-9
- *Patty's Industrial Hygiene and Toxicology*, 4th ed., G. D. Clayton and F. E. Clayton, Part A (1-50197-2), Part B (1-50196-4)
- *Radiation Detection and Measurement*, R. G. F. Knoll, 0471-81504-7
- *Radioactive Waste Management*, Berlin and Stanton

- *Radioisotope Laboratory Techniques*, Fairies and Parks

- *Radiology Departments: Planning, Operation and Management*, H. W. Fisher, Edward Brothers, Inc., Ann Arbor, MI

- *Radon and Its Decay Products in Indoor Air*, W. W. Nazaroff and A. V. Nero, Jr., Eds., 1-62810-7

- *Safe Handling of Chemicals in Industry*, Carson and Mumford

- *Safe Storage of Laboratory Chemicals*, 2nd ed., D. A. Pipitone, Ed., 1991, 1-51581-7

- *The Risk Assessment of Environmental Hazards: A Textbook of Case Studies*, D. J. Paustenbach, Ed., 1-84998-7

- *Toxicology Laboratory Design and Management for the 80's and Beyond*, A. S. Tegeris, Ed.

31. Handbooks and references available from **Wiley Law Publications**, A Division of John Wiley & Sons, Inc., 7222 Commerce Center Drive, Suite 240, Colorado Springs, CO 80919-9810

- *Environmental Liability Transaction Guide: Forms and Checklists*, J. A. Tarantino, 1-54268-7

- *Hazardous Substances in Buildings: Liability Litigation, and Abatement*, C. J. Berger, 1-52777-7

GOVERNMENT AGENCY PUBLICATIONS

32. *Clinical Laboratory Improvement Amendments* (CLIA '88), Public Law 100-578- 31 Oct. 88, Public Health Services (PHS), Health Care Financing Administration (HCFA), for sale by the Superintendent of Documents, U.S. Government Printing Office, Washington, DC 20402

33. *Code of Federal Regulations* (CFR), for sale by the Superintendent of Documents, U.S. Government Printing Office, Washington, DC 20402

- *Americans with Disabilities Act* (ADA), P. L. 101-336, explained in U.S. House of Representatives Report HR 2273; and U.S. Senate Report 101-116

    — Additional ADA Information Sources (Government)

— ADA *Accessibiliy Guidelines* (ADA-AG) lists many technical requirements of the ADA; call the Architectural and Transportation Barriers Compliance Board (ATBCB) at 1-800- USA-ABLE for a copy.

— Equal Employment Opportunity Commission (EEOC), Office of the Legal Counsel, 1801 L Street, NW, Washington, DC 20507; call 1-800-669-EEOC for information about "The Technical Assistance Manual for Compliance to the ADA, Title 1, Employment"; for legal questions about Title 1, call 202-663-4691 to reach the EEOC's "Attorney of the Day."

— President's Committee on the Employment of People with Disabilities, 1111 20th Street, NW, Suite 636, Washington, DC 20036; call 202-653-5044 for information about the ADA.

— Department of Justice (DOJ), Washington, DC 20530, Office of the Deputy Chief responsible for the enforcement of the public accommodations section of the ADA; call 202-307-2227 for information about the ADA.

— Additional ADA Information Sources (Private Business)

— *BOMA International's ADA Compliance Guidebook: A Checklist for Your Building*, The American Institute of Architects (AIA), 1735 New York Avenue, NW, Washington, DC 20006-5292; 1-800-365-2724.

— National Federation of Independent Business (NFIB), 600 Maryland Avenue, SW, Suite 700, Washington, DC 20024; call 202-554-9000 for information about the ADA.

— Additional ADA Information Sources (Disability Groups)

— Center for Independent Living, 2539 Telegraph Avenue, Berkeley CA 94704; call 415-841-4776 for information about workshops on the ADA.

— Disability Rights Education and Defense Fund, Inc. (DREDF), 2212 Sixth Street, Berkeley,

CA 94710; call 415-644-2555 or 415-644-2629 (Telecommunications Device for the Deaf number) for information about the ADA. The DREDF has an office also at 1616 P Street, NW, Washington, DC 20036; call 202-328-5185. The DREDF sells *The Layperson's Guide to the ADA*, for $75.

— Legi-Slate Publications, P.O. Box 96006, Washington, DC 20090-6006; customer service and information 1-800-274-2360; publishers of *ADA News & Regulations*, extensive information monitored from the *Federal Register* covering all four regulatory agencies involved with developing and interpreting ADA regulations.

- Atomic Energy Commission, 10 CFR 20

- *Clean Rooms*, FED-STD-209b, General Services Administration (GSA), 18th and F Streets, Room 3044, NW, Washington, DC 20405

- *Radiation Control for Health and Safety Act* (42 USC 263b et seq.)

- *Title 40*; Parts 260, 261, 262, 263, 264, 265, 270, 300

- *Uniform Federal Accessibility Standards* (UFAS FED-STD-795-1988), first published in the *Federal Register*, August 7, 1984, (49 FR 31528)

34. **General Services Administration** (GSA), Specifications Section, Room 6039, 7th and D Streets, NW, Washington, DC 20407

   - Write for listing of *Federal Space Standards and Specifications* available for numerous building types.

35. **National Bureau of Standards** (NBS), Institute for Basic Standards, Washington, DC 20234

   - *Measurements for the Safe Use of Radiation*, for sale by the Superintendent of Documents, SD Cat. No. C13.10:456 Stock No. 003-003-01862-9, U.S. Government Printing Office, Washington, DC 20402

36. **National Council on Radiation Protection and Measurements** (NCRP), 7910 Woodmount Avenue, Suite 1016, Bethesda, MD 20814

   - NCRP-RP-8   *Control and Removal of Radioactive Contamination in Laboratories*

- NCRP-RP-9   *Recommendations for Waste Disposal of Phosphorus-32 and Iodine-131 for Medical Users*

- NCRP-RP-12   *Recommendations for Disposal of Carbon-14 Wastes*

- NCRP-RP-22   *Maximum Permissible Body Burdens and Maximum Permissible Concentrations of Radionuclides in Air and Water For Occupational Exposure*

- NCRP-RP-30   *Safe Handling of Radioactive Materials*

- NCRP-RP-32   *Radiation Protection in Educational Institutions*

- NCRP-RP-33   *Medical X-Ray and Gamma Ray Protection for Energies up to 10 MeV: Equipment Design and Use*

- NCRP-RP-35   *Dental X-Ray Protection*

- NCRP-RP-36   *Radiation Protection in Veterinary Medicine*

- NCRP-RP-37   *Precautions in the Management of Patients Who Have Received Therapeutic Amounts of Radionuclides*

- NCRP-RP-38   *Protection Against Neutron Radiation*

- NCRP-RP-39   *Basic Radiation Protection*

- NCRP-RP-48   *Radiation Protection for Medical and Allied Health Personnel*

- NCRP-RP-49   *Structural Shielding Design and Evaluation for Medical Use of X-Rays and Gamma Rays of Energies up to 10 MeV*

- NCRP-RP-51   *Radiation Protection Design Guidelines for 0.1-100 Particle Accelerator Facilities*

- NCRP-RP-53   *Review of NCRP Radiation Dose Limit for Embryo and Fetus in Occupationally Exposed Women*

- NCRP-RP-58   *A Handbook of Radioactivity Measurements Procedures*

- NCRP-RP-59   *Operational Radiation Safety Programs*

- NCRP-RP-65   *Management of Persons Accidentally Contaminated with Radionuclides*

- NCRP-RP-67   *Radiofrequency Electromagnetic Fields: Properties, Quantities and Units, Biophysical Interaction, and Measurements*

- NCRP-RP-71   *Operational Radiation Safety-Training*

- NCRP-RP-72   *Radiation Protection and Measurement for Low Voltage Neutron Generators*

- NCRP-RP-73   *Protection in Nuclear Medicine and Ultrasound Diagnostic Procedures in Children*

- NCRP-RP-74   *Biological Effects of Ultrasound: Mechanisms and Clinical Applications*

- NCRP-RP-78   *Evaluation of Occupational and Environmental Exposures to Radon and Radon Daughters in the U.S.*

37. National Institute for Occupational Safety and Health (NIOSH), 4676 Columbia Parkway, Cincinnati, OH 45226

- *Industrial Noise Control Manual*, for sale by Superintendent of Documents, U.S. Government Printing Office, USGPO No. 1979-657-061/5827, Washington, DC 20402

- *Industrial Ventilation Guidelines*, for sale by Superintendent of Documents, U.S. Government Printing Office, USGPO No. 1976-657/5543, Washington, DC 20402

- *Pocket Guide to Chemical Hazards*, DLAH 4145.6, for sale by Superintendent of Documents, U.S. Government Printing Office, Washington, DC 20402

38. National Institutes of Health (NIH), 9000 Rockville Pike, Bethesda, MD 20205, for sale by the Superintendent of Documents, U.S. Government Printing Office, Washington, DC 20402

- *Guidelines for Research Involving Recombinant DNA Molecules*, Federal Register 49(227): 46266-46291 (App. G: Physical Containment; App. GII-A: BSL-1; App. G-II-B: BSL-2; App. G-II-C: BSL-3: App. G-II-D: BSL-4; App. I: Biological Containment; App. J: Federal Interagency Advisory Committee on Recombinant DNA Research; App. K: Physical Containment for Large Scale Uses of Organisms with Recombinant DNA Molecule; App. K-1: Selection of Physical Containment Levels)

- *Laboratory Safety Monograph: A Supplement to the NIH Guidelines for Research Involving Recombinant DNA*

- NIH 75-900   *Safety Standards for Research Involving Oncogenic Viruses*, Office of Research Safety

- NIH 76-891   *Design Criteria for Viral Oncology Research Facilities*

- NIH 76-900   *Safety Standards for Research Involving Chemical Carcinogens*, Office of Research Safety

- NIH 81-2305   *Design of Biomedical Research Facilities*

- NIH 81-2385   *Guidelines for the Laboratory Use of Chemical Carcinogens*

- NIH-83-2624   *Chemical Emergencies in Laboratories: Planning and Response*

- NIH 88-8395   *Biosafety in Microbiological and Biomedical Laboratories* (GPO #17-40-508-3)

- NIH 30Dec91   *Laboratory Hood Specifications for the National Institutes of Health, Facilities Engineering Branch, Division of Engineering Services, National Institutes of Health, Patricio Ochoa, Sr. Mechanical Engineer, FEB/DES, 9000 Rockville Pike, Bethesda, MD 20205*

- *Proceedings of the National Cancer Institute Symposium on the Design of Biomedical Research Facilities*, NCI, 5333 Westbard Avenue, Bethesda, MD 20205

39. **Oak Ridge National Laboratory** (ORNL), Oak Ridge, TN 01379

   - *Minimum Acceptable Face Velocities of Laboratory Fume Hoods and Guidelines for Their Classification*

40. **Occupational Safety and Health Administration** (OSHA), Publications Office, 200 Constitution Avenue, NW, Washington, DC 20210

   - *Instruction CPL 2-2.38A*, Appendix A

   - OSHA Field Operations Manual: *Inspection Guide*

   - OSHA Technical Manual: *Inspection Preparation Guide*

   - OSHA 51   *Proposed Standards for Laboratories Using Toxic Substances*, FR 26660

   - OSHA 2206   *General Industry, Safety and Health Regulations*, 29-CFR-1910

   - OSHA 3084   *Chemical Hazard Communication*

   - OSHA 3088   *How to Prepare for Workplace Emergencies*

   - OSHA 2236   *Materials Handling and Storage*

   - OSHA 3077   *Personal Protective Equipment*

   - OSHA 3079   *Respiratory Protection*

   - *Proposed Rules* (rules are revised annually)
     - 29-CFR-1900-1910.999
       General Industry Standards: OSHA Subparts A-T
     - 29-CFR-1900-1000-end
       General Industry Standards: OSHA Subparts Z (Z Tables), Haz-Com
     - 29-CFR-1910.35-37
       Standards for Means of Egress
     - 29-CFR-1910.101
       Flammables Cabinet Specifications Based on Reagent Classifications, Carcinogenic Chemicals, Volumes to Be Stored, Chemical Compatibility, etc.

— 29-CFR-1910.120
Hazardous Waste Operations and Emergency
Response: HAZWOPER

— 29-CFR-1910.130
Bloodborne Pathogen Standard

— 29-CFR-1910.133
Standards for Emergency Shower and Eye Wash
Stations

— 29-CFR-1910.146
Permit Required for Confined Spaces

— 29-CFR-1910.155-165
Standards for Fire Suppression Systems

— 29-CFR-1910.1030
Regulated Medical Waste

— 29-CFR-1910.1200
Hard Communication Standard

— 29-CFR-1910.1450
Occupational Exposures to Hazardous
Chemicals in the Laboratory Including Fume
Hood Controls

— 29-CFR-1910.1926
Construction

41. **U.S. Department of Agriculture** (USDA), Animal and
Plant Health Inspection Service—Veterinary Services
(APHIS-VS), Office of the Deputy Administrator, 6505
Belcrest Road, Federal Building, Room 756, Hyattsville,
MD 20782

■ *Animal Welfare Standards*, CFR-Title 9, Subchapter
A, Parts 1, 2, and 3

■ *Laboratory Animal Welfare Act* (PL 89-544, PL 91-
579, PL 94-279, PL 99-198)

■ *The Good Laboratory Practices Act*, Federal Register
43FR59986-60025.

42. **U.S. Department of Health, Education and Wel-
fare/Public Health Service** (DHEW/PHS), 330 In-
dependence Avenue, SW, Washington, DC 20201

■ *Classification of Etiological Agents on the Basis of
Hazard*, 4th ed.

■ *Lab Safety at the Center for Disease Control*, DHEW
Publ. (CDC) 75-8118.

43. U.S. Department of Transportation (DOT), 400 7th Street, SW, Washington, DC 20590

- *Emergency Response Guidebook*, Publ. DOT-P-5800-4
- *Hazardous Materials Regulations*, HM-181, Parts 100–177, 178–199
- *Transportation*, Parts 100-177, Sections 173.115, 173.150

44. U.S. Environmental Protection Agency (EPA), 401 M Street, SW, Washington, DC 20460

- *Air Programs*, Parts 52, 53–60, 61–80, 81–85, 86–99
- *Air Regulations*, Parts 1–51
- *Laboratory Fume Hood Standards*, R. Chamberlin, Report 68-01-4661, 1978
- *National Emission Standards for Hazardous Air Pollutants*
- RCRA, Hazardous Waste, Parts 260–299
- RCRA, Radiation, Solid Waste, Parts 190–259
- *Water Effluent Guidelines and Standards*, Parts 400–425, 425–699
- *Water Programs*, Parts 100–149

45. U.S. Food and Drug Administration (FDA), 5600 Fishers Lane, Rockville, MD 20857

- *Title 21, Code of Federal Regulations*
  - Part 25, *Environmental Impact*
  - Part 58, *Good Lab Practice*
  - Part 211, *Good Manufacturing Practice for Finished Pharmaceuticals*
  - Part 312, *New Drugs for Investigation*
  - Part 314, *New Drug Applications*
  - Part 330, *Over the Counter Drugs*
  - Part 511.1, *Investigational New Animal Drugs*
  - Part 558.4, *Medicated Feeds for Animal*
  - Part 570, *Food Additives* (including Parts 571, 573)
  - Part 600, *Biological Products: General*
  - Part 606, *Good Manufacturing Practice Regulations for Blood and Blood Components*

— Part 820, *Good Manufacturing Practice for Medical Devices: General* (including Parts 860, 862 through 890)

46. U.S. Nuclear Regulatory Commission (NRC), Medical, Academic, and Commercial Use Safety Branch, WF1, Mail Stop 6H06, Washington, DC 20555

- Title 10 CFR Parts 20, 34, 71, and 150

- Write for additional data, publications, etc., on planning, design, and management of facilities using radioactive materials

SPECIAL FACILITIES PUBLICATIONS

47. Publications relating to the use and care of animals in the laboratory and animal facilities

- *Animal Welfare Information Center of the National Agricuitural Library*, USDA, 10301 Baltimore Boulevard, Beltsville, MD 20705; write for *Quick Bibliography Series, Laboratory Animal Facilities and Management*, Jan. 1979–Mar. 1989, NAL-BIBL. QB 89-66

- *Animals and Animal Products*, Title 9, Subchapter A, Animal Welfare, Parts 1, 2, and 3, for sale by the Superintendent of Documents, U.S. Government Printing Office, Washington, DC 20402

- *Beyond the Laboratory Door* and *Comfortable Quarters for Laboratory Animals*, Animal Welfare Institute (AWI), P.O. Box 3650, Washington, DC 20007

- *Certfication Requirements for Animal Technologists and Technicians*, American Association for Laboratory Animal Science (AALAS), 70 Timbercreek Drive, Suite 5, Cordova, TN 38018

- *Design and Management of Animal Facilities*, Hessler and Moreland, in *Laboratory Animal Medicine*, J. G. Fox, Ed., Academic Press, Orlando, FL 62328

- *Design of Laboratory Animal Homes*, R. C. Simmonds, Aeromedical Review, Vol. 2, USAF School of Aerospace Medicine, Brooks AFB, San Antonio, TX 35782

- *Endangered Species Act, CFR-Title-50, Chapter 1, Subchapter B, Part 17*, Office of Endangered Species,

U.S. Department of the Interior, Fish and Wildlife Service, Washington, DC 20240

■ *Good Laboratory Practice Regulations* (GLP)

— Food and Drug Administration (FDA), Bioresearch Program Office, Parklawn Building, Room 12A-55, HFC-230, 5600 Fishers Lane, Rockville, MD 20857

— Environmental Protection Agency (EPA), Office of Pesticides and Toxic Substances, Laboratory Data Integrity Programs, 401 M Street, NW, Washington, DC 20460

■ *Guide for the Care and Use of Agriculture Animals in Agricultural Research and Teaching* (Agri-Guide), American Dairy Science Association, 309 West Clark Street, Champaign, IL 61820

■ *Guide for the Care and Use of Laboratory Animals*, NIH Publication NIH-86-23, for sale by the Superintendent of Documents, U.S. Government Printing Office, Washington, DC 20402; contains selected bibliography on publications related to animal care and facilities

■ *Guide to Techniques in Mouse Development*, P. M. Wassarman and M. L. DePamphilis, Eds.; available from Academic Press, Order No. 182126-9, A Division of Harcourt Brace & Company, Order Fulfillment Department, 6277 Sea Harbor Drive, Orlando, FL 32821-9816 (1-800-321-5068)

■ *Guidelines for Lay Members of Animal Care Committees*, Canadian Federation of Humane Societies, 30 Concourse Gate, Suite 102, Nepean, Ontario, Canada K2E 7V7

■ *Institutional Administrator's Manual for Laboratory Animal Care and Use*, NIH Publication NIH-88-2959, for sale by the Superintendent of Documents, U.S. Government Printing Office, Washington, DC 20402

■ *Laboratory Animal Housing*, National Academy of Sciences (Institute of Laboratory Animal Resources—Committee on Laboratory Animal Housing), 2101 Constitution Ave., NW, Washington, DC 20418

■ *Principles for the Utilization and Care of Vertebrate Animals Used in Testing, Research and Education,*

Office for Protection from Research Risks (OPRR), National Institutes of Health (NIH), Building 31, Room 5B59, 9000 Rockville Pike, Bethesda, MD 20892

- *Public Health Service Policy on Humane Care and Use of Laboratory Animals*, rev. September 1986, Office for the Protection from Research Risks (OPRR), National Institutes of Health (NIH), 9000 Rockville Pike, Building 31, Room 4B09, Bethesda, MD 20892

- *Welfare and Housing of Laboratory Primates*, D. Harris, Animal Welfare Research Report 1, Universities Federation for Animal Welfare (UFAW), 8 Hamilton Close, South Mimms Potters Bar, Hertfordshire, EN63QD, England

48. Publications available from the **Scientists Center for Animal Welfare** (SCAW), 4805 St. Elmo Avenue, Bethesda, MD 20814

- *Canine Research Environment*

- *Effective Animal Care and Use Committees*, Special Issue, January 1987

- *Science and Animals: Addressing Contemporary Issues*, Conference of the SCAW-22/25 June 1988

- *Well-Being of Non-human Primates in Research*

49. Publications available from **CRC Press, Inc.**, 2000 Corporate Boulevard, NW, Boca Raton, FL 33431

- *Laboratory Animal Science*, Vol. I, Melby and Altman, Eds.

- *Necropsy Guide: Rodents and the Rabbit*, Donald B. Feldman, Cat. No. 4934BE

- *The Experimental Animal in Biomedical Research*, Vol. I: *A Survey of Scientific and Ethical Issues for Investigators*, Bernard E. Rollin, Cat. No. 4981BE

- *The Nude Mouse in Oncology Research*, Epie Boven

50. Additional publications and associations relating to the use and care of animals in the laboratory, and animal facilities may be secured by writing to:

- **American Association for Accreditation of Laboratory Animal Care** (AAALAC), 9650 Rockville Pike, Bethesda, MD 20814

- **American Association for Laboratory Animal**

Science (AALAS), 210 North Hammes Avenue, Suite 205, Joliet, IL 60435

- **American College of Laboratory Animal Medicine** (ACLAM), Department of Comparative Medicine, The Milton S. Hershey Medical Center, The Pennsylvania State University, P.O. Box 850, Hershey, PA 17033

- **American Society of Laboratory Animal Practitioners** (ASLAP), Lab Animal Resource Center, Washington State University, Pullman, WA99164-1165

- **American Veterinary Medical Association** (AVMA), 1023 15th Street, NW, Suite 300, Washington, DC 20005

- **Animal Industry Foundation** (AIF), 1701 Fort Myer Drive, Suite 1200, Arlington, VA 22209

- **Animal Welfare Information Center** (AWIC), National Agricultural Library, Room 301, 3rd Floor Library, Beltsville, MD 20705

- **Applied Research Ethics National Association** (ARENA), 132 Boylston Street, Boston, MA 02116

- **Institute of Laboratory Animal Resources** (ILAR), National Academy of Sciences, 2101 Constitution Avenue, NW, Washington, DC 20418

- **National Agricultural Library** (NAL), Jean Larson, Beltsville MD, 20705

- **National Association for Biomedical Research** (Foundation for Biomedical Research), 818 Connecticut Avenue, NW, Washington, DC 20006

- **National Library of Medicine** (NLM), Dr. Fritz Gluckstein, 8600 Rockville Pike, Bethesda, MD 20894

- *Scientists Center for Animal Welfare* (SCAW), 4805 St. Elmo Avenue, Bethesda, MD 20814

GLOSSARY OF TERMS

The following terms and phrases have been excerpted from:

- The Lab Safety Supply, Inc.
  1994 General Catalog,
  Winter/Spring Edition
  Personal Environmental Safety
  P.O. Box 1368
  Janesville, WI 53547-1368

- The American Institute of Architects
  Glossary of Construction Industry
  Terms with Particular Emphasis on
  Use in the AIA Documents
  1735 New York Avenue, NW
  Washington, DC 20006

Although many of the terms and phrases are not included in the text of this book, they relate to the many and various phases involved during the process of planning, design, and construction of laboratory and other facilities.

Abrasive Blasting: The process of cleaning surfaces using materials such as sand, alumina, or steel grit mixed in a stream of high-pressure air.

Absolute Zero: (−458.8°F or −273.1°C): Temperature at which all molecular activity is presumed to cease.

Absorption: The process by which a liquid penetrates the solid structure of the absorbent's fibers or particles, which then swell in size to accommodate the liquid.

ACGIH: American Conference of Governmental Industrial Hygienists; an organization that annually determines standards of exposure to toxic and otherwise harmful materials in the workroom air, commonly known as TLV.

Acoustics: The science of sound. The study of building materials for sound transmission properties.

Action Level: The exposure level (concentration of the material in the air) at which cer-

tain OSHA regulations to protect employees take effect (CFR 1910.1-1047) (e.g., workplace air analysis, employee training, medical monitoring, and record keeping). Exposure at or above the action level is termed occupational exposure.

ADA: Americans with Disabilities Act: On January 26, 1992, the world's first civil rights law preventing discrimination against people with disabilities was enacted. This act can be found in the code of federal regulations (36 CFR Part 1191).

Addition: (1, to the contract sum) Amount added to the contract sum by change order. (2, to a structure) A construction project physically connected to an existing structure, as distinct from alterations within an existing structure. (3, to contract time) Extension of the contract time authorized by a change order. (4, to the Work) Increase to the scope of work included in the contract authorized by a change order.

Additional Services (of the Architect): Professional services which may, if authorized or confirmed in writing by the owner, be rendered by the architect in addition to the basic services or designated services identified in the owner–architect agreement.

Adsorption: The process by which a liquid adheres to the surface of the adsorbent material but does not penetrate the fibers or particles themselves.

Advertisement for Bids. Published public notice soliciting bids for a construction project or designated portion, included as part of the bidding documents. Most frequently used to conform to legal requirements pertaining to projects to be constructed under public authority, and usually published in newspapers of general circulation in those political subdivision from which the public funds are derived.

Aerosols: Liquid droplets or solid particles dispersed in air that are of fine enough particle size (0.1 to 100 micrometers) to remain so dispersed for a period of time.

AHERA: Asbestos Hazard Emergency Response Act (1986); federal law requiring local education agencies (LEAs) to identify asbestos hazards and develop abatement plans.

AIHA: American Industrial Hygiene Association.

Aliphatic: Pertaining to an open-chain carbon compound. Usually applied to petroleum products derived from a paraffin base and having a straight or branched chain and saturated or unsaturated molecular structure. Substances such as methane and ethane are typical aliphatic hydrocarbons.

Alpha Particle: A small electrically charged particle of very high velocity thrown off by many radioactive materials. It is made up of two neutrons and two protons and has a positive electrical charge.

Alterations: (1) A construction project (or portion of a project) comprising revisions within or to prescribed elements of an existing structure, as distinct from additions to an existing structure. (2) Remodeling. *See also* Addition.

Alternate Bid: Amount stated in the bid to be added to or deducted from the amount of the base bid if the corresponding change in the Work, as described in the bidding documents, is accepted.

Anemometer: A device that measures air velocity. Common types include the rotating vane, the swinging vane, and the hot-wire anemometer.

ANSI: American National Standards Institute; a private organization that provides the mechanism for creating voluntary standards through consensus. Over 8000 standards are approved and used widely by industry and commerce.

Application for Payment: Contractor's certified request for payment of amount due for completed portions of the Work and, if the contract so provides, for materials or equipment delivered and suitably stored pending their incorporation into the Work.

Approved Equal: Material, equipment, or method approved by the architect for use in the Work as being acceptable as an equivalent in essential attributes to the material, equipment or method specified in the contract documents.

APR: Air-purifying respirator.

Arbitration: Method of settling claims or disputes, between parties to a contract, rather than by litigation, under which an arbitrator or a panel of arbitrators, selected for specialized knowledge in the field in question, hears the evidence and renders a decision.

Architect's Approval: Architect's written or imprinted acknowledgment that materials, equipment, or methods of construction are acceptable for use in the Work, or accepting a contractor's or owner's request or claim as valid.

Architectural Area of Buildings: The sum of the adjusted areas of the several floors of a building, computed in accordance with AIA Document D101, The Architectural Area and Volume of Buildings.

Architectural Volume of Buildings: The sum of the products of the architectural areas of a building (using the area of a single story for multistory portions having the same area on each floor) and the height from the underside of the lowest floor construction system to the average height of the surface of the finished roof above the various parts of the building. *See also* Architectural Area of Buildings, and AIA Document D101, *The Architectural Area and Volume of Buildings.*

Aromatic: Applied to a group of hydrocarbons and their derivatives characterized by presence of the benzene nucleus (molecular ring structure).

As-Built Drawings: *See* Record Drawings.

ASTM: American Society for Testing and Materials; a technical organization that develops standards on characteristics and performance of materials, products, systems, and services. It is the world's largest source of voluntary consensus standards.

ATSDR: Agency for Toxic Substances and Disease Registry, federal agency in the Public Health Service charged with carrying out health-related responsibilities of CERCLA and RCRA.

Background Radiation: The radiation coming from sources other than the radioactive material to be measured. This "background" is due primarily to cosmic rays, which constantly bombard the earth's surface from outer space.

Basic Services (of the Architect): The architect's basic services consist of the phases described in the *Owner-Architect Agreement*, AIA Documents B141, B151, B171, B181, and B727.

Beta Particle: A small electrically charged particle thrown off by many radioactive materials. It is identical to the electron. Beta particles emerge from the radioactive material at high speeds.

Bidding Documents: The advertisement or invitation to bid, instructions to bidders, the bid form, other sample bidding and contract forms, and the proposed contract documents, including an addendum issued prior to receipt of bids.

Bidding or Negotiation Phase: The phase of the architect's service during which competitive bids or negotiated proposals are requested as the basis for awarding a contract.

Bolt Ring: Closing device used to secure a over to the body of an open-headed drum. This ring requires a bolt and nut to secure the closure.

Bonding: A safety practice. The interconnecting of two objects (tanks, cylinders, etc.) with clamps and bare wire. This will equalize the electrical potential between the objects and help prevent static sparks that could ignite flammable material. Flammable liquid dispensing/receiving requires dissipating the static charge by bonding between containers.

Bonus and Penalty Clause: A provision in the contract for payment of a bonus to the contractor for completing the Work prior to a stipulated date, and a charge against the contractor for failure to complete the Work by such stipulated date.

Breakthrough Time: The time from initial chemical contact to detection.

Buna Rubbers: Synthetic rubbers from butadiene with a sodium catalyst.

Bung: A threaded closure that is located in the head or body of a drum.

Bureau of Explosives: Division of the Association of American Railroads that regulates shipping specifications for hazardous products.

CAA: Clean Air Act—Public Law PL91-604. Found at 40 CFR 50-80. EPA jurisdiction. Effective December 31, 1970, and amended significantly several times. The regulatory vehicle that sets and monitors airborne pollution that may harm public health or natural resources. The EPA sets national ambient air quality standards. Enforcement and issuing of discharge permits are carried out by their state and are called state implementation plans.

Carpal Tunnel Syndrome: A common affliction caused by compression of the median nerve in the carpal tunnel. Often associated with tingling, pain, or numbness in the thumb and first three fingers.

CAS Number: An assigned number used to identify a material. CAS stands for Chemical Abstracts Service, a Columbus, Ohio organization that indexes information published in *Chemical Abstracts* by the American Chemical Society and provides index guides by which information about particular substances may be located in the abstracts when needed. CAS numbers identify specific chemicals and are assigned sequentially. The numbers have no chemical significance. The CAS number is useful because it is a concise, unique means of material identification.

Ceiling: Maximum allowable exposure limit for an airborne substance, not to be exceeded.

Ceiling Concentration: Maximum concentration of a toxic substance allowed at any time or during a specific sampling period.

Ceiling Limit: In TLV and PEL, the maximum allowable concentration to which an employee may be exposed.

Ceiling Value, C: The concentration that should not be exceeded during any part of the working exposure. "An employee's exposure [to a hazardous material] shall at no time exceed the ceiling value" (OSHA). *See also* TLV.

CERCLA: Comprehensive Environment Response, Compensation and Liability Act of 1980. Also Superfund: federal law authorizing identification and remediation of abandoned hazardous waste sites.

CFM: Cubic feet per minute.

CFR: *Code of Federal Regulations*; a codification of rules published in the *Federal Register* by the executive departments and agencies of the federal government. The code is divided into 50 Titles representing the broad areas subject to federal regulations.

CGA: Compressed Gas Association; usually used to refer to a cylinder valve outlet connection detailed in CGA pamphlet V-1.

Change Order: A written order to the contractor signed by the owner and the architect, issued alter the execution of the contract, authorizing a change in the Work or an adjustment in the contract sum or the contract time. The contract sum and the contract time may be changed only by change order. A change order signed by the contractor indicates the contractor's agreement, including the adjustment in the contract sum or contract time.

Changes in the Work: Changes ordered by the owner within the general scope of the contract, consisting of additions, deletions, or other revisions, the contract sum and the contract time being adjusted accordingly. All such changes in the Work shall be authorized by change order, and shall be performed under the applicable conditions of the contract documents.

Characteristics Wastes: Hazardous wastes exhibiting one of four characteristics: ignitability, explosivity, EP toxicity, or corrosivity.

CHEMTREC: The CMA Chemical Transportation Emergency Center; provides immediate information for members on what to do in case of spills, leaks, fires, or exposures on receipt of a phone call from the scene of the chemical transportation accident. The toll-free number is 1-800-424-9300.

Chime: The connection between the side and ends of a metal drum or pail.

CHRIS: Chemical Hazards Response Information System; an organization of the U.S. Coast Guard which provides information on hazard response and accident prevention.

Class A Fire: Wood, paper, cloth, trash, or other ordinary materials.

Class B Fire: Gasoline, grease, oil, paint, or other flammable liquids.

Class C Fire: Live electrical equipment.

Class D Fire: Flammable metals.

Clerk of the Works: Term (title) used to mean the owner's inspector or owner's site representative.

Combustible: A term used by the NFPA, DOT, and others to classify certain liquids that will burn on a basis of flash points. Both NFPA and DOT generally define combustible liquids as having a flash point of 100°F (38°C) or higher. *See also* Flammable. Nonliquid substances such as wood and paper are classified as ordinary combustibles by the NFPA. OSHA defines combustible liquids within the Hazard Communication Law as any liquid having a flash point of or above 100°F (39°C), but below 200°F (93.3°C) Also, any mixture having components with flash points at 200°F (93.3°C) or higher, the total volumes of which make up 99% or more of the total volume of the mixture.

Comprehensive Services: Professional services performed by the architect, including traditional services and such other services as project analysis, programming, land-use studies, feasibility investigations, financing, construction management, and special consulting services.

Conditions of the Contract: Those portions of the contract documents that define the rights and responsibilities of the contracting parties and others involved in the Work. The conditions of the contract include general conditions, supplementary conditions, and other conditions.

Construction Budget: The sum established by the owner as available for construction of the project, including contingencies for bidding and for changes during construction.

Construction Cost (for Calculating Compensation to the Architect): The total cost or estimated cost to the owner of all elements of the project designed or specified by the architect, including at current market rates (with a reasonable allowance for overhead and profit) the cost of labor and materials furnished by the owner and any equipment that has been designed, specified, selected, or specially provided for by the architect, but not including the compensation of the architect and the architect's consultants, the cost of land, rights-of-way, or other costs which are the responsibility of the owner.

Construction Documents: Drawings and specifications setting forth in detail the requirements for the construction of the project.

Construction Documents Phase: The phase of the architect's services in which the architect prepares from the approved design development documents, the construction documents, and assists the owner in the preparation of the bidding documents.

Construction Management: Special management services provided to an owner by an architect or other person or entity possessing requisite training and experience during the design phase and/or construction phase of a project. Such management services may include advice on the time and cost consequences of design and construction decisions, scheduling, cost control, coordination of contract negotiations and awards, timely purchasing of critical materials and long-lead items and coordination of construction activities.

Construction Manager: As used in AIA documents, the term refers to an individual or entity who provides construction management services with a fiduciary duty to the owner for both the design phase and/or construction phase of a project. As used in other contexts in the construction industry, it may refer only to a commercial, arm's-length relationship between an owner and construction manager, or a combination of a fiduciary and commercial relationship over the life of a project.

Construction Phase—Administration of the Construction Contract: The phase of the architect's services that includes the architect's general administration of the construction contract(s).

Contract Administration: The duties and responsibilities of the architect during the construction phase.

Contract Documents: The owner–contractor agreement, the conditions of the contract (general, supplementary, and other conditions), the drawings, the specifications, and all addenda issued prior to and all modifications issued after execution of the contract and any other items that may be specifically stipulated as being included in the contract; documents.

Corrosive: A substance that causes visible destruction or permanent changes in human skin tissues at the site of contact.

CSA: Canadian Standards Association; a nonprofit voluntary membership association that develops standards through consensus. Also offers certification and testing services.

CWA: Clean Water Act. Public Law PH 95-500. Found at 40 CFR Parts 100-140 and 400-470. Effective November 18, 1972, and amended significantly since then. EPA and Army Corps of Engineers have jurisdiction. CWA regulates the discharge of nontoxic and toxic pollutants into surface waters. Its ultimate goal is to eliminate all discharges into surface waters. Its interim goal is to make surface waters usable for fishing, swimming, and so on. EPA sets guidelines and states issue permits (NPDES, Natural Pollutant Discharge Elimination System permit) specifying the types of control equipment and discharges for each facility.

Date of Commencement of the Work: The date established in a notice to the contractor to proceed or, in the absence of such notice, the date of the owner–contractor agreement or such other date that may be established.

Date of Substantial Completion: The date certified by the architect when the Work or a designated portion thereof is sufficiently complete, in accordance with the contract documents, so the owner can occupy the Work or designated portion thereof for the use for which it is intended.

Decibel (dB): A unit for expressing the relative intensity of sounds on a scale from 0 (average least perceptible) to 130 (average pain level).

Design–Build Process: A process in which a person or entity assumes responsibility under a single contract for both the design and construction of a project.

Design Development Documents: Drawings and other documents that fix and describe the size and character of the entire project as to architectural, structural, mechanical, and electrical systems, materials, and such other elements as may be appropriate.

Design Development Phase: The phase of the architect's services in which the architect prepares from the approved schematic design studies, for approval by the owner, the design development documents, and submits to the owner a further statement of probable construction cost.

Detailed Estimate of Construction Cost: A forecast of construction cost prepared on the basis of a detailed analysis of materials and labor for all items of Work, as contrasted with an estimate based on current area, volume, or similar unit costs.

Dielectric: A material that is an electrical insulator or in which an electric field can be sustained with a minimum dissipation of power.

DOT Identification Numbers: Four-digit numbers, preceded by UN or NA, used to identify particular substances for regulation of their transportation. See DOT publications that describe the regulations. CFR 49 172.102.

Drawings: Graphic and pictorial documents showing the design, location, and dimensions of the elements of a project. Drawings generally include plans, elevations, sections, details, schedules, and diagrams. When capitalized, the term refers to the graphic and pictorial portions of the contract documents.

Drop Test: A test required by DOT regulations for determination of the quality of a container or finished product.

Dry-Bulb Temperature: The temperature of air measured with a dry-bulb thermometer in a psychrometer to measure relative humidity.

Dusts: Solid particles generated by handling, crushing, grinding, rapid impact, detonation, and decrepitation of organic or inorganic materials, such as rock, ore, metal, coal, wood, and grain. Dusts do not tend to flocculate, except under electrostatic forces; they do not diffuse in air but settle under the influence of gravity.

EDA: Emergency Declaration Area; officially designated area for cleanup of hazardous waste or materials, as at an NPL hazardous waste site.

Elastomer: A term used to describe elastic polymers with rubberlike behavior. A substance that can be stretched at room temperature to at least twice its original length, and after having been stretched returns with force to its approximate original length in a short time.

Elevation: (1) A two-dimensional graphic representation of the design, location, and dimensions of the project, or parts thereof, seen in a vertical plane viewed from a given direction. (2) Distance above or below a prescribed datum or reference point.

Engineering Controls: Methods of controlling employee exposures by modifying the source or reducing the quantity of contaminants released into the workroom environment.

Environmental Design Professions: The professions collectively responsible for the design of the human physical environment, including architecture, engineering, landscape architecture, urban planning, and similar environment-related professions.

EPA: U.S. Environmental Protection Agency; a federal agency with environmental protection regulatory and enforcement authority. Administers the Clean Air Act, Clean Water Act, RCRA, TSCA, and other federal environmental laws.

EP Toxicity: Extraction-procedure toxicity; toxicity test performed on RCRA wastes.

Ergonomics: A multidisciplinary activity dealing with interactions between workers and their total working environment plus stresses related to such environmental elements as at-

mosphere, heat, light, and sound, as well as tools and equipment of the workplace.

Etiologic Agent: Organisms, substances, or objects associated with the cause of disease or injury.

Exhaust Ventilation: The removal of air usually by mechanical means from any space. The flow of air between two points is due to the occurrence of a pressure difference between the two points. This pressure difference will cause air to flow from the high pressure to the low-pressure zone.

Explosion Class 1: Flammable gas/vapor.

Explosion Class 2: Combustible dust.

Explosion Class 3: Ignitable fibers.

Explosion-Proof: An electrical apparatus so designed that an explosion of flammable gas or vapor inside the enclosure will not ignite flammable gas or vapor outside.

Exposure Level: The level or concentration of a physical or chemical hazard to which an employee is exposed.

Exposure Limits: Concentration of substances (and conditions) under which it is believed that nearly all workers may be repeatedly exposed day after day without adverse effects. ACGIH limits are called TLV and OSHA exposed limits are called PEL (permissible exposure limits).

Face Velocity: Average air velocity into the exhaust system measured at the opening into the hood or booth.

FDA: U.S. Food and Drug Administration.

Feasibility Study: A detailed investigation and analysis conducted to determine the financial, economic, technical, or other advisability of a proposed project.

Federal Register: Publications of U.S. government documents officially promulgated under the law, documents whose validity depends on such publication. It is published on each day following a government working day. It is, in effect, the daily supplement to the *Code of Federal Regulations* (CFR).

FEMA: Federal Emergency Management Agency; body responsible for administering certain training funds under SARA Title III.

Final Acceptance: The owner's acceptance of the project from the contractor upon certification by the architect of final completion. Final acceptance is confirmed by the making of final payment unless otherwise stipulated at the time of making such payment.

Final Completion: Term denoting that the Work has been completed in accordance with the terms and conditions of the contract documents.

Final Inspection: Payment made by the owner to the contractor, upon issuance by the architect of the final certificate for payment, of the entire unpaid balance of the contract sum as adjusted by change orders.

First Responder: The first personnel trained to arrive on the scene of a hazardous material incident. Usually, officials from local emergency services, firefighters, and police.

Fixed Limit of Construction Cost: The maximum construction cost established in the agreement between the owner and the architect.

Flame Arrestor: A mesh or perforated metal insert within a flammable storage can which protects its contents from external flame or ignition.

Flammable: Flash point less than 100°F (and a vapor pressure of not over 50 psia at 100°F) (definition may vary by organization).

Flammable Liquid: A liquid with a flash point below 100°F (37.8°C), excluding gases.

Flash Back: The phenomenon characterized by vapor ignition and flame travel back to the vapor source (the flammable liquid).

Flash Point: The lowest temperature at which a flammable vapor–air mixture above the liquid will ignite when the ignition source is introduced.

FM: Factory Mutual; a nationally recognized testing laboratory and approval service recognized by OSHA.

Frazier Air Test: A testing method of the ASTM for material breathability.

Fumes: Particulate matter consisting of the solid particles generated by condensation from the gaseous state, generally after violation from melted substances, and often accompanied by a chemical reaction, such as oxidation.

Gamma Rays: The most penetrating of all radiation. High-energy photons, especially as emitted by a nucleus in a transition between two energy levels.

Gas: A state of matter in which the material has very low density and viscosity; can expand and contract greatly in response to changes in temperature and pressure; easily diffuses into other gases; readily and uniformly distributes itself throughout any container.

Gauge: Thickness of the steel used to manufacture a drum. The lower the gauge, the thicker the material, also used to measure glove thickness in inches.

General Conditions (of the Contract for Construction): That part of the contract documents which sets forth many of the rights, responsibilities, and relationships of the parties involved particularly those provisions that are common to many construction projects. *See also* Conditions of the Contract. AIA Document A201 has become the construction industry "standard" general conditions.

General Contract: (1) Under the single-contract system, the contract between the owner and the contractor for construction of the entire Work. (2) Under the separate contract system, a contract between the owner and a contractor for general construction consisting of architectural and structural Work.

Guaranteed Maximum Cost: Sum established in an agreement between owner and contractor as the maximum cost of performing specified Work on the basis of cost of labor and materials plus overhead expenses and profit. Preferable to guaranteed maximum price.

Hazard Classes: A series of nine descriptive terms that have been established by the UN committee of experts to categorize the hazardous nature of chemical, physical, and biological materials. These categories are: flammable liquids, explosives, gases, oxidizers, radioactive materials, corrosives, flammable solids, poisonous and infectious substances, and dangerous substances.

Hazardous Material (DOT): A substance or material that has been determined by the Secretary of Transportation to be capable of posing an unreasonable risk to health, safety, and property when transported in commerce and so designated (49 CFR 171.8).

Hazardous Waste: Under RCRA, any solid or combination of solid wastes, which because of its physical, chemical, or infectious characteristics, may pose a hazard when managed improperly.

HCS: Hazard Communication Standard; the OSHA standard cited in 29 CFR 1910.1200 requiring communication of risks from hazardous substances to workers in regulated facilities.

Hearing Conservation: The prevention or minimizing of noise-induced deafness through the use of hearing protection devices, the control of noise through engineering methods, annual audiometric tests, and employee training.

HEPA: High-efficiency particulate absolute; a filter that removes from air 99.97% or more of monodisperse dioctyl phthalate (DOP) particles having a mean particle diameter of 0.3 micrometer. Common use: "HEPA filter"—high-efficiency particulate air filter.

High/Low-Pressure SCBA: Respiratory apparatus available with a high-pressure cylinder with air compressed at 4500 psi or a low-pressure cylinder with air compressed at 2216 psi.

HMAC: Hazardous Materials Advisory Council; national organization representing the hazardous materials industry. Members are devoted to domestic and international safety in transportation and handling of hazardous materials and waste.

HMIG: Hazardous Materials Identification Guide.

HMR: Hazardous materials regulations; regulations administered and enforced by various agencies of DOT governing the transportation of hazardous materials by air, highway, rail, water, and intermodal means.

Hoop-Wrapped Cylinder: A cylinder for a SCBA made of heavier construction; won't dent as easily as aluminum.

HSWA: Hazardous and Solid Waste Amendments; 1984 amendments to RCRA establishing a timetable for RCRA land bans and more stringent requirements for RCRA activities.

IDLH: Immediately dangerous to life and health; maximum concentration of a chemical in air to which one can be exposed without suffering irreversible health effects (function of time, usually).

I.D./O.D.: Inside diameter of a container, outside diameter of a container.

Indoor Air Quality (IAQ): Sick-building syndrome, tight-building syndrome. The study, evaluation, and control of indoor air quality related to temperature, humidity, and airborne contaminants.

Infectious: Capable of invading a susceptible host, replicating, and causing an altered host reaction, commonly referred to as a disease.

Inspection: Examination of Work completed or in progress to determine its conformance with the requirements of the contract documents. The Architect ordinarily makes only two inspections of the Work, one to determine substantial completion, and the other to determine final completion. These inspections should be distinguished from the more general observations made by the architect on visits to the site during the progress of the Work. The term is also used to mean examination of the Work by a public official, owner's representative, or others.

Instruction to Bidders: Instructions contained in the bidding documents for preparing and submitting bids for a construction project or a designated portion(s).

Invitation to Bid: A portion of the bidding documents soliciting bids for a construction project.

Isotonic: Having the same osmotic pressure as the fluid phase of a cell or tissue.

Joule: Unit of energy used in describing a single pulsed output of a laser. It is equal to 1 watt second or 0.2390 calorie, or 10^7 erg.

Kinesiology: The study of human movement in terms of functional anatomy.

Lab Pack: Generally refers to any small container of hazardous waste in an overpacked drum, but not restricted to laboratory wastes.

Laser: Light amplification by simulated emission of radiation.

LCD: (liquid crystal display); a constantly operating display that consists of segments of a liquid crystal whose reflectivity varies according to the voltage applied to them.

LED: (lower explosive diode); a semiconductor diode that converts electric energy efficiently into spontaneous and noncoherent electromagnetic radiation at visible and near-infrared wavelengths.

LEL: (lower explosive limit); the minimum percent by volume of a gas which when mixed with air at NTP will form a flammable mixture.

LEPC: Local emergency planning committee; groups defined in SARA as responsible for developing emergency plans.

Letter Form of Agreement or Letter Agreement: A letter stating the terms of an agreement between addressor and addressee, usually prepared to be signed by the addressee to indicate acceptance of those terms as legally binding.

Letter of Intent: A letter signifying an intention to enter into a formal agreement, usually setting forth the general terms of such agreement.

Level A Clothing: Should be worn when highest level of respiratory, skin, and eye protection is needed.

Level B Clothing: Should be worn when highest level of respiratory protection is needed but a lower level of skin protection.

Level C Clothing: Should be worn when the criteria for using air-purifying respirators are met.

Level D Clothing: Should be worn only as a work uniform and not on any site with respiratory or skin hazards.

Local Exhaust Ventilation: A ventilation system that captures and removes the contaminants at the point they are being produced before they escape into the workroom air.

Lumbar: The section of the lower vertebral column immediately above the sacrum. Located in the small of the back and consisting of five large lumbar vertebrae, it is a highly stressed area in work situations and in supporting the body structure.

Maximum Use Concentration (MUC): The product of the protection factor of the respiratory protection equipment and the permissible exposure limit (PEL).

mil: One mil equals 1/1000 of an inch. Used in reference to glove thickness.

Minor Changes in the Work: Changes of a minor nature in the Work not involving an adjustment in the contract time or an extension of the contract time and not inconsistent with the intent of the contract documents, which shall be effected by written order issued by an Architect.

Mists: Suspended liquid droplets generated by condensation from the gaseous to the liquid state or by breaking up a liquid into a dispersed state, such as by splashing, foaming, or atomizing. Mist is formed when a finely divided liquid is suspended in air.

Modification (to the Contract Documents): (1) A written amendment to the contract signed by both parties. (2) A change order. (3) A written interpretation issued by the architect. (4) A written order for a minor change in the Work issued by the architect.

Module: (1) A repetitive dimensional or functional unit used in planning, recording, or constructing buildings or other structure. (2) A distinct component forming part of an ordered system.

MPPCF: Million particles per cubic foot.

MSDS: Material safety data sheet (OSHA Form 20); contains descriptive information on hazardous chemicals under OSHA's Hazard Communication Standards (HCS). These data sheets also provide precautionary information on the safe handling of the gas as well as emergency and first-aid procedures.

MSHA: Mine Safety and Health Administration; a federal agency that regulates the health and safety of the mining industry.

NFPA: National Fire Protection Association; an organization that promotes knowledge of fire protection methods.

NFPA Hazard Rating: Classification of a chemical by a four-color diamond representing health, flammability, reactivity, and specific hazard by a numbered hazard rating from 0 to 4.

NIOSH: National Institute for Occupational Safety and Health; independent federal agency charged with performing research on occupational disease and injury.

NOAA: National Oceanic and Atmospheric Administration; scientific support organization serving regulatory agencies charged with enforcing environmental laws affecting oceans and the atmosphere.

Notice to Bidders: A notice contained in the bidding documents informing prospective bidders of the opportunity to submit bids on a project and setting forth the procedures for doing so.

Notice to Proceed: Written communication issued by the owner to the contractor authorizing him to proceed with the Work and establishing the date of commencement of the Work.

NPL: National priority list. Official list of hazardous waste sites to be addressed by CERCLA.

NPT: National pipe thread.

NRR: Noise reduction rating.

NTP: (1) National toxicology program. (2) Normal temperature and pressure, which is defined as 70°F and 14.696 psia.

Observation of the Work: A function of the architect in the construction phase, during visits to the site, to become generally familiar with the progress and quality of the Work and to determine in general if the Work is proceeding in accordance with the contract documents.

Odor Threshold: The minimum concentration of a substance at which a majority of test subjects can detect and identify the characteristic odor of a substance.

Oleophillic: Having an affinity for, attracting, adsorbing, or absorbing oil.

Optical Density (OD): A logarithmic expression of the attenuation afforded by a filter.

ORM-D: A material such as a consumer commodity which, although otherwise subject to the regulations of this subchapter, presents a limited hazard during transportation due to its form, quantity, and packaging. They must be materials for which exceptions are provided in 171.101 of this subchapter. A shipping description applicable to each ORM-D material or category of ORM-D materials is found in 49 CFR 171.101.

OSHA: Occupational Safety and Health Administration; oversees and regulates workplace health and safety. Also OSHA: Occupational Safety and Health Act of 1970; law calling for establishment of the administrative OSHA body.

Outline Specifications: An abbreviated listing of specification requirements normally included with schematic or design development documents.

PAPR: Powdered air-purifying respirator.

Part B Permit: The second, narrative section submitted by generators in the RCRA permitting process; covers in detail the procedures followed at a facility to protect human health and the environment.

Partial Occupancy: Occupancy by the owner of a portion of a project prior to final completion.

PCB: Polychlorinated biphenyl; a pathogenic and teratogenic industrial compound used as a heat-transfer agent; PCBs may accumulate in human and animal tissue.

PEL: Permissible exposure limit; the OSHA limit of employee exposure to chemicals; found primarily i 29 CFR 1910.1000.

Permeation Rate: An invisible process by which a hazardous chemical moves through a protective material. Measured in $mg/m^2/sec$.

pH: Means used to express the degree of acidity.

Poison A: Poisonous gases or liquids of such toxicity that a very small amount of the gas or vapor mixed with air is dangerous to life.

Poison B: Substances, liquid or solid, other than class A poisons or irritating material which are known to be so toxic to humans as to afford a hazard to health during transportation, or which, in the absence of adequate data on human toxicity are presumed to be toxic to humans based on prescribed tests on laboratory animals.

Polymerization: Chemical reaction where simple materials, either one or more, are converted to a complex material that possesses properties entirely different from original materials used at the start of the reaction.

Post-construction Services: (1) Under traditional forms of agreement, additional services rendered alter issuance of the final certificate for payment, or in the absence of a final certificate for payment, more than 60 days after the date substantial completion of the Work; or (2) under designated services forms of agreement, services necessary to assist the owner in the use and occupancy of the facility.

PPE: Personal protection equipment; devices worn by the worker to protect against hazards in the environment (e.g., respirators, goggles, face shields, gloves, and hearing protectors).

ppm: Parts per million (1×10^{-6}); a convenient means of expressing very low concentrations of a substance in a mixture or as a low-level contaminent in a pure product.

Prefilter: A filter used in conjunction with a cartridge on an air-purifying respirator.

Preliminary Drawings: Drawings prepared during the early stages of the design of a project.

Prime Professional: Any person or entity having a contract directly with the owner for professional services.

Principal (in Professional practice): Any person legally responsible for the activities of a professional practice.

Principal-in-Charge: The architect or engineer in a professional practice firm charged with the responsibility for the firm's services in connection with a given project.

Program: A written statement setting forth design objectives, constraints, and criteria for a project, including space requirements and relationships, flexibility and expandability, special equipment and systems, and site requirements.

Programming Phase: That phase of the environmental design process in which the owner provides full information regarding requirements for the project, including a program.

Project: (1) The total construction of which the Work performed under the contract documents may be the whole or a part. (2) The total furniture, furnishings, and equipment and interior construction of which the Work performed under the contract, documents may be the whole or a part.

Project Architect: The architect designated by the principal-in-charge to manage the firm's services related to a given project.

Project Costs: Total cost of the project, including construction cost, professional compensation, land costs, furnishings and equipment, financing, and other charges.

Project Managers: A term frequently used interchangeably with project architect to identify the person designated by the principal-in-charge to manage the firm's services related to a given project. Normally, these services include administrative responsibilities as well as technical responsibilities.

Project Manual: The volume(s) of document(s) prepared by the architect for a project, which may include the bidding requirements, sample forms, and conditions of the contract and the specifications.

Project Representative: The architect's representative at the project site who assists in administration of the construction contract.

psi: Pounds per square inch.

psis: Pounds per square inch absolute; the absolute thermodynamic pressure, measured by the number of pounds-force exerted on an area of 1 in. square.

PVC: Polyvinyl chloride; a member of the family of vinyl resins.

Qualitative Analysis: The analysis of a gas, liquid, or solid sample or mixture to identify the elements or compounds composing the sample.

Quantitative Analysis: The analysis of a gas, liquid, or solid sample or mixture to determine the precise percentage composition of the sample in terms of elements or compounds.

Quotation: A price quoted by a contractor, subcontractor, material supplier, or vendor to furnish materials, labor, or both.

Radionuclide: A radioactive nuclide, one that has the capability of spontaneously emitting radiation.

Ratchet: A knob on the back of a respirator mask or hard hat headband for tightening.

RCRA: Resource Conservation and Recovery Act; regulates materials and wastes currently being generated, treated, stored, disposed, or distributed.

Reactivity: A substance's susceptibility to undergoing a chemical reaction or change that may result in dangerous side effects, such as an explosion, burning, and corrosive or toxic emissions.

Record Drawings: Construction drawings revised to show significant changes made during the construction process, usually based on marked-up prints, drawings, and other data furnished by the contractor to the architect. Preferable to as-built drawings.

Regulated Material: A substance or material that is subject to regulations set forth by the Environmental Protection Agency (EPA), the Department of Transportation (DOT), or any other federal agency.

Reimbursable Expenses: Amounts expended for or on account of the project which, in accordance with the terms of the appropriate agreement, are to be reimbursed by the owner.

Rejection of Work (by the Architect): The act of rejecting work that is defective or does not conform to the requirements of the contract documents.

Relative Humidity: The ratio of the quantity of water vapor present in air to the quantity that would saturate it at any specific temperature.

Rendering: A drawing of a project or portion(s) with an artistic delineation of materials, shades, and shadows.

Resident Engineer: An engineer employed by the owner to represent the owner's interests at the project site during the construction phase; term frequently used on projects in which a governmental agency is involved.

Retainage: A sum withheld from progress payments to the contractor in accordance with the terms of the owner–contractor agreement.

Retainer Ring/Cap: A plastic ring that will hold a cartridge or filter on a respirator mask or hold a prefilter on a cartridge.

Safety Can: An approved container, of not more than 5-gallon capacity, having a spring-closing lid and spout cover designed to safely relieve internal pressure when subjected to fire exposure.

Sanitize: To clean, not to sterilize.

SARA: Superfund Amendment and Reauthorization Act; federal law reauthorizing and expanding the jurisdiction of CERCLA.

SARA Title III: Part of SARA mandating public disclosure of chemical information and development of emergency response plans.

SCBA: Self-contained breathing apparatus; designed for entry into and escape from atmospheres immediately, dangerous to life or health (IDLH) or oxygen deficient.

Schematic Design Documents: Drawings and other documents illustrating the scale and relationship of project components.

Schematic Design Phase: The phase of the architect's services in which the architect consults with the owner to ascertain the requirements of the project and prepares schematic design studies consisting of drawings and other documents illustrating the scale and relationship of the project components for approval by the owner. The architect also submits to the owner a statement of probable construction cost based on current area, volume, or other unit costs.

SEI: Safety Equipment Institute.

Shade Number: Comparative darkness or obscurity caused by the interception of light rays. Used in reference to goggles or safety glasses.

Shop Drawings: Drawings, diagrams, schedule, and other data specially prepared for the Work by the contractor or any subcontractor manufacturer, supplier, or distributor to illustrate some portion of the Work.

SITE: Superfund Innovative Technology Evaluation; EPA-supported research, development, and demonstration projects designed to develop new remediation technologies.

Solution: Mixture in which the components lose their identities and are uniformly dispersed. All solutions are composed of a solvent and the substance dissolved, called the solute.

Solvent: A substance that dissolves another substance. Usually refers to organic solvents.

Specifications: A part of the contract documents contained in the project manual, consisting of written requirements for materials, equipment, construction systems, standards, and workmanship. Under the Uniform Construction Index, the specifications comprise 16 divisions.

Spectrum: A range of frequencies within which radiation has some specified characteristic, such as audio-frequency spectrum, ultraviolet spectrum, or radio spectrum.

Standard Net Assignable Area: That portion of the area of a project that is available for assignment or rental to an occupant, including every type of space usable by the occupant, computed in accordance with AIA Document D101.

Staphylococcus: Any of various spherical parasitic bacteria occurring in grapelike clusters and causing infections such as septicemia.

Statement of Probable Construction Cost: Cost forecasts prepared by the architect during the schematic design, design development, and construction documents phases of basic services for the guidance of the owner.

Static Pressure: The potential pressure exerted in all directions by a fluid at rest. When added to velocity pressure, it gives total pressure.

STEL: Short-term exposure limit; maximum concentration for a continuous 15-minute exposure period. (Maximum of four such periods per day, 60 minutes minimum between exposure periods, and the daily TLV-TWA must not be exceeded.)

Sterile: Free of living microorganisms.

Streptococcus: Any of various rounded, disease-causing bacteria that occur in pairs or chains.

Study: Preliminary sketch or drawing to facilitate the development of a design.

Superfund Sites: *See* NPL.

Supplemental Services (of the Architect): Those services described in the schedule of designated services are in addition to the generally sequential services (from predesign through postconstruction) of the architect, including such items of service as renderings, value analyses, energy studies, project promotion, expert testimony, and the like.

Supplementary Conditions: A part of the contract documents that supplements and may also modify, change, add to, or delete from provisions of the general conditions.

Supplied Air: Breathable air supplied to a worker's mask/hood from a source outside the contaminated area.

Supported Gloves: Gloves that are constructed of a coated fabric.

Survey: (1) Boundary, topographic, and/or utility mapping of a site. (2) Measuring an existing building. (3) Analyzing a building for use of space. (4) Determining owner's requirements for a project. (5) Investigating and reporting of required data for a project.

Systems (a Process): Combining prefabricated assemblies, components, and parts into single integrated units utilizing industrialized production, assembly, and methods.

Terne: A lead alloy having a composition of 10 to 20% tin and 80 to 90% lead; used to coat iron or steel surfaces.

Tier I or Tier II: Inventory form required under SARA Title III for reporting quantities and locations of hazardous substances.

Time (as the Essence of a Construction Contract): Time limits or periods stated in the contract. A provision in a construction contract that "time is of the essence of the contract" signifies that the parties consider punctual performance within the time limits or periods in the contract to be a vital part of the performance, and failure to perform on time is a breach for which the injured party is entitled to damages in the amount of loss sustained.

Timely Completion: Completion of the Work or designated portion thereof on or before the date required.

TLV: Threshold Limit Value; an estimate of the average safe airborne concentration of a substance and represent conditions under which it is believed that nearly all workers may be repeatedly exposed day after day without adverse effect. The TLV values are published yearly by the ACGIH in the TLV Booklet. TLV values should be prefaced with the year issued. TLV is a trademark of ACGIH.

TWA: Time Weighted Average; usually, a personal, 8-hour average exposure concentration to an airborne, chemical hazard; ppm and mg/m^3.

Type I: A safety can with a single spot.

Type I Duty Rating: A safety rating applied to ladders, indicating a load limit of 250 lb.

Type IA Duty Rating: A safety rating applied to ladders, indicating a load limit of 300 lb.

Type II: A safety can with two openings, one for pouring and one for filling.

UFC: Uniform Fire Code; prescribes regulations consistent with nationally recognized good practice for the safeguarding to a reasonable degree of life and property from the hazards of fire and explosion arising from the storage, handling, and use of hazardous substances, materials, and devices, and from conditions hazardous to life and property in the use or occupancy of buildings or premises.

UL: Underwriters' Laboratories; an independent, nonprofit organization that operates laboratories for the investigation of devices and materials in respect to hazards affecting life and property.

ULPA: Ultra low penetration air; a filter that removes from air 99.9995% of particles at 0.12 micrometer or larger.

Ultraviolet: Wavelengths of the electromagnetic spectrum which are shorter than those of visible light and longer than x-rays. Wavelength of 10^{-5} to 10^{-6} cm.

Uniform Construction Index: A published system for coordination of specification sections, filing of technical data and product literature, and construction cost accounting organized into Divisions.

Unit Price: Amount stated in the bid as a price per unit of measurement for materials or services as described in the bidding documents or in the proposed, contract documents.

UN: (United Nations) Number: The DOT (Department of Transportation) Number printed on the cylinder label. For example, in UN1066, the "UN" prefix indicates that 1066 is recognized throughout the world as identifying nitrogen. Sometimes "NA" (North America) will appear as a prefix. NA identification numbers are recognized in the United States and Canada.

Unsupported Gloves: Unlined gloves without any type of fabric lining.

UST: Underground storage tank; regulated by RCRA; tank with 10% or more of its volume underground, with connected piping; used to store CERCLA regulated hazardous chemicals or petroleum products.

Vapors: The distance in the line of advance of a wave from any point to a similar point on the next wave. It is usually measured in angstroms, microns, micrometers, or nanometers.

Vendor: A person or entity who furnishes materials or equipment not fabricated to a special design for the Work.

Viscosity: The property of a fluid that resists internal flow by releasing counteracting forces.

Visible Radiation: Wavelengths of the electromagnetic spectrum between 10^{-4} and 10^{-3} cm.

Volume Method (of Estimating Cost): Method of estimating probable construction cost by multiplying the architectural volume by an estimated current cost per unit of volume.

Wavelength: The distance in the line of advance of a wave from any point to a similar point on the next wave. It is usually measured in angstroms, microns, micrometers, or nanometers.

Work: As used in AIA documents, the completed construction required by the contract documents, including all labor necessary to produce such construction and all materials and equipment incorporated or to be incorporated in such construction. The word "work" as contrasted with capitalized "Work" is used in its ordinary sense.

X-Ray: Highly Penetrating Radiation): Unlike gamma rays, x-rays do not come from the nucleus of the atom but from the surrounding electrons.

Zoning Permit: A permit issued by appropriate governmental authority authorizing land to be used for a specific purpose.

AIA STANDARD FORMS

The following synopses is a partial list of the standard forms developed and published by the American Institute of Architects, 1735 New York Avenue, NW, Washington, DC 20006-5292. These forms are widely used and have become the standard for use by those institutions contemplating the planning, design, and construction of buildings. The Supreme Court of the United States has used these documents as examples of industry standard practice when adjudicating cases involving construction disputes.

The author strongly recommends that an institution considering the construction of *any* building, particularly a laboratory facility, secure a copy of *The Architect's Handbook of Professional Practice.* This handbook is a valuable resource for construction industry practices, owner–architect and owner–contractor relationships, agreements, and so on. Copies are available from the AIA.

A-SERIES DOCUMENTS

AIA Document A101, Owner–Contractor Agreement Form: Stipulated Sum

Document A101 is a standard form of agreement between owner and contractor, for use where the basis of payment is a stipulated sum (fixed price). The document has been prepared for use with AIA Document A201, *General Conditions of the Contract for Construc-*

tion, providing an integrated pair of documents. This pair of documents is suitable for most projects; however, for projects of limited scope, use of AIA Document A107 should be considered.

AIA Document A201, General Conditions of the Contract for Construction

The general conditions are a part of the contract for construction and set forth rights, responsibilities, and relationships of the parties involved. Since conditions vary by locality land project, supplementary conditions are usually required to amend or supplement portions of the general conditions as required by the individual project. Although not a party to the owner–contract or agreement and the general conditions, the architect does participate in the preparation of the contract documents and performs certain of the duties and responsibilities assigned thereunder.

AIA Document A201/SC, Federal Supplementary Conditions of the Contract for Construction

Document A201/SC is published and distributed only with A201, and the documents are intended for joint use on certain federally assisted construction projects. For such projects, A201/SC adapts A201 by providing (1) necessary modifications of the general conditions, (2) additional conditions, and (3) insurance requirements for federally assisted construction projects.

AIA Document A305, Contractors Qualifications Statement

An owner about to request bids or to award a contract for a construction project needs a vehicle for verifying the background, history, references, and financial stability of any contractor being considered. The construction time frame, the contractors performance, history and previous similar experience, as well as financial capability are important factors for an owner to consider. This form provides a sworn, notarized statement with appropriate attachments to elaborate on the important facets of the contractors qualifications.

AIA Document A401, Standard Form of Agreement Between Contractor and Subcontractor

Document A401 establishes the contractual relationship between prime contractor and subcontractor. It spells out the responsibilities of both parties and lists their respective obligations as enumerated in the General Conditions, AIA Document A201. The appropriate sections of A201 are included as part of the document. Blank spaces are provided where the parties can supplement the details of their agreement for each project.

AIA Document A501, Recommended Guide for Competitive Bidding Procedures and Contract Awards for Building Construction

Document A501 is intended to establish desirable objectives in the bidding procedure and the award of contracts. The guide is for use when competitive lump-sum bids are requested in connection with building and related construction, and is a joint publication of the AIA and the Associated General Contractors of America (AGC).

AIA Document A511, Guide for Supplementary Conditions

AIA Document A201, the general conditions, is the foundation document supporting the legal framework for the construction contract. Although extremely important, it is obvious that as a standardized document A201 cannot cover all the requirements which must be included for purposes of bidding or construction. This guide points out the kinds of additional information most frequently required to cover local situations and variations in project requirements. Even though it suggests standardized language, it is not meant to be a standardized for of supplementary conditions.

AIA Document A512, Additions to the Guide for Supplementary Conditions

Document A512 is used primarily to incorporate important recent developments in construction-related law and practices into the AIA Documents occurring since the issuance of the latest edition of either A201 or A511. Thus A512 may be revised on a shorter cycle than other AIA document, depending on the frequency and extent of changes in the construction industry. The document collects the changes cumulatively, and where appropriate, its provisions will be incorporated into new editions of the other AIA documents.

AIA Document A521, Uniform Location of Subject Matter

Document A521 recognizes that there are widely varying approaches to the question of where in the contract documents a particular matter should properly be covered. The practice of many architects of addressing the same subject matter in more than one location has caused confusion and unanticipated legal problems when the exact language is not repeated each time. This tabulation is intended to guide the user in determining the proper location of information in those documents customarily used on a construction project. The listing was not created for the exclusive use of design professionals, but also for owners, attorneys, contractors, subcontractors, lenders, sureties, and others who work with construction documents.

AIA Document A701 Instructions to Bidders

Document A701 provides a base upon other documents and project requirements build. It is complementary to the AIA General Conditions; it is meant for general use and anticipates some additions, modifications, and other provisions. The usual, rather than specific project provisions for instructions to bidders are included.

B-SERIES DOCUMENTS

AIA Document A701 Instructions to Bidders

This is the standard form of agreement between owner and architect, for use where services are based on the five traditional phases. The document has been prepared for use when AIA Document A201, General Conditions of the Contract for Construction, is used in the contract between the owner and the contractor. It sets forth the duties and responsibilities of the architect and the owner in each phase of a project.

AIA Document B161, Standard Form of Agreement Between Owner and Architect for Designated Services

Document B161 is a standard form of agreement between owner and architect for designated services and is intended to be used in conjunction with AIA Document B162, Scope of Designated Services. These documents are designed to work together in describing the terms and conditions of the agreement, the amounts of compensation (B161), and the

responsibilities and services to be undertaken by the owner and the architect (B162). The separation of B161 and B162 provides for the flexibility of using B162, Scope of Designated Services, with other agreement forms. B161 may be used as the terms and conditions with other forms of scope of services statements. However, neither document may be used alone. B161 provides a description of the architect's construction phase services which is coordinated with AIA Document A201, General Conditions of the Contract for Construction.

AIA Document B352, Duties, Responsibilities, and Limitations of Authority of the Architect's Project Representative

Document B352 relates to the construction phase and is coordinated with AIA Document A201, General Conditions of the Contract for Construction. It should be attached to the owner–architect agreement as an exhibit when the architect's project representative is employed.

AIA Document B431, Architect's Qualification Statement

The Architect's Qualification Statement may be used to list in a clear, concise manner information about an architect's qualifications to performing architectural services for a specific project.

AIA Document B727, Standard Form of Agreement Between Owner and Architect for Special Services

Document B727 is a standard form of agreement between owner and architect for special services, intended for use when other B-series documents are not appropriate. It is often used for planning, feasibility studies, postoccupancy studies and other services that require a specialized description.

C-SERIES DOCUMENTS

AIA Document C141, Standard Form of Agreement Between Architect and Engineer

Document C141 is a standard form of agreement between architect and engineer, establishing their responsibilities to each other and their mutual rights under the agreement. The document is most applicable to engineers providing services for architects who are providing the traditional five phases of "Basic Services" for owners under the provisions of AIA Document B141, Standard Form of Agreement Between Owner and Architect. Its provisions are in accord with those of B141 and of AIA Document A201, General Conditions of the Contract for Construction.

AIA Document C161, Standard Form of Agreement Between Architect and Engineer for Designated Services

Document C161 is meant to be used in conjunction with the architect's use of AIA Document B161, Standard Form of Agreement Between Owner and Architect for Designated Services, and B162, Scope of Designated Services. The architect identifies the services that each consultant will perform under this agreement by marking them by a symbol in the column marked "By Architect As Outside Services" in the owner–architect agreement, which must be attached to this agreement. This procedure allows the architect and engineer to conform their agreement to the owner–architect agreement for designated services.

AIA Document C431, Standard Form of Agreement Between Architect and Consultant for Other Than Normal Engineering Services

Document C431 is intended for use between the architect and a consultant for other than normal structural, mechanical or electrical engineering services. The consultant's services parallel the traditional five phases of ser-

vices described in AIA Document B141, Standard Form of Agreement Between Owner and Architect.

D-SERIES DOCUMENTS

AIA Document D101, The Architectural Area and Volume of Buildings

Document D200 establishes definitions for and defines methods for calculating the architectural area and volume of buildings. The document also covers interstitial space, single-occupant net assignable area, and store net assignable area.

AIA Document D200, Project Checklist

Document D200 is a convenient listing of tasks the practitioner normally would perform on a given project. The use of this checklist will assist the architect in recognizing the tasks required and in locating the data necessary to carry out assigned responsibilities. By providing space to note the date of actions taken, it may serve as a permanent record of the owner's, contractor's, and architect's actions and decisions.

G-SERIES DOCUMENTS

AIA Document G611, Owner's Instructions Regarding Bidding Documents and Procedures

Since the owner, with advice of legal counsel, should decide on the requirements for the construction agreement and bidding procedures for the project, AIA Document G611 is a standard form that enables the architect to request written instructions from the owner regarding this information.

AIA Document G701, Change Order

A change order is the instrument by which changes in the work and adjustment in the contract sum or contract time under the owner–contractor agreement are formalized. The form provides a space for a complete description of the change, modifications to the contract sum, and adjustments in the contract time.

AIA Document G702, Application and Certificate for Payment, and AIA Document G703, Continuation Sheet

Documents G702 and G703 provide convenient and complete forms the contractor can make application for payment. The architect certifies on the form that the payment is due. The forms require the contractor to show the:

- Status of the contract sum to date, including total dollar amount of the work completed and stored to date
- Amount of retainage
- Total of previous payments
- Summary of change orders
- Amount of current payment requested

Document G703, Continuation Sheet, breaks the contract sum into the portions of work in accordance with a schedule of values required by the general conditions. The form serves two purposes: (1) the contractor's application, and (2) the architect's certification. Its use can expedite payment and reduce possibility of error. If the application is properly completed and acceptable to the architect, the architect's signature certifies to the owner that a payment in the amount indicated is due to the contractor. The form also provides for the architect to certify an amount different than the amount applied for, with explanation by the architect.

AIA Document G704, Certificate of Substantial Completion

Document G704 is a standard form for recording the date of substantial completion of the

work or designated portion(s). The contractor prepares a list of items to be completed or corrected, and the architect verifies and amends this list. If the architect finds the work is substantially complete, a form is completed for acceptance by the contractor and the owner. A list of the items to be completed and corrected is appended to the form. The form provides for agreement as to the time allowed for completion or correction of the items, the date upon which the owner will occupy the work or designated portion(s), and description of responsibilities for maintenance, heat, utilities, and insurance.

AIA Document G709, Proposal Request

Document G709 is a form used to secure price quotations which are necessary in the negotiation of change orders. The form is not a change order nor a direction to proceed with the work. It is simply a request to the contractor for information related to a proposed change in the construction contract.

AIA Document G710, Architect's Supplemental Instructions

The Architect's Supplemental Instructions are used by the architect to issue supplemental instructions or interpretations or to order minor changes in the work. The form is intended to assist the architect in performing obligations as interpreter of the requirements of the contract documents in accordance with the owner–architect agreement and the general conditions of the contract. This form should not be used to change the contract sum or contract time. If the contractor believes that a change in contract sum or time is involved, different documents must be used.

AIA Document G711, Architect's Field Report

The Architect's Field Report is a standard form for the architect's project representative to use to maintain a concise record of site visits or, in the case of a full-time project representative, a daily log of construction activities.

AIA Document G712, Shop Drawing and Sample Record

Document G712 is a standard form by which the architect can schedule and monitor shop drawings and samples. Since this process tends to be complicated, this schedule, showing the progress of a submittal, is an aid in the orderly processing of work and will serve as a permanent record of the chronology of this process.

AIA Document G713, Construction Change Authorization

Document 713 is an authorization form for immediate changes in the work which, if not processed expeditiously, might delay the project. These changes are often initiated in the field and usually affect the contract sum or the contract time. This is not a change order, only an authorization to proceed with a change for subsequent inclusion in a change order. It establishes a basis for change in time or cost.

INDEX